ORDNANCE SURVEY MEMOIRS OF IRELAND

Volume Twenty-nine

PARISHES OF COUNTY ANTRIM XI
1832–3, 1835–9

Published 1995.
The Institute of Irish Studies,
The Queen's University of Belfast,
Belfast.
In association with
The Royal Irish Academy,
Dawson Street,
Dublin.

Grateful acknowledgement is made to the Economic and Social Research Council and
the Department of Education for Northern Ireland for their financial assistance at different
stages of this publication programme.

British Library Cataloguing-in-Publication Data.
A catalogue record for this book is available from the British Library.

Paperback ISBN 0 85389 518 X
Hardback ISBN 0 85389 519 8

Printed by W. & G. Baird Ltd, Antrim.

Ordnance Survey Memoirs of Ireland

VOLUME TWENTY-NINE

Parishes of County Antrim XI
1832–3, 1835–9

Antrim town and Ballyclare

Edited by Angélique Day and Patrick McWilliams

The Institute of Irish Studies
in association with
The Royal Irish Academy

ACKNOWLEDGEMENTS

During the course of the transcription and publication project many have advised and encouraged us in this gigantic task. Thanks must first be given to the Royal Irish Academy, particularly former librarian Mrs Brigid Dolan and her staff, for making the original manuscripts available to us. We are also indebted to Siobhán O'Rafferty for her continuing help in deciphering indistinct passages of manuscript.

We should like to acknowledge the following individuals for their special contributions. Dr Brian Trainor led the way with his edition of the Antrim Memoir and provided vital help on the steering committee. Dr Ann Hamlin also provided valuable support, especially during the most trying stages of the project. Professor R.H. Buchanan's unfailing encouragment has been instrumental in the development of the project to the present. Without Dr Kieran Devine the initial stages of the transcription and the computerising work would never have been completed successfully: the project owes a great deal to his constant help and advice. Dr Kay Muhr's continuing contribution to the work of the transcription project is deeply appreciated, as is that of former editor Nóirín Dobson. Mr W.C. Kerr's interest and expertise have been invaluable. Professor Anne Crookshank and Dr Edward McParland were most generous with practical help and advice concerning the drawings amongst the Memoir manuscripts. We would like to thank the Director of the Ordnance Survey, Dublin and the keepers of the fire-proof store, among them Leonard Hines. Finally, all students of the nineteenth-century Ordnance Survey of Ireland owe a great deal to the pioneering work of Professor J.H. Andrews, and his kind help in the first days of the project is gratefully recorded.

The essential task of inputting the texts from audio tapes was done by Miss Eileen Kingan, Mrs Christine Robertson, Miss Eilis Smyth, Miss Lynn Murray and, most importantly, Miss Maureen Carr.

We are grateful to the Linen Hall Library for lending us their copies of the first edition 6" Ordnance Survey Maps: also to Ms Maura Pringle of QUB Cartography Department for the index maps showing the parish boundaries. For providing financial assistance at crucial times for the maintenance of the project, we would like to take this opportunity of thanking the trustees of the Esme Mitchell trust and The Public Record Office of Northern Ireland.

Right:
Map of parishes of County Antrim. The area described in this volume, the parishes of Antrim town and Ballyclare, has been shaded to highlight its location. The square grids represent the 1830s 6" Ordnance Survey maps. The encircled numbers relate to the map numbers as presented in the bound volumes of maps for the county. The parishes have been numbered in all cases and named in full where possible, except those in the following list: Aghagallon 1, Aghalee 2, Ballyclug 9, Ballycor 10, Ballylinny 11, Ballymartin 12, Ballynure 14, Ballyrashane 15, Grange of Ballyrobert 16, Grange of Ballyscullion 17, Grange of Ballywalter 18, Ballywillin 19, Blaris and Lisburn 21 & 60, Grange of Carmavy 23, Carncastle 24, Carnmoney 25, Cranfield 28, Derryaghy 30, Derrykeighan 31, Grange of Doagh 32, Donegore 33, Drumbeg 34, Grange of Drumtullagh 36, Dunaghy 37, Grange of Dundermot 38, Dunluce 40, Glynn 44, Inver 46, Island Magee 47, Kilbride 48, Killagan 49, Grange of Killyglen 51, Kilraghts 52, Kilroot 53, Kilwaughter 54, Kirkinriola 55, Lambeg 56, Larne 57, Granges of Layd and Inispollan 59 & 45, Magheragall 62, Magheramesk 63, Mallusk 64, Grange of Muckamore 65, Newtown Crommelin 67, Grange of Nilteen 68, Rashee 73, Rathlin Island 74, Grange of Shilvodan 75, Templecorran 77, Templepatrick 78, Tickmacrevan 79, Tullyrusk 81, Umgall 82.

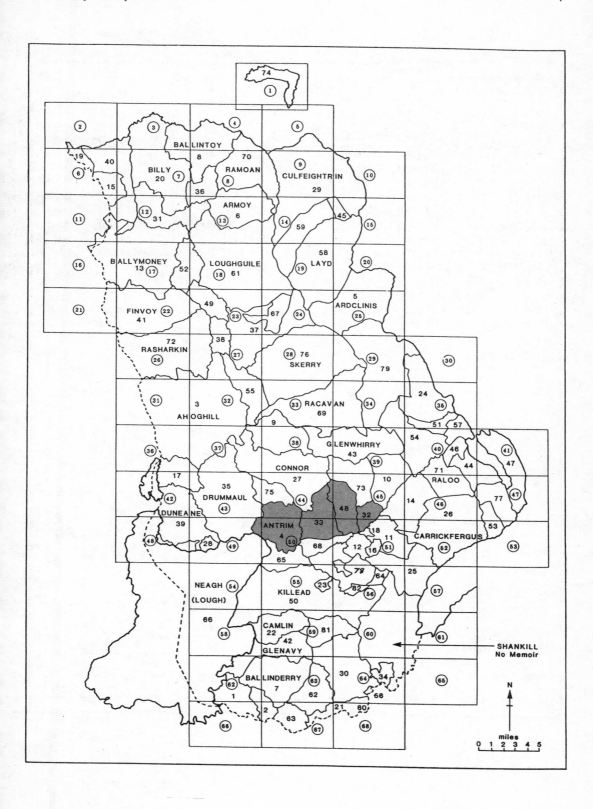

Map of County Antrim, from Samuel Lewis' *Atlas of the counties of Ireland* (London, 1837)

CONTENTS

Parishes in County Antrim

List of selected maps and drawings

List of O.S. maps, 1830s

INTRODUCTION AND GUIDE TO THE PUBLICATION OF THE
ORDNANCE SURVEY MEMOIRS

The following text of the Ordnance Survey Memoirs was first transcribed by a team working in the Institute of Irish Studies at The Queen's University of Belfast, on a computerised index of the material. For this publication programme the text has been further edited: spellings have been modernised in most cases, although where the original spelling was thought to be of any interest it has been retained and is indicated by angle brackets in the text. Variant spellings for townland and lesser place-names have been preserved, although parish and major place-names have been standardised and the original spelling given in angle brackets. Names of prominent people, for instance landlords, have been standardised where possible, but original spellings of names in lists of informants, emigration tables and on tombstones have been retained. We have not altered the Memoir writers' anglicisation of names and words in Irish.

Punctuation has been modernised and is the responsibility of the editors. Editorial additions are indicated by square brackets: a question mark before and after a word indicates a queried reading and tentatively inserted information respectively. Original drawings are referred to in the text, and some have been reproduced. Manuscript page references have been omitted from this series. Because of the huge variation in size of Memoirs for different counties, the following editorial policy has been adopted: where there are numerous duplicating and overlapping accounts, the most complete and finished account, normally the Memoir proper, has been presented, with additional unique information from other accounts like the Fair Sheets entered into a separate section, clearly titled and identified; where the Memoir material is less, nothing has been omitted. To achieve standard volume size, parishes have been associated on the basis of propinquity.

There are considerable differences in the volume of information recorded for different areas: counties Antrim and Londonderry are exceptionally well covered, while the other counties do not have quite the same detail. This series is the first systematic publication of the parish Memoirs, although individual parishes have been published by pioneering local history societies. The entire transcriptions of the Memoirs made in the course of the indexing project can be consulted in the Public Record Office of Northern Ireland and the library at the Queen's University of Belfast. The manuscripts of the Ordnance Survey Memoirs are in the Royal Irish Academy, Dublin.

Brief history of the Irish Ordnance Survey in the nineteenth century and the writing of the Ordnance Survey Memoirs

In 1824 a House of Commons committee recommended a townland survey of Ireland with maps at the scale of 6", to facilitate a uniform valuation for local taxation. The Duke of Wellington, then prime minister, authorised this, the first Ordnance Survey of Ireland. The survey was directed by Colonel Thomas Colby, who had under his command officers of the Royal Engineers and three companies of sappers and miners. In addition to this, civil assistants were recruited to help with sketching, drawing and engraving of maps, and eventually, in the 1830s, the writing of the Memoirs.

The Memoirs were written descriptions intended to accompany the maps, containing information which could not be fitted on to them. Colonel Colby always considered additional information to be necessary to clarify place- names and other distinctive features of each parish; this was to be written up in reports by the officers. Much information about parishes resulted from research into place-names and was used in the writing of the Memoirs. The term "Memoir" comes from the abbreviation of the word "Aide-Memoire". It was also used in the 18th century to describe topographical descriptions accompanying maps.

In 1833 Colby's assistant, Lieutenant Thomas Larcom, developed the scope of the officers' reports by stipulating the headings or "Heads of Inquiry" under which information was to be reported, and including topics of social as well as economic interest. By this time civil assistants were writing some of the Memoirs under the supervision of the officers, as well as collecting information in the Fair Sheets.

The first "Memoirs" are officers' reports covering Antrim in 1830, and work continued on the Antrim parishes right through the decade, with special activity in 1838 and 1839. Counties Down and Tyrone were written up from 1833 to 1837, with both officers and civil assistants working on Memoirs. In Londonderry and Fermanagh research and writing started in 1834. Armagh was worked on in 1835, 1837 and 1838. Much labour was expended in the Londonderry parishes. The plans to publish the Memoirs commenced with the parish of Templemore, containing the city and liberties of Derry, which came out in 1837 after a great deal of expense and effort.

Between 1839 and 1840 the Memoir scheme collapsed. Sir Robert Peel's government could not countenance the expenditure of money and time on such an exercise; despite a parliamentary commission favouring the continuation of the writing of the Memoirs, the scheme was halted before the southern half of the country was covered. The manuscripts remained unpublished and most were removed to the Royal Irish Academy, Dublin from the Ordnance Survey, Phoenix Park. Other records of the Ordnance Survey, including some material from the Memoir scheme, have recently been transferred to the National Archives, Bishop Street, Dublin.

The Memoirs are a uniquely detailed source for the history of the northern half of Ireland immediately before the Great Famine. They document the landscape and situation, buildings and antiquities, land-holdings and population, employment and livelihood of the parishes. They act as a nineteenth-century Domesday book and are essential to the understanding of the cultural heritage of our communities. It is planned to produce a volume of evaluative essays to put the material in its full context, with information on other sources and on the writers of the Memoirs.

Definition of descriptive terms

Memoir (sometimes Statistical Memoir): an account of a parish written according to the prescribed form outlined in the instructions known as "Heads of Inquiry", and normally divided into three sections: Natural Features and History; Modern and Ancient Topography; Social and Productive Economy.

Fair Sheets: "information gathered for the Memoirs", an original title describing paragraphs of information following no particular order, often with marginal headings, signed and dated by the civil assistant responsible.

Statistical Remarks/Accounts: both titles are employed by the Engineer officers in their descriptions of the parish with marginal headings, often similar in layout to the Memoir.

Office Copies: these are copies of early drafts, generally officers' accounts and must have been made for office purposes.

Ordnance Survey Memoirs for County Antrim

This volume, the eleventh for the county and twenty-ninth in the series, contains the Memoirs for 3 parishes and 1 grange in mid Antrim, an area stretching from Lough Neagh to Doagh along the course of the Six Mile Water. The towns of Antrim and

Ballyclare, the latter famous for its fairs, and the villages of Doagh and Parkgate, are the main areas covered.

The Memoir for Antrim was among the first to be transcribed. Edited by Dr Brian Trainor, it was published by the Public Record Office of Northern Ireland in 1969, a pioneering and remarkable achievement. This new edition of Antrim parish contains the complete Memoir, early and draft accounts as well as school statistics and other material, together with an exceptionally full weather journal kept between 1836 and 1838. This material was not included in the earlier edition and will be an indispensable reference to those interested in this area and in the development of the economy and society of this important country town, with Antrim Castle and its important gardens.

The other parishes in this volume provide an interesting context for the description of Antrim town, and a good comparison to Randalstown and district (vol.19). The main Memoirs are written by James Boyle between 1836 and 1838, with Fair Sheets by John Bleakly and earlier accounts by J.R. Ward, J. Fleming Tait and others, and contain some engagingly frank commentaries on the local inhabitants. There is a fascinating account of time spent on the drawings in Donegore, 244 out of 414 hours writing up the Memoir, and all these parishes are exceptionally well illustrated.

While a rich heritage of ancient monuments indicated settlement from early times, this area had a variety of manufacturing works such as paper, tanning and brewing as well as textile, and experienced the effects of early mechanisation of various processes in the linen industry, thereby providing interesting material on the effects of industrialisation.

The political and economic independence of the predominantly Presbyterian landholders was strongly marked and noted, and there is a great emphasis on education, both through schools, book clubs and libraries in Antrim, Ballyclare, Kilbride and Doagh, particularly the latter, as well as farming societies. A remarkable example of this is given in the career of a self- taught mechanic, John Rowan, who ran an engineering works at his forge in Doagh and invented a very early steam-coach or locomotive carriage.

In this prosperous district there is evidence of a well developed social life: dancing, home entertaining, good dress sense amongst the local farmers, although the Antrim Hunt, formerly patronised by the Donegalls who had maintained a hunting lodge at Fisherwick in Doagh, had lapsed by that time.

The editors would like to acknowledge the help they derived from the transcription of the Donegore Memoir published by Queen's Extra Mural Department and PRONI (1974).

Drawings in the Memoir papers are listed below and are cross-referenced in the text; some are illustrated. The manuscript material is to be found in Boxes 2, 9, and 12 of the Royal Irish Academy's collection of Ordnance Survey Memoirs, and section references are given beside each parish below in their printed order.

Antrim   Box 2 I 4, 2, 3, 4, 1

Doagh   Box 9 III 4, 3, 2, 1, 3a

Donegore   Box 9 IV 4, 3, 5, 2, 6 and 2, 2, 1

Kilbride   Box 12 I 6, 5 (also Box 9 III 3a), 2, 4 and 3, 1

Drawings

Antrim (sections 2 and 4):

Ground plan of Arian meeting house, with dimensions.

Ground plan of Roman Catholic chapel, with dimensions.

Massereene bridge, with riverside buildings [illustrated].

Antrim church with tower and steeple, south east view [illustrated].

New meeting house, Antrim, front elevation.

Roman Catholic chapel, Antrim, from a vista in the Wilderness.

Antrim round tower, with dimensions; vertical section and 4 cross sections with dimensions and scale.

Antrim round tower, 3 views, with figures at base for scale.

Antrim round tower, apex of tower, view of the spear, with dimensions, base and mortice, with dimensions.

Antrim round tower, drawings of windows, specimen of the masonry, with scale.

Cross over the doorway of Antrim round tower, with scale.

Antrim church, drawings of small window with dimensions, and east window with dimensions.

Fort in Rathenraw, with 2 sections and scale.

Fort in Dunsilly, with 2 sections and scale.

Plans and sections of 2 forts in Dunsilly.

Plans and sections of 3 forts in Ballycraigy.

Plans and sections of 3 forts in Lady Hill.

Plans and sections of 3 forts in Crevery.

Plans and sections of 3 forts in Antrim Town Parks and Crosskennan.

Plans and sections of 3 forts in Maghereagh and Carngranney.

Plans and sections of 2 forts in Shane's Castle townland.

Plans and sections of 2 forts in Kilbegs and Bleerick.

Tumuli in Antrim Town Parks and Crosskennan, with sections and scale.

Plan of cove in Lady Hill, with 3 sections, dimensions and scale.

Witches Stone in Steeple, with dimensions.

2 Danish pipes, 3 flint arrowheads, town of Antrim.

10 coins, both faces.

Antique chair in Antrim Castle [illustrated].

Doagh (section 3):

Specimen of masonry of Doagh church, 3 stones with dimensions and scale.

Annotated plan of fort, coves and old church of Doagh, with scale [both by J. Boyle].

Donegore (sections 2, 3 and 6):

Ground plan of Parkgate meeting house.

Plan of cove in Ballysavage, with orientation.

Plan of cove near Parkgate meeting house [by J. Bleakly].

Ground plan of Parkgate meeting house [by J.R. Ward].

Donegore Moat and landscape from the west, 5 miles distant [illustrated].

Map of Browndod hill, with scale.

Plan of Browndod hill, showing location of antiquities, with annotations, key and scale.

Plans and sections of 4 druidical altars in Browndod and Tobergill, with orientation and scale.

Ground plan of druidical altar in Browndod, with scale.

Druidical altar at point A, showing figure of man standing.

Ground plan of druidical altar at point B, with scale.

Ground plan of druidical altar in Tobergill, with scale.

Druidical altar in Browndod at point B, with figure of a man [illustrated].

Plan of enclosures in Browndod at point E, with sections and scale.

Enlarged plan of enclosure at point E, showing tumuli, with section and scale.

Enlarged plans and sections of enclosures at points O, F; enlarged plans and sections of tumuli at H and G, with scale.

Plans of enclosures in Browndod, with dimensions and scale.

Standing stone in Browndod, height 3 feet 9 inches.

Standing stone in Browndod, with dimensions.

Druidical altar in Tobergill.

Map of Donegore Moat, showing position of monuments, with scale.

2 standing stones in Donegore, with dimensions.

Plan of Donegore Moat, with 2 sections and scale.

Annotated plan of cyclopean fort in Ballywee, with sections, orientation and scale.

Plan of cyclopean fort, with sections, orientation and scale.

Enlarged plan of cove in cyclopean fort, with sections and scale.

Style of construction of cyclopean fort.

Fort and cove in Dunamuggy, with section and scale.

Enlarged plan of cove in Dunamuggy, with style of construction, dimensions and scale.

Plan of Browndod Fort, with 2 sections and scale.

Plan and section of tumulus in Dunamuggy; plan of grave at point B, with dimensions and scale.

Plan of Rathmore Trench, with section and scale.

Plan and sections of 3 forts in Ballynoe and Ballysavage, with scale.

Plans of sections of 2 forts in Tobergill, with scale.

2 forts in townlands of Browndod and 1 in Ballygowan, with sections and scale.

Artificial cave under Rathmore Trench, ground plan with sections and scale.

The Priest's Chair in Donegore.

Plan of enclosures on Donegore hill, townland of Tobergill, showing position of ancient fence and standing stone, with scale.

Brazen hatchet and 2 stone hatchets, full size.

Brazen pin in Browndod; iron spear and 3 flint arrows in Donegore.

Brazen celt in Donegore, full size.

Ornamented quern in Durhamsland, overhead view and section.

2 views of stone celt in Durhamsland, full size.

Stone amulet in Durhamsland, full size.

Plan of Ballygowan Fort and another tumulus in Ballygowan, with sections and scale [all the above by James Boyle].

Kilbride (sections 2 and 5):

Ground plan of giant's grave and cromlech in Drumadarragh.

Ground plan of cove in Kilbride [both by J. Bleakly].

Giant's grave in Drumadarragh, ground plan with annotations, dimensions and scale.

The Holestone, townland of Holestone.

Forts: 2 in McVickersland, 1 in Ballybracken, 1 in Loonburn, 2 in Drumadarragh, with scale.

Square enclosure in Drumadarragh, showing hollows in parapet, with section and scale.

Coves in Douglassland, with sections, dimensions and scale [all the above by J. Boyle].

Parish of Antrim, County Antrim

Memoir by James Boyle, May 1838

NATURAL FEATURES

Hills

The surface of this parish does not present any very striking features, its most abrupt slopes being smooth and comparatively gentle.

Along the eastern side of the parish a ridge, gradually declining in height from 780 to 120 feet above the sea, extends southward from Carnearny mountain in the adjoining parish of Connor and terminates in a high and steep bank along the Six Mile Water.

The declivity of this ridge is traversed by numerous minor ones, again intersected by several ravines and valleys formed by the little rivulets flowing down it and also by some curious little gravelly features resembling artificial embankments.

The western descent of this ridge terminates near the centre of the parish, more than half of which is almost flat, its inclination not exceeding that of an inclined plane falling towards Lough Neagh from the north and east.

The highest point in the parish, 780 feet above the sea, is at its north east corner. The principal points are Black rock, 457 feet, Crosskennan Lower, 413 feet and Rathenraw, 305 feet above the level of the sea.

Lakes

Lough Neagh, which washes the south west side of the parish: the northern extremity of the part of this vast sheet of water called Antrim Bay is formed by the southern side of this parish, the eastern and western sides of the bay being formed by the opposite shores of the grange of Muckamore and the parish of Drummaul.

The extreme length of Lough Neagh from north to south is 16 and a half miles and its breadth from east to west 12 miles. 48,342 acres, 3 roods 19 perches are included within the limits of this county and 523 acres 27 perches of its surface within the boundary of this parish.

In this parish its bottom, like its low beach, is sandy. Along its shore it is very shallow, deepening very slowly and gradually but finally within the parish attaining extreme summer depth of 49 feet. Its average rise in winter is 6 feet; sometimes it rises to 7 feet and sometimes its rise does not exceed 5 feet. Its lowering, of course, depends

upon the wetness of the season, as most of numerous tributary streams flow from the surrounding mountains.

By its rise neither benefit nor injury is sustained in this parish. Its low sandy shore is not susceptible of injury or improvement and were the lake to be drained or lowered, the only result to this parish would be that a dreary sandy strip along its coast would be laid bare.

In this parish the extent of shore is 1 and a half miles, extending from south east to north west. The shore is wooded almost to the water's edge and from a distance has a rich and beautiful appearance. The views from it embrace the shores of the lake, the surrounding mountains, the beautifully wooded grounds along the eastern side of Antrim Bay and the densely planted demesne of Shane's Castle, with its venerable ruins on its opposite side, combining all the ornaments of the richest rural scenery.

Rivers: Six Mile Water

The tradition concerning the orthography of this river is that it derived its name from being supposed to take its rise just 6 miles from the eastern extremity of the county. The supposition is, however, quite erroneous, its source being 10 and a half English miles from Black Head, the most easterly point of this county.

The Six Mile Water takes rise in Shane's hill in the parish of Kilwaughter, near the eastern coast of the county, at an elevation of about 1,000 feet above the sea. From this it pursues a south westerly course for 18 and a half miles through the fertile valley to which it gives its name. After receiving the contributions of numerous minor streams, supplying water power to 23 mills and manufactories, irrigating and enriching some of the districts through which it flows, and draining others, it discharges itself into Lough Neagh at Antrim Bay, five-sixths of a mile west of the town of Antrim through which it flows. Its average fall from its source to its mouth is 1 foot in 95 feet, but its fall is interrupted by 9 carries for the purpose of turning off water to machinery which it propels. On entering this parish the Six Mile Water is 99 feet above the level of the sea and 51 feet above the level of Lough Neagh.

It enters the parish at its south eastern corner, and from this it pursues a very irregular and

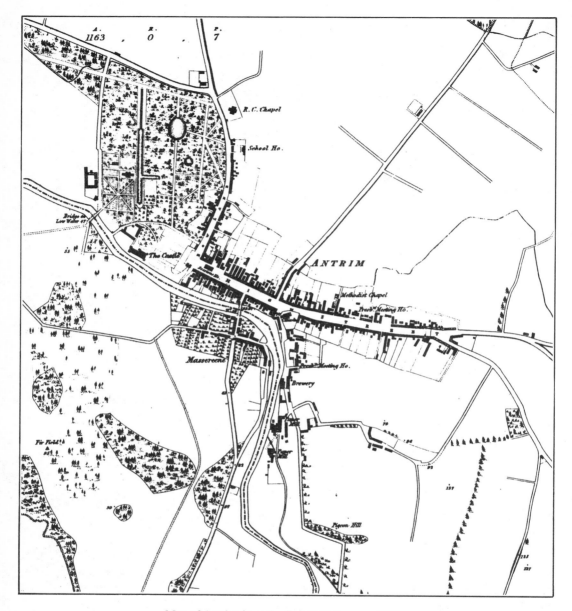

Map of Antrim from the first 6" O.S. maps, 1830s

circuitous course for 3 and a half miles along its southern boundary, separating it from the grange of Muckamore. Its breadth (in summer) at its mouth is 417 feet, at Antrim bridge 82 feet and on entering the parish 49 feet. Its least breadth in this parish is 37 feet and its average breadth 59 feet.

Its depth is very variable, depending upon the proximity of 4 carries or dams thrown across it for the purpose of turning off water to machinery. The first of these carries is one-sixth of a mile from where it enters the parish; it is raised 7 feet

above the bed of the river. The second is nearly half a mile further down and is 5 feet high; the third is nearly half a mile from the last and is 5 feet high; and the fourth and last, which turns off the water for the Antrim mills, is three-quarters of a mile from the last carry and is raised 9 feet above the bed of the river.

From the summit of the first to the base of the last-mentioned carry there is a fall of 36 feet in a distance of 10,490 feet, while from the base of the last carry to the mouth of the river, a distance of

7,990 feet, there is an inclination of only 15 feet, the average fall in the former distance being 1 foot in 291 feet and in the latter 1 foot in 532 feet.

Much of the intermediate spaces between the carries is in moderate weather almost dry, and only during wet weather does the river flow over the carries. Still, from the beautiful arrangement of the reservoirs and mill-races, a constant supply of water is preserved throughout the year.

The river gradually deepens from Antrim downwards and attains an extreme summer depth of 6 feet, but at its mouth there is a bar of sand which in summer is covered by not more than 18 inches to 2 feet of water and is easily fordable. The bed of this stream is rocky and very rough and uneven, until it approaches Antrim where it becomes clayey, and on nearing the lake is sandy.

For the 2 miles of its course in this parish it flows through the beautiful glen of Moylinny, the banks of which tower on each side to a height of from 30 to 100 feet, are very steep and clothed with a rich and beautiful planting, and here the scenery is quite romantic. Towards Antrim the banks are low and the country flat, but ornamented by the timber and young planting about Antrim Castle.

Near its mouth it overflows in winter a small extent of level hoame <holme> but without affecting the land either as to its benefit or injury. From the number of its tributary streams and the circumstance of its taking its rise in the mountains, it is subject to very violent and sudden floods which rise and fall with great rapidity.

This stream might at little expense be rendered navigable to the town of Antrim for lighters carrying from 30 to 40 tons. This was contemplated about 50 years ago and a pier erected at its mouth, but it would be of little advantage to Antrim as a few loads of coal from Belfast and 3 or 4 lighters of bricks or grain from Coalisland at present constitute the annual imports of Antrim.

Rivulets

There are 2 other little rivulets which flow through a portion of the western side of the parish and may be rendered useful in propelling machinery. The more important of these is the Dunsilly burn. It takes its rise at the north eastern side of the parish, at an elevation of 680 feet above the level of the sea and 632 feet above the level of Lough Neagh. From this it pursues a south westerly course across the parish, forming a portion of the boundary between the baronies of Upper Toome and Upper Antrim, and also between the estates of

Lords O'Neill and Ferrard; and, after receiving the waters of several minor streams, discharges itself into the Six Mile Water near the mouth of that river.

Its total length is 4 miles; its breadth is trifling, not exceeding 11 feet; its depth varies from a few inches to 2 and a half feet. Towards its source its bed is rocky and stony; in the low and almost level grounds near its mouth it is clayey and at its mouth it is sandy. For the latter half of its course it flows through an almost level country which, from its inconsiderable banks, it formerly injured by its frequent inundations, large tracts being laid under water by it in winter. From the fertility of its soil and its high state of cultivation it was found necessary to raise embankments to protect it, and it is no longer exposed to its inundations.

It is applicable to machinery, drainage and irrigation. It is usefully situated for the last two purposes and is partially applied to them. Its average fall is 1 foot in 34 feet.

The Mill burn takes its rise in the townland of Lenagh, in the adjoining parish of Drummaul. From this it flows easterly and, entering this parish at its western side, pursues a southerly course for 1 and one-eighth miles through the townlands of Maghereagh and Shane's Castle, and discharges itself into Lough Neagh after a total course of 3 miles.

Its source is 187 feet above the sea and 139 feet above Lough Neagh. Its average fall is 1 foot in 114 feet. Its bed is sometimes stony but more generally soft and clayey. Its banks are low and it sometimes overflows them without making any deposit or producing any effect on the inundated land; it soon naturally subsides.

This little brook, though not exceeding 12 feet in extreme width or 18 inches in ordinary depth, is applied to machinery and is usefully situated for the purposes of irrigation and drainage, particularly for the latter, there being some tracts of bog in the parish of Drummaul which might easily be drained by it. In this parish it would not be required for this purpose.

Mineral Spring

Adjoining the south side of the town of Antrim, but in the grange of Muckamore and townland of Balloo, is a highly impregnated chalybeate spring which, as it is known by the name of Antrim Spa, may here be noticed.

It is situated within 20 yards of the left bank of the Six Mile Water and trickles through an iron pipe set in a wall into a stone trough. The adjacent soil is gravelly and it is not elevated more than 4 feet above the surface of the river. It is but little used or noticed by anyone. A bottle of the water is herewith sent.

In the townland of Holy Well near the centre of the parish, 1 and one-third miles north of Antrim and a little to the left of the road leading from that town to Connor, is a spring well situated in a gravelly hill and 115 feet above the sea. The well is about 6 feet deep and the water of an agreeable flavour, in no respect differing in flavour from drinking water, but said to possess some tonic or strengthening powers.

It is more than probable that its properties are imaginary and founded only on tradition, as it is known by the name of Holy Well and seems to have been somehow connected with the round tower which is 5 and a half furlongs south of it; and there is also a tradition that charms or miracles were wrought at it and that stations were made from it to the Witches Stone near the tower. Its use for healing purposes is trifling, but still not confined to the ignorant or superstitious. A bottle of it is herewith sent.

The parish is amply supplied with spring and river water for domestic uses, though in some of its lower districts, particularly in the townland of Dunsilly within a few yards of Dunsilly burn, the spring water is so strongly impregnated as to be unfit for use. One person in that townland sunk a pump to a depth of 16 feet through a reddish clay, but the water found was incapable of being used. A bottle of Dunsilly spring water is herewith sent.

Woods

Except a few old thorns, a little hazel brushwood, usually to be found about the old forts of the country, and a little oak or fir timber found in the trifling patches of bog, there is not any natural wood in the parish.

Bogs

There is no bog in this parish which is cut for fuel. The inconsiderable patches to be met with in it are very few and are usually situated either in a little hollow in which water may have been lodged, or on the acclivity of a hill from which a spring issues. These patches are cultivated. They mostly contain a little fir or oak timber of trifling dimensions and seemingly very old and decayed. They have, however, been but partially explored.

Climate

The climate of Antrim is moist and very variable.

Notwithstanding this and its low situation, it is rather healthy and the air mild and pure.

From its proximity to Lough Neagh and the mountainous districts, and its situation between the former and the latter, and the prevalence of south west and westerly winds, it is subject to frequent rains. For the vapours which collect about the lake and the marshy districts along its southern shores are wafted by the prevailing winds to its northern extremity and, being there attracted by the mountains, are by them condensed into rain.

The west wind is more frequently followed by rain than the other winds, for most of the vapours carried by the south wind are attracted by either the Bann or Main rivers and descend upon the marshy and boggy districts along their banks.

About Antrim the north wind is commonly followed by cold dry weather, the north west by showery and stormy, the west by rainy, the south west by showery, the south (if in summer) by dry, if in winter by wet, the south east by showery, and the east and north east by dry but cold weather. Frost during a northerly or easterly wind is likely to continue for some time; with south or west, rain will soon follow. The shifts of wind are incessant during the twenty-four hours and of course attended by a variety of temperatures.

The aspect of the parish is good. It is also, except towards its north east corner, well sheltered either by the bushy hedgerows in its higher and more eastern grounds and the low situation of its western districts.

Crops

The ripening of crops throughout the parish is much alike in its different districts and the seasons may be noted as follows: wheat and barley are commonly reaped from the 12th August to 12th September, oats from the 20th August to the first week in October, and potatoes are dug during the month of November. Wheat is commonly sown soon after the raising of potatoes, and oats and barley during the month of March. Potatoes are generally planted during the last week in April and the early part of May. The above statement may be taken as generally applicable to this parish.

There have been some exceptions, particularly in the year 1836, when much of grain in the higher grounds remained uncut in the ridges in the month of December. During this season the weather was unusually rainy and there was not sufficient dry or warm weather to ripen or harden the crops (vide Metereological Register at the end).

MODERN TOPOGRAPHY

Antrim: Situation and Locality

The town of Antrim is beautifully situated at the south western side of the county, in the parish of the same name, in the barony of Upper Antrim and manor of Moylinny, diocese of Connor and north east circuit of assize.

It is situated in 54 degrees 40 minutes north latitude and 5 degrees 30 minutes west longitude, and is 120 statute miles north of Dublin, 17 and a half north west of Belfast, 12 and two-thirds south of Ballymena and 11 and a half miles west of Toome Bridge, which forms the nearest means of communication between the counties of Antrim and Londonderry.

Antrim is well watered by a copious stream known by the name of Six Mile Water, which flows close to the rear of the houses on the south side of the town and discharges itself into Lough Neagh, five-sixths of a mile west of the town. At Antrim bridge this stream is 82 feet broad and averages 3 feet deep. Its situation here is most advantageous to the town, affording a constant supply of water for its machinery and for the domestic uses of its inhabitants.

Antrim is the great thoroughfare or pass between Belfast and the northern and western towns and districts of this county, the county of Londonderry and the northern parts of Tyrone. The main street extends for half a mile along the great leading road from the northern metropolis to these districts and it is also the mail coach road from Belfast to Derry. The direct and post road to Dublin by Hillsborough diverges from the centre of the town. The extreme length of Antrim is half a mile from east to west and one-fifth of a mile from north to south.

The situation of Antrim, though low and not exceeding an elevation of 35 feet above Lough Neagh, is remarkably cheerful and interesting. From the eastern extremity of the town to its centre there is a gentle fall of about 20 feet, the rest of the town being almost perfectly flat and elevated but a few feet above its river.

It is almost embosomed in the numerous and tastefully disposed plantings immediately about it and but for the handsome and cathedral-like spire of its church, which rises gracefully above the groves of Antrim Castle, it would not be discernible from a distance.

East of the town the ground rises a little and north of it assumes a hilly and almost mountainous character, presenting an agreeable contrast to the almost level tracts towards the west and south.

The whole surrounding scenery is in a high state of cultivation. The country is diversified and ornamented with the handsome residences of neighbouring gentry, numerous clumps and groves of planting, watered by a copious stream, and possessing exquisite views of the neighbouring lake and its more distant shores, and abounding in delightful drives and walks in almost every direction.

HISTORY

Early History

Antrim is said to be a place of such antiquity that its early history, embracing the date and origin of its erection, is involved in obscurity or at least in uncertainty. The traditions concerning it are numerous and some of them appear reasonable and probable, but when it is remembered that scarce a descendant of the original possessors of the country now inhabits it, much faith cannot be placed in them.

The most probable and commonly believed tradition is that Antrim formerly stood near the ancient round tower (known by the name of the Steeple) in the townland of Steeple and three-quarters of a mile north of the present town. It is said that the town then bore the name of Entrumnia, but that its site was changed from that to its present one on account of its proximity to water, and some say also because of a ferry or bridge which crossed the river at this point. Its name was then changed to Anthrona, which is said to signify a ford or ferry, and hence the name of Antrim, which indeed some say was that of a witch who was very troublesome during the erection of the round tower, and at its completion expressed her dissatisfaction by jumping from its summit and, lighting on a stone 120 yards north of it, left in it the impressions of her knee and elbow, which still remain in it, and to this day it is known as the Witches Stone (see Ancient Topography).

The tradition respecting the former situation of Antrim is in some degree borne out by the circumstance of very extensive foundations and great quantities of building stones having been found about the round tower, which is pointed out as having been its site, and large quantities of human bones having also been found there. [Insert query by C.W. Ligar: Might not this have been the remains of a burying ground and religious establishment?].

In a manuscript of the late Dr Stevenson of Belfast, he states that a church was erected at Antrim in 495 by a disciple of St Patrick, but that there was no later record of it than 761. Except the round tower alluded to, there is not now any monument of antiquity either in the town or in its immediate vicinity.

The houses are, with a few exceptions, comparatively modern in their appearance and construction. One little old house at the western extremity of the Main Street has a gable elevated on its front and there are still 4 houses constructed exclusively of wood; in two of these the upper storey projects beyond the lower one. Within memory many of these wooden houses have been pulled down. The town is said to have been at one time solely consisted of them. They were constructed in the grange of Ballyscullion, 8 and a half miles west of Antrim, and from thence they were brought in pieces to Antrim. The floors, walls and doors are all of oak. The spaces between the timbers are filled up with mud or mortar plastered over and roughcast. They are now thatched, but it is said they were formerly roofed with shingles.

Clotworthy Family

Antrim became of much greater importance than it had before been, on the settlement of the Clotworthy family in it, who, being zealous Presbyterians or Nonconformists, came over from England in 1603 and in 1613 built the castle of Antrim. Sir Hugh Clotworthy, an officer of rank in the English army, was the first of the family who settled here and he is said to have induced many of the English Presbyterians to follow his example.

Rebellion of 1641

"On the 23rd October 1641, and within a few days after, the Irish rebels made slaughter of all men, women and children which they could lay hands on within the county of Antrim, burning their houses and corn" (Reid's *History of Presbyterianism*, vol.1) and on this day 947 Protestants are said to have been butchered in Antrim by the Roman Catholics.

In January 1642 Sir John Clotworthy, having been appointed to command of a vessel of about 20 tons and mounting 6 brass guns, with several smaller boats which were launched upon Lough Neagh for the purpose of keeping in check the Irish garrisons on the opposite coast of Tyrone under Sir Phelim Roe O'Neill, obtained several victories over the rebel forces, who had several boats in which they used to sail down the Blackwater into the lake and plunder its coasts.

Several skirmishes occurred between these fleets until the July following, when the rebels were totally defeated with the loss of above 60 men killed, and their boats, with a considerable number of prisoners, were conveyed in triumph to Antrim.

In 1649 the town of Antrim was taken and partly burned by General Monroe.

Rebellion of 1798

On the 7th June 1798 an engagement took place in Antrim between the rebels and the king's troops, the former amounting to about 1,000 and the latter (consisting of a squadron of the 22nd Light Dragoons, under the command of Colonel Lumley and Major Seddon and a corps of yeomanry) to about 150 men.

A meeting of the neighbouring magistrates was on that day to have taken place in the market house of Antrim, for the purpose of adopting some measures with respect to the unfortunate rebellion then raging throughout the country. The rebels were aware of this and determined to attack the town and take some of the magistrates as hostages.

They came from Donegore and Templepatrick on the east and Drummaul on the west, intending to have entered the town at different extremities simultaneously, but a house in which a large quantity of pikes were concealed having been set on fire privately by some of the loyal inhabitants, the Donegore column rushed on, thinking from the smoke that the town had already been attacked, and entered in at 1 o'clock, 1 hour before the intended time.

The squadron of the 22nd, with 2 curricle guns then attached to that regiment, galloped into town from Blaris camp near Lisburn and, entering the town from the south over Massereene bridge, opened on them with round shot from the centre of the street. The rebels were at this moment marching down High Street and, in spite of the fire, some of them rushed down and got into the churchyard, from which they kept up a desperate fire upon the yeomanry and cavalry.

The latter were ordered to charge, which they did most effectually, cutting their way through the rebels from the one extremity of the street to the other and back again, but lost a cornet (Dunne), 16 privates and 40 horses killed and 27 men wounded. Finding their forces too weak they retired the yeomanry behind the castellated wall at the foot of High Street. The cavalry halted at the wall for a few moments and gave the column of rebels who were just then (2 o'clock) entering the town by Bow Lane from Drummaul a couple of rounds from the artillery, which obliged them to retreat. The cavalry then galloped down to the river, threw the guns into the watering places in it, at the foot of the High Street, and retreated towards the shore of the lake.

In the meantime Lord O'Neill, who as governor of the county had come in to attend the meeting, was attacked near the market house. He dismounted from his horse and attempted to run up the steps outside but was knocked down and piked to death at the north side of the house.

The yeomanry still continued behind the parapet wall at the foot and the rebels kept their ground in the churchyard, and at the opposite end of High Street, occasionally firing at each other, until 3 o'clock when 2 large columns, cavalry, artillery and infantry, unseen by the rebels, approached Antrim, one from the south and the other from the east from Blaris camp. The cavalry cut down without mercy all whom they met leaving Antrim, within a mile of it, and the artillery poured a destructive fire on them from the eastern extremity of High Street. They, of course, fled in every direction, those who took the Lisburn Road being cut to pieces by the troops entering on that side.

Upwards of 300 rebels were killed that day; 127 fell in the streets of Antrim and were interred in a heap near the lake shore. Numbers who had been wounded crawled to the cornfields about the town, where they perished and were discovered during the ensuing harvest. Altogether they received such a chastisement that they never after rallied in the neighbourhood.

The rebels brought with them 2 6-pounders, which they had sometime previously stolen from the military in Belfast and hid in the floor of Templepatrick meeting house, from which they were dug up the night previous to the action. One of them they mounted on the carriage of a gentleman's chaise and the other on a common car. They were, however, of little service to them as they were quickly dismounted by the shot from the curricle guns.

Had the rebels from Drummaul entered Antrim simultaneously with the other bodies, the consquences for the town and the few troops in it must have been dreadful. To this day they attribute their speedy retreat to the cowardice of their leader, Samuel Orr, who recently died in Carrickfergus jail where he had been confined for debt. The body of the rebels which he commanded was very numerous and was composed of those from the western parishes of Drummaul and Duneane, and of many who had been at the fight of Ballymena the day previous.

Samuel was a brother of the celebrated William Orr, a rebel leader who had been executed at Carrickfergus during the previous winter. He was greatly beloved by the people, who had medals commemorative of him struck and rings with "Remember Orr" inscribed on them. His widow is a member of the Orthodox Presbyterian congregation in Antrim.

Since this time Antrim has not been the scene of any remarkable events, and from the peaceful and industrious character of its inhabitants it seems little likely again to be of any celebrity.

MODERN TOPOGRAPHY

Public Buildings

The public buildings in Antrim consist of a church, 3 Presbyterian and a Quaker meeting house, 2 Methodist and 1 Roman Catholic chapel, a market and court house, a schoolhouse and a bridge.

Church

The parish church stands at the south side of High Street and near the centre of the town. It consists of a main aisle standing nearly east and west, and measuring outside 66 feet by 33 feet. Attached to its south side is a wing 21 by 21 feet, occupied by the Massereene family and fitted up partly as a pew and partly as a vault.

At the western end of the church stands a very handsome square tower built in ashlar masonry, ornamented by massive sandstone buttresses which are surmounted by crocketted pinnacles. There are 4 very handsome and chaste Gothic windows in the tower. The spire is of cut sandstone and forms, with the tower, a total elevation of 117 feet, presenting a beautiful and cathedral-like appearance. In the tower is a belfry and also an excellent clock with 4 dials.

The church is well lit by 4 square leaded windows on its north side, 2 of a similar description on its south and a lancet window in its eastern gable. These windows are of cut stone and very old (see plans). The main aisle of Antrim church contains 14 double and 21 single pews, and a gallery containing 6 single ones, in all capable of accommodating 420 persons.

In the southern wing is the seat of the Massereene family, being spacious, wainscoted and constructed of oak, and lit by a similar window of beautifully stained glass which was brought from the Continent by the late Lord Massereene.

The church is comfortable and warm, and in pretty good repair. It is said to be of great antiquity. Its masonry is certainly rather rude and it would seem to have [been] at one time used as a place of defence, as there are 4 loopholes in its northern side and 2 in its eastern gable. An entrance had been made in its northern side but this is now built up. On one of the cut stones forming the jamb of this doorway the date 1596 is inscribed. It is said to have been the fourth church in which the Protestant [worship] was celebrated in Ireland.

In the church, near the pulpit, is a very handsome white marble slab with a figure on each side representing 2 females weeping. It was erected by his wife and daughter to the memory of the fourth Earl and eighth Viscount Massereene, who died the 25th February 1816. This monument was executed by Westmacott.

Near the east side of the burial ground are interred the colours of the Dumbarton Fencibles, which were quartered in Antrim in 1801. They were first burned and their ashes enclosed in a little coffin which was interred here on the 27th April in that year. And in the same grave the remains of Major Gibson of the same regiment were interred on the 28th August 1800.

Unitarian Meeting House

The Unitarian meeting house stands near the eastern end of the town, on the northern side of the main or High Street. It was built about the year 1699. It is a plain old building, consisting of a main aisle standing east and west, and measuring 60 by 27 feet, and a lesser one attached to its north centre, measuring 24 by 18 feet. It is perfectly plain, roughcast and lit by a double row of small, square lead windows on each side. It contains a gallery and accommodation for 800 persons. It is in pretty good repair.

The Presbyterian meeting house in the Mill Row has, in consequence of its ruinous state, just been abandoned! It had been erected in 1731, 5 years after the separation which took place in the synod.

New Meeting House

The new meeting house erected by the congregation of the last-mentioned one, and in connection with the Synod of Ulster, is a handsome, substantial and spacious structure, situated 90 yards to the south of High Street and near the east end of the town. Its extensive dimensions are 78 feet long (from north to south), 58 feet wide from east to west and 29 feet high in the side walls. It is well lit by 2 rows of windows in each side and 2 ornamental windows in its northern or entrance front.

The windows in the upper row have circular heads; those in the lower are square. The house is well built of whinstone. The walls are 3 feet thick and the roof, which has a trifling pitch, projects considerably over a handsome cornice.

The entrance front at its northern end is in the Egyptian style and has a handsome and massive appearance. It consists of a portico (the ascent to which is by 6 spacious steps) supported by 2 massive white porphyry columns, with capitals of the Doric order. These support a frieze and pediment which, with the entire of this front, are stone finished and have a very good effect. From the portico doors open right and left leading to the body of the house and in the centre of the portico is a handsome Egyptian doorway leading to the vestibule, from which 2 flights of stairs lead to the galleries which extend along 3 sides of the house.

The aisle is well planned and contains a single row of seats extending along 2 sides of the house, and a double row in the centre, in all 74 seats. The gallery is well planned and contains 58 seats capable, with the aisle, of accommodating 1,000 persons.

At the south side of the house is the pulpit, the ascent to which is from the basement storey by a well-constructed hidden spiral stair.

The interior execution and finish of the house are in keeping with the exterior. The ceiling and cornices are plain and elegant. The walls are stone finished, the galleries are supported by metal pillars and the woodwork neat and substantial. It is an airy, cheerful and comfortable place of worship, well designed and executed.

Underneath the southern end of the meeting house is an apartment 24 feet square, intended for holding a Sunday school in. It is lit by 4 square windows and is entered by a door from its southern side.

The total cost of this building was 3,000 pounds, of which 130 pounds were collected at the sermons preached on its being opened and by the sale of the tickets of admission to them. The remainder has been raised among the congregation, by contributions and the sale of seats, and by collections made in Scotland and by the sale of the old meeting house.

The house was opened for divine service on Sunday the 18th June 1837, by the Revd Archibald Nesbit A.M., Moderator of the Presbytery of Glasgow.

Methodist Chapels

The Primitive Wesleyan Methodist chapel is situated on the south side of High Street, near the east end of the town. It is a neat, little roughcast house, presenting a gable front to the street and measuring 42 by 20 feet. It is sufficiently comfortable and commodious, and accommodates 100 persons. Forms are the only seats used in it. It was erected by subscription in 1823 and cost 200 pounds.

The Methodist chapel is situated in an obscure lane on the south side of High Street and nearly opposite the Wesleyan chapel. It is a plain roughcast house, slated and measuring 42 by 27 feet. It is fitted up with forms and can accommodate 130 persons. It was erected by subscription in 1805 and cost 200 pounds.

Roman Catholic Chapel

The Roman Catholic chapel is a neat-looking, substantially finished edifice of a cruciform figure, situated at the western extremity of the town, on the road leading to Randalstown and Ballymena.

Its extreme length from north to south is 66 feet and from east to west 70 feet; its width is 30 feet. The eastern wing is used solely as a schoolroom. The part appropriated to divine service consists of a spacious hall, well lit. The entrance to it is by 3 doors. From the hall 2 flights of stairs lead to the galleries, which extend along 3 sides of the house and are fitted up with seats. The hall is without seats and the congregation occupying it are obliged to stand; its floor is earthen.

The house is comfortable and well finished. It was erected in 1818 and cost 1,400 pounds, raised by subscription. It accommodates 600 persons.

Market and Court House

The market and court house is situated at the end and near the centre of High Street. It is a plain but neat-looking, stone-finished building, measuring in the clear 78 by 42 feet and 32 feet high. It consists of 2-storeys; the under one is divided into a market place or weigh-house and a bridewell or temporary prison. The former of these divisions is 51 feet long and opens to the street by 5 circular-arched gateways on each side and 3 similar ones at its east end. These gateways are secured by iron gates.

At the western end of the weigh-house is a temporary bridewell for confining drunkards, rioters and prisoners under trial at the quarter sessions. It consists of 2 cells 16 by 11 feet and 9 feet high, each fitted up with 2 beds and bedding. Between them and the weigh-house is a sort of corridor or passage extending across the house and 7 feet wide, enclosed from the weigh-house by a dwarf wall with iron railings. This serves to admit air and light to the bridewell. The upper storey is fitted up as a court house and contains the keeper's apartments.

The court house is a spacious, airy and well-lit room, 51 by 40 feet and 18 feet high. It receives light from 5 large windows on each side and is suitably fitted up with jury and other benches, a council table, dock and other similar requisites. At its eastern end, behind the magisterial bench, is a retiring room for the bench and at its western end, over the keeper's apartments, is a jury room.

The keeper's apartments consist of 2 rooms, one at each side of the doorway of the court house, immediately under the jury room and over the bridewell. The entrance to the court is by a neat doorway at the western end of the house, the ascent to which is by a double flight of stone stairs on the outside.

The market house has a handsome hipped roof with a projecting eave. It is surmounted by a neat octagonal cupola lit by 8 windows and from its summit rises a gilt spear, which at a little distance has a pretty effect.

The market house was erected in 1726 and repaired by the county in 1821. The cupola was erected by Lord Ferrard in 1817 and cost 150 pounds.

Schoolhouse

The schoolhouse is situated in Bow Lane, near the western end of the town. It is a plain building, built of stone and roughcast, measuring 50 by 36 feet and 20 feet high, 2-storeys and well lit by a double row of windows on each side. It contains 2 schoolrooms, that on the first floor, for the boys, measuring 44 by 24 feet and that on the second, for the female scholars, measuring 34 by 24 feet. This house was erected in 1815 at the expense of the late Viscount Massereene and cost [blank].

Bridge

Massereene bridge, over the Six Mile Water and on the road to Dublin, forms the communication between the town of Antrim and its suburb, the hamlet of Massereene which extends along the left bank of the river. This bridge is near the south centre of the town. It measures 130 feet long, 18 feet wide and consists of 6 elliptic arches. Its roadway is 16 feet above the level of the river. It

Massereene bridge

is plain but substantial in its masonry and is in good repair. From an inscription on a sandstone slab in the parapet, it appears it was erected in 1708. This bridge, from its height, its narrow arches and pretty situation, has a very picturesque effect when viewed from a little distance.

Hotels

There are 2 hotels in Antrim, the Massereene Arms and the King's Arms, the former kept by Mr Leetch and the latter by Mr McNally, and both situated on the south side of the High Street and within a few doors of each other.

The Massereene Arms Hotel is one of the best country inns in Ireland, combining comfortable accommodation with civility. The house is commodious and contains 4 sitting and 6 bedrooms, and there are 8 horses constantly attached to its posting establishment.

The King's Arms is a tolerably good specimen of an Irish country inn and is pretty comfortable and reasonable in its charges. It is less expensive than the former and has only 4 post horses attached to it.

Private Residences: Antrim Castle

The private residences are: Antrim Castle, the family mansion of the Massereene family and one of the seats of Viscount Ferrard (whose eldest son is Viscount Massereene).

The castle was erected in the reign of Charles I (in 1613) by Sir Hugh Clotworthy, a lineal ancestor of Lord Ferrard's. It has since then undergone several changes, the last of which, as appears from an inscription on its front, took place in 1813 when Lord Massereene ("Renov") repaired, restored and improved it.

It is situated 110 yards west of the western extremity of High Street, from which it is completely hidden and separated by a castellated wall. The entrance to the castle grounds from the street is through a handsome and massive gateway in a sombre-looking barbican flanked by an octagonal tower on each side and presenting to the street a handsome dungeon-like front (the barbican was erected in 1818).

The castle stands within 20 feet of the right bank of the river, with which it is almost on a level. The ground about it on that side of the river is almost perfectly flat but on the opposite side it falls gently towards it with an almost unvaried slope. The view from the castle, except from the upper windows, is therefore confined.

The castle is a rectangular building presenting 2 fronts, its eastern, or entrance, front measuring 90 and its southern front (containing on the first floor a regular suite of apartments) extending along the river for 180 feet.

The entrance front presents quite a baronial appearance, being stone-finished and having almost a third of its entire surface covered with armorial bearings of the family, surmounted by a bust of Charles I, all well executed in stone and having a singular but fine effect. 2 wings project a little from each side of this front and they are ornamented with little circular towers at their angles. The approach to the doorway is by a double flight of stone stairs with massive cut-stone balustrades.

With the exception of this front, the external appearance of the castle is far from imposing, its southern front being roughcast and only varied by 3 rows of lofty windows.

Having been occupied by a few domestics only in the last [blank] years, the castle is but scantily furnished and does not now look to much advantage. The eastern front contains a spacious and lofty hall, from which open off a few small apartments. The southern front contains a regular suite of apartments which are of tolerable size. Beyond those, and at its eastern end, are the billiard room and a beautiful little family chapel with a handsome stained-glass window. The library is a good sized room and contains a tolerable collection. There are a few family portraits, some of which are pretty good, and some other paintings of little merit. The offices are a little to the north of the castle. They are suitable as to size but in other respects unworthy of notice and in bad repair.

Wilderness

The grounds in this side of the river, known as the Wilderness, are in this parish and, including the gardens, extend over about 37 acres. Those in the opposite side of the river are in the grange of Muckamore and, stretching along the shore of the lake for about 2 miles, extend over about 1,090 acres laid down in pasture as a deerpark and sheep-walks, and beautifully ornamented with

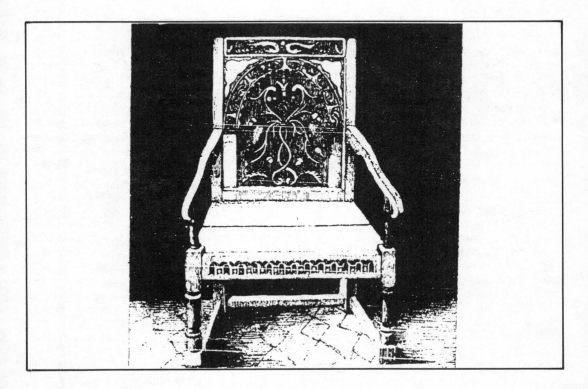

Antique chair in Antrim Castle

some old wood and numerous tastefully disposed clumps and belts of young planting.

The Wilderness is at once unique and curious in its arrangement, being a perfect specimen of the French style of gardening in the 17th century; and though almost flat and extending over no greater extent than 37 acres, it is so laid out as to seem more than double its real size.

It consists of a grove thickly wooded with very tall and tapering elms interspersed with a few other trees and shrubs, traversed by numerous perfectly straight alleys and walks, and these again intersected by several curiously contrived vistas cut through the planting, bearing on some interesting object such as the round tower, the church spire, the chapel etc.; and at the termination of two of them are handsome vases supported by pedestals.

The grounds are also ornamented by some beautiful ponds. One of these is 220 yards long and 10 yards broad. A walk and a splendid lime hedge 18 feet high extends along each side of it. There are 2 other ponds which are circular; the largest of these is 186 yards in circumference.

Towards the western side of the Wilderness is a curious little parterre [insert marginal note: 27] yards square, surrounded by a beautiful lime hedge 20 feet high and laid out in the most fantastic manner. Some of the beds contain flowers, but numberless little ones laid out in every variety of shape, enclosed by boxwood edging, contain only gravel, each containing a different colour. In the centre of the parterre is a yew tree 14 feet high, in the form of an obelisk.

A little to the north, and nearly opposite the castle, are the terrace gardens, which consist of a beautiful range of flower beds extending along 3 sides of a square 110 by 108 yards. They are 16 feet wide and raised 9 feet above the adjacent ground. A high wall encloses them from a kitchen garden in the centre and a lower one from the grounds on the outside. They contain a choice selection of flowers and shrubs, among which are some fine myrtles.

The kitchen garden contains 8 acres. It is situated on the west side of the Wilderness and contains a small hothouse. It is not walled nor is it very well stocked.

Close to the north side of the castle is a mount 37 feet high and 51 yards in diameter at the base and 12 at the summit. It seems to be one of the old Danish mounds commonly met with in the country. It is planted with a variety of trees and shrubs, and a well-constructed spiral walk leads to its summit.

There are several very fine old yews in the grounds. The elms grow to a great height and are immensely straight and taper. There are some fine beech, and cypress and rhododendrons are particularly luxuriant.

A plain bridge 87 feet long, and consisting of 6 semicircular arches, spans the river a little below the castle and leads to a drive and numerous delightful walks along the lake on its opposite side.

The grounds are kept in the nicest order. The public are admitted to them and the castle at all times, and it is much visited by strangers. The people of Antrim enjoy a most agreeable privilege in having at all times access to the delightful walks about the castle, and they are much frequented by them.

The other private gentlemen's residences are those of John Fowke Esquire, William Latham Esquire, M.D., John Hitchcock Esquire in the Mill Row, the Reverend James Carley in the High Street, [crossed out: Frederick William Macauley Esquire].

Streets

Antrim principally consists of one main street called High Street, which extends for half a mile from east to west along the Derry and Belfast road. From the western end of High Street, Bow Lane strikes off almost at right angles and extends along this same road for 410 yards. An irregular straggling lane called the Mill Row (from its leading to the mills) strikes off from the south side of the town and near its centre, and extends southerly for 400 yards. Paty's Lane branches from the north side of High Street opposite the Mill Row and extends northerly along the road to Connor for 148 yards. A single row of 6 cabins branches from the north side of High Street near its eastern end.

On the south side of the river, and in the grange of Muckamore, is a collection of 59 cabins, 10 2-storey and 3 3-storey houses forming 4 narrow and irregular streets or lanes known by the name of Massereene, and forming a portion of the town of Antrim, or more properly its suburb, and will therefore be included in the description of that town. Though it is situated in the grange of Muckamore and the barony of Lower Massereene, still it is the only part of the grange included in the manor of Moylinny in which Antrim is situated.

Antrim consists of 470 houses, of which 54 are 3-storeys, 223 2-storeys and 193 1-storey high. In the erection of these little or no regard has been paid to uniformity or regularity, and from the mixture of good with bad, and 2-storey houses with cabins, the appearance of all has suffered by the contrast and the irregularity of the town rendered more striking.

There are but few which have a modern look. Many, even about the centre of the town, are ruinous looking and towards its outlets, particularly in Bow Lane and Massereene, they tend to dwindle into wretched hovels of a miserable and filthy description, and with the narrowness of these streets tend to impress a stranger with a very unfavourable opinion of the town.

High Street is almost straight, having a slight curve near its centre. It is of a very fair width, averaging 44 feet clear of the footways which average 8 feet wide. The street is macadamized, kept in good order, cleanly and dries rapidly, owing to its having a sandy bottom and the crust of the road not exceeding 3 and a half inches in average thickness. From its western end nearly to its centre the footways are smoothly paved, in some instances flagged, and nearly entirely secured by a good curbstone. With the exception of a few spots, a roughly-paved footway extends along either side of the remainder of this street.

Bow Lane (as its name would imply) is slightly curved. Its width averages only 28 feet, its greatest breadth not exceeding 34 feet, while in some places it is only 23 feet wide. It is macadamized and has a narrow and uneven footway (in most places on a level with the street) for a short distance on both sides, but for the greater part on only one.

From its being the only entrance to Antrim from the northern and western towns, and its being so narrow and quite flat, it is in general very dirty, though in tolerable repair. Few of the houses in it are good, many of them very middling and some of them wretched mud hovels. There are 19 of the latter extending along its east side to its northern extremity. This street will, however, soon be much improved by its being widened and most of the worst houses thrown down, as the intended turnpike road from Antrim to Coleraine will pass through it.

Paty's Lane is an irregular little street only 19 feet wide and inhabited by tradespeople and labourers. It is macadamized and kept rather cleanly.

The Mill Row principally consists of a single very irregular row of houses and cabins extending along the river. It is built on a lane not more than 18 feet wide and which opens only to the street. Near the centre are 3 gentlemen's residences which look down the river and are prettily situated. This lane is usually in a very dirty state.

Massereene

Massereene, though beautifully situated in a grove of orchards along the south side of the river, consists with a very few exceptions of wretched mud or mud and stone huts, very small and huddled closely together in little narrow lanes. Three-quarters of them are in a ruinous state and they are almost all filthy and comfortless, and most of them are inhabited by labourers' families, fishermen or old and helpless people.

Massereene is little more than a hotbed of fever, from which it is seldom free, and in the spring, when there is not sufficient employment for agricultural labourers, nearly a third of its poor population are dispensary patients. It would be a matter of much importance to the town were Massereene thrown down, as from it infection is disseminated. The houses are rapidly falling into decay and will not be rebuilt, and in a few years there will probably not be 10 of them remaining.

The entrance to Antrim by the Dublin road is through a little street in Massereene not more than 17 feet wide.

Houses

With the exception of the mud cabins and houses constructed of wood, all the houses in Antrim are built of stone and lime and nearly all of them roughcast.

The best houses are situated between its centre and western end, and are almost exclusively inhabited by persons employed in trade or dealing, this being the business part of the town. As they approach the outlets of the town the houses diminish in size and comfort, and are occupied by a less affluent class.

The houses in High Street along the side of the river are so near to it that few of them possess sufficient accommodation in offices or outhouses, and with the exception of a few inconsiderable patches, there are no gardens immediately attached to them.

The entrance to most of the yards is by a narrow entry or archway common to 2 and sometimes 3 contiguous tenements. These entries seldom exceed between 4 and 5 feet in width, and at some seasons, particularly in spring, very much affect the appearance and cleanliness of the town, as the manure from the different yards being carried or drawn on barrows must be laid on the street, where it generally lies for some time previous to its being carted to the fields. At this season the appearance of Antrim is absolutely disgusting.

The 2 and 3-storey houses are in general

comfortable, but there are some which are old and nearly ruinous. The larger houses are of reasonable proportions and in general comfortable and cleanly, and are inhabited by persons in trade or business.

The smaller 2-storey houses and the better description of cottages are occupied principally by mechanics or tradespeople. They are rather roomy, substantial and comfortable in their appearance, and are kept rather neatly internally.

The smaller cottages or cabins are nearly all confined and comfortless huts, nearly ruinous, badly thatched, smoky and damp. Far from being cleanly or warm, most of them are constructed either entirely or partly of mud and many of them consist of but 1 apartment. They are inhabited chiefly by the labouring class. Of late, there has been considerable improvement in the appearance of the streets: several new houses have been erected on the sites of old ones and the fronts of many of the old houses have been modernised and improved.

Recent Improvements

Within the last year improvement has been more general than for many years previous. Towards the west end of High Street a spacious 3-storey house of a superior description has been erected by Surgeon Molyneaux (an inhabitant of Antrim). It is of stone and lime, neatly finished and is divided into 2 tenements each having a shop in the first floor. 2 other good 2-storey houses have been built in the same street; one is now occupied as a police barrack and the other suited for a tradesman. In this street the appearance of at least half a dozen houses has been much improved within the last year.

The great drawback to the improvement of the town is the circumstance of the tenements being held in perpetuity and the few persons who have got any capital being unwilling to embark it in building or improving, when there is neither trade, business nor manufacture sufficient to create a demand for, or increase the value of, houses.

Antrim does not come under the act for lighting, paving, watching or cleansing, though few towns would be more benefitted by it.

SOCIAL AND PRODUCTIVE ECONOMY

Local Government

Viscount Ferrard (who is also Baron Oriel and whose eldest son is Viscount Massereene) is the representative of the family of Clotworthy, who settled here in 1603 and built Antrim Castle in 1613. Lord Ferrard is the lord of the soil, his estate, in which Antrim is situated, producing him about [blank] pounds per annum. The family have latterly resided at Oriel Temple since 1834, previous to which Antrim Castle had been their constant residence.

Previous to the union of Great Britain with Ireland, Antrim had been a borough and had returned 1 member to the Irish Parliament. It does not now, however, enjoy that privilege and all trace of the former charter or corporation is lost. It had been what was termed "a potwalloping borough", that is, any person who boiled a pot inside the town, provided he held a hut no matter how bad, had a right to vote, and to this circumstance the erection of so many cabins in Antrim is attributed.

Quarter sessions are held in Antrim in the months of June and December, the alternative terms being held in Belfast; Philip Fogarty Esquire, assistant barrister. Manor courts for the manor of Moylinny are held in Antrim on every third Thursday; Mr Arthur Adair Gamble, seneschal. Sums not exceeding 2 pounds are recoverable by civil bill, and not exceeding 20 pounds by attachment at these courts, and manor courts for the same manor are held on every third Thursday. Petty sessions are held in Antrim on every second Thursday; George Jackson Clarke of Steeple and Thomas Montgomery of Birch Hill (both within a mile of Antrim) Esquires are the presiding magistrates. Special and road sessions under the grand jury bill are held in Antrim for the barony of Upper Antrim.

Occupations

About two-thirds of the population of Antrim (which amounts to 3,000 persons) are engaged in some trade, dealing or handicrafts and the remainder of the population is made up of agricultural and other labourers, servants, professional persons, unemployed females and children.

Almost all the dealers and most of the mechanics hold more or less land. Few of the labouring class hold any. They usually rent land in the town parks wherein to plant their potatoes, the quantity they plant depending on the quantity of manure they have accumulated. They take the land by the perch of the ridge, for which they pay 2d.

Few are engaged exclusively in farming and there are not any persons living upon fixed incomes independent of some profession or calling. Though there are not any who can be termed wealthy, still there are many of the better class of shopkeepers who are above the world, living frugally, though comfortably, and persevering in the same industrious habits, by which almost all, without having capital to begin upon, have rendered themselves independent. This class of shopkeepers are a respectable branch of the community, very cautious and prudent and punctual in their engagements, the consequence of which is that a failure or bankruptcy is rarely known among them.

The inferior class of petty dealers are not so steady. It embraces most of the publicans and tradesmen, who are rather improvident and consequently far from being independent. There is a great deal of intemperance and not much morality among them, though they might by common prudence and industry be independent and comfortable in their circumstances.

The labourers are also a very improvident class and though, with the exception of about 6 weeks at the season previous to seed time, they are in constant employment and can earn always 6s and sometimes 7s per week, still scarce a spring passes without subscriptions being called for to relieve the misery and sickness consequent on their previous improvidence. Of late years, however, there has been a perceptible improvement in their habits and morals, and they have become more temperate and provident.

Reading Society

A book club or reading society was established in this neighbourhood in the year 1834. It embraces 16 families in this and the surrounding parishes, of whom 5 reside in this. The subscription amounts to 2 pounds and 2s per annum for the first year, and by its regulations each member may order one work in the year. At the end of the year the books are auctioned and the person who ordered the work may have it at half-price, provided no one bids higher for it.

Library and Taste for Reading

A lending library, consisting of 176 volumes of useful and religious works, chiefly adopted for the middle class, was established here in 1830. There are 16 annual subscribers to this library, who pay from 2s 6d to 5s per annum. The circulation of the books among so small a proportion of the inhabitants is too limited to promote any perceptible moral or intellectual improvement in them.

Though there are few towns so free from party spirit or political discords, and though there is no actual taste for literature or intellectual recreation, still their taste for political and the other information contained in the different public journals is very strong; and this, as well as their political feelings, will be found more clearly illustrated by a reference to Appendix.

There is not, however, any news room. Each person prefers taking his own favourite paper, with which he amuses himself after the labours of the day.

Remarks on Economy

Antrim is by no means a place of trade or commerce, and its manufactories are confined to a brewery, a paper mill and a corn mill. Its proximity to Belfast and the great facility of communication with that town is a serious drawback to any improvements in the trade of Antrim, and as the large establishments or families procure almost all their groceries and other household necessaries from Belfast, the shops in Antrim merely supply those articles more commonly required by the middle or lower classes; the shops, therefore, are not extensive. The woollen shops are much the best and neatest looking; but however confined their business may be, most of them present neat fronts and are respectably kept.

Manufactories

The manufactories of Antrim consist of a brewery, a paper mill and a corn mill. The brewery is situated in the Mill Row towards the south side of the town and on the river side. It was established here in 1807. It measures exclusively of its grain stores and yard 102 by 64 feet. It is 16 feet high and 120 barrels of ale can be manufactured weekly at it.

The paper mill consists of 2 separate houses situated near the brewery. One of these contains a paper machine (one of the first introduced into this country) and 3 engines for masticating the rags. The house is 38 feet high and measures [blank] and [blank] feet. The dimensions of the wheel which propels the machinery is 10 feet in diameter and 3 feet 6 inches broad; it is a breast water wheel. The other houses contain machinery connected with the finishing of paper, which is propelled by 2 breast water wheels, one of which is 16 feet in diameter and 6 feet broad; the other is 16 feet in diameter and 5 feet broad.

The corn mill adjoins the last-mentioned house. It measures 29 by 33 feet and 34 feet high. The machinery is propelled by a breast water wheel 17 feet in diameter and 5 feet broad.

These manufactories are the property of Messrs

Ferguson and Fowke, who employ annually 26 men and 34 women at the paper mills. The former can earn 18s to 6s per week, according to the description of their work, and the latter can earn from 3s to 3s 6d per week. The paper mills were originally established here in 1783.

The brewery affords employment to 12 labourers annually, who can earn from 10s to 6s per week. The Antrim ale is very superior and is in high estimation in the neighbouring districts.

The paper manufactured here is such as is usually sold by country shopkeepers, as letter copy and post paper, but the former is not of the first quality. A considerable proportion of their manufacture is used by linen bleachers for packing, lapping and ornamenting their linens, paper for the last purpose being manufactured, dyed and glazed here.

Bank

A branch of the Ulster Bank (in Belfast) was established in Antrim on 11th August [1836 or 1837] and has formed one of the few exceptions (as to the effect it has produced) to the numerous branch banks about that time established throughout the country. The bank in Antrim is managed by Mr William Crawford, a gentleman who is native of Antrim and intimately acquainted with the circumstances of the people in the surrounding districts.

The credit given by it is very limited and has been judiciously afforded, and the result has been that instead of bringing ruin upon numbers who would only too gladly have availed themselves of the means of speculating upon a fictitious capital, it has been a great convenience to the public. For instance, a farmer to meet a pressing demand for rent or some other claim would be obliged to take his cattle or crops to the market, and let prices be ever so low he must sell them, perhaps for not more than two-thirds of their real value. But now, by the interposition of the bank, a respectable farmer may obtain the means of liquidating his debt and by a little delay avail himself of a rise in the prices of farm produce. As a proof of the discretion used in giving credit, the bank in Antrim has not lost anything by bad payments since its establishment.

Savings Bank

A savings bank (a branch of that in Belfast) was established here in December 1830 and has succeeded, not only in the gross amount of its deposits, but in the more fortunate result of its object being attained, in the depositors being principally tradesmen and servants. This has been in a great degree owing to the praiseworthy exertions of the neighbouring gentry among those over whom they have influence. A reference to Appendix will more fully illustrate the description of the depositors by the amount of the deposits.

Loan Fund

The Antrim Loan Society was established in September 1835. It is flourishing and promises to be of incalculable benefit to the lower class, a greater proof of which can scarcely be adduced than that it has been very injurious to the interests of the pawnbrokers, of whom there are 2 in Antrim and by whom it was bitterly opposed. The people see the value of this institution and gladly avail themselves of its advantages. The original capital, 288 pounds, was nearly all subscribed by 3 gentlemen residing in the parish. For an account of the receipts and disbursements of this society, see Appendix.

Fairs

There are 3 annual fairs held in Antrim, namely on the 1st January, 12th May and 12th November. In the January fair 80 to 100 horses of a middling description, suited for small farms and averaging not more than 10 pounds each in value, are exposed for sale. About 150 cows and from 300 to 400 pigs are usually exposed at this fair.

The other commodities exposed for sale are pedlar's goods exposed on numerous stalls ranged along the side of the street, old clothes, huxter's commodities such as cakes, apples etc. similarly exposed, a few stands with woollen stockings, shoes, tinware and ironmongery, and 3 or 4 cars of brown crockery from the neighbourhood of Bellaghy in the county Derry.

The other fairs in May and November are more for the purpose of hiring servants and for amusement than for business. The numbers of cattle exposed in them are nearly alike; about 150 cows and from 200 to 300 pigs but no horses are exposed in them. These, with the articles mentioned in the January fair, but in much larger quantities, constitute almost all the commodities for sale. There are neither tolls nor customs demanded, these having been many years ago abolished by the Massereene family, the proprietors, from a wish to encourage farmers to come to the fair here.

A curious custom is practised at the May and November fairs, namely that of servants coming to them to be hired; and both farmers and servants, many of them residing 8 miles off, come [for] this express purpose. It matters not if the servant intends continuing with his former master: he comes to the fair, where his master re-engages him by giving him a shilling. The male servants who come to be hired carry a rod; the women have no sign of any kind. The numbers who attend the May and November fairs are very great, particularly in the former; and as they are chiefly for amusement, they present towards evening disgraceful scenes of drunkenness and brawling.

Antrim is very well supplied with butcher's meat of the best quality, poultry, fish, milk and butter. The supply of vegetables is confined to potatoes, cabbage, leeks and onions, which are abundant and cheap. The only fruits for sale are apples, pears, plums, cherries and small fruit, which are also abundant.

Cost of Produce

Beef sells at from 4d to 6d per lb, mutton at from 4d to 5d ha'penny, veal at from 4d ha'penny to 5d ha'penny, slink at from 10d to 1s 6d per quarter. Geese at from 1s 6d to 2s 6d each, turkeys at from 1s 6d to 3s each, hens at from 6d to 1s, ducks at from 3d to 1s, chickens at from 5d to 1s per couple, young ducks 8d to 1s 6d. Lough Neagh trout at from 3d ha'penny to 4d ha'penny per lb, Lough Neagh pullen at from 10d to 1s per dozen, Lough Neagh salmon from 6d to 1s 2d per lb, Coleraine salmon from 6d to 2s, Carrickfergus codfish from 1d to 1d ha'penny; Myroe oysters from 1s to 5s per hundred, Strangford cockles from 1d per quart.

New milk from 2d per quart, skim milk from 1d ha'penny per quart, buttermilk from a ha'penny per quart; fresh butter from 8d to 11d per lb, crock butter from 7d to 9d per lb; Antrim cheese from 4d to 1s per lb. Turkey eggs from 8d to 9d per dozen, duck eggs from 5d to 6d per dozen, hen eggs from 4d to 6d per dozen.

Potatoes from 2s to 3s in spring per cwt, potatoes from 1s to 1s 3d in winter per cwt. Apples from 1s 6d to 4s per bushel, plums from 1s to 1s 8d per 100, cherries from 3d to 3d ha'penny per lb, gooseberries from a ha'penny per quart.

Turf from 1s to 3s per load, Scotch coals from 18s to 25s per ton (laid down), English coals from 25s to 30s per ton (laid down), bog wood from 4s to 5s per load.

Building stones 1s 4d to 1s 6d per ton (laid down), Tardree stone 4d to 6d per cubic foot uncut, bricks from Belfast 20s to 40s per 1,000 laid down; Queen ton slates, Countesses slates, Cardigan slates [blank] per ton, fluctuating and are brought from Belfast; pine timber 1s 6d to 1s 10d per cubic foot laid down, Memel timber 2s to 2s 6d per cubic foot laid down, lime 1s 3d to 1s 6d per barrel laid down.

The prices of the above articles vary, of course, according to the season and to their quality.

Cheese and Fish

Antrim is remarkable for the excellence of its cheese, a considerable quantity of which was formerly made; but now not more than 30 cheeses are annually made in the town, and these for private use.

The Lough Neagh trout is considered very fine and is abundant in the season.

Fuel

Firing is scarce and dear, particularly in spring. Turf are brought from the bogs in Lord O'Neill's estate in the parish of Drummaul, 3 to 4 miles distant.

Building Materials

Tardree stone, a description of white porphyry, is procured from the quarries in the parish of Connor, 6 miles distant. It cuts well and is a handsome and durable stone. Whinstone is chiefly used for building. It is brought from a quarry about 1 mile distant, near the east side of the parish. Lime is procured from the kilns in Carnmoney parish, 11 and a half miles distant. Sand is procured from the shores of the lake. Timber, slates, coals, iron and brick are procured from Belfast, 17 and a half miles distant. The carriage per cwt from Belfast is 6d.

There are 5 regular carriers or carmen to Belfast, who perform the journey there and back in from 1 day to 1 day and a half, but usually in the former time.

Water

Antrim is well supplied with water, not only from the river but from numerous pumps in the yards, and from an excellent town pump near the market house. The water is good and is usually found at depths varying from 26 to 32 feet.

Grazing

There is a good deal of stall feeding and some grazing of beef cattle about the town. The sheepwalks are very extensive and well stocked, and upwards of 1,000 acres of excellent grazing are contained in the Fir Field and Deerpark, Lord Ferrard's property, which lets for grazing as follows.

Black cattle: year-olds, 1 pound 10s; 2-year-olds, 2 pounds 4s; aged, 3 pounds.

Horses: year-olds, 3 pounds; 2-year-olds, 3 pounds 15s; aged, 4 pounds 10s.

[Crossed out: The above relate to the Deerpark, the Fir Field being stocked with Lord Ferrard's sheep].

Grazing for milch cows lets at from 50s to 60s per head.

There is not any market gardening.

Insurances

There are 18 houses insured from fire, and there are not any life insurances.

Employment

Combinations do not exist. Except for about 6 weeks in the beginning of spring, agricultural labourers do not suffer from want of employment. They can, on an average throughout the year, earn 5s per week and those who are in constant employment can earn 6s. Some of the inhabitants who have large farms give their labourers a free house and 5s per week, but they are a very improvident class and whenever unemployed are in great want.

Weavers, of course, are more or less affected by the frequent fluctuations in the linen trade and have for the last year been badly off; but the other trades are comparatively comfortable and in good employment.

Since the introduction of mill-spun yarn, that manufactured by the hand has fallen to such a low price that females cannot earn more than 2d per day spinning. They are therefore almost out of employment except in the busy seasons of seed time and harvest, when they can earn 6d per day.

Flowering muslin was introduced about 2 years ago, and for some time upwards of 100 girls were employed at it and could earn on an average 2s 6d per week; but now not more than half the number can obtain employment and these cannot earn more than 2s per week.

Communications

Few towns possess so great facility of communication with the neighbouring districts as Antrim. From its being such a thoroughfare, conveyances are passing through or leaving it at almost every hour and the constant arrivals and departures tend very much to enliven the town (a table of the different conveyances will be found in Appendix).

The mail from Dublin is conveyed in a taxed cart from Banbridge, and arrives in Antrim at 9 a.m. in summer and 10 a.m. in winter, and is despatched 3.30 p.m.

The mail coach from Belfast for Derry arrives at 9 a.m. in summer and 10 a.m. in winter. It arrives from Derry for Belfast at 4.30 a.m.

Dispensary

The dispensary was established in Antrim in 1817 and has been a most valuable institution in the effects it has had on the health of the lower class, where, from their inability to procure fuel from its scarcity and dearness in the inclement seasons, and their distance from lime, they are so subject to fever in the seasons of winter and spring. The prompt assistance afforded by the dispensary checks the prevalence of the complaint, or no doubt the poor families in the suburbs of the town would seldom be free of it.

Mendicity and Poor

A mendicity society was established in Antrim in 1825 and continued up to September 1836 when, from a variety of causes, it was abandoned. There is not now any regular support for the poor of the town. Further particulars under the head of Poor will be found in Social Economy.

The charitable schools in Antrim are: the Lancasterian male and female school, supported by the bequest of Erasmus Smith; the infant school, supported wholly by local subscription; and 3 sabbath schools similarly supported.

The private subscriptions in Antrim are liberal and will be found detailed in the Table of Benevolence. They are applied to the purposes which have already been stated and there are few towns where the wants of the aged, the helpless and infirm are more carefully attended to.

To Antrim, poor laws would be an important measure and would lighten the weighty load which is borne by a comparatively small proportion of its inhabitants in alleviating the misery of its poor. The better classes of society, including the wealthier shopkeepers, are those upon whom almost the entire burden falls, while there is a middle or lower class who, while they are deriving their support from the profits obtained from the poor and are comfortable in their circumstances, contribute little, if anything, to relieve their distress.

Character of the People

The inhabitants of Antrim are in general very industrious and domestic, peaceable, civil and obliging, and hospitable to the extent of their means. There is scarcely any society in the town, but a stranger will find the neighbourhood of Antrim the best in the country. There are many nice families in it who are very independent in their circumstances and proverbial for their hospitality.

Antrim is happily quite free from party schisms or political discords, all classes on the most friendly footing with each other. There is but little taste for amusement and a day in the Fir Field (which adjoins the town) at Easter may be said to be the only recreation they have.

Among the lower class there is a great deal of drunkenness, though this is decreasing, and there is also much immorality. The want of a resident magistrate is sadly felt in Antrim, as from its being such a thoroughfare it is subject to visits of numerous vagrants and improper characters, who frequent its streets without any steps being taken to remove them. It is very badly managed in this respect and is the only small town in the county where such characters are allowed to remain.

It would appear that its inhabitants have been contaminated by their intercourse with strangers, as there are at present 28 illegitimate children of various ages residing in it, and the charge on the parish applotted at the last Easter vestry for deserted children was 43 pounds 3s 6d.

There is not any shop-lifting in Antrim and petty thefts are unusual.

Conveyances

3 post chaises, 10 post cars, 1 phaeton, 1 gig and 18 post horses are kept for hire, independent of the numerous vehicles plying between the neighbouring towns. The charge for chaises are for 1 or 2 perons 1s per mile and for 3 persons 1s 2d per mile. For cars and gigs the charges are for 1 or 2 persons 8d per mile, for 3 persons 10d and for 4 persons 1s per mile Irish. These conveyances are in general well horsed and appointed, and travel at the rate of 5 miles Irish per hour.

Inns

From its being the stage next to Belfast, to Ballymena, to Magherafelt and to Lisburn, the posting done by the Antrim innkeepers is very great, particularly in summer, when the number of parties on their way to the Giant's Causeway and Shane's Castle is almost incredible. The visitors to the latter place make the town look quite gay, it being the favourite resort of the Belfast people.

General Remarks

Antrim is almost at a stand as to improvements. During the last year it has improved more than in many preceding ones. The grain market was established here in September 1836 and is flourishing. This, of course, causes an increased circulation of capital amongst the people in business and it is supposed that they are thriving. The improvement in the outward appearance of the houses would imply this, and failures or bankruptcies are almost unknown.

The improvements in Antrim must, it is feared, be very limited, as from its proximity to the important towns of Belfast and Ballymena, which absorb all the trade of the intervening districts, it cannot expect ever to attain any eminence in a commercial or trading point of view.

MODERN TOPOGRAPHY

Hamlet: The Milltown

The hamlet so called derives its name from its having, within memory (and it is said for ages), been the site of the mill which ground the corn of the inhabitants of the village, which within memory stood in the demesne of Shane's Castle. There is still an excellent corn mill in the village and as both are situated on Lord O'Neill's estate, the village is by some termed Shane's Castle Milltown.

The Milltown is situated partly in the townland of Kilbegs and partly in that of Shane's Castle, near the confines of the parishes of Antrim and Drummaul, and on a by-road a few yards to the right of the main road from the town of Antrim to that Randalstown, from the former of which it is [blank] miles distant.

Nothing whatever is locally known concerning the history or origin of the Milltown, nor are there remains of antiquity to throw any light on it; but it is probable that the mill formed a nucleus for the cottages which stand about it and that it never has been of greater extent or consequence than at present.

Until within about 30 years ago 2 annual fairs were held at the Milltown. They were almost [solely] for amusement and their having been given up was considered as a benefit to the neighbourhood.

The Milltown consists of 1 straggling and irregular street containing 37 cottages and houses, including a corn mill and 2 corn kilns. 3 of the houses are slated and 2 of them 2-storeys high. Some of them are cleanly, comfortable and in good order, but the majority are dirty and carelessly kept. They are all built of stone and lime, of good dimensions, well lit and consist of a kitchen and from 1 to 2 other apartments.

The inhabitants are chiefly of the humblest class and are not remarkable for their industry or sobriety, though they have improved in both respects within a few years. By referring to Appendix, a table of their trades and occupations will be found.

There is not any public building in the Milltown. A description of the corn mill will be found under the head of Machinery.

Public Buildings in the Parish

The pier was erected in 1785 by a Mr Bristow, then agent to the Massereene family. The sum said to have been expended upon it and in improving the navigation of the river, and which was granted by the government, was 2,000 pounds (about the expenditure of which there is still considerable doubt). The object in building the pier was to improve the town of Antrim by providing a place at which the vessels from the coasts of Lough Neagh, particularly those of Tyrone, could discharge their cargoes of grain and crockery ware. A pier was to be built on the southern side of the estuary of the Six Mile Water and the mouth of the river was to have been confined by a row of piles and stones parallel to the pier, by which its breadth would have been contracted and its depth increased.

The pier is 231 yards in length and 36 feet broad. Its direction is somewhat curved and crescent like. It is constructed solely of large stones secured at piles at its extremity next the lake. The stones have been firmly laid down, but from want of care and the heavy swells rolling in from the southward in winter, many of them have been washed away and the pier much injured. It rises from 3 to 6 feet above the summer level of the lake, which at that season is about 5 and a half feet deep at its point and 2 and a half deep in the side next the river. It is only a few inches deep at the other side but here it is of much importance to the fishermen, as it protects them by its curvature from the prevailing swell from the southward. Except for a few lighter loads of coals from Belfast, bricks from Tyrone or Derry, or brown earthenware from Coalisland in the former county, there is not any merchandise landed at this pier.

A row of piles extends from the outer extremity of and parallel to the pier for 467 yards, the intervening space being 98 feet. Some stones still remain which had been laid down with the piles, but they are below the surface. The piles are of oak and seem to have been about 1 foot asunder but many have disappeared. Those that remain appear about 18 inches above the summer level of the river.

The pier is now of little use. It certainly has tended to confine and deepen the river at its mouth, though at the "bar" where it meets the lake, and inside the pier, it is not in summer more than 18 inches deep.

Gentlemen's Seats

Ballycraigy, the residence of William Chaine Esquire Senior, is agreeably situated 1 and a quarter miles south east of the town of Antrim and within a few yards of the road from that town to Belfast. It takes its name from the townland in which it is situated.

The house is 2-storey and very spacious, consisting of 12 successive apartments which have from time to time been added to it during the last 30 years. The lawn is rather confined in front of the house and towards its western side it is used as a bleach field. There are several rows and belts of planting about it, and the view from some of the windows embraces the beautifully wooded bank on the opposite side of Moylinny glen.

Birch Hill, the residence of Thomas Montgomery Esquire, J.P., is delightfully situated in the townland of the same name, on the gentle acclivity of the ridge extending along the east of the parish and commanding one of the most beautiful and varied views that the county can boast of: embracing in the foreground Antrim, its numerous plantings and round tower, and the extensive demesne and woods of Shane's Castle, Antrim deerpark stretching along the shore of Lough Neagh, which is clearly seen from its northern to its southern extremity; beyond it rise the Derry mountains, which may be traced diminishing into the lower grounds of Tyrone, and sometimes the view extends into [the] still lower and more distant county of Armagh.

The lawn, which slopes gently from the house, contains 54 acres and is tastefully laid out and ornamented with clumps of planting and banks of evergreens, and possesses some pretty walks.

The gardens, though not large, are suitable and the flower garden contains a valuable collection of plants. The house is not modern in its appearance but is in good order and is [a] comfortable and gentleman-like family residence. It is 2-storey and spacious. It was erected about the year 1785 by the late [blank] Bristow Esquire and has had several owners.

The office houses are only recently finished. They form a handsome square and are very superior in their finish and design.

Birch Hill is 1 mile north east of Antrim and near the road from that town to the village of Connor.

The Steeple, the residence of George Jackson Clark Esquire, J.P., is cheerfully situated on a gentle swell three-quarters of a mile north of the town of Antrim. It, as well as the townland in which it is situated, takes its name from the ancient round tower which stands in the lawn and within 125 yards of the house.

The ground about the house is almost flat but rises sufficiently above the lake to admit of a view of it over the plantings in Shane's Castle and Antrim Castle demesnes. There is also a pretty view from the house of Antrim and of some of the neighbouring hills and groves. The lawn with the flower gardens contains 45 acres and is ornamented with some thriving young timber. There are also some pretty shrubberies of evergreens and 2 very neat and well laid out flower gardens. The kitchen garden contains 1 acre 1 rood 20 perches and is enclosed by a capital stone wall 9 feet high.

The dwelling house, which is spacious and modern, presents rather a handsome appearance. It is 2-storeys high and was erected by the late Mr Clark in 1827.

Moylinny Cottage, the residence of William Chaine Esquire Junior, is beautifully situated 1 mile south east of Antrim, near the road from that town to Belfast, in the townland of Moylinny and on the bank overhanging the romantic glen of that name.

Bush, in the townland of the same name and [blank] miles north east of Antrim, the residence of James Arthur Esquire: a cottage forming with its offices a compact hollow square. The house is situated on an elevated table land and commands a most extensive and varied prospect, comprising Lough Neagh and its low and wooded shores from its northern to its southern extremity and the distant mountains of Derry, Tyrone and Mourne. There is no planting about the house, which was erected in the year 1835.

Potters Walls, the residence of Alexander Montgomery, situated in the townland of the same name, [blank] miles north east of Antrim and near the road from Antrim to Connor: the house is somewhat in the cottage style and neat and modern in its appearance. Its situation is very

retired and near the mountains. Mr Montgomery made his residence in 1833, since which time he has considerably improved the neighbouring grounds. The offices, though small, are sufficiently commodious.

Mills and Manufactories

The machinery of the parish, besides that described under the head of Towns, consists of 2 beetling mills, 2 flax mills and 1 corn mill.

The beetling mills are in the townland of Moylinny and are the property of William Chaine Esquire. The machinery of one is contained in a house 50 by 33 feet and is propelled by a breast water wheel 22 feet in diameter and 6 feet broad. The machinery of the other is contained in a house 52 by 38 feet and is propelled by an undershot water wheel 17 feet in diameter and 12 feet broad.

52 acres of spreadfield attached to these mills are in this parish.

The arrangement of the water for these mills is so judicious as always to ensure a supply. The race which supplies the former is 1,166 yards long; it also supplies the latter. Both mills are situated on the Six Mile Water.

The flax mill in the townland of Tullycrenaght is propelled by a breast water wheel 14 feet in diameter and 2 feet 9 inches broad. The second flax mill in the same townland is propelled by a breast water wheel 11 feet in diameter and 2 feet 9 inches broad.

The corn mill is situated in the townland of Milltown and is propelled by a breast water wheel 15 feet 6 inches in diameter and 2 feet 10 inches broad. There is not any obstruction whatever to the erection of machinery.

Communications

The means of communication are throughout the parish ample in every respect, all its districts being traversed by roads which are in general good and not too numerous.

The main roads are: the mail coach road from Belfast to Antrim. Of this road, there are 2 miles traversing the southern side of the parish. Its breadth throughout is 33 feet, exclusive of the footpath which is 8 feet broad. This road was completed in 1831, having cost 21,000 pounds, its total length being 17 and three-quarter miles. The original engineer was Mr Edgeworth, but in consequence of his death it was completed under Mr Stevenson. The expense was defrayed by the county.

There are 2 toll-gates on the road, one at Antrim

and another at the Belfast end, and there is another toll-gate on the Carrickfergus road near Belfast which, from the communication between the roads, is let with the 2 others.

In the first year the road was managed by the trustees. The next year the tolls were let at 2,500 pounds, afterwards at the rent of 2,300 and 2,370 pounds, and the last year (1837) at 2,500 pounds.

It is now in the hands of the Board of Public Works, by whom it is managed. Its repair is let by them to a contractor, who receives 3s 6d per cubic yard for broken stones which are laid on by a person appointed by the board. It is a beautifully laid out and gently undulating road, and is kept in admirable order. Turf, manure and milk are exempt from toll on it.

The mail coach road from Antrim to Derry, through Randalstown and Ballymena, is a continuation of the former road and extends from the western end of High Street in the town of Antrim along the southern end to the western side of the parish. Its total length in this parish is 2 miles 4 furlongs and 18 perches; its average breadth is 51 feet, exclusive of the footpath which is 6 feet broad. That part of it in the town of Antrim does not average more than 27 feet broad, but this is about to be widened by the removal of some old houses. This road was made and is kept in good repair by the county. It is almost flat and its direction could not be improved.

The coach and direct road from Antrim to Ballymena extends northward from the western end of Antrim for 3 miles 2 furlongs and 29 perches through this parish. Its average breadth is 28 feet. Towards Antrim this road is tolerably level and in good order, but for the last mile and a half in this parish is very hilly and kept in but middling repair. It was made and is kept up at the expense of the baronies through which it passes. It is now about to be superseded by the new mail coach and turnpike road from Antrim to Coleraine, which has just been commenced at the expense of the county. Little of the old road will be found available, as the latter is carried too high along the acclivity of the hills while the new road will be laid out through the almost level valley at their base. This will be a matter of vast importance to the county, the intercourse between Ballymena and Belfast being very considerable and increasing daily.

One mile and 5 furlongs of the road from Antrim to Ballyclare through Parkgate extends from Antrim to the eastern extremity of this parish. Its average breadth is 23 feet. It is a hilly road and badly laid out, though lying almost in a right line between its 2 points. It was made and is kept in repair by the barony of Upper Antrim. It is in but middling repair at present.

3 miles 6 furlongs of the road from Antrim to Kells and Connor are situated in this parish. Its average breadth is 22 feet. It is kept in repair at the expense of the baronies of Upper Antrim and Upper Toome. It is not in very good order and is badly laid out, running over hills and valleys, while had it been carried a little lower down the face of the hill, it might have preserved an almost level line. The thoroughfare on it is inconsiderable.

By-roads

The by-roads are made and kept in repair at the expense of the baronies through which they pass. They are in general good, pretty well laid out and average 19 feet in breadth. They are sufficiently numerous without being too much so.

The material used in the repair of the roads in this parish is broken stone, chiefly whinstone and the harder kinds of basalt. The stones are procured mostly from the fields and are sufficiently abundant.

Bridges

The bridges are: Antrim bridge, on the road from Antrim to Lisburn and over the Six Mile Water at the town of Antrim. A description of it will be found under the head of Towns.

The only other bridge is that over the Six Mile Water, on the old road from Antrim to Belfast. It is a plain old structure measuring 94 feet long and 22 feet wide, and consists of 5 small semicircular arches. It is in sufficient repair.

These are the only public bridges; they are, however, sufficiently commodious as to situation and for the means of intercourse.

Scenery

Few rural districts possess the same attractions as this, either as regards its own appearance, the exquisite scenery along its shore or the delightful and extreme views from the higher grounds.

In the diversity of its surface and the splendid sheet of water bounding its southern side, nature has largely contributed to its ornament, while in the numerous wooded grounds around the gentlemen's seats occupying its more gentle slopes, its venerable and interesting round tower, gracefully raising its grey head above its groves, the cathedral-like spire of its church and the general aspect of fertility, industry and comfort, the hand of art has not been sparingly bestowed.

The views from almost every point in the parish are extensive and delightful: Lough Neagh, stretching southwards almost as far as the eye can reach, its low shores jutting out numerous little promontories and gradually ascending inwards until towards the west they terminate in a lofty chain of mountains. Towards the south east the more distant Mourne Mountains, elevating their blue peaks, present in their jagged outline a beautiful termination to the view, while nearer home the ancient ruins of Shane's Castle, with its vast and wooded demesne, the fertile shores of Killead and the more wild and mountainous scenery towards the east and north of the county present all the features of the richest landscape.

SOCIAL ECONOMY

Early Improvements

The great event which may undoubtedly be regarded as the earliest and almost the sole cause of improvement in the habits, morals and general character of the people of this country was its colonisation by the Scots in the early part of the 17th century.

Several important and partial settlements of Scots, English and a few French Huguenots had taken place here during the reign of Elizabeth, and even at a much earlier period the parish would seem to have been visited by strangers, from the number of ancient coins which are to this day found throughout it. But the most important settlement, and that which led to the subsequent beneficial results, was that under Sir Hugh Clotworthy (an ancestor of the Massereene family), who settled here in 1603 and in 1613 built the castle of Antrim.

He was a zealous Presbyterian and had resided in England, and his coming here induced many, both of the English and Scottish Presbyterians, to follow his example.

On 7th July 1619 the Revd John Ridge A.M. was admitted to the vicarage of Antrim on the presentation of Sir Arthur Chichester. [Insert footnote: From a single pamphlet on the parish of Templepatrick, published in 1824 by Dr Stevenson of Belfast].

On 6th May 1611 he had been admitted to the order of deacon by the Bishop of Oxford, but having no freedom for the exercise of his ministry in England, without submitting to impositions contrary to his conscience, he removed to this country. He was considered a very eminent man and, according to Blair, "a great urger of charitable works and a very humble man."

First Presbyterian Congregation

It was in 1619 that the first Presbyterian congregation in Antrim and the fourth in Ireland was established; and Antrim, as would appear from entries in some old session books, was the focus or headquarters of Presbyterianism.

Meetings which lasted for 2 days were held in it, the neighbouring clergy assembling there on the first Friday in each month. They continued to fast and pray during these days, 2 clergymen preaching in the forenoon and 2 in the afternoon.

Clotworthy Family

The Clotworthy family continued in their steadfast adherence to Nonconformity, Sir John Clotworthy (son of Sir Hugh) being obliged to fly to England to escape the hostility of Strafford <Stafford>, then Governor of Ireland.

He had been a member of the Irish House of Commons in 1634, and in 1636 seems to have first rendered himself obnoxious to Strafford by refusing to support his plans for establishing a monopoly of linen yarn. While in England he was one of the few double returns to the Long Parliament, having been elected for the boroughs of Bossing in Cornwall and also for Malden, but took his seat for the latter. [Insert footnote: Reid's *History of Presbyterianism*, vol.1].

He was also one of the committee appointed to prepare the charges against Strafford, against whom on his trial he appeared as a witness; and it was also he who in 1641 presented the petition from the Irish Presbyterians praying for the enjoyment of liberty of conscience.

Progress of Improvement

In subsequent years the Clotworthys (the proprietors of the soil) granted leases in perpetuity to the inhabitants of both town and country, which tended to create a spirit of independence and encouraged many to make improvements.

Afterwards, about 1642, the linen trade sprung up, which afforded to many a profitable employment.

The religious instruction regularly and powerfully inculcated, as it seems to have been, an enjoyment of property free from disturbance, combined with the rewards arising from industry, served to raise the character of the people and render them industrious, independent, peaceable and religious.

It seems, however, that some changes took place, for the successors of those who had obtained leases in perpetuity, on finding their properties increase in value, began to aspire to a higher sphere in society. Many of them educated their sons more liberally and sent them abroad into the world, where some of them distinguished themselves. These, on the decease of their fathers, inherited properties here, but being absentees and having acquired tastes and habits which could not be indulged in at home, they generally let their properties at a handsome profit rent and took no further interest in them.

Another cause of injury to the people was the contested elections which, from the system of bribery and perjury, drunkenness, etc., seem to have had a very injurious effect on their morals; and the town of Antrim also suffered in many respects from the number of small cabins which were erected for the purpose of creating voters.

In 1776, and for some years after, these contests were carried on very keenly, engrossing the attention of the people and at the same time demoralising them. Not long after, and before the fatal effects of these elections had begun to disappear, the spirit cherished by United Irishmen began to spread itself very generally through the community, and few in this or the neighbouring parishes were uncontaminated by it. The results of these events were that the people had descended from a very high to a very low and degraded state of society.

In 1726, owing to the Arian doctrines held by the celebrated Doctor Abernethy, then minister of Antrim, a separation took place in his congregation. A new one was formed here and the presbytery of Antrim (consisting of those holding opinions of doctrines similar to the doctor's) was then formed, and separated from the great body of Presbyterians, and in 1731 the second meeting house was built in Antrim.

The union between Great Britain and Ireland, by defranchising Antrim, [crossed out: and putting an end to rebellious organisations] seems to have been the means of bringing the people back to their former tranquil state; and subsequently religious instruction and the spread of education, which during the previous unsettled times had been almost wholly neglected, have tended to bring the minds of the people to a very improved state and place them on a footing with those of any part of Ireland.

Remarks on Improvements

Their proximity to the important and commercial towns and the great weekly pork, grain and linen markets in Ballymena, and the excellent means of communication with these markets, are important advantages to the farmer. A good grain market has lately been established in Antrim and is flourishing, and there is besides a ready market for wheat at the neighbouring mills in the adjoining grange of Muckamore. The lime-kilns in Carnmoney are [blank] miles distant and on the Belfast road, so that a farmer returning from that market may bring home lime.

The constant residence of an influential, wealthy and respected landed gentry, who by their example and influence tend to promote habits of comfort and regularity, and the number employed in the manufacture of linen or at the extensive bleach greens or mills in the neighbourhood, have been the means of rendering the working class independent in their circumstances, regular in their habits and comfortable in their manner of living.

From the circumstances of Antrim being such a thoroughfare or pass, their intercourse with strangers, though it may in some respects have tended towards their civilisation, still it has also had its injurious effects, in bringing many strolling and improper characters to the country, who, so long as they can, make it their residence. In this respect Antrim is very much exposed and it is to be regretted that no steps are taken for the extirpation of the many loose characters at present infesting it, and who must by their example eventually contaminate others.

Drunkenness never received such a check as from the late act which empowers magistrates to fine drunkards on the spot. Since that act has come into force there has not been a fourth of the drunkenness that was formerly to be seen in Antrim, and for which it had at one time been proverbial. [Insert marginal note: Authority for this?].

Prevalent Names

The most prevalent names in this parish are those of Frew (formerly spelled Ffrew) of French extraction, Fleming of English, and Agnew, Adair, Bell, Johnson, Miller, Campbell, Montgomery, Kerr, Hanna and Reid.

There are 3 Quaker families in the parish. The first establishment of that body took place here in 1669, the first in Ulster having taken place at Lurgan (22 miles distant) in 1654.

Obstructions to Improvement

There are not any obstructions to improvement.

Local Government

There are 2 magistrates in this parish, George

Jackson Clarke Esquire of Steeple and Thomas Montgomery of Birch Hill, Esquire, whose residences are conveniently situated within 1 mile of the town of Antrim. These gentlemen are respectable and possess the confidence of the people. Still, however, the want of an active magistrate resident in the town of Antrim is sadly felt.

A chief constable and 8 constabulary are stationed in Antrim. [Crossed out: The chief constable is rarely effective, being most of his time absent or unwell, and might as well be anywhere else as he has no duty to do, or rather does no duty farther than connected with the payment or management of the affairs of his men. Half the number of constabulary would be sufficient for the duty of Antrim district. Insert marginal note: See article on "Outrages", to prove they do their duty well].

The parish of Antrim is included in the manor of Moylinny, which extends to the parish of Larne on the east side of the county, including all Lord Donegall's estates on the north side of the Six Mile Water and north of a line produced from it to the town of Larne.

The jurisdiction of this court extends to sums not exceeding 2 pounds, which are recoverable by civil bill process, and not exceeding 20 pounds recoverable by attachment.

The manor courts of this manor are held in Antrim on every third Thursday and in the village of Doagh on every third Tuesday. The courts leet for the manor are held twice a year. The Marquis of Donegall is lord of the manor and Mr Arthur Adair Gamble, seneschal.

Petty sessions are held in the court house of Antrim on every alternate Thursday. The presiding magistrates are Mr Clark and Mr Montgomery. The business at these sessions is trifling and unimportant, and seldom occupies more than from 2 to 3 hours. Trespasses, disputes about wages and petty assults constitute almost the entire business disposed of at them. Quarter sessions are held here in June and December, the alternate terms being held in Belfast; Philip Fogarty Esquire, assistant barrister.

The Crown business at these sessions is comparatively trifling and the cases unimportant. The number of prisoners convicted at them varies from 8 to 15, and averages 11. The civil bill business usually occupies about 2 days.

Outrages, party riots, faction fights and agrarian disturbances are quite unknown here, a drunken brawl being almost the most serious case of disturbance known.

The only description of smuggling known is in the manufacture of paper. Within [blank] years there have been [blank] convictions by the revenue of the proprietors of the paper mills, for breaches of the revenue laws.

Insurances

There are not more than 31 fire insurances within the parish. Losses by fire have rarely been sustained and the insurance of property is therefore seldom resorted to.

Dispensary

Antrim dispensary was established in 1817, a house for the purpose having been built partly by the county and partly by local subscription. It cost 200 pounds, of which Lord Ferrard contributed 50 pounds. It has since then been supported by local subscriptions and grand jury presentations.

This institution has had a salutary effect on the health and comforts of the poor. And in Antrim, which is so much exposed to the communication of infection and disease by the numerous itinerant mendicants and vagrants, the speedy relief it affords has been particularly necessary in checking the prevalence of disease.

Fever, from the increased moisture of the climate [insert marginal query], is on the increase and its prevalence is encouraged by the privations which the poor endure from the scarcity and dearness of sufficient fuel, their inability to procure lime, and latterly from there being less employment for women and their consequent want of the means to purchase nutritious food.

Consumption is also on the increase and seems to be hereditary in many families; but withal, the inhabitants of this parish, contrasted with those of many others, are comparatively healthy. By reference to Appendix, a statement of the funds of this institution and the number and description of the cases will be found.

Schools

The means of obtaining instruction for their children are within the reach of almost all. The expense of education has been so much lessened by the support which the schools in this parish receive from charitable societies and individuals that there are few who cannot afford to educate their children. The benefits of intellectual and moral education are more or less appreciated by all classes, and to them in a great degree may be attributed the moral improvement which has of late years taken place here. With some there is still a degree of apathy as regards instruction, but on the whole people are anxious for the education of their children and at this moment 829 children, being one-sixth of the entire population, are receiving instruction.

There are few who cannot read; writing and arithmetic are not usually included in the female education but the majority of the males can write. English grammar is now generally taught and the course of education has within a few years been greatly improved.

The effects of sabbath schools have been very perceptible, and from the infant school which was established in 1830 much good is expected to result.

Poor

Since the Antrim Mendicity Society ceased to exist (in September 1836) there has not been any regular provision for the poor further than the collections on Sundays at the different places of worship, detailed accounts of which will be found by reference to Appendix.

On the discontinuation of the Mendicity Society a soup shop was established and rations, consisting [insert marginal query: unfinished?].

The Mendicity Society had been established in 1825, with a view to supply the old and infirm with necessary support by a weekly allowance of money or provisions, to furnish materials of industry to the poor that were able to work and to remunerate them according to their exertions. The benefits of the society extended to the adjoining granges of Muckamore and Shilvodan.

In their first report the committee announced that "the objects of the society had been realised: the system of public begging had been abolished in the district; habits of industry had been encouraged among those who could work; and the town and neighbourhood was no longer infested by strolling mendicants from other parishes."

They further stated that in the course of the year the committee had distributed 27,670 lbs of oatmeal and in money 126 pounds 8s 3d, and had thereby afforded assistance to 136 mendicants or families; and the quantity of yarn spun by the poor, and for which they were liberally paid, was 2,673 hanks.

In subsequent years the affairs of the society became gradually less prosperous. The country inhabitants relaxed in their subscriptions and others who had before subscribed removed from the neighbourhood. Still, however, it continued to exist, affording assistance to many objects of charity, until the month of September 1836, when it wholly and entirely ceased from want of sufficient funds to carry it on.

Its loss has been severely felt by many. For, though the inhabitants of the parish are particularly humane and charitable, still the town is so frequented by strollers from neighbouring towns and districts, by families under pretence of seeking for employment and by many with much less stronger claims upon their benevolence, that it is impossible for them to relieve the daily increasing objects of compassion.

There are at present 18 paupers on the parish books, among whom the annual sum of 31 pounds, collected in church, is distributed and there are 6 deserted illegitimate children supported by the parish, the assessment for whose support amounted at the Easter vestry, 1837, to 43 pounds 3s 6d.

Religion

In the parish of Antrim there are [blank] Episcopalians, [blank] Presbyterians, [blank] Quakers and about [blank] other Protestant Dissenters, and [blank] Roman Catholics [insert marginal note: incomplete].

Antrim is a vicarage in the united diocese of Down and Connor, and in the presentaton of the Marquis of Donegall. The Revd William Greene is the present vicar. The vicarial tithes amount to 272 pounds per annum.

There are 2 Presbyterian congregations in Antrim; the members of these are not confined to the immediate parish, many of them coming from the several surrounding ones, as is generally the case in the Presbyterian Church. The Antrim congregations are of the second class.

One congregation consists of about 813 families and is in connection with the Synod of Ulster. The minister is the Revd Robert Magill A.M., whose stipend amounts to 92 pounds 6s 2d and regium donum to 75 pounds per annum.

The other and first established congregation is in connection with the Presbytery of Antrim and comprises about 250 families, the Reverend James Carley, minister. His stipend amounts to 80 pounds per annum and regium donum to 75 pounds.

Original Clergy

The Revd George Macartney L.L.D. was appointed vicar of Antrim in 1773. He died on the 2nd December 1824 at the age of 84, having been vicar of Antrim for 51 years.

The Revd Lord Edward Chichester succeeded Dr Macartney and held the vicarage of Antrim until 22nd July 1832, when he was promoted to the deanery of Raphoe. Lord Edward Chichester was succeeded by the Revd William Greene, who is the present vicar of Antrim.

Presbyterians

The first Presbyterian minister of Antrim was the Revd John Ridge A.M., who was ordained vicar of it in 1619; he died in 1656. To him succeeded the Revd James Cunningham in 1656; he died in 1670. Thomas Cowan in 1672; he died in 1683. Anderson in 1685; removed elsewhere in 1688. Adair in 1690; he died in 1698. Dr John Abernethy in 1703; removed to Dublin in 1730. Revd Mr Duchall in 1730; removed to Dublin in 1741. Alexander Maclean (no record). Dr Campbell (no record). Revd William Bryson in 1764; resigned 1810, died 1815. James Carley in 1811, the present minister.

In the second congregation (Presbyterian) formed in 1726 and in connection with the Synod of Ulster the first minister was the Reverend William Holmes, ordained 1731, died 1750. To him succeeded the Revd John Ranken who died 1793, the Revd Alexander Montgomery who died in 1820 and the Revd Robert Magill A.M. (the present minister), ordained 20th June 1820.

Methodists

The Wesleyan Methodists have a resident minister, the Reverend Bayley, who preaches alternately with a minister from Ballymena. He receives 16 pounds per annum and free lodgings.

The Primitive Wesleyan Methodists, who worship at the chapel to the north of High Street: their ministers are frequently changed. The present one, the Revd William Lendrum, receives 16 pounds per annum salary, 16 pounds per annum for his wife, 4 pounds per annum for his child and free quarters. He is paid by the Methodist Conference.

Catholics

In the Roman Catholic Church this parish is united to those of Connor and Drummaul and grange of Shilvodan. The parish priest, the Reverend Daniel Curoe, resides at Randalstown. His income, being derived from his congregation in a variety of ways, of course fluctuates. [Crossed out: For instance he receives 2s 6d for each christening, 1 pound for each marriage, besides confessions, which, with the stated sums paid by each family in his congregation, are said to amount to from 300 to 400 pounds per annum]. [Insert note: The fees [? administered] for the various roles of that religion [are] said to amount to about [?] 300 pounds per annum].

Habits of the People

Nearly one-half of the adult male rural population of this parish are engaged in the manufacture of linen. A considerable number are employed at the neighbouring bleach greens, and the paper mills in Antrim afford the means of support to 26 men and 34 women. 235 families are engaged in farming. The resident gentry, who hold large farms, afford employment to many agricultural labourers. The majority of the remainder of the adult male population is made up of the traders, dealers and mechanics in the town of Antrim, servants and professional men.

About 8 females throughout the parish are employed in working flowers upon muslin, at which they can earn about 2s per week; but, except these and the comparatively small number employed as servants and dressmakers, the females may now be said to be without any employment, except during the seasons of seed time and harvest. In the former they can earn 6d and in the latter 1s per day. Spinning is now resorted to more as an alternative to being idle than from anything it can produce, as they cannot earn more than 2d per day by it.

The weavers have for the last year been suffering from the depression to which the trade has been subject, and are frequently in great want; and as it had for so many years been so prosperous they derived their entire support from it, while their daughters and wives spun the yarn they manufactured into linen. Farming was quite neglected by them and few of them have it now as an alternative.

Those who are employed at the mills and very extensive bleach greens in the neighbourhood can earn at least 1s per day constantly and are therefore well off.

Farmers

The farmers are in general independent and comfortable in their circumstances. Their farms vary in size from 10 to 40 acres and might average 18 acres. They are a decent respectable class and the mere aspect of their comfortable and substantial residences, generally 1-storey but roomy, neatly roughcast and whitened, and enclosed in a little planting, are almost sufficient indications of their being a [crossed out: civilised] and industrious race. Many of their houses, particularly those lately erected, are slated and nearly all have neat little vegetable gardens attached to them. Their system of farming is advanced and their fields squared and enclosed by bushy hawthorn hedgerows.

Bacon, salt and dried meat, some Lough Neagh fish when in season, baker's bread, eggs, milk and potatoes constitute the principal food of the farmers. Oaten bread has in a great measure been superseded by baker's, the cheapness of the latter and the convenience of procuring it from the bread carts from neighbouring towns and the numerous petty grocers' shops throughout the country giving it an advantage over the oaten cake. Tea is generally used by the farmers but not more than once a day. They are rather addicted to whiskey drinking but are otherwise frugal.

The weavers and labourers are now almost on a par as to circumstances, but the houses of the former are better than those of the latter. A good house is required for the manufacture of fine linen, which is easily spoiled by damp or soot, while it is almost immaterial how bad the house may be in which calico or coarse linen is manufactured.

Weavers and Labourers

The weavers' houses in this parish are 1-storey, mostly consist of 2 tolerable good apartments, are thatched, roughcast and well lit. They are rather cleanly and comfortable. The cottages of the labouring class are, with a few exceptions, inferior in size, comfort and cleanliness to the weavers'. They are all thatched and many of them damp and smoky. A few of them are of mud, but almost all the houses in the parish are of stone and lime. Many of the agricultural labourers are cottiers living on their landlord's farm and paying their rent in labour. They also in general spread their manure and plant their potatoes on his land, for which they pay per perch by the ridge. Except in spring and in the dead of winter the agricultural labourers seldom suffer from want of employment and at all other seasons they can earn from 10d to 1s per day.

The females are now, except during the seasons of seed time and harvest, almost out of employment. In those seasons they work in the fields. In harvest a woman can earn as much as a man, in other seasons not more than 6d per day.

Many of the weavers keep a cow each. Few of the labourers can afford to do so. Potatoes is the chief food of both these classes. Bacon and salt meat is consumed in but small quantities. The supply of milk is not plentiful.

During the summer large quantities of the pullen or freshwater herring are taken along the shore of Lough Neagh. 3 boats, each manned by 3 men, are daily engaged in fishing. The pullen sell on an average for about 10d per dozen and furnish a cheap and palatable meal for all classes.

The lower orders consume them in large quantities. A dozen of these fishes may average about [blank] lbs weight.

Some of the weavers and a few of the labourers have little gardens, and the consumption of vegetables is more general here than in most westerly and northerly parishes. Tea has not been so constantly used during the last 2 years, from want of the means of procuring it. Baker's bread is much more generally used than formerly. Stirabout was at one time the usual breakfast but less meal is now made and the raw corn is generally sent to market.

The weavers and labourers are much addicted to whiskey drinking, particularly at fairs and markets, and are therefore an improvident race. They are otherwise quiet, peaceable and industrious, quite free from party feuds and very honest. There is, however, much immorality among them and the farmers.

Bastards are numerous and the crime of exposing children is on the increase. The latter is attributed more to poverty and it is considered that the people are much more moral than formerly.

Dress

All classes dress well and neatly in their respective stations. Their clothes are both substantial and comfortable, and put on with a degree of taste. The numerous stalls and shops for the sale of ready-made and old clothes, and the low prices of calicoes have brought the prices of male and female apparel, even in these times, within the reach of all and there not only is not a falling-off in their appearance at fairs and markets, but on the contrary their style of dressing seems to be improving.

Dark blue coats with gilt buttons, coloured waistcoats, drab or blue trousers and castor hats are usually worn by the men. Calico, stuff and frequently silk gowns, neat cloaks, straw bonnets, gloves and well-made shoes and stockings are commonly worn by the females on Sundays and holy days.

Watches are common among most classes and an umbrella is considered an indispensable appendage to the equipment of both males and females.

Observance of Sabbath

The sabbath is nowhere in Ireland (outwardly) more strictly observed than here, but it is to be feared that the public houses are too much frequented on that day by those who come to town from the country to attend worship.

Fuel

Except among the upper class, turf is the only fuel. It is procured from the adjoining and westerly parish of Drummaul, and is both dear and scarce in the southern and eastern districts in this parish, where the poorer class suffer much in winter from want of sufficient fuel; and to this cause may be attributed much, if not most, of the disease and sickness which annually visits the parish in spring.

The autumn of 1836 was so wet that the turf could not be got out of the bogs where they lay cut, and such was the want of firing that the hedgerows were actually sold by the perch and cut down for firing.

Marriage

They marry rather early than otherwise. Females frequently marry at the age of 17 and males at that of 20 years. It is a curious fact that though there is a large and respectable congregation in Antrim, still there have been only 2 couples married by the present vicar, who has been incumbent of Antrim for [blank] years. The Protestants prefer being married in their own houses to avoid the bustle, noise and staring attendant on a marriage in the church, and therefore apply to the Presbyterian ministers.

The usual number in a family is 5 persons.

Amusements

Previous to 1798 the people here were very prone to amusement and recreation in public, and assembled for several days at Christmas and Easter; but since the act which was passed at that troublesome period to prevent public meetings, their spirit for amusement has greatly declined. The want of means of enjoying themselves has also checked or debarred them from their recreations and there is besides a necessity for every increased exertion they can put forth to make up the deficiency in the circulation of capital among them. Attending the summer fairs, a little dancing, an idle day at Christmas and games in the Fir Field at Easter are now their only amusements.

The sports at Easter consist in the males and females running in pairs between 2 certain points in the Fir Field, which adjoins Antrim, on Monday, and performing the same ceremonies at Ann's hill, just outside the east of the town, on Tuesday; and after spending each day at these innocent games they all come into town and, taking hands to the number of perhaps from 80 to 100, "thread the needle" from one extremity of Antrim to another. They then retire to their houses and thus terminate the Easter sports at Antrim.

Cock-fighting was at one time a favourite amusement, but it is now prevented by the magistrates. There is little or no card-playing, nor have they any patrons nor patrons' days, such things being unknown in Presbyterian districts. There are not any local customs. Wakes are not now attended for amusement.

There is no doubt but that many beneficial effects are produced by checking among the lower class the naturally strong taste they have for meeting in public; but this step, however sensible it may at first appear, is attended with worse consequences.

The people here seem bent on having some recreation and assemble they will, whether it be in public or in private. If they be prohibited from the former, as they have been, they will have recourse to the latter, which is the case at present; and to such private meetings seven-eighths of the immorality of the parish may be traced.

Traditions

They have not got any legendary tales nor ancient music among them.

The lower class are almost all superstitious, having an implicit belief in the existence of fairies and of ghosts, in witchcraft and charms, and perfectly convinced that cows are blinked and deprived of their milk by the fairies and can only be cured by a charm.

Old thorns and forts are held as sacred and considered as "gentle places", that is, that fairies assemble about them. To remove either is considered as sacrilegious and the person who would do so is looked on as insane, for he is sure never after to prosper. The favourite punishments for such transgressions seem to be the death of the offender's cattle, sickness of some of his family or the burning of his house. These superstitious notions do not seem to be much on the decline.

Emigration

Emigration is, as contrasted with former years, considerably on the decrease. The causes for this are numerous, but the principal are: there not being the same encouraging accounts as formerly from those who had emigrated; the ravages caused by cholera when it visited America and many from the neighbourhood of Antrim having been carried off by it. Few now emigrate who had been prospering at home, though almost all who have lately gone have been industrious and respectable characters. A reference to Appendix will more clearly illustrate the nature and extent of emigration in this parish.

Remarkable Events

The parish has not given birth to any remarkable character, nor has it been the scene of any remarkable event except those alluded to under the head of Towns.

Superstitions

An implicit belief exists in the sanctity of forts, and this is not confined to any particular persuasion. The forts are considered as the abodes of fairies, who are religiously respected. To remove a fort or injure one by cultivation is sacrilege and invariably attended by some domestic visitation, usually the death of a cow or depriving it of its milk. A man in the townland of Crosskennan removed or rather cultivated a fort in the year 1836. Within a few days his cow died and he has never since prospered in anything he undertook. [Insert footnote: I had this from the man himself; he is about 50 years old]. To this superstition may be attributed the preservation of so many forts throughout the country, even where they interfere with the cultivation of the land.

The existence of fairies is confidently and generally believed in, particularly by old women and men, many of whom assert that they have seen them; but of late they say they have almost disappeared, owing to the circulation of the Scriptures.

Old thorns are sacred and few, even of the more enlightened class, would venture to cut them down. The results of such an act would be undoubtedly fatal and the stories concerning them are very numerous and ridiculous. They generally grow singly and are termed "gentle."

Witches are believed in and are supposed to have the power of taking away the luck or milk of a cow, or preventing cream from rising in the milk. They are supposed to be old haggard-looking women who can transform themselves into hares.

The Devil has been seen by many: his favourite mode of appearance is in the person of a black dog, but he is said to have the power of assuming any form but that of a sheep.

Charms are believed in and resorted to but not so frequently as formerly. Giving a cow a drink in which a little salt, a flint arrow and a crooked sixpence have been dipped is considered an infallible cure for being "elfshot" or deprived of her milk by the fairies.

Flint arrowheads are termed "elf stones", being considered as charmed as the missiles of the fairies.

A strange dog or cat coming to a house is sure to bode prosperity to it.

The ears feeling warm indicates that you are the subject of conversation, and eyes being itchy that a stranger will soon sleep in your house.

Traditions

A tradition exists, and is in common acceptation, that the valley of the Six Mile Water, particularly that part of it in this parish, was a favourite abode of Ossian's, and that it is described or alluded to in his poems. This is very doubtful, as neither the valley by that or its other ancient names, namely Owen Nivien (the Irish name of the river) or Moylinny (the name of a townland in the parish and also the name of the manor) are mentioned, nor is there any description which is quite applicable to this district.

ANCIENT TOPOGRAPHY

Ecclesiastical: Round Tower

The round tower of Antrim, or the Steeple as it is more commonly called, is situated in the townland of Steeple near the south centre of the parish, three-quarters of a mile north of the town of Antrim, a similar distance north of the nearest point of the Six Mile Water and 1 and a quarter miles north east of the north eastern coast of Lough Neagh. It is 16 miles north of the round tower which formerly stood at Trummery near the south of the county, 10 miles north north east of that in Ram's Island in Lough Neagh and 28 and a quarter miles south by west of that at Armoy near the north of the county.

Its situation, though low (111 feet above the sea and 63 feet above Lough Neagh), is very picturesque and beautiful, seated on a trifling swell in the almost level tract extending along the eastern shores of Lough Neagh and at the western base of a ridge extending from the neighbouring mountains, which falls towards it with a varied and undulating slope.

From the wooded state of the surrounding country, its low situation and grey and indistinct colour, the round tower of Antrim is not now discernible from any distance; but were the country more bare of planting it would no doubt be a very conspicuous object from Lough Neagh and the higher grounds along the west of the county. Its grey head now faintly appears in the landscape above the surrounding woods which threaten yet to outtop it, but it is still from its venerable and picturesque appearance an interesting and peculiar ornament to the scenery.

Dimensions of Tower

Its elevation from the point where it first touches the ground to its summit is 92 feet. A little mound 3 feet high has been formed around it by drawing away a quantity of the rich earth to manure the neighbouring land. From the surface of this mound its foundations sink to a depth of 4 feet.

The circumference of the tower at its base is 49 feet 6 inches, but near the surface of the ground there is an offset which adds 14 inches all round the circumference of its foundations. Its interior diameter at the first entrance or doorway (7 feet 4 inches from the ground) is 9 feet and here its walls are 3 feet 1 inch thick. From this its diameter gradually diminishes as it ascends, until it reaches the base of the cone forming its summit, where it is 6 feet, and here the wall is 1 foot 8 inches in thickness.

From its base to the first doorway the tower is a mass of solid masonry. The upper 6 feet of the cone forming its summit (which is 12 feet high) is also solid, so that the elevation of the internal open space is 79 feet 8 inches; see drawings.

Masonry of Tower

The profiles of the tower, as taken from the 3 different points, are almost similar. They present a trifling variation from the rectilinear and seem to have always existed, there being no indication of the tower having been built or increased in height at different periods; on the contrary the masonry (except in the cone) is quite similar.

The stones used in its construction are, with the exception of the lintels and jambs, of a description of basalt (rather soft) which would seem to have been procured from the townland of Lady Hill, 3 miles north of the tower. They are not quarry stones, there being no quarry, but stones of a similar description are abundant in that townland and are not commonly to be found elsewhere in the neighbourhood. They are in general of an oblong form, bear trifling marks of the hammer and are laid lengthwise. Few of them are bond stones or go "through and through." They are generally very unshapely and (in the inside) apparently loosely laid, so much that the light appears through the wall in 2 places.

A fair idea of the masonry cannot be formed from the external appearance of the tower, as it has been pointed and the spaces between the stones carefully [filled] up; but in the inside it seems to have undergone little change as here there is very little mortar used. The tower seems to have been for about the first 22 feet (above its floor) built in courses of 4 feet each; in some instances these courses do not appear horizontal. Above this the stones diminish in size and seem to be badly laid and bedded, the spaces very open, less mortar being used.

At the base of the cone is a cordon or ring which projects about 8 inches and under this cordon is an oak beam about 8 by 6 inches, upon which the centering of the cone seems to have been raised. The arch seems to have been constructed of wickerwork, as the marks of their twigs are to this day quite perceptible in the mortar. The interior of the cone is more spherical than conical.

The upper 6 feet of the cone (which is 12 feet high) are solid, almost the entire of which had been knocked off, apparently by lightning, at some remote period, the stones having been found riven and splintered. The remaining portion is carefully built in courses of well-dressed Tardree or white porphyry stones. It was rebuilt and repaired in 1819.

On the summit of the cone there had stood a handsome stone spear, octagonal, and of a description of stone very rare in this neighbourhood. [Insert footnote: NB a specimen of the stone is now sent. I found one of similar description in the window of Muckamore Abbey, one in a fragment of the wall of Toome Castle and 4 besides the lintels of the door in Cranfield old church. It appears to be composition and the spear seems to have been cast, not cut]. It had been morticed into a moulded circular block of similar stone, with a torus or ring round it. This seems to have been thrown down at the same period with the cone and its fragments are now to be found inside the tower.

The lintels and sills of the doorway, and some of the windows, are of what is termed by masons "field granite", a description of greenstone quite as hard as granite. These, particularly in the doorway, are very well dressed. Many of them, however, are cracked through.

The mortar is similar to that now used, save that it is very coarse, the lime being found in large half-burnt lumps and the sand being uneven, coarse and unriddled.

There are 8 windows and 1 doorway in the tower. 4 of these windows are immediately under the cone of the tower and each opposite one of the cardinal points. Their dimensions are similar, each measuring 3 feet 6 inches by 1 foot 6 inches, including a very little towards the top. A high slab forms the top and another the bottom of each, as regards their width. There is no arch of any kind about them and their jambs are of smoothly dressed stones. Of the 4 other windows, 2 are on the southern side of the tower (under the upper one), 1 is on the west side and 1 on the north east side.

The bottom of the lower southern window is 35 feet 4 inches from the ground and that of the centre one 27 feet 8 inches above the latter. Their dimensions are alike, being 3 feet 6 inches by 1 foot 10 inches.

The bottom of the lower western window is 25 feet 4 inches and that of the north east 20 feet 4 inches from the ground. The dimensions of the former are 3 feet 5 inches by 1 foot 6 inches, of the latter 3 feet 6 inches by 1 foot 8 inches.

All the windows are similar as to masonry, there being no attempt at an arch but merely the stone slab extending across their summits. Their sides are all well formed of faced and jointed greenstone. There are not traces of beams or frames having been in them.

Doorway of Tower

The doorway is in the north side of the tower, 7 feet 4 inches from the ground and its threshold is nearly on a level with the floor formed by the summit of the solid masonry. The masonry of the doorway is massive, solid and well finished, a single solid slab forming its threshold and with 2 slabs laid longitudinally forming its top. A rough beam of oak extends across the top between the slabs. This beam is not more than 5 inches square at the thickest.

A second beam of oak extends across the threshold towards the inside (the floor being 9 inches higher than the step of the doorway), its extremities being received into a recess or groove extending round the doorway in the inside and which evidently seems to have been intended for the door frame. This recess is rather singular as the door frame must have been built in it and could not have been inserted in it, from its being grooved into the wall in either side.

The sides of the doorway are of hard greenstone similar to that before mentioned. They are quite smooth in their faces and are dressed square.

The doorway measures 4 feet 4 inches high, 1 foot 11 inches wide and the wall is 3 feet 1 inch thick.

The sill and lintels are worn very smooth,

apparently from constant use at some remote period.

From the sockets for ends of joists <joices> or beams, and the manner in which they occur in the wall, it is evident that a spiral stair extended from the bottom to the top of the window. Wooden sleepers or plugs of oak are also found in similar positions. It is therefore improbable that there could have been floors except at the top just above the upper windows, where there is 1 oak beam 8 inches square, perfectly sound except where it enters the wall, where its ends are a little decayed. Opposite each window, or rather immediately under it, there is a beam of oak thrown across like a joist, and from there being but 1 beam it is probable that there may have been a sort of landing place or half-stage at these points.

And another reason for this conjecture is that the windows are at different heights and (except at the top) not opposite each other. For instance, the doorway is 7 feet 4 inches from the ground, the next window 20 feet 4 inches, the second 35 feet 4 inches, the third 45 feet 6 inches, the fourth 63 feet and the 4 upper windows 77 feet from the ground. There would therefore have been 4 of these stages and upper and lower floors. There are not now either lofts nor floors in the tower, nor are there any means of ascending it except such as may be constructed for the purpose.

It was repaired and pointed in 1819 by the late William Clark Esquire and is in good preservation, not manifesting any signs of decay. This may to a great degree be attributed to its being in the grounds of Steeple, the residence of George Clark Esquire, which stands a few yards to the north west of the tower.

On a large granite stone immediately up above that forming the upper part of the doorway of the tower a cross has been raised. A description of it will be found [later] and a drawing of it.

Spear

On the summit of the tower there formerly was a stone spear (see drawings) which must have formed a beautiful termination to the cone. On repairing the cone in 1819 the fragments of the spear and block into which it had been morticed were found scattered about, but it had not been noticed before.

The spear consisted of a single stone and would seem to have been hexagonal. It had been morticed into a hewn circular block of composition stone (see specimen) 20 inches in diameter at the base, 17 at the top and 10 inches deep. A torus or ring 3 and a half inches in depth is cut round the outside of the block and the mortice which receives the spear is well squared and cut.

The spear is now in 2 pieces and only 2 portions of the base, forming about two-thirds of its entire, remain. They are lying inside the steeple among a heap of rubbish.

The stone of which the spear and its base are formed is composition and quite similar to that alluded to in the window of Muckamore Abbey. A specimen of the stone is herewith sent.

Ancient Church

The tradition of the country is that a church, abbey or monastery once stood beside the Steeple, and that the town of Antrim, then called Entrumnia, formerly stood there, but was removed to its present site from the want of water. The former of these traditions is in a good measure confirmed by a variety of circumstances which will be afterwards detailed.

The late Dr Stevenson of Belfast, who died within a few years, stated in a manuscript that a religious house was founded in Antrim in 495 by a disciple of St Patrick, but that there are no further records of it than 766.

In eradicating the ruins of some barns and outoffices attached to the old dwelling house of Steeple (which stood 30 yards north of the tower) in the year 1819, a huge block of freestone, which had evidently been the architrave of the door of some public building, was dug up. This block, which was a cube of 3 feet, had what is termed by masons "the egg and dart" (a device somewhat like the fleur de lis) carved on it; it was somewhat defaced, but one side of the stone had been chiselled and ornamented. From this stone the apex of the cone now on the tower was formed.

The site of the garden at Steeple House was until about 7 years ago traversed by foundations of old buildings and quantities of loose building stones, the expense and labour of removing which was very great.

The site of some old foundations, now removed, but said to be those of a church, is pointed out within 70 yards west of the tower. Little credit, however, is to be attached to this.

The quantities of human bones which have been dug up about the round tower are almost incredible and scarce a spadeful of earth can even now be turned up that does not contain some fragments of them. The extreme richness and depth of the mould would infer that it had been long used as burial ground, and these facts tend to confirm the truth of the tradition concerning the church.

Some of the bones found were of unusually large proportions, and from the statements of some medical men who examined and measured the thigh-bones, it would appear that they were those of men from 6 to 7 feet high.

5 and a half furlongs north of the round tower is a holy well, and 120 yards north of the tower is a stone known by the name of the Witches Stone; see description and drawing.

MODERN TOPOGRAPHY

Church

The parish church of Antrim is situated on a low sloping ground near the centre of the town of the same name, within 50 yards of the north bank of the Six Mile Water, above which it is elevated about 12 feet.

The church consists of an aisle standing east north east and west south west, and measuring outside 65 feet 6 inches in length, 33 feet in width. The side walls are 14 feet high and the eastern gable 26 feet. Attached to the south side of this aisle is another (now occupied by the Massereene family, part fitted up as a pew and part as a vault). This portion or aisle measures 21 by 21 feet but is lower than the main aisle by 4 feet.

In the north side of the church are 4 large square-headed windows (see sketches), and in the south side 2 and southern gable 1 of a similar description. They measure in the inside 5 by 5 feet and are of cut sandstone. In the lesser aisle are 2 old windows of smaller dimensions but similar architecture (see plan), measuring inside 5 feet high and 1 foot 6 inches wide. [Insert marginal note: One is larger].

In the eastern gable is a Gothic or other lancet-shaped window (see plan). The doorway is of similar architecture and style with the east window, and measures 8 feet 7 inches high and 4 feet wide. It is in the western gable but is now inside the church, the tower and spire having been erected in 1817 to 1818, previous to which time there had not been one or other.

The walls of the church are 4 feet thick. The masonry seems to have been very rude, as in the exterior of the lesser aisle, which has not been pointed, the stones (quarry stones, chiefly whinstone) are very rudely dressed or shaped, very loosely or openly laid and but little mortar between them. This, however, is not so apparent in the walls of the main aisle, which are well pointed.

Antrim church

There are 3 loopholes or embrasures for mus-
ketry in the north side and 2 in the eastern gable
of the church, and it is probable there may be
more, as from their small size externally they
might be easily plastered over. These holes are
about 2 feet from the ground. The exterior aper-
ture is cut through a block of sandstone and is
about 3 by 4 inches. The embrasure expands at a
considerable angle but there is no mark inside
whereby it can be measured. The loopholes in the
gable are perforated or formed obliquely, both
bearing north east upon the street of Antrim. The
edges of the hole are much worn to the outside.

From the masonry and the architecture of the
church, and its windows and door, it would seem
to have been erected at the same period, as the
strictest uniformity in every respect pervades it;
and it is rather remarkable that the sandstone in
the quoins is similar to that found near the round
tower and now on its summit, and that it must
have been brought across the lake from Coalisland,
as it perfectly resembles the sandstone of that
district and is different from any in this.

It should have been mentioned that 28 feet
from the western gable on the north side there are
a number of quoins extending from the top to the
bottom of the side wall, their faced ends and sides
facing the north and west.

A doorway many years ago, but within memory,
stood here. A window in uniformity with the
others (square) now occupies part of the space.

On one of the quoins or door-jambs alluded to
the date 1596 is inscribed quite legibly. This, it is
said, is the date of its being first used as a Protestant church. It is said to be the fourth church in
which the Protestant religion was celebrated in
Ireland.

No ancient families being in this churchyard,
the oldest tombstone bears the date of 1666. The
only family of rank who bury in it are the
Massereene family, whose ancestors (the
Clotworthys) settled in Antrim in 1603. Their
burial place or vault is under the southern wing of
the church, the remainder of which is occupied by
their seat.

Only 1 Roman Catholic has been interred here
during the last 20 years.

The graveyard is well enclosed but crowded
with graves and not kept with care, neatness or
regularity.

Cross

On the stone above that forming the top of the
doorway in the round tower, and on the outside, a
cross has been sculptured. The stone measures

externally 2 feet 3 inches long and 1 foot 4 thick,
and is of granite. It is cracked through close to one
side of the cross.

The cross is neatly executed and is raised about
one-sixth of an inch. There is not the slightest
trace of any inscription or of any other sculpture.
A drawing of the cross, which more clearly illus-
trates it, will be found by reference to drawings,
and a plan of the doorway showing its position
will be found in drawings.

ANCIENT TOPOGRAPHY

Holy Well

In the townland of Holy Well near the centre of
the parish, 5 and a half furlongs north of the round
tower and at an elevation of 115 feet above the
sea, is a spring well on the acclivity of a hill. The
well is 6 feet [high] and 4 and a half feet in
diameter. The water is slightly chalybeate and is
by some said to possess tonic or strengthening
properties, and is still used as such by a few.

These properties are, however, imaginary and
originated in the tradition of the well being a holy
one, that stations were formerly made at it and
penances from it to the round tower, but these
have not occurred for ages. It is used for domestic
purposes and has lately been cleared and faced
inside with stones. There are neither old thorns,
stones, paths or anything about it which could
indicate its former use.

Witches Stone

In the garden at Steeple, 120 yards from and
nearly due north of the round tower, is a broad flat
stone measuring 6 feet by 4 feet 7 inches, known
by the name of the Witches Stone (see drawings).
2 holes, one 9 inches deep, 15 inches long and 12
broad, and another 3 inches deep and 6 inches in
diameter are sunk in the stone, which is a sort of
whin or hard basalt.

Formerly a little rivulet ran along 2 sides of this
stone but on the enclosing of the garden about 7
years ago the course of the stream was altered
considerably.

This stone is said to derive its name from the
circumstances of a witch jumping from the summit of the round tower when it was completed
and, lighting on this stone on her knees, she left
the impressions it still retains.

Another tradition is that the larger hole was
used as a baptismal font and the smaller one for
containing the holy oil or chrism; that stations
were formerly made from the holy well (5 and a
half furlongs north of it) to this stone; and that in

the still earlier ages the converted pagans who inhabited or worshipped at the round tower were here baptised and anointed.

The latter tradition is in many respects reasonable and probable. The large hollow is well adapted for the purpose of a baptismal font and its former proximity to water strengthens this idea. Both holes are neatly and smoothly cut but the surface of the stone, though naturally tabular, is otherwise undressed.

Forts

In the parish of Antrim there are 2 mounds and 28 raths or forts, of which plans and sections will be found by reference to drawings. One of the mounds is situated in the demesne of, and within 6 feet of, Antrim Castle, occupying a low situation within 36 yards of the river and [not] discernible except from the very high grounds.

Its form is that of a truncated cone 51 yards in diameter at the base and 11 yards at the top. Its elevation is 37 feet and it seems to be composed of a rich earthy soil. There is neither ditch nor parapet round it. Its sides are planted with some lofty Scotch firs and shrubs. An old thorn grows near its summit and on its east side, about 10 feet from its base, there is a venerable old yew (3 feet in girth at the butt) which, from the extent of its spreading boughs, must have been coeval with the erection of the castle (1613). A well laid out spiral walk renders the ascent of the mound very easy.

The other mound occupies a conspicuous situation on the summit of a ridge (in the townland of Crosskennan) 500 feet above the sea. Its form is semiglobular, its diameter 73 feet and its height 12 feet. The traces of a parapet may still be found round it. This mound seems to be composed of earth. It is not well preserved and may have been, at one time, higher.

The forts in the townlands of Dunsilly and Rathenraw differ from all the others and evidently seem intended for different uses. They are composed of earth. The situation of that in Rathenraw is conspicuous and commanding, being 305 feet above the sea, while that in Dunsilly is low, only 102 feet above the sea and only discernible from the higher grounds.

The other forts, 26 in number, vary little in any respect. They are all composed of earth, mostly circular and differ only in the number of their parapets. They generally occupy a sloping situation and are almost invariably in the immediate vicinity of a stream or spring.

These structures are, in this as in most districts,

indebted for their preservation to the superstitious feeling regarding their mutilation or removal, an attempt at either being invariably attended by some dreadful affliction or visitation in the family of the individual; and this feeling is by no means confined to any one sect or persuasion (see Superstitions).

Some of the forts are cultivated and in several instances a blackish mould resembling ashes has been found on their summit.

Coves

Coves are common in this parish. 2 only now remain open but several have been closed up or wholly removed within memory, from having interfered in the labours of the farmer.

The principal cove now remaining open is that in the townland of Lady Hill, near the north side of the parish. A plan and sections of it will be found in drawings, which will illustrate the form and construction. The branches which extend westward have not been explored, but they have been traced by the removal of the earth from their coping stones, which are near the surface of the ground. The falling-in of earth which has choked them up prevents them being wholly explored. It is more than 40 years since they were discovered and no one remembers the discovery of anything in them.

In the townland of Craiggy Hall, near the eastern boundary of the parish, is a very large cave which extends in a right line for 78 yards from south west to north east and across the summit of a gravelly ridge, at the eastern side of which and within 30 yards of the extremity of the cove is a stream forming the eastern boundary of the parish. This cove was accidently discovered by the falling-in of one of the huge stones forming its roof, but from there being 1 foot deep of water in it where it is open, and its total height being only 4 feet, no attempt has been made to explore it.

In its construction and form it resembles the cove just before mentioned. Its dimensions are 4 feet high, 8 feet wide at the bottom and 2 feet wide at the top. It seems to have had 2 entrances, one at each end as it terminates there, but no trace of them remains. A chamber or branch extends north from its east end but the quantity of spring water in it prevents its being explored.

In the townland of Gally Hill, near the centre of the parish, are a number of coves or one cove consisting of several branches. They are constructed in a curious little gravelly ridge, but after being open for many years were closed up about 2 years ago and no trace of them is now visible.

Bones, said to be those of the fox, were found in this cove.

In the townland of Steeple, within 70 yards of the round tower, a small cove was discovered but was destroyed about 8 years ago.

Coins

Coins of silver, brass and copper are frequently found throughout the parish, but the former are almost as soon as found disposed of to watchmakers, who give the mere value of the siver for them. Silver coins of the reign of Elizabeth are rather common. The other silver coins which are usually found are those of the Alexanders (Kings of Scotland), a few of Henry II, more of the other Henrys and many of Charles I and II.

2 very perfect specimens of the base coins of James I (brass shillings) were in the year [blank] dug up in the churchyard of Antrim, when sinking the foundations of the church tower. They were found at a depth of [blank] feet from the surface of the ground. One of these bears the date 1636, the other that of 1690.

Many local copper tokens issued by persons residing in Newry, Carrickfergus, Drogheda, Ballymena and Antrim have been found in the parish. The dates are commonly from 1656 to 1666. The Newry and Drogheda tokens are of brass.

The following are some of the inscriptions on these coins: "Samuel Shennan, marchant in Antrim; William Craford, marchant in Antrim, 1656; John Stewart, marchant of Antrim; Matthew [blank], postmaster in Antrim; Anthony Hall in Carrickfergus; Hugh Fowkes Svr, Drogheda; Walter [blank] of Newry; William Adair in Bellimenoch" (see table of coins for drawings of the more ancient ones).

Standing Stones

About 150 yards from the eastern end of the town of Antrim, and at the right side of the road from that town to Ballyclare, is a portion of a standing stone, the dimensions of which are at present 6 by 4 by 3 feet; but it has been reduced to less than half its former size by blasting, and some of its fragments lie near it. It stands near the summit of a little hill to which it gives the name of the Grey Stane Brae. It is almost due south of the round tower, from which it is distant [blank] furlongs.

226 yards south by east of the last is a second stone partly concealed in a fence. It appears to be about 5 feet high and about 2 feet square. The third is due south of the last and is 220 yards

distant from it. It also lies in a ditch and seems to have been reduced in size. It measures 4 feet 10 inches by 2 feet 1 inch by 1 foot 8 inches.

The fourth is 62 yards east south east of the third. It has been broken and the portion now remaining measures only 4 feet 5 inches by 1 foot 9 inches by 1 foot 3 inches. (For continuation of these stones see grange of Nilteen).

The traditions concerning these stones is that they form part of a line which extended from Carrickfergus to the town of Antrim and which is to be much more easily traced in some of the intervening parishes. From their direction it would seem that they bore upon the round tower, but further particulars concerning them will be found in the adjoining grange of Nilteen, in which they present a remarkable appearance from their size and number.

Miscellaneous Discoveries

The pipes shown in the drawings were found near an old fort which stood near the town of Antrim but has been demolished many years since. Similar pipes have been frequently found near the old forts in this parish.

The arrowheads shown in the drawings were found in a field adjoining the town of Antrim. Similar arrowheads have been found in almost every townland in the parish but have been either sold to strangers or lost.

Stone hatchets of various sizes have been found in this parish but none are at present to be had in it, as the parish is sometimes visited by strangers for the purpose of collecting antiquities for public and private museums.

Appendix to Memoir by James Boyle

SOCIAL AND PRODUCTIVE ECONOMY

Table of Trades and Occupations

Attorneys 4, architects 1, apothecaries and surgeons 4; bricklayers 3, managers of bank 1, bakers 6, barbers 1, brewers 1, butchers 3, blacksmiths 5, bonnetmakers 4, blue dyers 1; clergymen 3, constabulary 9, cabinetmakers 1, carpenters (houses) 7, [?] cartmakers 2, carmen 5, clock and watchmakers 1; dressmakers and mantuamakers 11, drapers (woollen) 3; flax dressers 2, fruit sellers 3; glaziers and painters 3, grocers 22, grocery and spirit shops 6, gardeners 2, gaugers 2; hotel keepers 2, houses of lodging and entertainment 23, hatters 1, hosiers 7, haberdashers and milliners 3, hardware and grocery shops 2; inn-keepers and spirit sellers 25; labourers (agricultural) 16, labourers (otherwise employed) 22, leather cutters and grocers 2; midwives 1; nailers 5; pawnbrokers 2, physicians 1, prostitutes 16, pensioners 13; ragmen 2, reedmakers 1; shoemakers 13, schoolmasters 5, schoolmistresses 5, saddlers 2, sawyers 4; thatchers 2, turners and wheelwrights 2, tailors 7, turnpike keepers 2; whitesmiths 2, weavers (linen) 33, washerwomen 4; surgeon 1; fishermen 6, fisherwomen 2; meal, flour and bran shop 1; timber, coal, iron and grocery shops 1; [total] 352.

Grain sold about Antrim

[Table] Wheat: 1826 500 tons, 1827 436 tons, 1828 673 tons, 1829 200 tons, 1830 300 tons, 1831 190 tons, 1832 280 tons, 1833 332 tons, 1834 200 tons, 1835 291 tons, 1836 314 tons.

Oats: 1826 285 tons, 1827 310 tons, 1828 297 tons, 1829 305 tons, 1830 420 tons, 1831 541 tons, 1832 300 tons, 1833 901 tons, 1834 875 tons, 1835 675 tons, 1836 721 tons.

Barley: 1826 196 tons, 1827 205 tons, 1828 216 tons, 1829 199 tons, 1830 200 tons, 1831 210 tons, 1832 230 tons, 1833 299 tons, 1834 205 tons, 1835 200 tons, 1836 197 tons. NB The oats only are sold in the market. The barley is sold at the brewery and the wheat at the mills at Muckamore.

Mendicity Society Funds

A statement of the funds of the Antrim Mendicity Society for the years 1825 and 1835.

[Table] Amount of subscriptions: 1825, 268 pounds 10s 11d, 1835, 158 pounds 16s 7d; amount of donations: 1825, 6 pounds 4s 4d, 1835, 17 pounds 18s; collections at the parish church: 1825, 50 pounds 11s 1d, 1835, 20 pounds 15s 5d ha'penny; collections at the 1st Presbyterian meeting house: 1825, 12 pounds 15s, 1835, 7 pounds 10s; collections at the 2nd Presbyterian meeting house: 1825, 13 pounds, 1835, 5 pounds; collections at the Roman Catholic chapel: 1835, 2 pounds; amount of fines from magistrates: 1825, 23 pounds 8s 3d, 1835, 11 pounds 13s 9d; from the foreman of a jury: 1835, 1 pound; [totals]: 1825, 374 pounds 9s 7d, 1835, 224 pounds 13s 9d ha'penny.

[Insert footnote: The Mendicity Society was given up in September 1837 from want of funds, but as it may again be revived this statement is given].

Expenditure of Mendicity Society

[Table contains the following headings: year, annual expenditure, average number relieved weekly].

1825, 344 pounds 4s 4d ha'penny, 98 relieved; 1826, 375 pounds 11s 5d, 107 relieved; 1827, 329 pounds 10s 8d farthing, 124 relieved; 1828, 265 pounds 3s 9d, 126 relieved; 1829, 255 pounds 15s 8d ha'penny, 137 relieved; 1831, 236 pounds 15s 8d ha'penny, 135 relieved; 1832, 244 pounds 13s 2d ha'penny, 135 relieved; 1833, 230 pounds 11s 2d, 130 relieved; 1835, 226 pounds 4s 3d, 98 relieved.

Belfast Savings Bank

Antrim branch of the Belfast Savings Bank. [Table contains the following headings: number of deposits in the year, amount of sums deposited in the year, number of deposits amounting to 5s, 1 pound, 5 pounds, 20 pounds, over 20 pounds].

1831, 116 deposits, 216 pounds 16s deposited; 1832, 320 deposits, 811 pounds 6s 10d deposited; 1833, 149 deposits, 692 pounds 4s 11d deposited; 1834, 243 deposits, 686 pounds 6s 8d deposited; 1835, 163 deposits, 680 pounds 1s 9d deposited; 1836, 65 deposits, 184 pounds 14s deposited; number of deposits amounting to 5s: 385; above 5s, not exceeding 1 pound: 172; above 1 pound, not exceeding 5 pounds: 180; above 5 pounds, not exceeding 20 pounds: 98; above 20 pounds: 34.

Antrim Dispensary

[Table] Annual amount of county presentment: 1826, 44 pounds 18s 1d; 1827, 46 pounds 11s; 1828, 46 pounds 11s; 1829, 49 pounds 14s; 1830, 52 pounds 4s 8d; 1831, 35 pounds 10s; 1832, 35 pounds; 1833, 10 pounds; 1834, 33 pounds.

Private subscriptions: 1826, 44 pounds 18s 1d; 1827, 46 pounds 11s; 1828, 46 pounds 11s; 1829, 49 pounds 14s; 1830, 52 pounds 4s 8d; 1831, 35 pounds 10s; 1832, 35 pounds; 1833, 37 pounds 10s; 1834, 33 pounds; 1835, 30 pounds 10s.

Surgeon's [annual] salary: 1826 to 1835 50 pounds.

Expense of medicines: 1826, 22 pounds; 1827, 27 pounds 3s; 1828, 19 pounds; 1829, 22 pounds 10s; 1830, 19 pounds 7s 2d; 1831, 25 pounds 5s; 1832, 22 pounds 10s; 1833, 23 pounds 8s; 1834, 29 pounds 4s; 1835 5 pounds.

Antrim Loan Fund

[Table] Original capital 268 pounds, total issue since commencement 585 pounds, sum now outstanding 256 pounds 11s 11d ha'penny, average issue weekly 15 pounds 9s 8d ha'penny.

Collections

Collections at the different places of worship. [Table] 1827: average weekly collection at church 1 pound 1s 7d, Unitarian meeting house 6s, Trinitarian meeting house 11s 3d ha'penny, Roman Catholic chapel 7s.

1837: average weekly collection at church 14s, Unitarian meeting house 5s, Trinitarian meeting house 10s 7d, Roman Catholic chapel 7s 6d.

Periodicals

Political and other periodicals taken in the parish of Antrim. [Table contains the following headings: name of publication, number of copies, politics].

Quarterly Review, 1, Conservative; *Blackwood's Magazine*, 3, Conservative; *University Magazine*, 4, Conservative; *Penny Magazine*, 5; *Saturday Magazine*, 3; *Age* newspaper, 1, Conservative; *Courier*, 1, ministerial; *Dublin Evening Mail*, 2, Conservative; *Dublin Evening Packet*, 2, Conservative; *London Times*, 2, Conservative; *London [?] Market Lane Express*, 1; *St James' Chronicle*, 1, Conservative; *Belfast Commercial Chronicle*, 9, moderate; *Belfast Ulster Times*, 10, Conservative; *Belfast Northern Whig*, 7, radical; *Belfast Newsletter*, 6, uncertain; *Dublin Advertiser*, 4; *Glasgow Courier*, 1, Conservative; Chambers' *Edinburgh Journal*, 8; Wilson's *Tales of the Borders*, 4.

Conveyances from Antrim

[Table contains the following headings: conveyance, hours of departure, arrival in Antrim, arrival at destination, distance from Antrim in English miles, fare, days of travelling].

Mail coach from Derry to Belfast: departure 6 p.m., arrival in Antrim 4.45 a.m., arrival 7 a.m.; 17 and three-quarter miles; fare 4s inside, 2s 6d outside; daily.

Same coach from Belfast to Derry; departure 7 a.m., arrival in Antrim 10 a.m., arrival 8 p.m.; 69 miles; fare 21s inside, 17s 6d outside; daily.

Champion stage-coach from Coleraine to Belfast; departure 8 a.m., arrival in Antrim 2.30 p.m., arrival 4.30 p.m.; 17 and three-quarter miles; fare 3s 6d inside, 2s 6d outside; Sunday, Tuesday and Thursday.

Same coach from Belfast to Coleraine; departure 12 noon, arrival in Antrim 2 p.m., arrival 8.30 p.m.; 52 miles; Monday, Wednesday and Friday.

Lark stage-coach from Cookstown to Belfast; departure 5 a.m., arrival in Antrim 8.45 a.m., arrival 11 a.m.; 17 and three-quarter miles; fare 2s 6d inside, 1s 6d outside; daily, Sunday excepted.

Same coach from Belfast to Cookstown; departure 3 p.m., arrival in Antrim 5 p.m., arrival 9.15 p.m.; 38 and a half miles; fare 6s inside, 4s outside; daily, Sunday excepted.

Commerce stage-coach from Ballymena to Belfast; departure 4 a.m., arrival in Antrim 6 a.m., arrival 8 a.m.; 17 and three-quarter miles; fare 2s 6d inside, 1s 6d outside; daily, Sunday excepted.

Same coach from Belfast to Ballymena; departure 4 p.m., arrival in Antrim 6 p.m., arrival 8 p.m.; 13 miles; fare 2s inside, 1s outside; daily, Sunday excepted.

4-wheeled caravan from Magherafelt to Belfast; departure 6 a.m., arrival in Antrim 8.30 a.m., arrival 11 a.m.; 17 and three-quarter miles; fare 1s 6d; daily, Sunday excepted.

Same conveyance from Belfast to Magherafelt; departure 3 p.m., arrival in Antrim 5 p.m., arrival 8 p.m.; 18 miles; fare 2s 6d; daily, Sunday excepted.

4-wheeled caravan from Antrim to Belfast; departure 8 a.m., arrival 10 a.m.; 17 and three-quarter miles; fare 1s 6d; daily, Sunday excepted.

Same conveyance from Belfast to Antrim; departure 4 p.m., arrival 6.15 p.m.; 17 and three-quarter miles; fare 1s 6d; daily, Sunday excepted.

3 jaunting cars from Antrim to Belfast; departure 8 a.m., arrival 10 a.m.; 17 and three-quarter miles; fare 1s 3d; Friday.

Same cars from Belfast to Antrim; departure 4 p.m., arrival 6.30 p.m.; 17 and three-quarter miles; fare 1s 3d; Friday.

4-wheeled caravan from Antrim to Ballymena; departure 8 a.m., arrival 10 a.m.; 13 miles; fare 1s; Saturday.

Same conveyance from Ballymena to Antrim; departure 4 p.m., arrival 6 p.m.; 13 miles; fare 1s; Saturday.

Antrim Dispensary

Table of cases for the years 1827 and 1829.

1827: asthma 11, abcess 39, bilious affections 63, bruises and sprains 44, burns 14, bowel complaints 54, consumption 13, cutaneous diseases 59, croup 2, cholera and colic 54, diarrhoea and dysentery 14, diseases of the urinary organs 12, dropsy 16, dislocations 4, dyspepsia 43, epilepsy 7, fevers 86, fractures 9, febrile and pulmonary affections 83, hernia 4, hysteria 4, hip diseases [blank], hydrocele 2, inflammation of the bowels 6, inflammation of the chest 17, inflammatory sore throat 17, incontinence of urine 29, jaundice 13, local inflammations 35, opthalmia 39, palsy 2, piles 25, rheumatism 67, scrofula and scorbutic eruptions 25, sprains and contusions 44, ulcers (68) and worms (42) 110, [total] 1,086.

1829: asthma 29, abcess 17, bilous affections 59, bruises and sprains 68, burns 8, consumption 10, cholera and colic 59, coughs 67, diarrhoea and dysentery 52, diseases of the urinary organs 7, dropsy 9, dislocations 3, epilepsy 4, fevers 89, fistulae 2, fractures 10, febrile and pulmonary affections 35, hernia 5, hysteria 29, hydrocele 4, inflammation of the bowels 6, inflammation of the chest 21, inflammatory sore throat 6, incontinence of urine 3, indigestion 111, itch 41, jaundice 5, local inflammations 37, mortification 2, necrosis 3, opthalmia 33, piles 9, paronychia 5, paralysis 5, ruptures 3, retention of urine 3, rheumatism 57, scrofula and scorbutic eruptions 38, ulcers (29) and worms (97) 126, [total] 1,092.

Rules of the Antrim Loan Society

That this institution be conducted agreeably to the 4th George IV chapter 32.

That the funds be lent in sums not exceeding 5 pounds nor less than 1 pound, to honest, sober and industrious inhabitants on 2 securities, on the borrower signing an unstamped promissory note to be repaid weekly at the rate of 1s for each pound until the entire be discharged, with interest at the rate of 4d for each pound to be paid in the first 4 weeks.

That a fine of 2d per pound be levied for the first neglect of payment of the weekly instalment, 5d per pound for the second, and any borrower in arrears for 3 sucessive weeks shall be disqualified to receive a new loan and the debt shall be sued for.

That no person shall receive out of the fund more than 9 pounds in 1 year.

That any attempt to impose on the society shall forever disentitle each person concerned from relief.

That all applications for loans must remain for a week for consideration, and a private certificate of the sobriety, honesty and industry of the applicant must be previously signed by some member of the society and by the persons becoming sureties.

That no person engaged in the sale of spirituous liquors shall receive a loan.

That no member, treasurer or other officer shall receive any benefit from the society by loan or otherwise, and any clerk or other persons who may be employed shall alone receive any salaries or wages, etc.

The other rules relate to the appointment of officers, etc.

Antrim Petty Sessions

[Table showing number of cases] 1836: number of summonses issued 195, assault 41, rescue 3, larceny 4, trespass 14, disputes as to wages 25, breaches of game laws 4, breaches of excise laws 1, drunkenness 8, miscellaneous cases 117; number of cases tried 217, number of convictions [blank], number of warrants issued nil, cases sent to assizes nil, cases sent to quarter sessions 2.

1837: number of summonses issued 322, assualt 61, rescue 8, larceny 6, trespass 6, disputes as to wages 34, breaches of game laws 3, breaches of excise laws 3, drunkenness 4, miscellaneous cases 110; number of cases tried 235, number of warrants issued 5, cases sent to assizes 4, cases sent to quarter sessions 3. 7th May 1838.

Pawnbrokers

The number of tickets issued by one pawnbroker in the town of Antrim are as follows. [Insert footnote: This pawnbroker's name is John Birnie. There is another whose shop is and has for some time been closed but will shortly reopen].

In the year 1834, 10,056; 1835, 10,502; 1836, 15,198; 1837, 11,702. The number of tickets for sums not exceeding 1s in each year averaged 2,374; for sums not exceeding 2s 6d and over 1s, one-quarter of the entire; for sums not exceeding 5s and over 2s 6d, one-quarter of the entire; for sums not exceeding 1 pound and over 5s, one-quarter of the entire; for sums above 1 pound, 6 tickets.

Trades and Occupations: Milltown

Table of trades and occupations in the Milltown: cottiers and labourers 9, cottiers and fishermen 4, farmer and publican 1, farmer and nurseryman 1, farmers 5, carpenters 2, blacksmith 1, grocer (on a very humble scale) 1, painter 1, plasterer 1, widows 7, total 33.

SOCIAL ECONOMY

Benevolence: Education

[Table contains the following headings: name, situation and description, when established, income and expenditure, physical, intellectual and moral education, number of pupils subdivided by age, sex and religion, name and religion of master and mistress].

In a suitable 2-storey house containing a separate room each for the males and scholars, and also apartments for the male and female teacher; built at the expense of Lord Massereene and situated in Bow Lane, town of Antrim, established 1815; income: the male teacher receives as parish schoolmaster 2 pounds annually from the vicar, the sum of 60 pounds (Irish) is allotted from the legacies of Erasmus Smith, total 57 pounds 7s 6d, 4 pounds from pupils; expenditure: the male and female teachers have each apartments and a cow's grass; the former has 29 pounds 13s 9d, the latter 27 pounds 13s 9d per annum, total 55 pounds 7s 6d; other expenses: replacing and repairs of seats and forms etc. 4 pounds; intellectual education: spelling, reading and writing, arithmetic, geography, book-keeping, books of the Kildare Place Society; the females learn sewing; moral education: visited occasionally by the vicar, Authorised Version of the Scriptures daily, church catechism on Saturdays; number of pupils: males, under 10 years of age 28, from 10 to 15 years of age 23, total males 51; females, under 10 years of age 31, from 10 to 15 years of age 16, total females 47; total number of pupils 98, Protestants 28, Presbyterians 51, Roman Catholics 19; master Richard Leighton, Protestant, mistress Esther Kempston, Protestant.

For the education of infant children, held in the Methodist chapel, town of Antrim, established 1830; income: supported by a voluntary annual subscription amounting to 18 pounds; expenditure: teacher's salary amounts to 15 pounds, books and stationery 3 pounds; intellectual education: the course of instruction is that usually pursued in infant schools; moral education: Authorised Version of the Scriptures and church catechisms daily; number of pupils: males, under 10 years of age 13, total males 13; females, under 10 years of age 41, total females 41; total number of pupils 54, Protestants 48, Roman Catholics 6; mistress Jane Leighton, Protestant.

Sunday school, held in the Orthodox Presbyterian meeting house, town of Antrim; intellectual education: spelling and reading books of the Sunday School Society; number of pupils: males, under 10 years of age 29, from 10 to 15 years of age 23, above 15 years of age 7, total males 59; females, under 10 years of age 18, from 10 to 15 years of age 18, above 15 years of age 5, total females 41; total number of pupils 100, Protestants 7, Presbyterians 81, Roman Catholics 11; gratuitous teachers.

Sunday school, held in the Wesleyan Methodist meeting house, town of Antrim; intellectual education: spelling and reading books of the Sunday School Society; moral education: Authorised Version of the Scriptures; number of pupils: males, under 10 years of age 31, 10 to 15 years of age 18, above 15 years of age 9, total males 58; females, under 10 years of age 37, 10 to 15 years of age 32, total females 69; total number of pupils 127, Protestants 105, Presbyterians 13, Roman Catholics 9; gratuitous teachers.

Sunday school, held in the Roman Catholic chapel, town of Antrim, established 1832; intellectual education: spelling and reading books of the Sunday School Society; moral education: Authorised and Douai Version of the Scriptures, and Roman Catholic catechism; number of pupils: males, under 10 years of age 51, 10 to 15 years of age 54, total males 105; females, under 10 years of age 39, 10 to 15 years of age 29, total females 68; total number of pupils 174, Roman Catholics 174; taught by gratuitous teachers.

In a suitable house built by the Kildare Society in the townland of Crevery <Creavery>, established 1828; income from pupils 13 pounds; intellectual education: spelling, reading, writing, arithmetic, books of the London Hibernian Society; moral education: visits from the Presbyterian clergyman, Authorised Version of the Scriptures; number of pupils: males, under 10 years of age 15, 10 to 15 years of age 14, total males 29; females, under 10 years of age 8, 10 to 15 years of age 5, total females 13; total number of pupils 42, Protestants 3, Presbyterians 36, Roman Catholics 3; master David Chisholm, Presbyterian.

In a suitable house built by the Kildare Society in the townland of Potters Walls, established 1825; income from pupils 18 pounds; intellectual education: spelling, reading, writing, arithmetic, books of the London Hibernian Society; moral education: visits from the Presbyterian clergyman, Authorised Version of the Scriptures; number of pupils: males, under 10 years of age 8, 10 to 15 years of age 10, total males 18; females, under 10 years of age 6, 10 to 15 years of age 7, total females 13; total number of pupils 31, Protestants 2, Presbyterians 26, Roman Catholics 3; master John Donaghy, Roman Catholic.

In a house built by the Kildare Society in the townland of Bush, established 1823; income from pupils 15 pounds; intellectual education: spelling, reading, writing, arithmetic, books of the London Hibernian Society; moral education: visits from the clergy, Authorised Version of the Scriptures daily; number of pupils: males, under

10 years of age 9, 10 to 15 years of age 15, total males 24; females, under 10 years of age 2, 10 to 15 years of age 4, total females 6; total number of pupils 30, all Presbyterians; master Robert Heslip, Presbyterian.

[Totals]: income from public societies 75 pounds 7s 6d, from pupils 47 pounds; expenditure: salaries 70 pounds 7s 6d, other expenses 7 pounds; number of pupils: males, under 10 years of age 184, 10 to 15 years of age 157, above 15 years of age 16, total males 358; females, under 10 years of age 182, 10 to 15 years of age 111, above 15 years of age 5, total females 298; total number of pupils 656, Protestants 193, Presbyterians 237, Roman Catholics 225.

Private Schools

A day school for boys in which a classical and mercantile education is afforded; kept in the house of the teacher in the town of Antrim, established 1812; income from pupils 120 pounds; intellectual education: boys are instructed in the sufficient works necessary for a classical, mercantile or English education; moral education: none; number of pupils: males, under 10 years of age 6, from 10 to 15 years of age 21, above 15 years of age 3; total number of pupils 30, all male, Protestants 4, Presbyterians 26; master the Revd James Carley, Presbyterian.

In a house the property of the teacher in the town of Antrim, established 1834; income from pupils 20 pounds; intellectual education: the classics, English and mercantile education; moral education: Authorised Version of the Scriptures and Church of England and Scotland catechism on Saturdays; number of pupils: males, under 10 years of age 9, from 10 to 15 years of age 7, total males 16; females, total 4; total number of pupils 20, Protestants 3, Presbyterians 17; master Nathaniel White, Presbyterian.

In a house the property of the teacher in the town of Antrim, established 1815; income from pupils 50 pounds; intellectual education: mathematics, spelling, reading, writing, arithmetic, English grammar; moral education: Authorised Version of the Scriptures; number of pupils: males, under 10 years of age 33, from 10 to 15 years of age 17, above 15 years of age 4, total males 54; females, under 10 years of age 15, from 10 to 15 years of age 11, total females 26; total number of pupils 80, Protestants 14, Presbyterians 32, Roman Catholics 34; master John McGill, Roman Catholic.

Ladies' boarding and day school, in a house the property of the teacher in the town of Antrim,

established 1834; income from pupils 60 pounds; intellectual education: needlework, music, French, history, geography, spelling, writing, arithmetic, grammar; moral education: Authorised Version of the Scriptures and church catechisms; number of pupils: females, under 10 years of age 6, from 10 to 15 years of age 16, above 15 years of age 3; total number of pupils 25, all female, Protestants 3, Presbyterians 22; mistress Miss McClune, Presbyterian.

Ladies' day school, held in the teacher's house in the town of Antrim, established 1810; income from pupils 30 pounds; intellectual education: needlework, spelling, reading, writing, arithmetic, geography, history; moral education: Protestant and Presbyterian catechism on Mondays, Authorised Version of the Scriptures daily; number of pupils: females, under 10 years of age 3, from 10 to 15 years of age 5; total number of pupils 8, all female, Protestants 2, Presbyterians 6; mistress Miss Bryson, Presbyterian.

Day school, held in the teacher's house in the town of Antrim, established 1833; income from pupils 15 pounds; intellectual education: needlework, spelling, reading, writing, arithmetic, grammar; moral education: Authorised Version of the Scriptures and Protestant catechism; number of pupils: females, under 10 years of age 7, from 10 to 15 years of age 3; total number of pupils 10, all female, Protestants 5, Presbyterians 5; mistress Miss Lorinan, Protestant.

[Totals]: income from pupils 295 pounds; number of pupils: males, under 10 years of age 48, from 10 to 15 years of age 45, above 15 years of age 7, total males 100; females, under 10 years of age 31, from 10 to 15 years of age 35, above 15 years of age 3, total females 73; total number of pupils 173, Protestants 31, Presbyterians 108, Roman Catholics 34.

Benevolence: Establishments for the Indigent

[Table contains the following headings: name, object, management, number relieved, funds from public bodies and private individuals, annual expense of management, relief afforded, when founded].

9 schools supported wholly or partly by benevolent individuals or societies; object: the removal of ignorance; management: by sundry societies, local committees or patrons; number relieved: 656 children receiving instruction; funds: from the Board of National Education annually [blank], Erasmus Smith's legacy 57 pounds 7s 6d, local subscriptions amount to 18 pounds, from the vicar 2 pounds, total annual amount 77 pounds 7s 6d; expenditure: re-

pairing and replacing of furniture 4 pounds; the teachers receive the sums (except 4 pounds) paid by the scholars, also 70 pounds 7s 6d; instruction: the different education societies contribute grants of books and school requisites, 3 pounds; when founded: at different times.

Mendicity Society, object: the suppression of street begging and affording a support to the aged, helpless and infirm; management: by a committee, treasurer and secretary; number relieved: the average number relieved weekly for the last 9 years has been 121; funds: the amount of fines annually received from magistrates would average 8 pounds; the sums annually subscribed for the last 9 years would average 278 pounds; relief afforded: sometimes a little meal has been distributed; sums varying from 4d to 1s 6d are given weekly to each poor person; when founded: 1825.

Savings Bank, object: to enable the working class to amass the fruits of their industry; management: a committee, directors, secretary and treasurer; number relieved: 176 depositors on an annual average; funds: 3 per cent paid by government on the sum in bank; relief afforded: interest of 3 per cent paid on the sum deposited; when founded: 1830.

Loan Fund, object: to assist the working class by loans at moderate interest, and to suppress the vicious system of pawnbroking; management: a committee, treasurer and secretary; number relieved: fluctuating; funds: the sum of 288 pounds was advanced to be paid by instalments; relief afforded: sums not less than 1 pound nor exceeding 5 pounds are lent, to be repaid in weekly instalments; when founded: 1835.

[Totals] funds: from public bodies 8 pounds, from private individuals 355 pounds 7s 6d; annual expense of management: house rent 4 pounds, salaries 70 pounds 7s 6d; relief afforded: 3 pounds.

Establishments for Mental and Bodily Diseases

Dispensary: managed by a committee, secretary and treasurer; the average number of patients annually relieved is 1,200; funds: the annual grant from the county grand jury would average 38 pounds, the average annual amount of subscriptions is 41 pounds; annual expense of management: surgeon's salary 50 pounds; total annual average expense of patients 71 pounds; when founded: 1817.

MODERN AND ANCIENT TOPOGRAPHY

Drawings

Massereene bridge, Antrim, with riverside buildings.

Antrim church with tower and steeple, south east view.

New meeting house, Antrim, in connection with the Synod of Ulster, front elevation.

Roman Catholic chapel, Antrim, from a vista in the Wilderness.

Antrim round tower, with dimensions; vertical section from north to south, 4 cross sections with dimensions of windows and doorway, scale 1 inch to 12 feet. [Insert note by Boyle: The horizontal sections are taken where windows occur, which are not shown in the vertical sections].

Antrim round tower, north east view, south view, west view, with figures at base for scale.

Antrim round tower, apex of the tower revived, bird's eye view of the spear, dimensions 1 foot 10 inches by 12 and a half inches, base and mortice, dimensions 1 foot 6 inches.

Antrim round tower: detail drawings of east window, upper west window, upper south window, north window, specimen of the masonry in the windows, doorway, the doorway from the inside, north east window, middle south window, lower south window, lower west window, scale of half an inch to 1 foot. [Insert note: The stones are all drawn to scale].

Cross inscribed on a stone over the doorway of Antrim round tower, scale of 4 inches to 1 inch.

Antrim church: detail drawings of small window, dimensions 5 feet by 18 inches; east window, dimensions 9 feet 6 inches by 5 feet 10 inches.

Fort in townland of Rathenraw, with 2 sections, scale of 1 inch to 80 feet.

Fort in townland of Dunsilly, with 2 sections, scale of 1 inch to 80 feet.

Forts in townland of Dunsilly (7), plans and sections of 2 forts.

Forts in townland of Ballycraigy (4), plans and sections of 3 forts.

Forts in townland of Lady Hill (6), plans and sections of 3 forts.

Scale for the plan and horizontal section 1 inch to 80 feet, scale for the vertical section 1 inch to 40 feet. [Insert note: NB The number prefixed to each fort denotes the number of that description in that townland. The forts wanting here will be found in suceeding pages].

Forts in townland of Crevery (3), with plans and sections.

Forts in Town Parks of Antrim (2) and townland of Crosskennan (1), with plans and sections.

Forts in townlands of Maghereagh (2) and Carngranney (1), with plans and sections.

2 forts in townland of Shane's Castle, with plans and sections.

Forts in townlands of Kilbegs (1) and Bleerick (1), with plans and sections.

Tumuli in Town Parks of Antrim and townland of Crosskennan, with sections, scale of 1 inch to 80 feet.

Plan of cove in townland of Lady Hill, with 2 sections and transverse section, showing construction, dimensions 7 feet by 8 feet at bottom and 2 feet at top, scale 33 feet to 1 inch.

The Witches Stone, townland of Steeple, main dimensions 6 feet by 4 feet 7 inches, showing large hollow 9 inches deep, diameter 15 by 12 inches, lesser hollow 3 inches deep, diameter 6 inches.

2 Danish pipes, 3 flint arrowheads, town of Antrim.

10 coins, both faces.

Antique chair in Antrim Castle.

Draft Memoir by J. Fleming Tait, April 1835

MODERN TOPOGRAPHY

Town of Antrim

Refer to Mr Boyle [initialled] R.K. Dawson, September 1835.

Is situated on the north eastern border of Lough Neagh, at the mouth of the Six Mile Water. The situation of the town is low, being only 20 feet above the level of the lough and about 68 above the level of the sea. It is 16 miles distant from the town of Belfast and 120 from Dublin. Its latitude is 54 degrees 40 minutes, longtitude 5 degrees 30 minutes west.

It is in the diocese of Down and Connor, province of Ulster, county of Antrim, barony of Upper Antrim, parish of Antrim and the north east circuit of assize.

Its length from the commencement of Bow Lane to the end of the High Street is three-quarters of an English mile. Bow Lane and the High Street, with a few cottages on the opposite bank of the river which are called Massereene, form the town. It is situated very prettily with regard to the scenery of the surrounding country.

General History

It appears that there was a small village here at the time of the general colonization of the north. The church bears the date of 1596. There is no very remarkable house. The oldest one is said to be that one in the High Street, opposite to Massereene bridge. It is now covered with plaster, but it is

principally built of wood said to be wrought at, and brought from, Toome. There is nothing curious in the appearance of the house, unless that it looks rather more dirty and misshapen than its neighbours.

Public Buildings

The town contains 1 church, 1 Roman Catholic chapel, 2 Presbyterian meeting houses, and a handsome Presbyterian meeting house is at present building. It contains also a Methodist meeting house and a Wesleyan meeting house, a sessions and a market house. 2 very good inns and a bridge called Massereene bridge, also a dispensary, a mendicity association and 9 schools. The above buildings are all of stone, as is also the whole town.

The principal private residences in the town are those of Messrs McAuley, Williamson, Fowke, Campbell, Laidley and Carley, and Massereene House, which is situated at the western end of the High Street. There is a savings bank in the town, which is kept by Mr Gwyn.

Roads

The High Street composes the principal part of the town. Its average breadth is 85 feet and it is half a mile long. The are some good substantial houses in it, chiefly, however, at the west end, which is also generally slated. Bow Lane bears a great resemblance in its appearance to Barrack Street in Dublin. [Crossed out: It has also the sweet savour of that noted spot and would doubtless be peculiarly grateful to the nasal organs of those who have been accustomed to the latter place]. Its average breadth is 50 feet and its length is about a quarter of a mile.

Massereene

Massereene is a collection of about 60 cottages situated in an irregular street on the southern bank of the river (Antrim being on the northern side). The inhabitants are of the poorer class and there is no public building there.

General Appearance

The town of Antrim is paved with the common round stones (and edged with freestone in the High Street). The centre of the road is macadamized <McAdamized>. It is not lighted nor watched, but there is a party of policemen and a sergeant stationed here. The town contains 463 houses, of which number 29 are houses of 3-storeys in height, 224 are 1-storey in height and the remaining 215 are cabins and cottages on the ground floor. There are about 224 houses roofed with slate and 244 thatched.

Church

The church was built in the year 1596. The clergyman is Mr Green and who declined giving the account of his salary as vicar. It is said to be about 275 pounds per annum. The congregation consists of about 1,000 persons and the average attendance is 300. The building is 60 feet in length and 33 in breadth.

Presbyterian Meeting Houses

Presbyterian meeting house of Mill Row, of which Mr Magill is pastor, is in such a bad state of repair that it has been judged expedient to build a new one. The date and cost of the old building is not known, and of the new Presbyterian meeting house the foundation was laid in 1834 [insert marginal note: 9th June]. The length of it is 93 feet, the breadth is 56 feet. It is unfinished at present, but promises to be a handsome building. The estimated expense of it is 2,000 pounds.

[Insert note: The clergyman is the Revd R. Magill. The salary is nearly 100 pounds (Irish) and the regium donum 75 pounds per annum. The congregation consists of 3,500 persons and the average attendance is nearly 1,000, the number of seatholders being heads of families, 320. He was ordained in June 1820, since which period he has united in matrimony 321 couples and baptised 1,402 children, viz. 710 males and 692 females. The deaths in the congregation during that period amounted to 600, 55 of whom died of cholera.

The old Arian Presbyterian meeting house was built about the year 1699. The repairs within the last 20 years have cost upwards of 250 pounds. It is a plain whitewashed building and its dimensions are: [ground plan, main dimensions 60 feet by 53 feet, "T" shape]; the pastor is Mr Carley. The seatholders are 200 in number. The total is 1,241 people and the average attendance varies from 150 to 400 people. Mr Carley receives 80 pounds per annum from his congregation and the regium donum amounting [to] 50 pounds.

Roman Catholic Chapel

The Roman Catholic chapel was built in the year 1818; it cost 1,400 pounds and its dimensions are: [ground plan, main dimensions 60 feet by 69 feet, cruciform]. It is rather sweet in its appearance and it is adorned with a figure of the Virgin Mary and the Infant Jesus in the front. The parish priest is the Revd D. Curoe. He receives 200 pounds per annum from his parishioners here, and resides at Randalstown. The total congregation is 1,000 persons and the average attendance 600. The number of seatholders is 60.

Wesleyan Meeting House

The Wesleyan meeting house was built in the year 1823 and cost 200 pounds. It is 42 feet long and 20 broad, and of a neat appearance. Different clergymen serve in it (they reside in Belfast). The congregation on the average is 150. The total congregation is 300. The clergymen of this and the following establishment are paid by their congregations.

Methodist Meeting House

The Methodist meeting house was built in the year 1806; it cost about 200 pounds and is a small square building, being 42 feet in length and 27 feet in breadth. The average congregation is 50. The actual congregation is uncertain. The clergyman Mr Waugh receives from the congregation 16 pounds for himself, 16 pounds for his wife and 4 pounds for each child under 10 years of age, per annum.

SOCIAL ECONOMY

Table of Schools

[Table contains the following headings: type of school, number of pupils subdivided by religion and sex, master or mistress, when established, how supported].

Lancasterian: Episcopalians 34, Presbyterians 27, Roman Catholics 34, males 95, total 95; master R. Leighton; established 1815, supported by the legacy of Erasmus Smith, 30 pounds per annum cash.

Lancasterian: Episcopalians 30, Presbyterians 33, Roman Catholics 33, females 96, total 96; mistress Miss Kempton; established 1815, supported by the legacy of Erasmus Smith, 30 pounds per annum cash.

National school: [crossed out: Episcopalians 14, Presbyterians 32, Roman Catholics 34, males 54, females 26, total 80; master Mr McGill; established 1815, supported by payments from 2d to 4d a week from each].

Day school: Episcopalians 4, Presbyterians 26, males 30, total 30; master Mr Carley; established 1812, supported by scholars, 20s per quarter.

Day school: Episcopalians 3, Presbyterians 17,

males 16, females 4, total 20; master Mr White (classics); established 1834, supported by scholars, 5s per quarter.

Day school: Episcopalians 1, Presbyterians 16, Roman Catholics 1 (1 quarter), males 12, females 6, total 18; master [crossed out: S. Dixon]; established 1834, supported by scholars, 5s to 7s 6d per quarter.

Infants under 7: Episcopalians 19, Presbyterians allow 20, Roman Catholics 19, males 46, females 12, total 58; mistress Miss Leighton; established 1830, supported by 15 pounds per annum.

Females' school: Episcopalians 5, Presbyterians 5, females 10, total 10; mistress Miss McLorimer; established 1833, supported by scholars, 5s to 10s per quarter.

Females' school: Episcopalians 2, Presbyterians 6, females 8, total 8; mistress Miss Bryson; established 1810, supported by scholars, 20s per quarter.

Females' school: Episcopalians 1, Presbyterians 13, Roman Catholics 1, females 15, total 15; mistress Miss Dickey; established 1827, supported by scholars, 7s 6d to 10s per quarter.

Day school: Episcopalians 20, Presbyterians 12, Roman Catholics 18, males 30, females 20, total 50; master J. Sufferan; established 1831, supported by scholars, 2s per quarter.

Total: schools 10, Episcopalians 133, Presbyterians 207, Roman Catholics 140, males 283, females 197, total 480.

Population

In Antrim town (excluding the part called Massereene which is in the grange of Muckamore) there are 2,772 inhabitants, viz. 711 Roman Catholics, 607 Episcopalians, 1,323 Presbyterians and 131 other Dissenters. The population of Massereene added to this would make about 3,000.

Dispensary

Is supported by subscription from the neighbouring gentry and by an allowance of 50 pounds [crossed out: from government per annum] [insert correction: from the grand jury and subscriptions from neighbouring gentry. The dispensary was built in 1817, at an expense of 200 pounds, for its present use. It was paid by the grand jury and the wealthy inhabitants of the town].

The dispensary doctor is Mr E. Bryson. It has had a beneficial effect on the health and comfort of the poor.

Cases at Dispensary

[Table gives disease, followed by month and number of cases].

Fever: in May 11, June 2, July 8, August 7, September 8, October 6, November 12, December 10, January 10, February 8, March 12, April 20.

Inflammation of chest: in May 2, June 2, July 5, August 4, September 3, October 1, November 4, December 1, January 1, April 3.

Inflammation of bowels: in June 2, July 1, August 2, September 2, October 3, December 1, March 1, April 1.

Diarrhoea and dystentry: in May 10, June 11, July 13, August 8, September 6, October 10, November 9, December 13, January 34, February 81, March 53, April 23.

Colic: in June 4, July 3, August 6, September 5, October 6, November 6, December 3, January 4, February 2, March 1.

Indigestion: in May 3, June 3, July 7, August 7, September 10, October 7, November 9, December 11, January 5, February 4, March 5, April 4.

Bilious diseases: in May 2, June 5, July 6, August 6, September 3, October 4, November 4, December 1, January 4, February 2, March 1.

Jaundice: in May 2, June 3, July 1, October 3, November 1, December 2.

Dropsy: in May 2, August 4, September 2, October 1, November 2, December 2, January 1, March 1.

Palsy: in May 2, June 2, December 4.

Epilepsy: in June 1, September 1, January 2.

Hysteria: in May 1, June 1, July 5, August 6, September 2, October 4, November 5, December 2, January 5, February 2, March 5, April 3.

Asthma: in May 2, June 2, July 3, August 4, September 1, October 1, November 1, December 3, January 2, February 2, April 2.

Consumption: in May 3, June 3, July 4, August 4, September 3, October 1, November 1, December 2, January 6, February 2, April 1.

Worms: in May 2, June 7, July 3, August 10, September 5, October 5, November 8, December 5, January 6, February 2, March 4, April 1.

Uterine diseases: in May 1, June 3, July 4, August 5, October 6, November 1, December 9, January 7, February 6, March 6.

Local inflammation: in May 2, June 3, July 3, August 4, September 1, October 1, November 5, December 1, January 2, March 1, April 2.

Opthalmia: in May 4, June 4, July 5, August 3, September 5, October 3, November 3, December 6, January 2, February 2, March 1, April 3.

Rheumatism: in May 2, June 4, July 10, August 4, September 9, October 4, November 4, December 6, January 5, February 1, March 5, April 2.

Scrofula: in May 6, June 1, July 2, August 4,

September 5, October 3, November 1, December 3, January 1, February 9, March 4, April 3.

Inflammatory sore throat: in May 2, June 1, July 4, August 1, September 5, October 3, January 2, February 1, March 2, April 1.

Ulcered sore throat and mouth: in May 1, June 1, July 2, September 2, October 2, November 2, December 1, January 1, February 2, April 3.

Cutaneous diseases: in May 2, June 3, July 4, August 9, September 8, October 2, November 2, December 1, January 4, March 3, April 3.

Piles: in May 1, June 5, July 3, August 2, September 6, October 2, November 1, December 2, January 4, February 3, March 1, April 1.

Ulcers: in May 8, June 9, July 9, August 6, September 7, October 8, November 5, December 6, January 5, March 7, April 1.

Carbuncle: in May 1, October 1, January 1.

Abcess: in May 5, June 2, July 7, August 5, September 4, October 4, November 7, December 3, January 3, February 1, March 5, April 2.

Hydiscule [? hydrocele]: in August 1, October 1.

Hirncia [?hernia]: in May 1, December 1, February 1.

Wounds: in June 5, July 4, August 3, September 2, October 3, November 2, December 3, January 3, February 2, March 2, April 2.

Fractures: in June 1, July 1, August 1, September 4, October 1, November 1, January 2.

Dislocations: in June 1, September 2, October 1, November 1, January 1.

Burns: in May 3, July 5, October 4, November 3, December 2, January 1, March 1, April 3.

Contusions and sprains: in May 7, June 4, July 4, August 7, September 2, October 6, November 3, December 4, January 1, February 2, March 5, April 4.

Catarrhal and pulmonary affections: in May 7, June 8, July 3, August 8, September 11, October 4, November 5, December 4, January 5, February 6, March 3, April 4.

PRODUCTIVE AND SOCIAL ECONOMY

Trades and Occupations

Publicans 23, grocers 28, butchers 2, bakers 5, carpenters 12, chandlers 10, coopers 2, china shops 2, cloth merchants and linen 3, bonnetmakers and milliners 9, cartmakers 3, coachmakers 1, doctors 3, glaziers 2, paper mill 1, hairdressers 2, hardware shops 2, inns 2, nailers 4, pawnbroker 1, smiths 4, shoemakers 6, watchmakers 1, saddlers 2, turner 1, tailors 3, wheelwrights 2, policemen 9, brewery 1, corn mill 1, total 147.

Local Government

The most ancient family is the Clotworthy, represented by Lord Viscount Massereene.

A manor court is held every 3 weeks in the town by Mr Williamson, the seneschal of the Marquis of Donegall. Sessions are held in the market house in April and October, and from 4 to 7 magistrates attend. The magistrates of Antrim are Mr Thompson of Muckamore Abbey, Mr Clark of the Steeple and Mr Whittle.

General Remarks

The occupations of the men are agriculture in spring and autumn and generally weaving in winter. Antrim is said to be a very dissipated place, but I have not seen any signs of this in the men. It is in contemplation to establish a library.

Savings Bank

There is a savings bank here, under the management of Mr Gwyn. There were about 230 depositors in the year 1834 and the total amount deposited was 2,389 pounds 13s 3d. The depositors are principally farmers and servants.

Markets and Fairs

Markets are held here once a week (on every Thursday), but very poorly attended in consequence of the neighbourhood to Belfast. Flax is the principal thing disposed of. Larger markets are held on the last Thursday in the month and are rather better attended. There are no tolls levied: Lord Ferrard, who at present holds the Massereene estate, took them off in hopes of bettering the market, but without effect.

Fairs are held on the 12th May, on the 12th November and on the 1st January. Cattle is the principal commodity disposed of. The markets are never glutted with anything.

The town is well supplied with provisions, however, and with good trout from Lough Neagh in spring and summer.

Grazing

The cattle are stall fed. The ground round the town is let for about 2 pounds 15s an acre and is used for farming.

Building Materials

Timber is generally procured from Belfast; fir is principally used. Slates are procured from Belfast and Toome, large slates measuring 33 inches by

20 cost 2 pounds 9s per ton. Lime is procured from Belfast and Toome, and costs about 1s 8d a barrel. Stone for building is procured from several good quarries in the neighbourhood, at the low price of 1s a load. Turf is procured from a bog about 2 Irish miles to the north west of Antrim. It is very dear, as are also coals. To keep a single fire costs 5s a month; in consequence of this the poor suffer greatly in winter.

General Remarks

Neither houses nor lives are insured. There are no combinations of workmen. Agricultural labourers are subject to want in winter. Coopers are also liable to be unemployed during that period, as butter casks are not so much in request.

Conveyances

The mail from Belfast to Londonderry passes through here every morning at 9 o'clock and returns in the [crossed out: evening] at 4.30.

The Champion coach passes this town from Belfast to Coleraine at half past 3 o'clock on Monday, Wednesday and Friday, returns on Tuesdays, Thursdays and Sundays at 2.30 for Belfast.

The Commerce passes through for Belfast every morning at 6 o'clock and returns to Ballymena, passing Antrim at 6.30 p.m.

The Reformer passes through on the mornings of Monday, Wednesday and Friday for Londonderry at 9 a.m. and returns on Tuesdays, Thursdays and Saturdays at 4 for Belfast.

The Lark for Cookstown every weekday passes at 5 p.m.

There is a public car runs between this and Crumlin, and post chaises horses and cars may be hired at either of the inns.

Mendicity Association

Is supported by the collection which is made in the meeting houses and church, and by a small sum weekly from the Roman Catholic chapel. There are on the average 110 poor people who receive relief on every Friday. This weekly distribution amounts to nearly 5 pounds. The annual average amount is about 230 pounds.

Habits of the People

The general style of the houses is plain; they are commonly slated and have glass windows. Stone is used for building. The houses are all whitewashed and in general comfortable. The number of rooms in a house varies from 16 to 1. The usual number in a family is from 4 to 5.

The people commence work at 5 and 6 o'clock in the morning and leave at 6 or 7 in the evening, and consequently have no time for amusement. They are in general civil, but I have met with some few otherwise in the course of my enquiries among them. These latter, however, were not among what is generally termed the lowest class.

Amusements

Easter Monday and Tuesday are kept as holidays by the people. They assemble on these days at [?] greens situated outside of the town. The amusements are cock-fighting, a game called *Thread the Needle* and another game in which about 60 persons (male and female) form a ring where they challenge each other to kiss, and the person challenged is obliged to obey.

Emigration

Emigration prevails to a small extent in the spring to America; few return. A good number go annually to the harvest in England or Scotland. They leave their wives and family behind them. They rent ground and sow potatoes for winter support.

Remarkable Events

The most remarkable events that have occurred in Antrim are the burning of the town in 1641 by Lord Antrim, "Red Shanks", and the murder of the Earl O'Neill in 1798, in the rebellion of that year.

MODERN TOPOGRAPHY

Market and Sessions House

The market and sessions house was built in the year 1726 and repaired about 1821. It is an ornament to the town, although the inhabitants do not seem to think so. It is 78 feet long and 13 broad, and has a handsome projecting slate roof. It is but little use as a market house.

Mills and Brewery

Paper mill belongs to Messrs Ferguson and Fowke. The diameter of the first wheel is 16 feet and its breadth 6. The second wheel is 16 feet in diameter and 5 in breadth. They are both breast wheels. There is also a paper machine here, the wheel of which is 10 feet in diameter and the breadth 3 feet 6 inches. It is an overshot wheel.

The corn mill belongs to the Messrs Ferguson and Fowke. The wheel is breast and is 17 feet in diameter and 5 in breadth.

The brewery belongs to Mr Ferguson and has been established for upwards of 30 years. The ale is of good quality and much esteemed. Mr Ferguson declined giving the account of the quantity of ale etc. which is brewed in the year.

Massereene Castle and Bridge

Is built in the castellated style and is in length 180 feet and 90 in breadth. The building is very old, but was repaired in 1815, so that at present it has a very modern appearance. For the size of the building there might have been more taste displayed in the appearance. The paintings are nearly all family portraits and there is no piece of any note among them. The library is rather sparingly furnished for its size, being 40 feet by 20. There is a very pretty little family chapel.

There is a large mound on the northern side of the building. It is 360 feet in circumference at the base and about 40 feet high; its slope is 45 degrees.

There is an old, but strong, bridge across the river, about 200 yards below the house. It has 6 arches, is 15 feet broad and about 150 feet long. The principal entrance to the house is by a strong-looking tower, from which, on both sides, a turreted wall extends, which command the High Street and Bow Lane. It is from this place the rebels were peppered in 1798.

Massereene bridge is situated about half-way between Massereene Castle and Antrim church. It was built in the year 1708. It is 18 feet broad and 130 feet long and has 6 arches. It appears strong and good.

Social Economy

Character of the People

The general character of the people is that they are rather more civilized in their manners than we will meet with on going further north. Their hospitality I presume is gone out of fashion, as we experienced none of it during the time we were stationed here. Thus far to strangers, but they appear to be sociable among themselves. On an emergency the town would probably be able to accommodate 1,000 men. As to improvements, the new meeting house and a large dwelling house in the High Street, built by Mr Campbell, are the only signs at present. I think the town may be considered stationary in that respect.

Note: The only peculiarity of dress that I have remarked is that the women sometimes wear a dark cloth cloak, generally green, with a collar of bright red or light blue, which has a good effect. [Signed] J. Fleming Tait, April 1835.

Draft Memoir by M.M. Kertland, [before] April 1835

Natural Features

Hills

Received 25th April 1835 [signed] J. McGann. Refer to Mr Boyle, [signed] R.K. Dawson, 18th September 1835.

There are no remarkable hills in the parish. Along the eastern side of it a ridge runs from Carnmoney in a southerly direction, terminating at the Six Mile Water, or rather changing its direction and running westerly along its banks as far as the town of Antrim. The general fall is south west by west. The eastern or higher part of the parish is variegated and intersected, but gradually changes till it becomes almost perfectly level at its western termination.

Lakes and Rivers

Lakes none. [Insert marginal query by J. Boyle: Lough Neagh?].

The Six Mile Water forms part of the southern boundary, running in a north westerly direction (see Muckamore for particulars). There is no other river in the parish, but it is well supplied with water by springs and rivulets.

There are no hot or mineral springs in the parish. [Insert marginal query: Antrim spa well?].

Bogs and Woods

Bogs: there are none.

There are no natural woods in the parish, but a good deal has been planted through it, principally about Birch Hill, the Steeple and Antrim Castle. It consists chiefly of fir. About Antrim Castle there is a quantity of very fine elm, ash, beech, yew.

Climate and Crops

As far as may be judged by the experience of a month (from 22nd March to 22nd April), an idea of the climate may be given by the acompanying register.

Wheat is sown in the beginning of November, and oats and barley in April. The harvest is generally in the end of August but is much affected by the nature of the season. Potatoes are sown in the end of April or beginning of May, and are ready to be dug in October. Flax is very little sown in the parish.

MODERN TOPOGRAPHY

Towns and Public Buildings

Antrim is the only town in the parish (see Memoir of that place).

Public buildings: none beyond the town of Antrim.

Gentlemen's Seats

Birch Hill, the residence of Thomas Montgomery Esq., situated in the townland of the same name, lies about a mile to the north east of the town of Antrim. It is a large, but rather old-fashioned-looking house, commanding an extensive view of the Lough and the surrounding scenery. There is a good deal of wood about it, principally fir, but there are also a variety of other trees, ash, elm, beech.

Steeple, the residence of George Clarke Esq., is so denominated from a round tower in its vicinity commonly called the Steeple. It lies in the townland of the same name, about three-quarters of a mile to the north east of Antrim. It was built in 1819. There is nothing extraordinary in its style of architecture. It is a large and rather handsome building. There is a good deal of young fir planted about it.

Moylinny Cottage, the residence of William Chain Esq. Junior, is situated on the northern bank of the Six Mile Water, about a mile from the town of Antrim. It was built in the year 1832. There is a good deal of wood about it, principally fir.

Ballycraigy, the residence of William Chain Esq. Senior, is situated close to the main road from Belfast to Antrim and about 1 and a quarter miles from the latter. It is an old-fashioned, plain and rather large building. It is surrounded by bleach greens. There are a good many fir trees planted about it.

Bush House, the residence of James Arthur Esq., is at present being built. It is situated in the townland of Bush, in the northern part of the parish. It promises to be a large and rather handsome building. There is no wood or any ornamental ground about it.

Bleach Greens, Manufactories and Mills

On the northern bank of the Six Mile Water and in the townland of Ballycraigy there are about 39 acres employed as bleach greens. [Table contains the following headings: townland, diameter, breadth and nature of wheel, nature of mill].

Moylinny, diameter of wheel 22 feet, breadth 6 feet, breast wheel, beetling mill.

Tullycreenaght, diameter of wheel 14 feet, breadth 2 feet 9 inches, breast wheel, flax mill.

Tullycreenaght, diameter of wheel 11 feet, breadth 2 feet 9 inches, breast wheel, flax mill.

For paper mill and corn mill, see Memoir of town.

Communications

The main road from Antrim to Belfast traverses the parish for about 1 and a half miles. Its average breadth is 44 feet. It is kept in excellent order (for particulars see Ballymartin).

The road from Antrim to Parkgate passes through the parish for about 2 miles. Its average breadth is 25 feet. It is tolerably well laid out (considering the nature of the country). It was made by the county and is kept in middling repair by the barony.

The main road from Antrim to Connor and Kells runs through the parish for 2 and a half miles. Its average breadth is 26 feet. It is very well laid out and is kept in good order by the barony. It was made by the county.

The main road from Antrim to Ballymena runs through the parish for 1 and a quarter miles. Its average breadth is 30 feet. It was made by the county and is repaired by the barony and county. It is kept in very good order and very judiciously laid out [insert marginal query: judiciously?].

There is about half a mile of the road from Randalstown to Antrim in the parish. Its average breadth is 44 feet. It was made by the county and is kept in very good repair by the county and barony. It is very well laid out.

The parish is conveniently intersected with by-roads which are not unnecessarily numerous. They are kept in good order at the expense of the barony.

Bridge

On the road from Antrim to Lisburn there is a bridge over the Six Mile Water. It consists of 4 arches and is 94 feet by 22. It appears to be in very good repair. It was made by the county; the date and cost are not known.

General Appearance and Scenery

The parish is calculated to impress the beholder with an idea of fertility and a high state of cultivation. Its diversified undulations and the wood which is generally scattered through it serve to vary a landscape which would otherwise be tame and uninteresting from its changeless fertility. The town of Antrim, with its concomitant and conspicuous steeple and round tower, forms a pleasing addition to the view from almost all parts of the parish, while the whole scene borrows a foreign splendour from the extensive Lough Neagh and the opposite fertile and well wooded declivities of Muckamore.

Social Economy

Local Government

Obstructions to improvement: none.

Illicit distillation is not carried on; property is not insured (for particulars see town of Antrim).

Dispensaries: there is one in the town of Antrim (see Memoir of that town).

School

There is a school in the townland of Bush, consisting of 36 pupils; of these 30 are males and 6 females. There are no Catholics at it. It is supported solely by subscriptions from the parents, which vary from 2s 6d to 3s 6d per quarter. There is 1 at present paying 10s 6d. Writing, reading and arithmetic form the principal subjects of instruction, but Latin is taught to such as choose to pay for it. With the exception of those mentioned in the Memoir of Antrim, this is the only school in the parish. The average number in attendance is not more than two-thirds of the total, but the people seem to be aware of the advantages of education and anxious that their children should benefit by them.

Poor

There is a mendicity [society] in the town of Antrim (see Memoir).

Religion

Something more than half of the people are Presbyterians; the rest are divided between the Churches of England and Rome, the latter having the majority. The manner in which the clergy are supported will be seen by referring to the town of Antrim, where they all reside.

Habits of the People

The cottages are chiefly built of stone, have all glass windows and are in most cases thatched; a few are 2-storeys high. The number of rooms varies from 2 to 4. They generally have a neat exterior and in many cases display an internal attention to comfort.

The food of the working classes from August to April may be said to consist almost exclusively of potatoes; for the rest of the year oatmeal forms their principal support. Turf is their fuel, but owing to there being no bog in the parish it is dear, and therefore can not be much used by the lower orders, who are greatly inconvenienced for want of a substitute.

There is little attention paid to dress by the people generally, but on Sundays, market days and fair days they dress very well.

There are no extraordinary instances of longevity in the parish, but persons of 70 and 80 are not uncommon. The usual number in a family is 5 or 6. No marriages of persons under 18 are heard of.

Dancing appears to form the principal amusement of the people. No saints' days are celebrated in the parish; Easter Monday is kept as a holiday.

Emigration is not frequent.

Remarkable events: none.

Natural Features

Weather Journal in 1835

Journal of the weather at Antrim from 22nd March to 22nd April. [Table contains the following headings: date, state of the weather in the morning, noon, afternoon, direction of wind].

March, 22nd: fine, fine, fine, north easterly; 23rd: fair, fair, fair, north easterly; 24th: fair, fine, fine, north easterly; 25th: fair, fine, fine, easterly; 26th: fair, fine, fine, westerly; 27th: fair, fine, fine, easterly; 28th: fine, fine, fine, easterly; 29th: fair, fair, fair, south easterly; 30th: cloudy, showery, showery, south westerly; 31st: cloudy, cloudy, cloudy, south westerly.

April, 1st: fair, fair, fair, south westerly; 2nd: fine, fine, thunder showers, south westerly; 3rd: fair, fine, fine, easterly; 4th: rainy, rainy, fair, easterly; 5th: rainy, wet, light rain, southerly; 6th: wet, fair, fair, southerly; 7th: fair, fine, fine, south westerly; 8th: fair, fair, fair, south westerly; 9th: grey, wet, wet, westerly; 10th: fair, fine, very fine, north westerly; 11th: fine, very fine, very fine, south westerly; 12th: fair and cloudy, fair, fair, southerly; 13th: fair and cloudy, fair, fair, southerly; 14th: fair, fair, fair, south westerly; 15th: fair and light rain, fine, fine, north westerly; 16th: rain and hail, fair, fine, westerly; 17th: wet, rainy, rainy, south westerly; 18th: wet, heavy rain, rainy, north westerly; 19th: fair, fair, fair, south westerly by westerly; 20th: fair, fine, fine, south westerly; 21st: fair and cloudy, heavy rain, rainy, south westerly; 22nd: fair, fine, fine, westerly.

Meteorological Register by James Boyle

Weather Journal

Meteorological register kept at Antrim from the 4th May 1836 to the 30th August 1837 [sic]. [Table contains the following headings: date, state of the weather in the morning, noon, afternoon and night, direction of wind].

1836, May. 4th: windy, showery, dry, windy, northerly; 5th: dry cold, dry, dry, dry, northerly; 6th: mild, mild, mild, mild, northerly; 7th: mild, mild, mild, mild, northerly; 8th: mild, mild, mild, mild, south easterly; 9th: heat, mild, heat, dry, southerly; 10th: heat, heat, heat, dry, southerly; 11th: windy, windy, windy, windy, westerly; 12th: windy, dry, dry, windy, south westerly; 13th: slight showers, dry, dry, dry, south westerly; 14th: fine, fine, fine, fine, north westerly; 15th: fine, fine, fine, fine, south westerly; 16th: heat, heat, heat, dry, westerly; 17th: heat, cold, cold, dry, westerly; 18th: heat, cold, cold, dry, westerly; 19th: heat, sultry, sultry, dry, southerly; 20th: heat, heat, sultry, dry, southerly; 21st: heat, sultry, heavy rain, dry, south easterly; 22nd: heat, heavy rain, heavy rain, rainy, easterly; 23rd: heat, cold, cold, cold, north easterly; 24th: cold, cold, cold, dry, north north easterly; 25th: dry, cold, cold, dry, easterly; 26th: dry, cold, heat, dry, easterly; 27th: dry, heat, heat, dry, easterly; 28th: dry, heat, heat, frost, north easterly; 29th: dry, heat, heat, frost, north easterly; 30th: heat, windy, windy, windy, northerly; 31st: dry, heat, heat, dry, northerly.

June. 1st: fair, fair, fair, fair, south easterly; 2nd: fair, heat, heat, showery, southerly; 3rd: slight showers, heat, heat, slight showers, southerly; 4th: rainy, fair, fair, dry, south westerly; 5th: dry, fair, fair, dry, south westerly; 6th: showery, rainy, showery, showery, south westerly; 7th: dry, fair, fair, fair, southerly; 8th: dry, fair, rainy, rainy, westerly; 9th: rainy, rainy, rainy, rainy, westerly; 10th: showery, dry, dry, showery, south westerly; 11th: showery, showery, showery, rainy, south westerly; 12th: fair, fair, fair, fair, south easterly; 13th: fair, heat, fair, fair, south easterly; 14th: dry, fair, fair, dry, south easterly; 15th: dry, heat, fair, fair, south easterly; 16th: dry, dry, dry, dry, south easterly; 17th: showery, dry, heat, dry, westerly; 18th: showery, dry, dry, dry, north

westerly; 19th: dry, dry, dry, dry, north westerly; 20th: cold, cold, cold, cold, south easterly; 21st: dry, rainy, rainy, rainy, south easterly; 22nd: rainy, showery, showery, showery, south easterly; 23rd: dry, heavy showers, heavy showers, rainy, south westerly; 24th: showery, showery, dry, dry, south westerly; 25th: dry, showery, heavy showers, rainy, south westerly; 26th: fair, fair, fair, fair, south westerly; 27th: fair, showery, showery, rainy, southerly; 28th: fair, showery, fair, fair, south westerly; 29th: showery, dry, fair, fair, south westerly; 30th: showery, rainy, rainy, rainy, south westerly.

July. 1st: rainy, sultry, showery, fair, south westerly; 2nd: fair, sultry, sultry, dry, westerly; 3rd: rainy, fair, fair, fair, south westerly; 4th: fair, sultry, sultry, rainy, easterly; 5th: thunder and rain, sultry, thunder and rain, fair, easterly; 6th: fair, fair, showery, fair, north westerly; 7th: showery, showery, rainy, dry, north westerly; 8th: fair, sultry, rainy, rainy, south westerly; 9th: rainy, showery, showery, showery, westerly; 10th: rainy, fair, fair, fair, southerly; 11th: showery, rainy, rainy, rainy, westerly; 12th: showery, showery, squally, windy, south westerly; 13th: dry, cold, windy, showery, south westerly; 14th: showery, showery, dry, dry, south westerly; 15th: showery, showery, mild, mild, south westerly; 16th: dry, dry, showery, rainy, southerly; 17th: showery, windy, windy, windy, south westerly; 18th: windy, windy, windy, dry, westerly; 19th: rainy, showery, showery, dry, west north westerly; 20th: showery, showery, dry, dry, westerly; 21st: showery, showery, dry, mild, north westerly; 22nd: rainy, showery, showery, showery, north westerly; 23rd: fair, fair, fair, rainy, westerly; 24th: rainy, dry, dry, rainy, westerly; 25th: rainy, mild, mild, rainy, southerly; 26th: rainy, dry, fair, fair, westerly; 27th: fair, showery, rainy, rainy, south westerly; 28th: rainy, rainy, rainy, rainy, south westerly; 29th: rainy, rainy, rainy, rainy, north westerly; 30th: showery, showery, showery, showery, westerly; 31st: fair, fair, fair, rainy, south westerly.

August. 1st: rainy, windy, showery, showery, north westerly; 2nd: dry, fair, fair, rainy, southerly; 3rd: showery, fair, fair, dry, south westerly; 4th: dry, windy, windy, cold, easterly; 5th: fair, heat, heat, dry, south easterly; 6th: dry, sultry, sultry, dry, north westerly; 7th: dry, sultry, sultry, dry, southerly; 8th: dry, mild, mild, dry, southerly; 9th: dry, heat, sultry, dry, south westerly; 10th: dry, heat, sultry, fair, south easterly; 11th: dry, heat, sultry, fair, northerly; 12th: dry, heat, heat, fair, southerly; 13th: dry, heat, heat, fair, south westerly; 14th: dry, sultry, sultry, fair, north westerly; 15th: dry, windy, windy, dry, westerly; 16th: dry, windy, windy, rainy, westerly; 17th: dry, fair, fair, rainy, westerly; 18th: rainy, showery, showery, showery, westerly; 19th: dry, dry, fair, fair, westerly; 20th: rainy, showery, fair, fair, westerly; 21st: fair, fair, rainy, rainy, south westerly; 22nd: rainy, showery, showery, frost, south easterly; 23rd: frost, fair, fair, fair, easterly; 24th: fair, heat, heat, frost, south easterly; 25th: fair, showery, showery, frost, southerly; 26th: fair, fair, fair, rainy, south westerly; 27th: rainy, fair, fair, frost, westerly; 28th: rainy, showery, fair, fair, south westerly; 29th: fair, sultry, sultry, fair, south westerly; 30th: rainy, rainy, rainy, rainy, south westerly; 31st: rainy, rainy, rainy, rainy, westerly.

September. 1st: showery, showery, fair, frost, westerly; 2nd: fair, slight showers, fair, fair, south westerly; 3rd: rainy, rainy, rainy, rainy, south westerly; 4th: rainy, rainy, rainy, rainy, westerly; 5th: fair, fair, showery, frost, south westerly; 6th: fair, rainy, showery, rainy, north westerly; 7th: fair, fair, fair, frost, north westerly; 8th: fair, rainy, rainy, frost, north westerly; 9th: frost, rainy, rainy, frost, northerly; 10th: frost, fair, showery, frost, north westerly; 11th: fair, fair, fair, frost, westerly; 12th: fair, fair, fair, frost, westerly; 13th: fair, fair, fair, frost, westerly; 14th: fair, fair, fair, fair, south easterly; 15th: fair, fair, fair, fair, north westerly; 16th: fair, fair, fair, frost, easterly; 17th: fair, fair, fair, frost, easterly; 18th: fair, fair, fair, moist, north westerly; 19th: showery, showery, fair, fair, north westerly; 20th: fair, fair, fair, frost, westerly; 21st: fair, fair, fair, rainy, south westerly; 22nd: fair, showery, rainy, rainy, south westerly; 23rd: rainy, showery, showery, fair, southerly; 24th: fair, showery, showery, fair, south westerly; 25th: fair, showery, fair, rainy, southerly; 26th: fair, fair, fair, frost, south westerly; 27th: fair, fair, fair, fair, south westerly; 28th: fair, showery, showery, showery, westerly; 29th: fair, fair, fair, showery, westerly; 30th: showery, showery, showery, showery, north westerly.

October. 1st: rainy, rainy, rainy, rainy, easterly; 2nd: windy, windy, windy, windy, south westerly; 3rd: windy, dry, dry, frost, south westerly; 4th: fair, fair, fair, frost, north westerly; 5th: frost, showery, fair, fair, south westerly; 6th: frost, fair, fair, fair, south easterly; 7th: rainy, showery, fair, fair, south south easterly; 8th: showery, showery, fair, fair, south westerly; 9th: showery, showery, fair, frost, southerly; 10th: fair, fair, fair, frost, southerly; 11th: frost, fair, fair, fair, north easterly; 12th: fair, fair, fair, rainy, west-

erly; 13th: showery, fair, fair, frost, south westerly; 14th: frost, fair, showery, showery, south easterly; 15th: frost, fair, showery, showery, south easterly; 16th: showery, fair, fair, rainy, north easterly; 17th: fair, foggy, moist, tempestuous, north easterly; 18th: tempestuous, rainy, rainy, fair, south easterly; 19th: fair, fair, fair, frost, south westerly; 20th: frost, fair, rainy, rainy, south easterly; 21st: rainy, rainy, rainy, rainy, south easterly; 22nd: rainy, rainy, fair, fair, south south easterly; 23rd: showery, moist, frost, fair, southerly; 24th: moist, moist, fair, dry, west south westerly; 25th: fair, fair, mild, dry, westerly; 26th: fair, showery, showery, showery, south westerly; 27th: sleet and rain, fair, cold, frost, easterly; 28th: frost and snow, cold, cold, rain and sleet, north westerly; 29th: frost and snow, cold, cold, frost, northerly; 30th: frost, frost, fair, frost and snow, north north westerly; 31st: frost, fair, fair, rainy, south westerly.

November. 1st: dense fog, rainy, rainy, showery, southerly; 2nd: rainy, showery, fair, dry, south westerly; 3rd: rainy, showery, rainy, rainy, south westerly; 4th: fair, fair, showery, showery, westerly; 5th: rainy, sleet showers, dry, dry, west north westerly; 6th: rainy, showery, dry, dry, north westerly; 7th: frost, dry, dry, dry, westerly; 8th: frost, fair, fair, dry, westerly; 9th: rainy, rainy, rainy, showery, southerly; 10th: dry, dry, dry, dry, southerly; 11th: rainy, showery, moist, moist, westerly; 12th: fair, showery, rainy, rainy, south westerly; 13th: fair, dry, showery, dry, westerly; 14th: rainy, showery, showery, showery, westerly; 15th: rainy, dry, showery, dry, westerly; 16th: dry, showery, rainy, rainy, southerly; 17th: dry, showery, storm and rain, storm and rain, southerly; 18th: showery, dry, dry, dry, westerly; 19th: rainy, rainy, squally, rainy, south westerly; 20th: fair, fair, fair, dry, westerly; 21st: frost, showery, showery, dry, south westerly; 22nd: showery, dry, dry, frost, westerly; 23rd: dry, dry, dry, frost, north westerly; 24th: dry, dry, dry, showery, westerly; 25th: showery, dry, dry, dry, westerly; 26th: showery, showery, showery, dry, south westerly; 27th: rainy, rainy, storm and rain, storm and rain, southerly; 28th: dry, rainy, rainy, dry, west south westerly; 29th: dry, showery, showery, dry, south westerly; 30th: frost, dry, fair, dry, westerly.

December. 1st: frost, frost, showery, frost, south easterly; 2nd: showery, fair, showery, showery, south westerly; 3rd: showery, dry, dry, rainy, west south westerly; 4th: dry, stormy, stormy, dry, south westerly; 5th: tempestuous, stormy, stormy, stormy, south westerly; 6th: rainy, rainy,

rainy, rainy, westerly; 7th: dry, showery, showery, rainy, westerly; 8th: dry, dry, dry, dry, north westerly; 9th: frost, fair, frost, frost, easterly; 10th: frost, fair, fair, frost, south easterly; 11th: frost, fair, foggy, rainy, westerly; 12th: rainy, rainy, showery, showery, south westerly; 13th: stormy, stormy, rainy, rainy, south south westerly; 14th: rainy, rainy, squally, squally, westerly; 15th: showery, dry, showery, dry, south south easterly; 16th: frost, dry, dry, dry, south south westerly; 17th: moist, moist, showery, rainy, south westerly; 18th: moist, dry, dry, dry, southerly; 19th: moist, showery, dry, dry, south westerly; 20th: dry, dry, dry, dry, south westerly; 21st: moist, dry, dry, dry, south westerly; 22nd: fair, fair, dry, rainy, westerly; 23rd: snow and sleet, dry, frost, intense frost, northerly; 24th: intense frost, frost, frost, intense frost, northerly; 25th: frost, snow showers, snow, frost and snow, north easterly; 26th: intense frost, frost, frost, frost, north easterly; 27th: frost, frost, frost, frost, north easterly; 28th: frost, frost, frost, frost, north easterly; 29th: frost, frost, mild, mild, northerly; 30th: mild, mild, frost, snow, northerly; 31st: snow showers, mild, mild, frost, northerly.

1837, January. 1st: moist, showery, showery, showery, south westerly; 2nd: dry, fair, fair, frost, westerly; 3rd: dry, cold, cold, frost, south westerly; 4th: frost, dry, showery, rainy, southerly; 5th: frost, showery, showery, dry, south westerly; 6th: showery, dry, dry, dry, south westerly; 7th: frost, moist, moist, rainy, westerly; 8th: frost, showery, showery, showery, south westerly; 9th: showery, showery, showery, rainy, westerly; 10th: frost, cold, cold, rainy, northerly; 11th: frost, fair, fair, frost, northerly; 12th: rainy, rainy, rainy, frost, easterly; 13th: showery, dry, dry, rainy, southerly; 14th: frost, fair, fair, frost, north easterly; 15th: frost, fair, fair, mild, north easterly; 16th: showery, mild, mild, mild, northerly; 17th: mild, mild, mild, mild, northerly; 18th: moist, moist, mild, dry, south westerly; 19th: mild, mild, mild, dry, southerly; 20th: moist, dry, dry, dry, southerly; 21st: moist, moist, fair, showery, south easterly; 22nd: rainy, rainy, rainy, rainy, southerly; 23rd: moist, moist, moist, moist, south westerly; 24th: mild, mild, mild, rainy, westerly; 25th: rainy, dry, dry, dry, north westerly; 26th: dry, dry, dry, dry, north easterly; 27th: dry, dry, dry, snow showers, north easterly; 28th: snow showers, cold, sleet showers, frost, northerly; 29th: frost, snow showers, snow showers, snow showers, north easterly; 30th: moist, rainy, rainy, rainy, easterly; 31st: fair, mild, mild, mild, south easterly.

February. 1st: moist, foggy, foggy, foggy, easterly; 2nd: dry, dry, dry, dry, south easterly; 3rd: moist, showery, dry, rainy, southerly; 4th: dry, mild, mild, dry, south easterly; 5th: moist, showery, dry, moist, south easterly; 6th: showery, showery, rainy, rainy, easterly; 7th: dry, dry, dry, dry, south easterly; 8th: rainy, moist, mild, mild, east south easterly; 9th: showery, stormy, dry, stormy, south easterly; 10th: rainy, rainy, rainy, dry, south westerly; 11th: rainy, rainy, rainy, showery, south westerly; 12th: showery, dry, fair, dry, north westerly; 13th: fair, dry, fair, dry, west north westerly; 14th: fair, dry, fair, dry, west north westerly; 15th: rainy, rainy, rainy, dry, south westerly; 16th: rainy, rainy, rainy, dry, south south easterly; 17th: dry, dry, fair, dry, west south westerly; 18th: rainy, rainy, rainy, tempestuous, south westerly; 19th: tempestuous, tempestuous, stormy, dry, south easterly; 20th: snow, showery, dry, dry, south westerly; 21st: showery, showery, windy, snow storms, west south westerly; 22nd: snow showers, dry, dry, showery, west south westerly; 23rd: snow showers, snow storms, snow storms, snow, north westerly; 24th: snow showers, snow storms, snow storms, snow showers, north westerly; 25th: frost, dry, dry, mild, north westerly; 26th: frost, moist, showery, showery, north north westerly; 27th: moist, moist, showery, showery, north westerly; 28th: moist, mild, dry, dry, northerly.

March. 1st: dry, dry, dry, frost, easterly; 2nd: moist, moist, moist, dry, south easterly; 3rd: dry, fair, fair, dry, north westerly; 4th: dry, fair, fair, dry, northerly; 5th: frost, fair, fair, dry, northerly; 6th: fair, fair, fair, frost, northerly; 7th: fair, fair, fair, dry, north westerly; 8th: fair, windy, windy, dry, south westerly; 9th: fair, fair, snow showers, snow showers, south westerly; 10th: dry, dry, dry, frost and snow, southerly; 11th: dry, dry, dry, frost and snow, southerly; 12th: snow storms, snow storms, dry, frost, westerly; 13th: frost, fair, fair, frost, northerly; 14th: frost, fair, fair, dry, northerly; 15th: frost, fair, fair, frost, northerly; 16th: frost, fair, fair, frost, northerly; 17th: frost, fair, dry, dry, northerly; 18th: frost, dry, moist, dry, north easterly; 19th: frost, fair, fair, dry, north easterly; 20th: dry, fair, fair, frost, northerly; 21st: dry, fair, fair, dry, north easterly; 22nd: dry, cold, cold, dry, north easterly; 23rd: snow, cold, cold, snow, northerly; 24th: dry, cold, fair, frost, northerly; 25th: frost, dry, rainy, sleet and snow, northerly; 26th: snow showers, snow showers, snow showers, frost and snow, northerly; 27th: frost and snow, snow showers, snow showers, frost and snow, north westerly; 28th: dry, dry, dry, dry, north westerly; 29th: dry, fair, fair, dry, north westerly; 30th: frost, fair, fair, frost, north westerly; 31st: frost, fair, fair, frost, north westerly.

April. 1st: snow showers, windy, cold, frost, north westerly; 2nd: frost, fair, dry, snow, north westerly; 3rd: frost and snow, dry, cold, frost, northerly; 4th: frost, dry, dry, frost, northerly; 5th: frost, dry, cold, frost, north easterly; 6th: frost, cold, cold, frost, northerly; 7th: frost, dry, dry, frost, northerly; 8th: frost, dry, dry, dry, north westerly; 9th: frost, dry, dry, mild, north westerly; 10th: frost, cold, snow showers, frost and snow, south westerly; 11th: frost and snow, snow showers, snow showers, frost, easterly; 12th: frost, squally, squally, dry, south easterly; 13th: dry, dry, fair, frost, northerly; 14th: mild, cold, showery, rainy, south westerly; 15th: showery, windy, dry, frost, south westerly; 16th: windy, fair, dry, frost, north westerly; 17th: frost, dry, dry, frost, north westerly; 18th: frost, dry, dry, frost, north westerly; 19th: moist, showery, showery, rainy, south westerly; 20th: rainy, showery, showery, dry, south westerly; 21st: moist, showery, showery, mild, southerly; 22nd: moist, dry, dry, dry, north westerly; 23rd: dry, dry, dry, dry, north westerly; 24th: dry, dry, dry, rainy, north westerly; 25th: rainy, showery, showery, showery, southerly; 26th: showery, showery, mild, moist, southerly; 27th: mild, mild, mild, mild, south westerly; 28th: showery, showery, mild, mild, southerly; 29th: rainy, rainy, rainy, showery, southerly; 30th: stormy, showery, rainy, showery, southerly.

May. 1st: showery, showery, showery, showery, south westerly; 2nd: showery, showery, showery, dry, south westerly; 3rd: mild, showery, showery, dry, westerly; 4th: dry, fair, fair, mild, north westerly; 5th: dry, mild, mild, mild, northerly; 6th: mild, showery, mild, dry, north westerly; 7th: slight showers, mild, mild, showery, easterly; 8th: sleet showers, dry, dry, dry, northerly; 9th: hail, cold, dry, frost, northerly; 10th: frost, cold, cold, cold, northerly; 11th: dry, dry, windy, rainy, south westerly; 12th: sultry, sultry, sultry, mild, southerly; 13th: moist, slight showers, mild, mild, southerly; 14th: frost, dry, dry, dry, northerly; 15th: frost, heat, fair, fair, easterly; 16th: mild, heat, showery, mild, northerly; 17th: showery, moist, windy, showery, north westerly; 18th: dry, windy, windy, dry, north north westerly; 19th: windy, dry, dry, dry, north westerly; 20th: dry, dry, windy, windy, north westerly; 21st: windy, dry, windy, windy, north north westerly; 22nd: cold, cold, mild, mild, north westerly; 23rd: cold, windy, mild, mild, south westerly;

24th: windy, windy, windy, rainy, south south westerly; 25th: rainy, showery, mild, windy, southerly; 26th: showery, mild, heavy showers, mild, southerly; 27th: mild, heat, heat, heat, southerly; 28th: mild, showery, rainy, showery, southerly; 29th: sultry, heavy showers, heavy showers, mild, south westerly; 30th: showery, showery, hail storms, showery, north westerly; 31st: mild, mild, mild, mild, south westerly.

June. 1st: fair, fair, mild, fair, westerly; 2nd: fair, mild, mild, fair, westerly; 3rd: mild, heat, heat, mild, westerly; 4th: mild, mild, mild, mild, westerly; 5th: dry, dry, mild, mild, south westerly; 6th: dry, fair, fair, fair, northerly; 7th: dry, cold, cold, cold, northerly; 8th: cold, windy, windy, cold, easterly; 9th: cold, windy, windy, rainy, easterly; 10th: dry, dry, dry, cold, easterly; 11th: showery, showery, showery, rainy, south westerly; 12th: dry, showery, rainy, showery, south easterly; 13th: dry, fair, sultry, mild, easterly; 14th: mild, fair, fair, mild, southerly; 15th: fair, fair, fair, mild, southerly; 16th: showery, showery, sultry, mild, south westerly; 17th: sultry, thunder showers, thunder showers, sultry, south westerly; 18th: showery, showery, showery, mild, south westerly; 19th: mild, mild, dry, dry, south easterly; 20th: heat, heat, showery, dry, south easterly; 21st: dry, dry, showery, dry, north westerly; 22nd: heat, sultry, sultry, sultry, southerly; 23rd: sultry, sultry, sultry, sultry, southerly; 24th: heat, sultry, dry, dry, south westerly; 25th: heat, heat, fair, dry, northerly; 26th: heat, heat, heat, mild, north easterly; 27th: heat, heat, mild, mild, south westerly; 28th: sultry, sultry, sultry, sultry, south easterly; 29th: heat, heat, dry, mild, north westerly; 30th: heat, heat, heat, mild, northerly.

July. 1st: heat; 2nd: heat, heat, heat, mild, northerly; 3rd: mild, mild, mild, dry, westerly; 4th: mild, sultry, sultry, slight showers, westerly; 5th: mild, mild, sultry, mild, north westerly; 6th: mild, heat, heat, mild, north westerly; 7th: heavy dew, intense heat, heat, cool, northerly; 8th: heavy dew, heat, heat, mild, south easterly; 9th: heat, heat, heat, mild, south easterly; 10th: heavy dew, fair, fair, fair, easterly; 11th: fair, fair, windy, mild, east south easterly; 12th: fair, windy, windy, rainy, east south easterly; 13th: mild, mild, thunder showers, rainy, southerly; 14th: rainy, rainy, showery, showery, southerly; 15th: rainy, rainy, thunder showers, mild, south westerly; 16th: showery, dry, dry, dry, north westerly; 17th: showery, rainy, rainy, rainy, westerly; 18th: rainy, rainy, showery, fair, south westerly; 19th: fair, fair, fair, mild, north westerly; 20th: fair, fair, mild, mild, west north westerly; 21st: mild, heat, mild, rainy, westerly; 22nd: showery, sultry, showery, rainy, westerly; 23rd: fair, fair, mild, showery, north westerly; 24th: fair, fair, fair, rainy, west north westerly; 25th: fair, mild, mild, rainy, south westerly; 26th: fair, fair, mild, showery, south westerly; 27th: rainy, rainy, rainy, rainy, westerly; 28th: showery, sultry, sultry, rainy, south westerly; 29th: rainy, showery, showery, dry, north westerly; 30th: fair, showery, showery, mild, westerly; 31st: fair, showery, showery, mild, north westerly.

August. 1st: fair, fair, fair, fair, southerly; 2nd: rainy, showery, showery, showery, westerly; 3rd: rainy, rainy, showery, showery, westerly; 4th: showery, showery, showery, showery, north easterly; 5th: fair, fair, fair, fair, northerly; 6th: fair, fair, fair, fair, northerly; 7th: fair, heat, fair, mild, north easterly; 8th: fair, heat, heat, mild, easterly; 9th: fair, heat, heat, sultry, south easterly; 10th: mild, mild, mild, showery, easterly; 11th: sultry, sultry, sultry, heavy dew, south easterly; 12th: dewy, sultry, showery, mild, south westerly; 13th: heat, heat, heat, mild, southerly; 14th: heat, heat, heat, mild, south westerly; 15th: heat, heat, fair, mild, south easterly; 16th: fair, fair, fair, mild, easterly; 17th: mild, mild, mild, mild, westerly; 18th: heat, heat, heat, mild, easterly; 19th: mild, mild, mild, mild, easterly; 20th: slight showers, windy, windy, stormy, south easterly; 21st: stormy, stormy, stormy, stormy, south easterly; 22nd: fair, fair, mild, mild, northerly; 23rd: showery, heat, mild, mild, southerly; 24th: fair, fair, fair, fair, south easterly; 25th: dry, cold, slight showers, heavy rain, south westerly; 26th: dry, windy, windy, cold, north westerly; 27th: fair, fair, fair, mild, south easterly; 28th: mild, fair, fair, cold, south westerly; 29th: fair, fair, cold, cold, westerly; 30th: fair, fair, hail and rain, showery, north westerly; 31st: showery, cold and showery, cold and showery, showery, northerly.

September. 1st: moist, showery, showery, showery, north westerly; 2nd: dry, dry, cold, cold, northerly; 3rd: cold, cold, fair, mild, northerly; 4th: fair, cold, cold, rainy, south easterly; 5th: showery, mild, mild, mild, south easterly; 6th: showery, fair, fair, fair, west south westerly; 7th: rainy, rainy, fair, fair, westerly; 8th: fair, heat, fair, showery, south westerly; 9th: rainy, showery, fair, fair, south westerly; 10th: showery, stormy, stormy, stormy, south westerly; 11th: heavy rain, showery, fair, mild, west south westerly; 12th: mild, dry, dry, showery, south easterly; 13th: rainy, rainy, rainy, showery, south westerly; 14th: showery, showery, showery, fair, westerly; 15th: fair, showery, showery, moist, south west-

erly; 16th: rainy, rainy, rainy, showery, south south westerly; 17th: dry, dry, dry, moist, south south westerly; 18th: dry, dry, fair, fair, southerly; 19th: dry, showery, rainy, dry, south south easterly; 20th: windy, windy, fair, fair, easterly; 21st: mild, dry, dry, dry, easterly; 22nd: fair, fair, fair, fair, easterly; 23rd: fair, fair, fair, fair, easterly; 24th: fair, fair, fair, fair, easterly; 25th: fair, fair, fair, fair, easterly; 26th: fair, fair, fair, frost, easterly; 27th: fair, fair, fair, frost, easterly; 28th: fair, fair, cold, cold, easterly; 29th: fair, warm, fair, dry, easterly; 30th: fair, fair, showery, rainy, south easterly.

October. 1st: showery, fair, showery, fair, south easterly; 2nd: fair, fair, fair, fair, south easterly; 3rd: showery, dry, dry, dry, southerly; 4th: dry, showery, dry, mild, southerly; 5th: showery, showery, showery, stormy, south south easterly; 6th: showery, mild, mild, mild, south westerly; 7th: moist, moist, showery, rainy, south westerly; 8th: mild, mild, dry, dry, south south westerly; 9th: dry, mild, mild, mild, south south westerly; 10th: dry, dry, windy, windy, southerly; 11th: moist, rainy, showery, fair, south easterly; 12th: frost, fair, fair, frost, north westerly; 13th: frost, frost, fair, frost, north westerly; 14th: frost, frost, fair, frost, north westerly; 15th: frost, fair, fair, mild, south westerly; 16th: mild, mild, mild, mild, south westerly; 17th: mild, moist, moist, rainy, south westerly; 18th: fair, mild, mild, mild, south westerly; 19th: fair, fair, fair, fair, southerly; 20th: mild, moist, mild, showery, southerly; 21st: mild, mild, moist, mild, southerly; 22nd: dry, dry, dry, rainy, south westerly; 23rd: moist, showery, cold, frost, west north westerly; 24th: showery, showery, cold, frost, northerly; 25th: frost, cold, cold, showery, south westerly; 26th: showery, stormy, squally, squally, westerly; 27th: stormy, showery, rainy, rainy, westerly; 28th: rainy, showery, showery, stormy, westerly; 29th: moist, dry, dry, frost, south westerly; 30th: squally, squally, squally, stormy, west south westerly; 31st: squally, squally, squally, dry, westerly.

November. 1st: fair, fair, fair, moist, westerly; 2nd: cold, cold, cold, frost, westerly; 3rd: moist, showery, showery, rainy, westerly; 4th: dry, dry, showery, showery, south westerly; 5th: fair, dry, dry, dry, westerly; 6th: moist, rainy, rainy and foggy, moist, south westerly; 7th: fair, fair, fair, fair, south easterly; 8th: fair, fair, moist, moist, southerly; 9th: moist, mild, mild, showery, southerly; 10th: showery, moist, moist, dry, westerly; 11th: rainy, fair, fair, showery, westerly; 12th: showery, showery, fair, fair, westerly; 13th: moist, moist, rainy, dry, westerly; 14th: showery, fair,

fair, frost, north westerly; 15th: frost, frost, frost, frost, northerly; 16th: rainy, rainy, rainy, rainy, southerly; 17th: showery, moist, moist, dry, south westerly; 18th: showery, moist, dry, stormy, westerly; 19th: moist, showery, showery, frost, south westerly; 20th: showery, showery, sleet showers, rainy, westerly; 21st: showery, fair, fair, fair, west north westerly; 22nd: rainy, rainy, rainy, rainy, west south westerly; 23rd: showery, stormy, stormy, mild, westerly; 24th: fair, fair, fair, frost, west north westerly; 25th: frost, slight showers, slight showers, slight showers, westerly; 26th: showery, showery, showery, showery, westerly; 27th: sleet showers, sleet showers, showery, frost, north westerly; 28th: showery, showery, showery, snow, north westerly; 29th: snow, fair, fair, rainy, westerly; 30th: rainy, showery, showery, fair, south westerly.

December. 1st: frost, fair, fair, fair, north westerly; 2nd: fair, fair, fair, fair, westerly; 3rd: frost, fair, fair, fair, south easterly; 4th: mild, fair, fair, fair, south easterly; 5th: fair, fair, fair, fair, south easterly; 6th: fair, fair, fair, fair, east north easterly; 7th: fair, fair, fair, fair, north easterly; 8th: fair, moist, fair, rainy, north easterly; 9th: showery, fair, fair, slight showers, north easterly; 10th: showery, showery, cold, frost, north easterly; 11th: fair, fair, fair, frost, northerly; 12th: frost, moist, rainy, foggy, southerly; 13th: moist, fair, cold, cold, southerly; 14th: windy, windy, rainy, rainy, southerly; 15th: stormy, rainy, rainy, rainy, east south easterly; 16th: storm and rain, showery, fair, fair, southerly; 17th: stormy, rainy, rainy, storm and rain, east south easterly; 18th: rainy, rainy, rainy, showery, south westerly; 19th: rainy, rainy, rainy, rainy, south south westerly; 20th: rainy, rainy, rainy, rainy, south south westerly; 21st: showery, showery, rainy, rainy, south south easterly; 22nd: showery, moist, rainy, rainy, west south westerly; 23rd: fair, fair, fair, fair, westerly; 24th: moist, showery, moist, rainy, west south westerly; 25th: fair, fair, fair, fair, westerly; 26th: fair, fair, fair, fair, south westerly; 27th: showery, fair, fair, mild, southerly; 28th: rainy, mild, fair, fair, southerly; 29th: moist, showery, rainy, showery, south south westerly; 30th: showery, showery, fair, fair, south south easterly; 31st: fair, rainy, rainy, rainy, southerly.

1838, January. 1st: moist, showery, showery, fair, southerly; 2nd: moist, showery, showery, rainy, south south westerly; 3rd: showery, rainy, rainy, fair, southerly; 4th: fair, fair, fair, fair, southerly; 5th: fair, fair, fair, fair, southerly; 6th: fair, fair, fair, fair, south south easterly; 7th: fair, slight showers, slight showers, cold, south south

easterly; 8th: cold, cold, cold, frost, south easterly; 9th: frost, cold, cold, frost, east north easterly; 10th: frost, frost and snow, frost, frost, north north easterly; 11th: intense frost, frost, frost, intense frost, north north easterly; 12th: intense frost, intense frost, intense frost, intense frost, north north easterly; 13th: intense frost, intense frost, intense frost, frost, easterly; 14th: snow showers, cold, cold, thaw, east south easterly; 15th: sleet and rain, sleet and rain, sleet, moist, east south easterly; 16th: frost, frost, frost, snow, easterly; 17th: intense frost, frost, frost, mild, easterly; 18th: frost, frost, frost, snow, north north easterly; 19th: intense frost and snow, frost, frost, snow, north easterly; 20th: intense frost, frost, frost, snow, east south easterly; 21st: thaw, rainy, rainy, rainy, southerly; 22nd: rainy, moist, fair, stormy and frost, east south easterly; 23rd: fair, fair, fair, frost, east north easterly; 24th: sleet storms, snow storms, snow storms, intense frost, easterly; 25th: intense frost, intense frost, frost, intense frost, north easterly; 26th: frost and snow, snow, snow, slight snow, north easterly; 27th: mild, mild, mild, frost, easterly; 28th: snow, mild, mild, frost, easterly; 29th: moist, moist, moist, moist, south easterly; 30th: moist, showery, showery, moist, east north easterly; 31st: frost, fair, fair, fair, easterly.

February. 1st: mild, mild, mild, mild, easterly; 2nd: mild, slight snow, snow showers, snow, north easterly; 3rd: snow showers, snow showers, fair, frost, east north easterly; 4th: intense frost, intense frost, intense frost, intense frost, north easterly; 5th: frost, thaw, thaw, mild, south easterly; 6th: mild, moist, moist, mild, easterly; 7th: rain and snow, rainy, rainy, rainy, southerly; 8th: rainy, rainy, mild, mild, south easterly; 9th: mild, fair, frost, frost, northerly; 10th: frost, frost, frost, intense frost, northerly; 11th: intense frost, frost, frost, intense frost, northerly; 12th: intense frost, frost, frost, frost, north easterly; 13th: intense frost, frost, frost, windy, easterly; 14th: windy, stormy, stormy, tempestuous, easterly; 15th: tempestuous, tempestuous, tempestuous, snow storms, easterly; 16th: snow storms, snow storms, thaw, mild, easterly; 17th: snow showers, moist, thaw, thaw, north westerly; 18th: mild, moist, moist, moist, easterly; 19th: moist, showery, showery, mild, south easterly; 20th: frost, fair, fair, frost, easterly; 21st: frost, fair, fair, fair, easterly; 22nd: fair, fair, windy, fair, easterly; 23rd: snow showers, rainy, rainy, stormy, easterly; 24th: snow storms, snow storms, snow and tempest, snow and tempest, easterly; 25th: snow, rainy, rainy, showery, east south easterly; 26th: fair, windy, fair, fair, easterly; 27th: fair, slight snow, snow showers, snow showers, east south easterly; 28th: rainy, fair, fair, fair, north easterly.

March. 1st: rainy, rainy, rainy, rainy, south easterly; 2nd: rainy, mild, mild, mild, easterly; 3rd: mild, mild, mild, mild, south easterly; 4th: mild, mild, mild, fair, easterly; 5th: showery, fair, mild, fair, south easterly; 6th: fair, cold, cold, cold, east south easterly; 7th: showery, squally, squally, fair, west south westerly; 8th: showery, fair, fair, frost, west north westerly; 9th: frost, fair, fair, fair, east north easterly; 10th: rainy, rainy, rainy, squally, east south easterly; 11th: rainy, rainy, rainy, fair, easterly; 12th: fair, fair, fair, rainy, south westerly; 13th: showery, fair, cold, rainy, south westerly; 14th: rainy, rainy, windy, squally, north westerly; 15th: fair, fair, fair, fair, southerly; 16th: showery, snow and hail showers, snow showers, snow showers, south westerly; 17th: snow showers, squally, squally, moist, south westerly; 18th: fair, fine, fine, fair, southerly; 19th: fair, fair, rainy, showery, south south westerly; 20th: stormy, equinoctial gales and rain, storms and rain, storms and rain, westerly; 21st: stormy, fair, windy, storms and rain, west north westerly; 22nd: windy, cold, cold, frost, north north westerly; 23rd: frost, fine, fine, fine, northerly; 24th: frost and snow, fair, snow showers, stormy and rainy, south westerly; 25th: frost, fine, fine, fine, northerly; 27th: cold, fair, fine, mild, south easterly; 28th: moist, mild, mild, mild, south westerly; 29th: moist, fine, fine, mild, north north westerly; 30th: fine, fine, fine, mild, northerly; 31st: fine, fine, fine, mild, northerly.

April. 1st: frost, fine, fine, cold, northerly; 2nd: frost, cold, cold, cold, north easterly; 3rd: mild, moist, rainy, rainy, south westerly; 4th: showery, showery, showery, showery, west north westerly; 5th: showery, showery, showery, showery, westerly; 6th: moist, mild, fine, mild, northerly; 7th: moist, rainy, rainy, rainy, east south easterly; 8th: showery, windy, showery, rainy, west north westerly; 9th: showery, cold, showery, rainy, east south easterly; 10th: showery, showery, fair, fair, southerly; 11th: showery, squally, squally, showery, west north westerly; 12th: squally, squally, squally, fair, westerly; 13th: fair, mild, showery, showery, west south westerly; 14th: fair, fair, showery, rainy, west north westerly; 15th: windy, hail storms, hail storms, tempestuous, westerly; 16th: snow storms, snow storms, hail storms, snow, north westerly; 17th: snow storms, stormy, hail storms, snow, north westerly; 18th: stormy, stormy, stormy, stormy, north north westerly; 19th: cold, cold, cold, frost, northerly; 20th: cold,

fair, fair, cold, north north westerly; 21st: cold, cold, cold, rainy, north north westerly; 22nd: showery, showery, rainy, mild, south south westerly; 23rd: slight frost, rainy, mild, mild, southerly; 24th: slight showers, fair, fair, fair, north north westerly; 25th: fair, fine, fine, dry, north north easterly; 26th: fair, mild, mild, mild, east north easterly; 27th: slight frost, fine, fine, fine, northerly; 28th: slight frost, fair, fine, fine, north north westerly; 29th: slight frost, fine, fine, dry, west north westerly; 30th: cold, cold, warm, frost, north westerly.

School Statistics

SOCIAL ECONOMY

Table of Schools

[Table contains the following headings: name of townland where held, name and religion of master or mistress, free or pay school, annual income of master or mistress, description and cost of schoolhouse, number of pupils subdivided by religion, sex and the Protestant and Roman Catholic returns, societies with which connected].

Antrim, master John Alexander, mistress Jane Kelso, Protestant; free school, annual income 30 pounds each; schoolhouse very substantial, cost 800 pounds; number of pupils by the Protestant return: Established Church 53, Presbyterians 74, Roman Catholics 53, males 100, females 80; by the Roman Catholic return: Established Church 27, Presbyterians 31, Roman Catholics 26, males 84; the parish school; Erasmus Smith's trustees; Lord Ferrard gave 200 pounds towards building the schoolhouse.

Antrim, master Revd James Carley, Presbyterian; pay school, annual income 210 pounds; schoolhouse stone and brick, cost 100 pounds; number of pupils by the Protestant return: Established Church 18, Presbyterians 30, Roman Catholics 1, males 49; by the Roman Catholic return: males 54; associations none.

Antrim, master Pat Magill, Roman Catholic; pay school, annual income 20 pounds; schoolhouse stone and mortar, 5 pounds a year rent; number of pupils by the Protestant return: Established Church 12, Presbyterians 20, Roman Catholics 8, males 40; by the Roman Catholic return: Established Church 2, Presbyterians 30, other denominations 2, Roman Catholics 6, males 34, females 6; Presbyterian minister visits.

Antrim, master Nathaniel White, Presbyterian; pay school, annual income 50 pounds; schoolhouse stone and lime, cost 40 pounds; number of pupils by the Protestant return: Established Church 4, Presbyterians 22, Roman Catholics 2, males 24, females 4; by the Roman Catholic return: Established Church 4, Presbyterians 22, Roman Catholics 2, males 24, females 4; associations none.

Antrim, master John Martin, Presbyterian; pay school, annual income 12 pounds; schoolhouse stone and lime, cost 100 pounds; number of pupils by the Protestant return: Established Church 14, Presbyterians 21, Roman Catholics 15, males 38, females 12; by the Roman Catholic return: Established Church 10, Presbyterians 7, Roman Catholics 8, males 30, females 13; associations none.

Antrim, mistress Elinor Cosgrave, Church of England; pay school, annual income not stated, charges 3s 3d reading per quarter, 5s 5d writing and sewing; schoolhouse a hired room; number of pupils by the Protestant return: Established Church 2, Presbyterians 7, Roman Catholics 3, males 2, females 10; by the Roman Catholic return: Established Church 4, Presbyterians 6, Roman Catholics 2, males 2, females 10; associations none.

Antrim, mistress Elizabeth Wilson, Presbyterian; pay school, annual income: 5s 5d small children, 6s 6d others per quarter; schoolhouse a hired room; number of pupils by the Protestant return: Established Church 4, Presbyterians 4, Roman Catholics 2, males 2, females 8; by the Roman Catholic return: Established Church 4, Presbyterians 12, Roman Catholics 2, females 18; associations none.

Antrim, mistress Mary Thompson, Presbyterian; pay school, annual income 2s 2d and 5s 5d per quarter; schoolhouse a hired room; number of pupils by the Protestant return: Established Church 1, Presbyterians 20, Roman Catholics 3, males 4, females 20; by the Roman Catholic return: Established Church 4, Presbyterians 17, Roman Catholics 4, males 4, females 21; associations none.

Antrim, mistresses Mary and Jane Bryson, Presbyterian; pay school, annual income a guinea a quarter; held in their brother's house; number of pupils by the Protestant return: Established Church 2, Presbyterians 6, Roman Catholics 1, females 9; by the Roman Catholic return: Established Church 2, Presbyterians 7, Roman Catholics 1, females 10; associations none.

Maghareagh, master Daniel Dowling, Roman Catholic; pay school, annual income 12 pounds; schoolhouse stone and lime, cost 100 pounds; number of pupils by the Protestant return: Established Church 5, Presbyterians 10, Roman Catholics 14, males 14, females 15; by the Roman

Catholic return: Established Church 8, Presbyterians 16, Roman Catholics 23, males 29, females 18; connected with Kildare Place Society.

Antrim, master James Wallace, Presbyterian; pay school, annual income 2s 2d to 5s 5d per quarter; schoolhouse a hired room; number of pupils by the Protestant return: Presbyterians 2, Roman Catholics 4, males 6; by the Roman Catholic return: Established Church 3, Presbyterians 10, Roman Catholics 5, males 12, females 6; associations none.

Antrim, mistress Eleanor Kelso, Presbyterian; free school, annual income 30 pounds with house; schoolhouse built by Erasmus Smith's trustees; number of pupils by the Roman Catholic return: Established Church 21, Presbyterians 2, Roman Catholics 26, females 49; connected with Erasmus Smith's trustees.

Antrim, mistress Martha Mackey, Presbyterian; pay school, annual income 5s 5d per quarter; schoolhouse a hired room; number of pupils by the Protestant return: Established Church 5, Presbyterians 8, males 5, females 8; by the Roman Catholic return: Established Church 6, Presbyterians 3, males 7, females 2; associations none.

Irishtown, mistress Mrs McMillen, Presbyterian; pay school, annual income 10 pounds; schoolhouse a hired room; number of pupils by the Roman Catholic return: Presbyterians 24, males 6, females 18; associations none.

Grange of Doagh, County Antrim

Statistical Report by Lieutenant Edward
Durnford, October 1832

NATURAL STATE

Situation and Boundaries

It is situated in the barony of Upper Antrim and
county of Antrim; lies north of the Six Mile Water
and west of the town of Ballyclare, which is
nearly at the south eastern extremity of the grange.
It is extraparochial and tithe free.

It is bounded on the north by the parish of
Rashee, on the north east by that of Ballycor, on
the south east by those of Ballynure and Ballylinny,
Ballywalter grange and parish of Templepatrick,
and on the west by the parish of Kilbride.

Extent and Divisions

It extends from north east to south west about 3
British statute miles and from north west to south
east about a mile and a half. The grange contains
2,305 British statute acres. It is divided into 4
townlands, which are all in the manor of Moylena,
the property of the Marquis of Donegall.

NATURAL FEATURES

Surface and Soil

There is no remarkable feature of ground in this
small grange, which is generally well cultivated.
There is, however, some wasteland which appears
to have been bog cut out, but it is of no great extent.

Produce and Turbary

The general crops are potatoes, oats and some
flax. The acre commonly yields of corn, from 12
to 17 cwt of meal, and of potatoes from 300 to 400
bushels. These are taken to Belfast market. The
flax is only grown for the use of the inhabitants.

The land is chiefly held on leases of lives
renewable forever, about 1 pound 5s to be paid at
the fall of each life, and the rent from 3s to 7s an
Irish acre. The cause of the rent being so low is
that fines were paid to the Marquis of Donegall,
who then reduced it.

There is no good turbary in the grange: the
inhabitants are chiefly supplied from Ballyboley.

NATURAL HISTORY

Minerals

Basalt is the prevailing rock throughout the grange.

In the demesne at Fisherwick there is a pit sunk
to a considerable depth through a stratum of
amygdaloid or toad stone.

MODERN TOPOGRAPHY

Town of Ballyclare

The town of Ballyclare is situated in the townland
of the same name, near the south east extremity of
the grange, on the Six Mile Water, over which
there is a long stone bridge. It is a post town and
a large monthly market is held on the first Wednesday in every month. There are also 4 fairs held
annually, on the 31st January, 22nd May, 24th
July and 20th November.

There is no church in Ballyclare, but there is a
large meeting house for the New Light Presbyterians and another for the Methodists. The latter is
situated on the other side of the bridge, in Ballynure
parish. By the census of 1831 the population,
including the townland of Ballyclare, was 1,127.

Village of Doagh

The village of Doagh is situated near the south
west extremity of the grange, in the townland of
the same name. It is very small. There is a large
inn and post house, chiefly used by the gentlemen
of the Antrim Hunt, who meet here during the
season. The only place of worship is a small
meeting house for the Methodists. By the census
of 1831 the population, including the townland of
Doagh, was 435.

Manufactures

There are no manufactures carried on in the
grange. There is a bleach mill in the village of
Doagh, but it is not in use at present. The females
are generally employed in spinning.

Roads

The only roads of any consequence are: one from
Belfast to Broughshane which traverses the eastern end of the grange, passing through Ballyclare;
another from Ballyclare to Antrim which passes
through Doagh; and one from Belfast to Ballymena
(by Doagh) which traverses the south west extremity of the grange. These are all in good repair,
as also some crossroads which run through the
grange.

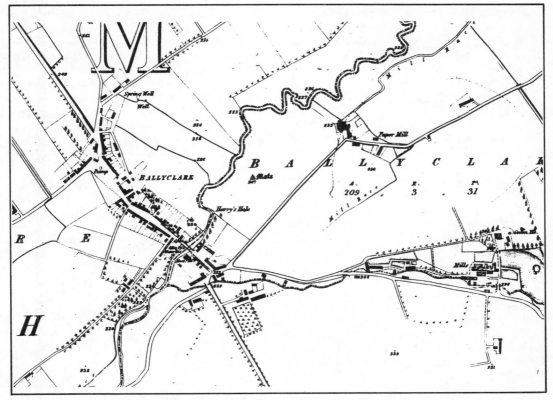

Map of Ballyclare from the first 6" O.S. maps, 1830s

NATURAL FEATURES

Rivers

The Six Mile Water forms the south east boundary of the grange and is crossed by the roads from Belfast to Broughshane and to Ballymena, mentioned above. A considerable stream called the Doagh river forms the western boundary of the grange, running into the Six Mile Water at the south west extremity of it.

Bogs and Woods

There are no peat bogs in the grange. There is some wasteland of a boggy nature, but it is not used for fuel. There are some plantations about Fisherwick, a hunting lodge of the Marquis of Donegall's, situated close to the village of Doagh.

SOCIAL ECONOMY

Population

By the census of 1831 the population of the grange only amounted to 1,814, and was by townlands as follows: Ballyclare, males 557, females 570, total 1,127; Cogree, males 123, females 129, total 252; Doagh, males 208, females 227, total 435.

ANCIENT TOPOGRAPHY

Antiquities

There is a fort or mound at Doagh in which was found an urn containing bones, some coins and spearheads, which are in possession of a person residing in the village, who has also a large collection of stone hatchets, arrowheads and several brazen celts.

In the village of Doagh is a graveyard, in which are the remains of a building; but when it ceased to be used as a place of worship is not known. [Signed] Edward Durnford, Lieutenant Royal Engineers, 15th October 1832.

Memoir by James Boyle, February 1839

MEMOIR WRITING

Composition of Memoir

The information contained in this Memoir is

complete to this date. It was originally commenced on the 2nd July 1836 and was completed on the 5th February 1839. The total time employed at it was 232 hours, equals 25 days. [Signed] James Boyle, 5th February 1839.

NATURAL FEATURES

Hills

The grange of Doagh occupies a portion of the southern extremity of the features spreading out from the mountains in the adjoining northern and eastern parishes, which terminate in a level holme on the right hand of the Six Mile Water and form the north western side of the extensive and fertile valley to which that stream gives its name. From an average elevation of 198 feet above the sea the ground rises somewhat gradually from the south east side of the grange. At its north east corner it attains at the Craig hill, which rises abruptly, an extreme elevation of 449 feet, but with the exception of this knoll its average elevation at its northern boundary does not exceed 350 feet.

The surface of the grange is considerably diversified, particularly towards its southern side, where there is much variety in the numerous little gravelly swells and knolls. The general appearance of the country is fertile and the formation of the ground presents sufficient diversity. The only remarkable point is Craig hill, a small basaltic knoll, 449 feet above the level of the sea.

Rivers: Six Mile Water

The Six Mile Water flows south westerly along the southern side of this grange, separating it from the parish of Ballylinny and grange of Ballywalter. This stream takes its rise at an elevation of about 1,000 feet above the sea and 952 feet above Lough Neagh, into which it discharges itself, on the south western side of Shaw's hill, in the more easterly parish of Kilwaughter. From this it pursues a south west [course] for 4 and a half miles and, descending to a level of 230 feet above the sea, enters the south east corner of this grange. It flows for 3 miles 4 furlongs 110 yards along its southern side and descends to a level of 162 feet. It afterwards pursues a more westerly but more irregular course, until it discharges itself into Lough Neagh, five-sixths of a mile west of the town of Antrim, through which [it] flows.

Its inclination in this grange is 1 in 278 feet. Its extreme breadth is 90 feet and average breadth 19 feet. Its ordinary depth varies from 1 to 6 and averages 3 feet. Its bed is chiefly composed [of] fine loose sand or gravel, occasionally alternating with small and worn pebbles. Towards the eastern side of the grange it is soft and clayey. Its banks are very low, being in several instances not more than a foot higher than the ordinary level of the stream. It frequently overflows them, and to a considerable extent in several places inundates the level holme through which it flows, in some instances enriching and benefitting the meadow land, while in others committing serious injury to that which is cultivated, by sweeping off the soil and injuring the crops, sometimes depositing gravel and stones.

Its deposit is nowhere beneficial. It chiefly consists of a sandy grit, which injures the quality of the hay and by some is said to sour the aftergrass and render it unpalatable to cattle. It is in one instance applied to machinery, and may easily be applied to the purposes of drainage and irrigation. Its floods are violent, rising rapidly but requiring some time to subside.

The ancient name of this stream was Amhuinna-Fiodh or the "river of the woods", which it is said to have derived from the dense forest which clothed the valley through which it flows. It also (subsequently) bore the name of the Loubar, and as such is mentioned in old deeds, leases etc. The derivation of this name is not known. Its present name is generally believed to have derived from the circumstance of it being crossed at a ford just 6 miles from the town of Carrickfergus, on the ancient leading road from that town to Antrim. With some it is thought that it was owing to the supposed and erroneous idea that its source was just 6 miles from the most eastern point of the county.

This stream flows for 18 and a half miles through the fertile valley to which it gives its name, and which traverses the county from its western to within 5 miles of its eastern side. In the neighbouring parishes it affords a most valuable supply of water power to the very extensive bleach greens and paper and flour mills along its banks. In this grange the scenery along it is rather devoid of interest, the ground being tame and destitute of planting, but in most of the adjacent districts the scenery along its banks is picturesque and interesting.

Doagh River

The Doagh river is a small stream which flows southerly for 2 and three-quarter miles along the western side of the grange, separating it from the parish of Kilbride. This stream issues from several sources (at an elevation of 830 feet above the sea and 634 feet above the point where it discharges itself into the Six Mile Water) from the adjoining parish of Rashee. After flowing southerly for 1 and three-quarter miles, it descends to a level of 290 feet above the sea and enters the north west corner of the grange. From this it pursues a southerly course for 2 and three-quarter miles along its western side and discharges itself into the Six Mile Water at an elevation of 162 feet above the sea.

Its total length is 4 and a half miles. Its average inclination is 1 in 46 feet, but its inclination is irregular, its bed being very rough and uneven, and its course being interrupted by several shallows and carries for the purpose of turning off water to machinery. Its average breadth is only 10 feet and its average ordinary depth 2 feet.

Its bed is very rough and is principally formed of large loose stones and gravel rolled down by it in its frequent and impetuous floods, which rise and subside rapidly without committing any mischief or extending beyond its channel, which it has worn to a considerable depth, its banks being in several instances, particularly at the village of Doagh, high and almost precipitous. It is usefully situated for the purposes of machinery, to which it is in several instances applied, and it is also applicable to drainage and irrigation. It is in many places easily fordable and does not impede communication. In the neighbourhood of the village of Doagh the scenery along it is pleasing, its banks being high and steep and diversified with planting.

Springs

The grange is amply supplied, from numerous springs and rivulets, with water for domestic uses.

Climate and Crops

The grange possesses a good southern aspect. The climate, particularly in its southern districts, is dry and the air is pure and healthy. Along the banks of the Six Mile Water and of the Doagh river frosts make their appearance at an early season, sometimes so soon as the middle of September, and are injurious to the potato crop.

The crops chiefly cultivated are oats, potatoes, wheat, barley and a little flax. Oats are sown during the months of March and April, and are reaped from the latter part of August to the end of September. The general planting of potatoes takes place during the last week in April and the first fortnight in May. A few early potatoes are planted about Patrick's Day and are fit for digging about the latter part of July. Wheat is sown immediately

after the raising of the potatoes and is reaped during the last fortnight in August. Barley is sown during the latter part of April and reaped during the middle of August. Flax is sown during the month of April and is pulled during the month of July.

Bogs

The bogs in this grange have been almost totally cut out and their subsoil has been laid bare. They occupied the little hollows between gravelly swells and banks along the Six Mile Water, which by its inundations seems at some remote period to have in rainy seasons deposited water in them. The subsoil is generally a greyish clay, in which a few oak trunks of but trifling dimensions and some oak stumps have been found imbedded. The trunks are said to have apparently been broken off from stumps.

Woods

A very little stunted brushwood of hazel and holly is now the only natural wood in the grange. In digging a trench in the gravelly soil near the Six Mile Water, some pieces of oak timber about 6 feet long, 8 inches in diameter and in good preservation were found at a depth of about 7 feet from the surface of the ground, and 2 feet lower than the bed of the river. The timber lay indiscriminately on a marshy bed, beneath a stratum of blue clay about 3 feet thick. There was no indication of their having been drifted there, nor was there any gravel or diluvial deposit immediately under or over them.

MODERN TOPOGRAPHY

Towns: Ballyclare

The little town of Ballyclare and the village of Doagh are situated in this grange.

The town of Ballyclare is chiefly situated in the grange of Doagh. A small portion of it, including 24 houses and cottages on the south side of the Six Mile Water which flows through the town, is included in the parish of Ballylinny, manor of Ballylinny and barony of Lower Belfast, but this portion will be included in the description given here. The remaining and principal part of the town is situated in the townland of Ballyclare, manor of Moylinny and barony of Upper Antrim. It is in the diocese of Connor and north east circuit of assize.

The town is built on the road from Kells and Connor and Broughshane to Carrickfergus, which also leads from the latter town to Belfast. This is intersected at the southern side of the town by the leading road from Antrim to Larne and Carrickfergus, and at this northern end it is joined by a road from Antrim through the village of Doagh. Its extreme length from north to south is 770 yards and east to west 200 yards.

Ballyclare occupies a low situation on the banks of the Six Mile Water, which here is 90 feet wide. It is not discernible from a distance, nor does it [in] any respect constitute an ornament [to] the scenery of the country. The town is built without the slightest regard to uniformity, regularity or neatness. It is anything but cleanly and its general appearance is uninteresting in the extreme. Its situation is cheerful and agreeable. The valley falls gently towards the Six Mile Water and presents in its fertile slopes a striking contrast to the wild and mountainous backgrounds which bound the view.

Ballyclare is 119 miles north of Dublin, 10 and a half miles north of Belfast, 10 miles south west of the seaport town of Larne and 9 miles east of Antrim.

History of Ballyclare

There is no local record concerning the origin and history of Ballyclare, and the traditions concerning it are vague and unsatisfactory. There is not any appearance of antiquity about it, nor is there anything to indicate its ever having been of greater importance or extent than at present. There are not any remains of antiquity in the town, nor in its immediate vicinity. The bridge across the Six Mile Water is the first which stood on that site. It has been erected about 80 years since, and the oldest house in the town has not been more than 75 years erected.

Ballyclare is said to have derived its name from the circumstance of there having been a floating bridge or raft across the river, both previously and subsequent to the erection of the town. It is difficult to account for this derivation. Its erection may have partly originated in the circumstance of there having been a ford here, and particularly so as it was on one of the ancient roads from Carrickfergus. The increase of the town may have been further promoted by the construction of the bridge, which at the period of its erection was the only one for several miles on the river.

The celebrated horse fairs and monthly markets of Ballyclare have been established beyond memory. The former still retains its character, but the latter have dwindled into insignificance. The town has within memory increased nearly one-half, but within the last 10 years it has not under-

gone any improvement. It formerly had a good linen market, which was given up about 40 years since, and there was also a good market for butter, but this also has been discontinued for 15 years. Its trade, which had ever been on a limited scale, is now confined to the pettiest dealing, and the circulation of money in it is very trivial, consisting merely in that expended by the humbler farmers, tradespeople and labourers in the purchase of their little necessaries.

Houses and Public Buildings

Ballyclare chiefly consists of one very irregular and crooked street, varying in width from 26 to 110 feet, and extending for 770 yards from north to south. From the northern end of this a few houses extend along the road leading westward to Doagh. The town contains 153 houses and cottages, of which 1 is 3[-storeys] and 30 are 2-storeys high, the remainder being 1-storey cottages and cabins. 28 of the 2-storey houses and 35 cottages are slated. The rest are thatched. All built of stone and lime. There are 7 uninhabited houses in the town.

The public buildings of Ballyclare consist of 2 Presbyterian and 1 Methodist meeting house, a Roman Catholic chapel and a bridge.

Presbyterian Meeting Houses

The Unitarian meeting house is situated near the centre of the town. It is a plain and rather clumsy structure, built of stone and roughcast. It measures 68 by 27 feet. It contains 2 galleries, 1 at each end, which are approached by flights of rude stone stairs at the outside of the house. It is fitted up with pews and contains accommodation for 400 persons. It is in but middling repair. This house was erected by subscription about the year 1770.

The Covenanting meeting house is situated at the north eastern side of the town. It is a plain but substantial little house, measuring 47 by 24 feet. It is fitted up with pews and contains accommodation for 217 persons. The floor is earthen and it is as yet in an unfinished state, from want of funds. It was erected in 1832 and has cost 400 pounds, which was raised by subscription.

Roman Catholic Chapel

The Roman Catholic chapel is situated on the road to Doagh and about 250 yards north west of the town. It is a plain and unfinished-looking house, measuring 48 by 24 feet. It is built of stone and slated. Though it was commenced in 1833 it still remains in quite an unfinished state, nothing more than the walls and roof having been erected. It is not even plastered, nor is it floored nor fitted up with pews. Its estimated expense when finished is 250 pounds, a considerable proportion of which has not been collected.

Methodist Chapel

The Wesleyan Methodist chapel is situated at the southern side of the town and on the south bank of the river. It is a plain but substantial and neatly finished house, well built of stone and lime, and slated. It measures in the extreme 54 by 39 feet and is lit by 3 rows of windows. It consists of 2 floors. The under one contains a schoolroom 34 by 36 feet and apartments intended for the preacher. The upper or first floor is used for worship and is fitted up with 30 single pews, each capable of accommodating 6 persons. There are also a few forms. It is altogether neatly and substantially fitted up.

The house is situated in a square plot of ground measuring 180 by 60, enclosed by a 6 foot wall and tastefully planted with shrubs and evergreens. It was erected by subscription in 1828 and cost 1,200 pounds.

Bridge and Streets

The bridge across the Six Mile Water consists of 4 circular-segment arches, and measures 151 feet in length between the abutments and 21 feet wide. It is a plain substantial structure.

The street of Ballyclare declines with a somewhat rapid and undulating slope towards the Six Mile Water. Its width is irregular and varies from 26 to 110 feet. In the erection of the houses not the slightest attention has been paid to uniformity of construction or regularity of position. Pretty good houses are built next wretched cabins, and the appearance of both thereby injured. Many of the houses and cabins are in bad repair. The use of lime seems to be but little known, and from its unfrequented application the external appearance of the houses is gloomy and sombre. Very little regard seems to be paid to cleanliness. The streets are dirty and manure heaps are frequently to be found before the doors of the cottages.

Ballyclare is not increasing in size. Within the last 10 years 15 cottages and 3 2-storey houses have been built in it. There is no one to take any interest in the improvement of the town. The tenements are held in perpetuity under the Donegall family, and from there being neither trade nor manufacture and but little capital, and there being so many trifling interests, it is but little likely to improve.

Population

3 constabulary are stationed in Ballyclare. A detailed statement of the occupations of the inhabitants of Ballyclare will be found in the Appendix. The people are all of the humbler class and are engaged in some profession, dealing or trade, or as labourers. With the exception of the labourers, most of them hold some land, and in addition to their other pursuits are engaged in farming. The tradespeople seldom hold more than a field, either for grazing or for raising potatoes.

They are a peaceable race, not very industrious nor temperate in their habits, nor do they possess much idea of neatness or comfort in the keeping of their dwellings or in their mode of living.

Libraries and Temperance Society

There are 2 libraries in Ballyclare. One of these was established in 1805 and contains 224 volumes. There are 20 subscribers, who pay 2s 6d per quarter. The second library or book club consists of 20 members, who pay 1 pound entrance and 6d per quarter. It was established in 1831 and possesses 100 volumes. The works in both clubs are well selected and are chiefly on biography, history and useful and religious subjects. They have tended greatly towards improving the tastes and amusements of the people.

A temperance society was established here in 1835 and at present consists of 60 members. It is rather on the increase and is said to have been attended with beneficial results.

PRODUCTIVE ECONOMY

Markets

There is neither trade nor manufacture in the village, its dealing or business being almost solely confined to supplying the common necessaries required by the lower classes in the neighbouring districts. Until about 40 years ago Ballyclare possessed a good linen market, and until about 15 years ago it had also a butter market. A market is now held on the third Wednesday in each month for the sale of cows, pigs, sheep, yarn, pedlar's goods, hardware, earthenware, wooden ware, old clothes, cheese and fruit. These markets are inconsiderable: scarcely 20 cows, about 30 pigs and a few sheep constitute the great bulk of the market, the quantities of the other articles being very trifling.

Fairs

4 annual fairs are held in Ballyclare, namely one on the second Tuesday in January, May, July and November. These fairs, particularly those held in May and November, are celebrated as horse fairs, and are attended by dealers from England and Scotland, and from distant parts of Ireland. At the latter the description of horses offered for sale is superior and consists of those suited for the field, the cavalry, for draught or as farm horses. They vary in price from 10 pounds to 150 pounds, and might average 30 pounds each. A considerable number is bought up by dealers for the English and Scottish markets. The January and July fairs are principally for farming horses and those for domestic purposes, which are exposed in great numbers. They might average 18 pounds each. A good many of these are also bought up by dealers from England and Scotland. The number of cows or pigs exposed at these fairs is inconsiderable, the great traffic being confined to horses.

There are also numerous stalls for the sale of pedlar's goods, old clothes, earthenware, hardware, huckstery and confectionery, but as no tolls or customs have been levied for 15 years, and from the extreme confusion and irregularity, no accurate statement of the numbers of horses and cattle can be afforded. The customs were the property of the Marquis of Donegall, but for the last 15 years the people have refused to pay them, as the fairs are held in the open street.

Trade and Commodities

Farm produce is conveyed to market in the carts of the farmers. There are 3 carmen who ply between Ballyclare and Belfast. The journey is generally performed within the 24 hours. The charge for carriage from Belfast, as also from Larne, is 6d per cwt.

Ballyclare is badly supplied with butcher's meat; very little, however, of that article is consumed here. Its want is therefore scarcely known. Poultry are abundant and cheap, as are also milk and butter. There is no market gardening and the sale of fruit and vegetables is confined to apples and gooseberries, and some leeks and onions. Meal is sold in the shops and potatoes are sold in small quantities by the farmers.

The town is abundantly supplied with water from the river and from 3 pumps which were sunk in the street at the expense of the inhabitants. Turf are brought into town almost daily from the mountain bogs in Rashee and Glenwhirry, and cost from 13d to 15d per cubic yard or gauge in

summer, and from 1s 8d to 2s per gauge in winter. Coal is procured from Belfast. There is not any stall feeding. Grazing for a milch cow during the summer half-year costs 3 pounds 10s, and for beef cattle 3 pounds per head.

Belfast is the great mart from whence merchandise, timber, iron and slates are procured. It is 10 and a half miles distant. The carriage of goods from thence cost 6d per cwt.

Building Materials

Pine timber for building and countess slates are the description commonly used. Lime is procured from the kilns at Carnmoney (on the road to Belfast), 5 and a half miles distant, and costs, when laid down, 14d per barrel. Bricks are usually procured from Carrickfergus, 8 and a half miles distant. Stone of an excellent description for building is everywhere abundant in the neighbourhood.

Insurances and Employment

There is scarcely a house insured from fire. There are not any life insurances. Neither tradesmen nor labourers suffer from want of employment at any particular seasons. There are 3 regular carriers who ply to Belfast. They perform the journey within the 24 hours and charge 6d per cwt.

SOCIAL ECONOMY

Dispensary and Schools

There is no dispensary in Ballyclare, but there is one at the village of Doagh, 2 miles distant, which extends its assistance to patients from this town. It was established in 1835, and though its effects are not as yet actually perceptible, still it has been of great benefit to the lower class here.

There are 4 day schools and 3 Sunday schools in Ballyclare (see Table of Schools). One of the former is partly supported by the Board of National Education. The 3 others are private schools. The education afforded at the Sunday schools is gratuitous.

There is no regular provision for the poor. The people, generally speaking, are humane and charitable. The beggars from the surrounding neighbourhood frequent Ballyclare on each Monday, when they receive assistance from the inhabitants.

Amusements

There is little or no taste for amusements. Dancing is now almost their only recreation. Their dances are now much less frequent than formerly. They are very social and among the more affluent class there are frequent convivial meetings, the recreations at which consist in card-playing and punch-drinking. There has always been much taste for reading, and the number of newspapers taken is considerable. There are 4 lodges of Free-masons in Ballyclare.

The people are civil and obliging, peaceable and generally well conducted. They are not, however, very temperate in their habits. On the subjects of politics and religion they are very bigoted, and are almost exclusively violent radicals. Though there are but a few individuals who can be termed affluent, still most of the better class are in independent circumstances.

Conveyances and Post Office

There are 3 post cars which ply regularly to Belfast market on Fridays and to Ballymena market on Saturdays. The fare to each of these towns for 1 passenger is 1s. When privately engaged during the week the charge per mile Irish is 7d. They are but indifferently horsed and appointed.

A post office (a penny post) was established here in 1801 and has been a great accommodation for the neighbourhood. The mail from Dublin and Belfast arrives here daily at 10 a.m. and is despatched at 2 p.m. Upwards of 50 newspapers are delivered at this office.

General Remarks

For several years Ballyclare has ceased to improve. Its trade and dealing, as has been before stated, has for the last 15 years continued to decline. There is not the slightest probability of its amendment, and in consequence, either as to extent or appearance, the town has not improved, nor is it likely to improve.

MODERN TOPOGRAPHY

Doagh Village

The little village of Doagh is cheerfully situated at the western side of the grange and townland of the same name, in the barony of Upper Antrim and manor of Moylinny. A small stream (the Doagh river) flows along the western side of the village, and the road from Carrickfergus to Antrim through Ballyclare, which had until within a few years been the leading road between these towns, passes through its southern side. The village straggles irregularly for 150 yards along the road from Kells and Connor to Belfast.

Doagh is 2 miles west of Ballyclare, which is its post town. It is 7 miles east of Antrim, 10 miles north of Belfast and 12 miles south west of Larne. Its situation on the steep bank of the Doagh river, and in the midst of the plantations on it and about the demesne of Fisherwick, is very pleasing. The village is neat and cleanly, though irregularly constructed, and the surrounding country is fertile and highly cultivated.

Origin of Doagh

The origin and history of Doagh are involved in obscurity, or at least in uncertainty. This is not to be wondered at when it is borne in mind that there is not among the present the slightest trace of the former inhabitants of the country. There is no record concerning it, and the only tradition (or perhaps conjecture) is that it derived its name and origin from a monastery of black friars which formerly existed here, and the name Doagh is a corruption of dhu or "black."

This is to a considerable extent borne out by the circumstance of there being an old burial ground, containing a small fragment of the wall of some building, contiguous to the southern side of the village and on the summit of the high bank which

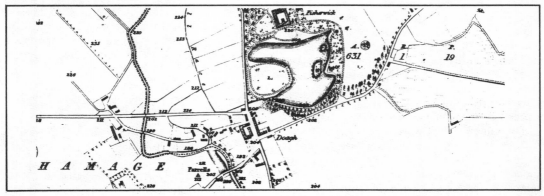

Map of Doagh from the first 6" O.S. maps, 1830s

overhangs the river. The masonry in the wall (see Ancient Topography) is of the rudest description, the stones being small, undressed and such as are picked up in the fields; or more probably they have been procured from the bed of the stream, as they are all water worn. The cement seems to have been a sort of coarse grout.

Between the burial ground and the edge of the bank is a circular earthen rath 64 feet in diameter and 5 feet high. A cove or gallery constructed in a manner precisely similar to that adopted in the coves of the country, but now quite closed up, extends under the burial ground from a field on its eastern side. The mouth or entrance of the cove was 43 yards from the church, to which it was found to extend, but no other outlet or entrance could be discovered. It is said to have been from 4 to 5 feet high and about 4 feet broad, but it occasionally contracted and again expanded. No remains were found in it.

It is also said that the grange was the mensal land of the abbey. This is probable, as it pays no tithe and is exceedingly fertile. It is alleged by some that it was attached to the celebrated abbey of Muckamore, 8 miles distant, while by others it is said to have been in connection with [the] abbey of Connor (9 miles), which was in ancient times the residence of the bishops of the diocese.

In 1798 a portion of the village was burned by the king's troops, in consequence of the part which its inhabitants took in the insurrection of that year.

Hunt Club

In 1815 the celebrated hunt club known as the Antrim Hunt, and composed of members from this and the adjoining counties, was formed under the patronage of the Marquis of Donegall, who had a splendid hunting establishment at his seat at Fisherwick which adjoins the village. The very extensive hotel was soon after enlarged to its present size. It contained a large and handsome clubroom, and spacious accommodation, besides stabling for 70 horses.

There were at one time 40 members belonging to this club. They held their meetings at stated periods, and for a long time it was well kept up, but on the decline of the Donegall family, caused by their embarrassments, and on the breaking up of the hunting establishment at Fisherwick, the club began to dwindle and was finally broken up in 1835. This was a serious loss to Doagh. The money circulated by the members and the retinues was very considerable. Now the spacious hotel is but partly occupied and but a few of its rooms are furnished, and it is now nothing more than an ale house.

Streets and Houses

Doagh consists principally of 1 street, 150 yards long and 38 feet wide. From the northern end of this a second branches off westerly for a few yards.

The village consists of 46 houses and cottages. Of these, 7 are 2-storeys high, 35 are thatched and the remainder are slated. All are built of stone and lime, and all are roughcast and whitened. They are in general substantial and neat-looking, and though there has not been any regard paid to uniformity or regularity, still from its cleanliness and situation the appearance of the village is not unpleasing.

Public Buildings

There is nothing to which the term of public building can properly be applied. The library is a plain 2-storey house containing a room on each floor. The upper is used as a library and the lower for holding school in. The extreme dimensions of the house are 24 by 18 feet. It is roughcast and kept neatly whitened. It was erected at the expense of the members of the club.

The Methodists celebrate worship in a house adjoining the national school. It measures 18 by 21 feet, is fitted up with forms and is in bad repair. It was built for the purpose by subscription in 1804.

Hotel

The hotel is a spacious building near the centre of the village. It measures in the exterior 68 by 26 feet and consists of a cellar and 2 lofty storeys. There is stabling for 70 horses attached [to] it. This hotel has been given up and is now occupied as a common ale house. It was enlarged by the Marquis of Donegall in the year 1815, for the accommodation of the members of the Antrim or Doagh Hunt, and it was until within the last 4 years admirably kept up. This hotel was originally built in 1799 by the late Edward Jones Agnew Esquire.

Manufactories

The manufactories of Doagh are confined to 2 beetling or bleach mills and a flax mill, on rather a limited scale, and a forge, where every variety of iron work, including steam engines, iron fittings etc., of the best description are manufactured. 16 hands are employed at this forge.

SOCIAL ECONOMY

Book Club

A book club was formed in Doagh in 1754 from among the inhabitants of the adjacent districts. In 1798 their library room was burned by the king's troops, in consequence of the active part the people [took] in the rebellion of that year. It was, however, soon after rebuilt by the members, and at present contains 800 volumes of very well selected works on every useful subject, novels, etc. There are 30 members who pay 3 pounds entrance and 1s 6d per quarter. The club continues to thrive. Its effects have proved most beneficial and are manifest in the tastes and pursuits of the people. A strong spirit for acquiring knowledge has been excited by it.

Trade

There is neither trade nor commerce of any kind in Doagh, the petty shops supplying nothing beyond the mere necessaries of its inhabitants.

Population

The population amount to 195 individuals, all of whom are of the humbler class and are engaged in some trade or dealing, or as farmers on a small scale. Almost all, in addition to their business, hold a little land. They are [a] peaceable and respectable class, and, particularly the more affluent, are enlightened and well informed; see Table of Trades and Occupations.

Commodities

Belfast is the mart from whence the inhabitants are supplied with their commodities, either for sale by retail or for private use. The carriage of goods from thence costs 6d per cwt.

Building Materials

Lime is procured from the kilns in Carnmoney, on the way to Belfast and 5 and a half miles distant. It costs, when laid down, 14d per barrel. Stone of an excellent quality is everywhere abundant in the neighbourhood.

A cow's grass in the vicinity of the village costs 3 pounds 10s for the summer.

Schools and Dispensary

There is a day school partly supported by the Board of National Education and by an annual bequest of 2 pounds 2s per annum from the late Edward Jones Agnew of Kilwaughter Castle, Esquire. 45 children are at present being educated at it. There is also a night school, in the evening, in the same house, at which 23 adults are at present receiving instruction.

A dispensary for the relief of the poor of this and some of the surrounding parishes was established here on the 1st April 1835 and has since been supported by equal sums locally subscribed and granted by the county grand jury. It has been a most useful institution in this retired district, but as yet its effects have not been perceptible.

Remarks on Doagh

Doagh has not within memory been of greater extent than it now is, but it is said that extensive foundations have been dug up in several spots about it. It has in its petty business greatly declined since the dissolution of the hunt club, which was the means of circulating a good deal of money among all classes. The farmers are not worse off than formerly, but the dealers and persons formerly employed about the hotel have felt its loss severely.

MODERN TOPOGRAPHY

Gentlemen's Seats

Fisherwick, the residence of James Agnew Esquire, J.P., is situated on the southern side of the grange and immediately adjoining the eastern side of the village of Doagh. The house is an elegant and uniform structure in the cottage style, forming with the offices a spacious quadrangular enclosure. It contains a regular suite of handsome apartments and is constructed and finished in the most modern style. The demesne and pleasure grounds, which are principally under pasture or meadow land, contain [blank] acres and are enclosed by a [blank] foot wall. A deep belt of thriving planting encircles the entire demesne, which is still further ornamented by numerous tastefully disposed clumps, principally consisting of fir, larch and beech, but also containing almost every variety of forest tree. The pleasure grounds about the house are very well laid out. Immediately in front of it is a handsomely formed artificial pond. The gardens are not extensive.

Fisherwick was built as a hunting residence in the year 180[remaining figure blank] by the Marquis of Donegall, who until within a few years back kept a very extensive hunting establishment at it.

Machinery and Manufactures

The machinery and manufactories of the grange

consist of 1 mill for beetling linen, 1 mill for washing linen, 1 paper mill, 2 corn mills, 1 flax mill and 1 forge for the manufacturing of machinery.

The beetling mill adjoins the village of Doagh and is situated on the Doagh river. The house is 2-storeys and measures in the clear 45 by 24 feet. The machinery is propelled by a breast water wheel 26 feet in diameter and 6 feet 2 inches broad, having a fall of water of 18 feet. This mill is the property of Mr Hugh Swan. It was established in 1835, previous to which it had been used as a corn mill.

The bleach mill, the property of Mr Henry Bragg, is situated in the same townland and on the same stream. The machinery is contained in a 2-storey house measuring 60 by 21 feet and is propelled by a breast water wheel 13 feet in diameter and 3 feet broad, having a fall of water of 6 feet.

The paper mill is situated on the Six Mile Water and in the townland of Ballyclare. It consists of 3 lofts and measures 36 by 30 and a half feet. The machinery, which is modern, is propelled by 2 breast water wheels, one of which measures 24 feet in diameter by 12 feet broad and has a fall of water of 21 feet. The other is 16 feet in diameter and 2 feet broad, and has a fall of water of 16 feet. The lesser engine wheels are of metal. 32 men and 15 women are employed at this establishment.

This paper mill is the property of Mr Robert Greenfield, by whom it was converted from a flour mill to its present purpose in 1836.

One of the corn mills almost adjoins the paper mill and is the property of the same person. It is 2-storeys high and measures externally 31 by 21 feet. The machinery is propelled by a breast water wheel 14 feet in diameter and 2 feet broad, having a fall of water of 14 feet. This mill is double geared. It has been nearly 150 years established, but was rebuilt of stone about 20 years ago.

The second corn mill is situated in the townland of Kilbride and on the Doagh river. The house containing the machinery is 3-storeys high and measures in the clear 62 by 26 feet. It is well built of stone and lime, and slated. The machinery is propelled by a breast water wheel 14 feet in diameter and 6 feet broad, having a fall of water of 14 feet. 2 extensive corn kilns with iron heads are attached to this mill. It was built in the year 1823 and is now the property of Mr William McFerran.

The flax mill, the property of Mr Hugh Swan, is situated on the Doagh river and in the townland of Doagh. The house consists of a single storey and is thatched. The machinery is propelled by a breast water wheel 14 feet in diameter by 1 foot 6 inches broad, having a fall of water of 13 feet.

Forge

The forge is situated in the townland of Doagh and on the Doagh river. It was built and established by its present proprietor, Mr John Rowan, in 1824. It consists of a neat quadrangular enclosure, measuring in the extreme 100 by 80 feet, containing the workshops and sheds which occupy 3 of its sides. The turning and fitting-up shop measures 35 by 16 feet, the grinding shop 25 by 10, and 2 other apartments or rooms 45 by 18 and 29 by 18 feet. The machinery is altogether propelled by water power. An undershot water wheel 16 feet in diameter and 2 feet 6 inches broad, equal to 6 horsepower, works it.

This establishment is kept in the neatest order and exhibits considerable economy of time and labour. All manner of fittings for machinery, steam engines, farming implements and ordinary smith work are executed here in a superior manner. Mr Rowan is a self-taught mechanic, and all his workmen (including his 3 sons), 16 in number, have served their apprenticeships to him.

There is not any obstruction to the erection of machinery in the grange.

Communications: Roads

There are 3 miles and 2 furlongs of main and 4 miles of by-roads in the grange, which afford ample means of intercourse between it and the neighbouring towns and districts, and are sufficiently numerous. They are all kept in repair at the expense of the barony of Upper Antrim.

The main roads are: that from Antrim to Ballyclare through Doagh, which passes in an almost right line for 2 miles along the southern side of the grange. Its average breadth is 21 feet. Its direction is pretty good, but it is not level nor is it kept in good repair. This road was in ancient times the only one in the grange and was the leading road between the towns of Antrim and Carrickfergus. It is now but little used by vehicles, the road from Antrim through Templepatrick to Ballyclare and Carrickfergus being much more preferable.

A road from Kells and Connor to Belfast through the village of Doagh passes for 7 furlongs through the western side of the grange. Its average breadth is 21 feet. Its direction so far as this grange is concerned is good. It is hilly, but is kept in pretty good repair. It is quite sufficient for the wants of the country.

A road from Broughshane through Ballyclare to Belfast passes for 1 mile and 3 furlongs from north west to south east along the eastern side of the grange. Its average breadth is 20 feet. For a considerable distance in this and the adjoining parishes the direction of this road is almost rectilinear, but it is badly and injudiciously laid out, being hilly, and is kept in but middling repair. There is but little traffic on it in consequence of its inequality, carriers and others preferring to go a considerable distance round by the road through Kells and Connor.

The by-roads average 17 feet in width and are generally in pretty good repair, but they are not judiciously laid out, either with respect to their direction or the inequality of the ground, and are therefore hilly. They are scarcely sufficiently numerous. A well-constructed by-road through the centre of the grange from north to south would be a matter of accommodation to the farmers and be attended with beneficial results to the grange.

The material used in the repair of the roads in the grange is broken whinstone, which is everywhere abundant. The roads seem to be permitted to run too far into bad order before any attempt is made to repair them.

Bridges

There are 7 bridges in the grange, namely 2 over the Six Mile Water and 4 over the Doagh river. They are sufficiently numerous and conveniently situated.

The bridge over the Six Mile Water on the road from Ballyclare to Belfast consists of 4 circular-segment arches and measures 151 feet in length and 21 feet in width.

The bridge over the same stream on the road from Doagh to Belfast consists of 2 small circular-segment arches and measures 165 feet in length and 21 feet in width.

The bridge across the Doagh river on the road from Doagh to Antrim consists of 3 circular-segment arches and measures 120 feet long and 18 feet wide.

The bridge over the same stream on the road from the village of Doagh to Ballymena, across the same stream, consists of 2 circular-segment arches and measures 36 feet long and 21 feet wide.

The bridge on the by-road from near the village of Doagh, and between the last 2 bridges across the same stream, consists of 3 circular-segment arches and measures 50 feet in length and 21 feet in width.

The fourth bridge is further up the stream by [?] 1 mile. It consists of 2 circular-segment arches and measures 36 feet long and 21 feet wide.

The fifth bridge is a quarter of a mile further up the same stream, consists of 2 circular-segment arches and measures 21 feet in width and 42 feet in length.

General Appearance and Scenery

The southern districts are fertile, well cultivated, thickly populated and prettily interspersed with planting. The demesne and extensive plantations about Fisherwick add considerably to the appearance of this district of the grange. Along the banks of the Doagh river, which bounds its eastern side, there [is] every indication of comfort in the substantial and neat residences of the farmers, and of civilisation and improvement in the advanced state of agriculture, the fields being tolerably spacious, well laid down and enclosed, and evidently fertile.

In the northern districts of the grange the aspect of the country is bare from the want of planting and uninteresting from its being less thickly inhabited. The adjoining northern districts are almost wholly mountainous and tend, still further, to diminish the appearance of this portion of the grange.

SOCIAL ECONOMY

Early Improvements

The grange of Doagh constitutes a portion of the vast estates which were granted by James I to the Chichesters, the ancestors of the Marquis of Donegall, the present proprietor. It is included in the manor of Moylinny and barony of Upper Antrim. There are, in the several forts and coves in the grange, indications of its having at a very early period been inhabited. The ruins of a church, said to have been a monastery of black friars, and from which (dhu) the grange derived its name, would indicate its having at a later period been frequented. It is also said that the forts in this and the adjoining parish of Rashee were thrown up by the Danes, one column of whom landed at Larne and from thence proceeded to the interior of the country by the valley watered by the Larne river, which is a continuation of that of the Six Mile Water. [Insert footnote: This tradition I had several years ago from a very old man near Larne].

During the latter part of the 16th and during the 17th century this grange became, in common with the surrounding districts, an exclusively Scottish colony. Its proximity to the then important garrison of Carrickfergus, and its situation along the road from that [town] to those of Toome and Antrim, rendered it considerably frequented in those days; and from its extreme fertility (the valley having principally been mensal lands) and its delightful situation, it is probable that it was among the earliest of the colonised districts.

The early settlers seem to have been something more than mere adventurers. The extent of the holdings and their general cultivation, the size of the houses and their description, and the names of the different localities and of some of the townlands, which would seem to have been the portion allotted to the family whose name they bore, are indications of this circumstance. The results attendant upon such an event have in this been similar to those in the adjoining districts, and to it may undoubtedly be attributed the numerous subsequent events which have from time affected the social, moral or political state of the inhabitants.

The first was the foundation of congregations by the ministers who came with the groups from Scotland, and by those who came over in 1611, the consequent erection of meeting houses, the establishment of schools, which seems to have been coeval with the latter, and the peace and quiet which ensued the peopling of the country by an industrious and civilised race.

The construction of roads, which took place within a century, seems to have been the next step towards improvement, for previously the grange and most of the district in this side of the Six Mile Water had but 1 road, namely that from Carrickfergus to Belfast. Now it possesses every facility of intercourse with the neighbouring districts and markets. This has been an important advantage to the grange, the centre of which is within 11 and a half miles of Belfast [and] 12 miles of the seaport town of Larne. The lime-works at Carnmoney are on the road to Belfast and within 7 miles of the grange.

Progress of Improvement

Cultivation has become more general and of a more systematic description of late years. The farmers can now at all times obtain the highest prices for their farm produce, and their milk, butter, grain, potatoes and pork all find their way to the Belfast market. From it in return they bring their timber and coals, and from Carnmoney their lime, which when laid down costs 14d per barrel. Their consequent increased intercourse with the world has also proved beneficial to them, for, being a shrewd and intelligent class, they are always ready to avail themselves of the improvements of others.

Book Club

In 1754 the Doagh Book Club was established. It has been the means of an immensity of good in this neighbourhood, which is looked on as one of the most enlightened, if not the most so, in the county, and even in the neighbouring districts it has excited a taste for acquiring knowledge.

The house containing the library was built by the members of the club. In 1798, owing to the disaffection of the inhabitants, it was burned down by the king's troops, and many of the books were destroyed. It was soon after rebuilt and now contains upwards of 800 volumes, upon the most useful, entertaining and religious subjects, besides maps, globes, etc.

The spirit for acquiring knowledge, and the description of information generally sought for here, is unusual in rural districts, and of the effects it has produced there are many striking instances. [Insert footnote: One of these is the person of Mr Rowan of the village of Doagh, who served his apprenticeship in the grange. His sons and journeymen, amounting to 16, were all instructed by him. He never worked elsewhere. Still, this individual constructed a steam-coach on a principle of his own, at a cost of about 1,150 pounds. It succeeded, having run along the roads and in the streets of Belfast. He intended to have taken out a patent for it, but has been discouraged by the expense. He is now employed in making steam engines and other finished machinery for Belfast and the surrounding districts. His forge is at Doagh. His taste for mechanics and his knowledge of mechanism was solely derived from this library].

Mechanics, history and divinity are among the most favourite studies. The formation of this library has led to that of others on a smaller scale, and more within the reach of some of the inhabitants in this grange.

Farming Society

In 1818 a farming society was established here. For 8 years this society was quite distinct from any other and was solely supported by local subscriptions. In 1826 it became connected with the North East Society. On the dissolution of the latter in 1836 it became again a distinct society, and has since continued as such. It at present consists of 45 members from this and the adjacent districts, who annually dine together. There is a

the Presbyterian Church. The remainder are divided between the Established and Romish Churches, and the Methodist Society. The grange is extraparochial. There are not either lay or rectorial tithes. There is no place of worship for the members of the Established Church. The nearest churches are that at Donegore, 4 miles, and that at Ballyeaston, 1 and a half miles from the centre of the grange.

There are 2 congregations of Presbyterians in the grange. One, a Unitarian congregation, is in connection with the Remonstrant Synod; the second is a Covenanting congregation of the Church of Scotland.

The Unitarian congregation worship at the meeting house in Ballyclare. The number of families belonging to it amounts to 120. Many of these come from the adjoining parishes. The annual stipend paid to their minister, the Revd William Heron, is 50 pounds and the regium donum 75 pounds. The Covenanting congregation have no fixed minister, but they are supplied with one by their synod on every second Sunday. A social meeting is held on every alternate Sunday and Thursday at their meeting house at Ballyclare, for the purpose of reading and expounding to each other the Scriptures. On Thursdays these meetings, which commence with and conclude with singing and prayer, begin at 12 and terminate at 3 o'clock. On Sundays they commence at 3 and conclude at 5 o'clock. There are 20 families in connection with this congregation. They have not as yet had a fixed minister here.

One of the Wesleyan Methodist congregations worship at their meeting house in Ballyclare. The usual attendance amounts to about 150 individuals. This congregation was established about 40 years ago. They have no stationed preacher, but are supplied with one by the conference. A social meeting is held at their meeting house on every Thursday evening.

The other Methodist congregation worships at their meeting house in the village of Doagh. It has been about 40 years established. They have no stationed minister, but are supplied by one who visits this place periodically in his circuit. There are about 70 members in connection with this congregation.

The Roman Catholics worship at the chapel at Ballyclare. The number of this persuasion in the grange is very trifling, and almost exclusively consists of labourers and persons who have migrated here in quest of employment about the neighbouring manufactories. Within memory there was scarcely a Roman Catholic in the grange.

The present chapel is the first which has stood here since the Reformation. It was erected in 1833 but is quite unfinished internally. There is no other place of worship for Roman Catholics within 10 miles. A priest attends here on Sundays from Belfast.

Habits of the People

According to the enumerative returns of 1831, the population of the grange of Doagh amounts to 300 families, consisting of 1,654 individuals, giving an average of 5 and a half to a family, and with reference to its extent (2,304 acres 2 roods 7 perches), of 1 individual to 1 and a third acres.

The occupations and habits of the inhabitants of the villages of Ballyclare and Doagh will be found detailed under the head of Towns. Of the rural population, the great majority are employed in agriculture, either as farmers or labourers. A few individuals are employed at manufactories in this and the adjoining districts, and there are about 40 linen weavers. Labourers are not more numerous than is necessary for the cultivation of the soil.

Farming

The size of the farms varies from 6 to 100 acres and averages 40. The system of farming is generally advanced and modern. With the more extensive farmers it is quite Scottish and of an improved and systematic style, potatoes being almost invariably planted by the plough, the farming implements, gates, homesteads and fences being of an improved description, and the cultivation of green crops being now pretty general.

Doagh is still behind the more fertile and almost adjoining grange of Nilteen as respects husbandry and appearance, but it has within the last 10 years undergone a very great improvement and still continues to improve.

Farmhouses

The residences of the better description [of] farmers indicate in their plain but substantial appearance a degree of comfort and independence as to circumstance on the part of their owners. They, as well as all the houses and cottages in the grange, are built of stone and lime. A few of the farmers' houses are 2-storeys high and are slated, but the majority of them are but 1-storey cottages roofed with thatch. All are sufficiently commodious and roomy, and most of them are in good repair. The better description of houses are roughcast and kept neatly whitened, and are lit by sash-frame windows, but almost all the others receive light from 4 or 5 leaden windows.

Most of the houses are situated in a little cluster of trees, and most of them are tolerably neat and cleanly in their appearance and in their internal keeping. The better description of houses are neatly and comfortably fitted up and furnished with modern furniture, each having a comfortable and well-furnished parlour and from 2 to 4 good bedrooms. Most of the houses have neat gardens with some little extent of shrubbery or planting attached to them. There is, however, but little taste for gardening or planting, the consumption of vegetables being but trifling.

Farmers

The farmers, that is those holding farms of from 25 or 30 acres and upwards, are among the most enlightened and civilised of the class to which they belong, though they at the same time possess many peculiarities of character. In their mode of living, in their habitations and in almost everything connected with them, there is a substance and comfort combined with a tolerable share of frugality and homeliness. Without possessing much mental activity, there is a persevering steadiness of purpose and a degree of inquiry and application which more than makes up their deficiency in actual talent. Their determination and perseverance in every pursuit amounts almost to obstinacy and cannot be stemmed. It is almost impossible to rouse or excite them, but still their energies are not less powerful on this account.

Food

Their food is both substantial and excellent, and they consume as much animal food, fresh and salted, as the inhabitants of any rural district. They enjoy much comfort at their meals, which are furnished with more than the mere necessaries of life. Tea is used generally twice a day, and many of them use whiskey almost daily.

There is not much difference between the food of the humbler class of farmers and that of the weavers and labourers. Potatoes constitute the great basis of the diet of all. Meal is less commonly used than formerly, more raw corn being now sent to market. The only difference now consists in the quantity of animal food consumed by them. With the farmers it is but trifling, and limited almost to a little salt or dried meat, while with the others its consumption is seldom, except at Christmas, Easter or on some particular occasion. Their chief food is potatoes and milk, with

salt herrings, meal and eggs. Milk is rather plentiful. Buttermilk is chiefly used by the labourers, who purchase it from the farmer who employs them at 1d ha'penny per gallon in winter and 1d per gallon in summer.

Labourers and Cottiers

The labouring class, being in constant employment, are in pretty comfortable circumstances, but are by no means provident. Their cottages are substantial, dry and warm, built of stone and lime, thatched, lit by from 2 to 3 little lead windows, and consist of 2 apartments which are pretty well furnished. They are less cleanly and neat in appearance than in reality. Few of them are roughcast or whitened, and the use of lime in their interior is but infrequent. Each cottage has a small garden, in which a few early potatoes, some leeks, onions and cabbage are raised.

Few of the cottiers hold land, and still fewer possess a cow. Each family has 1 pig; some of them have 2. These they kill and send to the Belfast market, and with their price pay their rent. They also keep a few hens for laying, but they are not allowed by their landlords to keep geese.

The cottier usually lives on the farm of his employer, to whom he partly pays his rent in labour. The usual rent for a cottage and garden, with permission to keep pigs and poultry (except geese), is from 30s to 40s per annum.

During harvest labourers are fed by their employers, and receive 8d per day besides. Women at this season receive as high wages as the men. During other seasons the latter receive but 6d per day, while men receive 6d per day with their food and 10d per day without it.

The usual wages of a farm servant who lives with his employer are from 3 pounds to 4 pounds 10s half-yearly. The wages of women servants vary from 25s to 30s the half-year. The labouring class are hard-working, honest and peaceable, but they are improvident and fond of whiskey, and have little or no notion of domestic economy or management.

Fuel

The farmers burn coal, which they buy from Belfast, in their parlours and grates, but in their kitchens turf only is used. The latter article is scarce and dear, and almost out of the reach of the poorer classes. It is procured from the bogs in the mountainous districts of the more northern parishes, from 3 to 5 miles distant. It costs, when laid down, 13d per gauge (a cubic yard) in summer and 15d in winter. The cottiers seize on brambles, old hedges, the husks of corn and anything combustible for firing. The hedgerows not unfrequently suffer from their depredations in quest of fuel.

Dress

In no district do the better class of farmers, particularly the females, dress with more taste, and at the same time with more comfort. Their appearance in public is very respectable, and at their dances and entertainments the costumes of the women is very neat and handsome. The clothes of both sexes are well made and put on with no little taste. During the week their attire is plain and homely, but they are by no means negligent in their persons.

Among the labouring class there is the same taste for dress, but they are either in rags or in finery. The men are comfortably and well clad, except during the week, when they and most of the females are slovenly and careless in their persons, and still more so in those of their children, who are half-naked and dirty; but at meeting, at fairs, or at dances it is surprising to see the contrast they then present. On the latter occasions they are nicely dressed in coloured calicos or stuffs, with neat bonnets, shawls, shoes, stockings and gloves. Many of the men, even among the labouring class, have watches, and an umbrella is with both sexes considered a necessary article in their equipment.

Longevity and Marriage

They are not remarkable for being long-lived, but at the same time there are in every townland individuals of from 70 to 80 years of age. About 10 years since, a man named John McClelland died at the age of 95 years, and about 6 years ago Sarah Ardiss died at the age of 90 years. There are several persons still living from 80 to 90 years old.

They are not remarkable for marrying early. Females usually marry at from 18 to 28 and men at from 25 to 35 years of age.

Amusements

The taste for amusement has here, as throughout the neighbourhood, greatly declined, and their recreations have also undergone considerable change for the better. Since the more general introduction of book clubs, cock-fighting has almost disappeared. Horse-races for saddles, bridles or some such stakes were some years ago of frequent occurrence, but latterly they have been given up.

Dancing is now the favourite amusement of all classes. Among the better class of farmers their dances are very well got up and are conducted with decorum. Even among the lower class dances are very rarely attended with excess or riot. Those given at the Doagh library are regulated by strict rules and conducted in a most respectable manner. Quadrilles, reels and country dances are the usual figures. The violin is the only music. There are several dancing schools in the neighbouring districts, and one is occasionally held at the Doagh library.

Attending one or two of the summer fairs in the neighbouring towns is a favourite recreation with all classes. There are a couple of idle days at Christmas and one or two at Easter, which are spent by the lower class chiefly in the ale houses. On the latter occasion, Easter Monday was formerly spent at cock-fights.

There is a great taste for card-playing among the farmers and particularly among the people of Ballyclare. The better class are very social and are in the habit of giving dinner and evening parties, the only amusements at which are drinking and card-playing. The favourite game is "The Fifteen" or "Spoil Five." The sums played for are not large, nor is much money lost or won.

At their entertainments the men drink deeply, but not to actual intoxication. They are "very hard headed" and they, as well as the lower grades, can by no means be termed temperate.

Religious Feeling

There are 5 Masonic lodges in the grange. There is no party feeling, but at the same time there is not in any part of Ireland a district in which there is a stronger or more bigoted antipathy towards the Established Church, or more political feeling. They have not since 1798 ever proceeded to any act of violence, but at the same time they are to a man united against it. They have held their meetings and published their resolutions, and subscriptions have been forwarded to those who are at law with its ministers, and to its bitterest enemy of a creed at variance with their own. Still no tithes have been demanded of, or been paid by, them at any period.

Character of the People

The general character of the people is strictly Scottish. Their accent is broad and unpleasing. Their idioms and old saws savour strongly of the country of their ancestors. Among a few of the better class of farmers their manners are courteous and civil, but with the majority they are cold, stiff and disagreeable, partly from habit, partly from the little intercourse they have with strangers and partly from a notion that they have no superiors and that courtesy is but another term for servility. The last notion is chiefly to be attributed to their independent circumstances, holding leases in perpetuity at trifling rents, and to the information they have obtained by reading, without its being matured by intercourse with the world.

They pique themselves not a little upon their independence, knowledge and liberality. With respect to the former they have some claim, but as to the last they are illiberal and bigoted, particularly on the subject of religion.

With the exception of some of the upper class of farmers, they cannot be termed a strictly moral class. They are not temperate and there is more than a little licentiousness in their morals. It is true that they are regular in their attendance at meeting, but it is equally true that they are quite as regular in their visits to the ale house on that same day. Otherwise the sabbath is strictly observed by them.

They are rather litigious. Their taste for going to law has been greatly encouraged by several public suits and appeals in which they have been engaged, with respect to applotments of cess and tithes. Upon legal matters they are too well versed. In their library *Blackstone's Commentaries*, NcNally's *Justice of the peace* and several other similar works of reference are to be found.

They are very punctual in fulfilling their engagements, and are cautious and canny in their transactions and dealings. The lower class are very honest and peaceable, except while under the influence of whiskey, when they are riotous, quarrelsome and obstinate, without possessing one particle of humour, fun or good nature.

Appearance

The men are above the middle stature and are generally tall and rather well made. They are sinewy and capable of undergoing much fatigue. They are calculated to make capital soldiers, but scarcely any inducement could tempt them to enlist.

The women are generally comely, but lose their looks at an early age. Their cheek-bones are high and their features are strongly marked. In those respects they retain the characteristics of their Scottish ancestry.

Emigration and Migration

During the last 3 years only 17 individuals have emigrated from this grange. North America was the destination of 1 of these, the United States of America that of 14 and Glasgow that of 2. None of the emigrants have returned. The capital taken out of the country by them was trifling. Emigration is greatly on the decline here; see Emigration Tables, Appendix.

There are 4 individuals who occasionally go to Scotland in search of employment during harvest, and return when it is over. They are young unmarried men.

ANCIENT TOPOGRAPHY

Ecclesiastical History

The grange of Doagh is now extraparochial. In ancient times it constituted the mensal lands of the monastery of Doagh, which according to some was in connection with the celebrated abbey of Muckamore (8 miles distant) and by others is said to have belonged to the great abbey of Connor, 9 miles north of it. For an extent of 9 and a half miles, including that portion of it west of this grange, the valley of the Six Mile Water had, since the 6th century, been the property of the church and formed the mensal lands of the numerous religious establishments which formerly existed in it.

From various old documents and leases it seems to have at an early period [been], as it still is, one of the most fertile districts in the county and to have been equally remarkable for its peaceful and retired situation and picturesque scenery. The woods and forests which once adorned it, and from which the river derived its ancient name (the Amhuin-na-Fiodh, "the river of the woods"), no longer exist; but on the other hand there is not an acre of waste or uncultivated ground in it, west of this grange.

The granges of Doagh, Ballywalter, Nilteen and Muckamore, and the parish of Templepatrick, which had been mensal lands, occupy with a trifling exception the portion of the valley of the Six Mile Water extending westward from this grange to the shore of Lough Neagh.

The grange is said to have derived its original name Dhu signifying "black", corrupted into Doagh, from a monastery of black friars which formerly stood in or near the old burial ground. When, or by whom, the monastery was built or destroyed is not locally known. The only remains are the burial ground, containing the foundations and a small fragment of the wall of some very old building.

Burial Ground

The burial ground includes a quadrangular space of 109 by 133 feet, pretty well enclosed by a quickset fence with a small iron gate. The graves are very numerous, but are kept in rows without being crowded. Its surface is tolerably level and it is altogether rather decently kept. There are not any old tombs or headstones. No particular family nor one of any note bury here. It is the usual place of interment for the people of the neighbourhood.

Ancient Church

The foundations of the church stand east and west. They measure in the extreme 60 by 26 feet. The walls are 4 feet thick. They are now faintly discernible, being lower than the surface of the ground, except at the western end where a mutilated fragment of the wall, 8 feet high, 6 feet long and 4 feet thick, deprived of most of its facing stones, still remains. Its masonry is of the very rudest description. The stones are not laid in courses; the largest stone above the foundations does not exceed 12 by 10 inches. They are all rude and undressed. There are no quarry stones and only such as are water-worn or field stones from 3 to 8 lbs weight.

The specimen of the masonry given includes all that remains of the facing stone, the remainder having from time to time fallen off, leaving the centre or heart of the wall, which consists of a mass of small stones from 1 to 4 lbs weight, confusedly thrown together but firmly cemented by an abundance of coarse mortar or grouting which, as it does not appear in the face of the wall or among the outside stones, has evidently been poured into the heart of the wall in a liquid state. There is not any indication of the positions of the doors or windows.

A great number of dressed and faced stones, and some which are moulded or sculptured, have been found about the graveyard but have been removed. Some are still in its vicinity and a few are standing as headstones. They are chiefly of Tardree stone, a species of white porphyry from Tardree quarry in the parish of Connor, 6 miles distant. A few of the merely faced or dressed stones, such as may have been used as door or window-jambs, are of basalt or trap. One of these, a square column with 4 smooth and equal sides 11 inches square, measures 3 feet 10 inches long. Another, presenting 1 face of 15 inches and an-

other of 10, measures 9 feet in length. The other stones are of much lesser dimensions, being mostly from 12 to [blank] inches long and from 6 to 8 inches square. They are smoothly cut and some of them are slightly sculptured (see drawings).

A considerable portion of the walls have fallen within memory and the site of the church is now occupied with graves.

Rath and Coves

A circular earthen rath is situated 30 feet west of the burial ground and on the verge of a precipitous bank 30 feet high which overhangs the Doagh river. In a field separated by a highway from the eastern side of the burial ground are several very large coves, one of which is said to extend underneath the church. A description of them will be found hereafter, and a plan of the ground will be found in Appendix.

Military and Pagan Remains

There are not any military remains in the grange, nor have any been remembered in it. The pagan antiquities of the grange are confined to some coves now closed up and 1 fort.

Coves

The grange of Doagh formerly abounded in coves. In the townland of Doagh 5 coves have been demolished and 8 closed up, and in the townland of Ballyclare 2 have been destroyed and 4 closed up within memory. None are now open. The coves about a fort in the townland of Doagh, which were almost totally removed, were very extensive, containing many chambers. It is said that a vast number of silver coins were found in them, but this is to be doubted.

The coves in a field immediately to the east of the old graveyard at Doagh were closed about 8 years ago. From the description given of them by several persons who explored them, they must be on an unusually extensive scale. They are said to contain more than a dozen chambers connected with each other by narrow passages, through which a man can, with difficulty, creep. In one of these coves the chambers measure 6 feet wide at the bottom and 3 at the roof, and are 8 feet high. In some of the others the chambers are 6 feet 6 inches high and 6 feet wide at the bottom. Their style of construction is precisely similar to that usual in such structures. Their floors are of earth and are smoothly and carefully formed.

White ashes of turf were found in several of them. In one a large heap of ashes, occupying the centre of the floor, was found. Around the heap were 3 smooth stones, which had evidently been used as seats.

The only other remains discovered in them were little clay pipes not unlike those now in use, and a few stone hatchets; but in the fields about them quantities of flint arrowheads, stone hatchets, clay pipes and a few silver coins have been picked up. No querns were found about these coves. One gallery is said by some to extend from the field into the burial ground to the foundations of the church, an extreme distance of 140 feet.

In addition to their being covered up these coves were, by means of a drain, converted into a receptacle for the waters of a neighbouring cesspool, which now utterly precludes their entrance.

Forts

Within memory 9 earthen raths have been demolished in this grange. One of them in the townland of Doagh contained a gallery, which also was destroyed.

The only fort now remaining is that near the old burial ground at the village of Doagh, of which a plan will be found in Appendix. It is situated on the summit of a precipitous bank overhanging the Doagh river, above which it is elevated 30 feet. On its opposite side, and within 30 feet of it, is the burial ground. On this side the fort is only 6 feet high. Its form is circular. It is 64 feet in diameter and is constructed solely of earth. It has not any outworks or defences, nor have any remains, except the burial ground and church, which do not seem to have been connected with it, been remembered about it.

Miscellaneous Discoveries

The only articles of antiquity which have been found in the grange are clay pipes, similar to those now used, only much thicker and shorter on the shank. These are not only found in the coves but also in the field. Stone hatchets and flint arrowheads of various sizes and degrees of finish have been found in the vicinity of the forts and coves.

It is said that great numbers of coins, of what reign it is not known, have from time to time been picked up throughout the grange; but these, as well as all the other articles alluded to, have either been lost or found their way into some of the collections in Belfast.

Several querns, some of which were ornamented, were found in some of the forts which have been demolished.

There are about 30 old hawthorns scattered throughout the grange. Some of them are large, but they do not in their positions bear any reference to each other.

Ancient Park

A small portion of an ancient fence known as the Thorn Dyke, which enclosed an extensive park, is still to be seen in the townland of Ballyclare, in the southern side of the grange. This dyke commenced at the Six Mile Water and, proceeding in a right line northwards, intersected the road from Ballyclare to Doagh at a place still known as the Thorn Dyke, about half-way between them. It then proceeded westward in a right line across the parish of Kilbride to Donegore hill in the parish of Donegore, where it struck off towards the south and, passing through the site of the present village of Parkgate, terminated at the Six Mile Water, at a point 3 miles and 3 furlongs below that at which it commenced.

The space included by it extended about 3 miles from east to west and 2 miles from north to south. It had 2 gates, one on the road near the Thorn Dyke in this grange, which is still known as the Parkgate. The second was on the site of the present village of Parkgate (to which it gave the name) in the parish of Donegore and on the same road. A toll of 1 ha'penny was paid by each person passing through either gate. Portions of the dyke (which is said to have been planted with enormous sloe thorns) are still to be traced in the adjoining parish of Kilbride. It is from 5 to 7 feet thick and rudely constructed of stones and earth.

This park is said to have been formed by Sir Arthur Chichester, Lord Deputy of Ireland, in the reign of James I, but whether it was public or private property is not locally known.

Appendix to Memoir by James Boyle

SOCIAL AND PRODUCTIVE ECONOMY

Ballyclare: Table of Trades and Occuptions

Attorney 1, apothecaries and surgeons 3, baker 1, besommaker 1, blacksmiths 2, bonnetmakers 1, butchers 3, car drivers 1, carriers and carmen 3, carpenters 2, clerks of meeting houses 2, cobblers 1, constabulary 3, dressmakers 2, dyers (blue) 1, linen drapers 1, woollen drapers 3, excise officer 1, excise officer superannuated 1, farmers 3, farmer and chandler 1, flax dresser 1, grocers 12, hosiers 1, hucksters 3, innkeepers and publicans 12, keepers of lodging houses 4, labourers 22, leather cutters 1, masons 2, general mechanic 1, nailers 2, paupers 2, pensioners 2, postmaster 1, ragmen 2, reedmakers 2, saddlers 2, schoolmasters 2, schoolmistresses 2, shoemakers 3, slaters 1, tailors 2, tinsmiths 2, victualling and provision dealer 1, wheelwright 1, widows, old and unemployed 11, total 134.

Doagh: Table of Trades and Occupations

Carmen 1, carpenters 2, cotton printers 1, farmers 5, grocers 2, innkeepers and publicans 2, labourers, agricultural 6, labourers employed at bleach green 1, milliners and dressmakers 2, surgeons 2, schoolmasters 2, smiths, general 1, weavers, linen 3, wheelwright 1, widows, old and unemployed 3, total 33.

Doagh Dispensary: Accounts

This dispensary was established in April 1835.

Receipts and expenditure from 1st April 1835 to 11th January 1836. Receipts: amount of subscriptions 41 pounds 13s 6d, presented by the county grand jury 41 pounds 13s 6d, total 83 pounds 6s. Disbursements: expenses including house rent, medicine, printing and an attendant 72 pounds 9s 6d, surgeon's salary 10 pounds 16s 6d, total 83 pounds 6s.

Receipts and expenditure from 11th January 1837 to 5th March 1838. Receipts: amount of subscriptions 43 pounds 9s, sum presented by the county grand jury 43 pounds 9s, total 86 pounds 18s. Disbursements: medicine 23 pounds 2s 2d, house rent 7 pounds, surgeon's salary 46 pounds 10d, attendant or porter 5 pounds 4s, stationery 1 pound 5s, printing and advertising 3 pounds, incidental expenses 2 pounds 6s, total 86 pounds 18s.

NB From the manner in which the books have been kept, and in consequence of the destruction of some documents, this is the only information which can be given respecting the funds of this dispensary. The papers relating to the year 1836 have been lost.

Patients at Dispensary

From 1st April 1835 until 11th January 1836 the number of patients treated was 261. Of these, 212 were visited at their own houses, [blank] were treated at the dispensary, 8 died and 41 remained on the books. During the same period 1,025 prescriptions were filled.

From 19th January 1837 until 5th March 1838 the number of patients admitted was 1,003. Of these, 966 were discharged cured, 16 remained on the books, 13 died and 8 were incurable; of these, 183 were treated at their own houses.

The papers containing the reports of this dispensary for the year 1836 have been lost.

Cases at Dispensary

Table of cases treated from 19th January 1837 till 5th March 1838: amenorrhoea 4, asthma 20, abscess 4, boils 6, burns 10, blood, spitting of 6, bronchocele 1, catarrh 11, colica 4, cancer 1, constipation 26, cough, chronic 22, croup 2, diarrhoea 58, deafness 3, debility 20, dyspepsia 22, dysuria 3, dysmenorrhoea 15, erysipelas 10, eruptions, cutaneous 30, epilepsy 1, fever 90, fractures 6, flatulence 6, gravel 2, haemorrhoids 6, whooping <hooping> cough 20, hysteria 9, inflammation of the throat 6, inflammation of the bowels 2, inflammation of the eyes 20, indigestion 60, influenza 90, jaundice 2, diseases of joint 4, leucorrhoea 4, lumbago 20, menorrhagia 2, measles 1, neuralgia 2, opthalmia 3, odontalgia 2, palpitations 20, psora 78, paralysis 6, pneumonia 4, quinsy 2, retention of urine 7, rheumatism 50, scrofula 6, scabies 4, smallpox 10, sprains 16, toothache 20, ulcers 32, vomiting 3, vertigo 6, worms 70, wounds 20, [total] 992.

Original Clergy

No authentic or accurate record of the Presbyterian clergy of Ballyclare, nor of the dates of their ordination to the congregation, have been preserved. Their names as they occurred in succession only are known. The first was the Revd Futt, who was succeeded by the Revd Thomas Wilson, the Revd James Marshall, the Revd Futt Marshall and the Revd William Heron, the present minister, who was ordained to the congregation in 1816.

The Covenanters have not had any fixed minister, but have been supplied with preaching by ministers sent by the synod on every alternate Sunday.

The Methodists have not had any resident ministers. Doagh and Ballyclare are included in circuits to which preachers are attached, who visit periodically each of the congregations under their superintendence.

Farming Society

The Doagh Farming Society is at present constituted of 45 members from the grange of Doagh and the adjacent granges and parishes. It was established in 1818 and in 1826 became connected with the North East Farming Society, and continued in connection with it until its dissolution in 1836, since which period it has been again dependent on its own funds. During the existence of the North East Society it received from it a sum equal to that locally contributed, which for the 7 years previous to 1838 amounted annually to 14 pounds. In 1838 the sums subscribed amounted to but 13 pounds. The subscriptions vary from 5s to 1 pound per annum. There are but 4 subscribers of the latter sum, and almost all the others are of the former. In 1831 the number of members was 45, in 1837 it was 50 and in 1838, 48.

The society meets twice a year at the village of Parkgate. The meetings were, until about 2 years since, held in the village of Doagh. A ploughing match takes place at the winter meeting, and the cattle show at that held in autumn.

Prizes of from 5s to 25s are given to the best ploughmen. For the best brood mare and foal 10s, second best brood mare and foal 5s. For the best 2-year old colt or filly 10s, for the best 1-year old colt or filly 7s 6d. For the best milch cow for dairy 10s, second best milch cow for dairy 5s, for the best grass fed cow 10s. For the best bull 10s, for the best 2-year old bull 7s 6d, for the best 1-year old bull 5s. For the best 2-year old heifer 7s 6d. For the best calf according to age 5s. For the best ewe and lamb 7s 6d, for the best ram 5s. For the best sow for breeding 7s 6d, for the best boar 5s. For the best firkin of butter 7s 6d, for the second best firkin of butter 5s. Challenges to produce the best crops of different kinds, and cattle, also take place at these meetings.

Emigration Table

[Table contains the following headings: year, age, capital, occupation and religion of emigrants].

1836: 1 under 40 and over 30 years, 3 under 30 and over 20, 1 under 20 and over 10; capital: 1 under 100 and over 50 pounds, 1 under 50 and over 20 pounds, 3 under 10 pounds; 1 farmer, 1 tradesman or mechanic, 2 labourers, 1 other; 3 Presbyterians, 2 Roman Catholic, 5 males, total 5.

1837: 1 under 40 and over 30 years, 3 under 30 and over 20; capital: 1 over 100 and under 50 pounds, 2 under 20 and over 10 pounds, 4 under 10 pounds; 2 farmers, 1 labourer, 4 others; 7 Presbyterians, 4 males, 3 females, total 7.

1838: 1 over 50 years, 2 under 40 over 30, 2 under 10; capital: 1 under 50 and over 20 pounds, 4 under 10 pounds; 1 farmer, 1 tradesman or mechanic, 1 labourer, 2 others; 4 Presbyterians, 1 Roman Catholic, 3 males, 2 females, total 5.

Traditions

It is said that the former name of Ballyclare was Ballybullion and that it derived it from the circumstance of there having been a sort of stage or "foot-go" across the river where the bridge now stands, by which pedestrians crossed the stream while their horses carrying panniers walked alongside. It is said that this led to the erection of the town.

It is said that at the time of the erection of the Thorn Dyke there was not a white hawthorn in this country, and that the first introduced to it were those brought from Dublin about the year 1630, when they cost 1 guinea a thousand. They were planted in a farm in the townland of Kilbride and were soon afterwards stolen.

National Schools

[Table contains the following headings: name, situation and description, when established, income and expenditure, physical, intellectual and moral education, number of pupils subdivided by age, sex and religion, name and religion of master and mistress].

Held in a schoolroom 22 by 16 feet, the property of the Doagh Book Club, by whom the house was built about the year 1754; the room is too small for the purpose. The room is given gratis by the club; it is situated in the village of Doagh. This school has been established for nearly a century; it was placed under the Board of National Education in 1832; income: 10 pounds per annum from the Board of National Education and 2 pounds 2s from the heirs of the late Edward Jones Agnew of Kilwaughter, Esq., [total] 12 pounds 2s, from pupils 30 pounds; expenditure on salaries: the teachers receive the sums paid by scholars and contributed by benevolent societies and individuals, [total] 42 pounds 2s; intellectual instruction: spelling, reading, writing, arithmetic, geography, English grammar, mensuration, algebra, books of the Board of National Education; moral instruction: Authorised Version of Scriptures and Presbyterian and Church of England catechisms at stated hours; visited by the Revd William Heron, Unitarian minister; number of pupils: males, 14 under 10 years of age, 4 from 10 to 15, 18 total males; females, 16 under 10 years of age, 10 from 10 to 15, 1 above 15, 27 total females; total number of pupils 45, 6 Established Church, 39 Presbyterians; master William Johnson, Presbyterian; visited 20th December 1838.

Held in a thatched house, the schoolroom measuring 16 by 16 feet, being too small for the purpose, situated in the village of Ballyclare; established 1838; income: from the Board of National Education annually 8 pounds, from pupils 10 pounds; expenditure on salaries: 18 pounds; intellectual instruction: spelling, reading, writing, arithmetic, geography, English grammar, algebra, books of the Board of National Education; moral instruction: Authorised Version of Scripture and Presbyterian and Church of England catechisms at stated hours; visited by the Revd William Heron, Unitarian minister; number of pupils: males, 10 under 10 years of age, 7 from 10 to 15, 10 above 15, 27 total males; females, 15 under 10 years of age, 8 from 10 to 15, 23 total females; total number of pupils 50, 28 Presbyterians, 16 Roman Catholics, 6 other denominations; master Thomas Kelly, Presbyterian; visited 18th December 1838.

Private Schools

Held in the national schoolroom during the winter evenings, situated in the village of Doagh; established 1831; income from pupils 4 pounds 16s; expenditure on salaries 4 pounds 16s; intellectual instruction: books of the day school are used; writing, arithmetic, book-keeping, grammar, mensuration; number of pupils: males, 5 from 10 to 15 years of age, 11 above 15, 16 total males; females, 1 under 10 years of age, 2 from 10 to 15, 5 above 15, 8 total females; total number of pupils 24, all Presbyterians; master William Johnson, Presbyterian; visited 20th December 1838.

Held in a private room 16 feet by 10 feet, the property of the teacher, situated in the village of Ballyclare; established 1831; income from pupils 8 pounds; expenditure on salaries 8 pounds; intellectual instruction: *Manson's Primer and spelling books, Gough's Arithmetic*, writing, reading, *Murray's Grammar*; moral instruction: Authorised Version of Scriptures and church catechism on Saturdays by the teacher; number of pupils: males, 11 under 10 years of age, 6 from 10 to 15, 17 total males; females, 3 under 10 years of age, 3 total females; total number of pupils 20, 3 Established Church, 14 Presbyterians, 3 Roman Catholics; master Patrick Gault, Presbyterian; visited 13th December 1838.

Held in a room 12 feet square, the property of the teacher, situated in the village of Ballyclare; established 1832; income from pupils 6 pounds; expenditure on salaries 6 pounds; intellectual instruction: spelling and reading in *Manson's Primer and spelling book*; moral instruction: reading, Authorised Version of Scriptures; number of pupils: males, 12 under 10 years of age, 12 total males; females, 8 under 10 years of age, 8 total females; total number of pupils 20, 8 Established Church, 8 Presbyterians, 4 Roman Catholics;

mistress Martha Henderson, Presbyterian; visited 13th December 1838.

Held in the schoolroom in the lower part of the Methodist meeting house in the village of Ballyclare; established 1838; income from pupils 8 pounds; expenditure on salaries 8 pounds; intellectual instruction: this is an infant school; *Manson's Primer and spelling books* are the only books used; moral instruction: Authorised Version of Scriptures read daily; visited by Miss Bell (a Methodist), who questions the children; number of pupils: males, 14 under 10 years of age, 14 total males; females, 9 under 10 years of age, 5 from 10 to 15, 14 total females; total number of pupils 28, 22 Presbyterians, 3 Roman Catholics, 3 other denominations; mistress Mary Curran, Methodist; visited 12th December 1838.

[Totals]: income from public societies or benevolent individuals 20 pounds 2s, from pupils 66 pounds 16s; expenditure on salaries 86 pounds 18s; number of pupils: males, 61 under 10 years of age, 22 from 10 to 15, 21 above 15, 104 total males; females, 52 under 10 years of age, 25 from 10 to 15, 6 over 15, 83 total males; total number of pupils 187, 17 Established Church, 135 Presbyterians, 26 Roman Catholics, 9 other denominations.

Sunday Schools

[Table contains the following headings: situation and description, when established, teachers, superintendence, number of scholars, instructions, hours of attendance, remarks].

Held in the Methodist chapel in the village of Ballyclare, established 1838; 1 male and 2 female teachers, total 3; superintended by Mr Samuel Thompson, a Methodist; number of scholars: 10 Established Church, 20 Presbyterians, 15 males, 15 females, total 30; instructions: spelling and reading the Scriptures and books given by the Sunday School Society; hours of attendance from 2 till 4 p.m.; commences and concludes with singing and prayer.

Held in the room in which one of the private day schools in the village of Ballyclare is held, established 1838; 1 teacher, female; superintended and taught by Mrs Martha Henderson, the teacher of the day school; number of scholars: 8 Presbyterians, 4 Roman Catholics, 2 males, 10 females, total 12; instructions: the books used are the Scriptures and those used at the day school; hours of attendance from 10 a.m. till 3 p.m.; the teacher of the day school is the only person who attends here.

Held in the Roman Catholic chapel at the

village of Ballyclare, established 1832; 1 male and 1 female teacher, total 2; superintended by the Revd Mr Hannah P.P.; number of scholars: 50 Roman Catholics, 36 males, 14 females, total 50, 36 exclusively Sunday school scholars; no scriptural books are used but only those taught at the day school; hours of attendance from 10 a.m. to 1 p.m.; no scriptural education is afforded at this school.

[Totals]: 2 male and 4 female teachers, total 6; number of scholars: 10 Established Church, 28 Presbyterians, 54 Roman Catholics, 53 males, 39 females, total 92, 36 exclusively Sunday school scholars.

Establishment for the Indigent

[Table contains the following headings: name, object, when founded, management, funds from public bodies and private individuals, expenditure, relief afforded, number relieved].

2 day schools and 3 Sunday schools wholly or partly supported by benevolent societies or individuals; object: the suppression of vice by the removal of ignorance and the diffusion of knowledge; founded at various periods; management: by sundry societies, local committees and patrons; funds: from the Board of National Education 18 pounds annually, from the heirs of the late Edward Jones Agnew of Kilwaughter Castle, Esq. annually 2 pounds 2s; expenditure on salaries: the teachers receive the sums contributed by benevolence and also that paid by the scholars; relief afforded: education and school requisites; number relieved: 95 day scholars and 36 children who are exclusively Sunday school scholars are being educated in the grange.

Clothing society; object: to provide clothing and blankets for the poor; founded 1837; managment: by a committee of [?] 2 ladies and 1 gentleman; funds: the average sum annually subscribed (locally) had been 6 pounds 15s; relief afforded: cloaks, petticoats, chemises and blankets; average number annually relieved has been 60.

Dispensary

[Table contains the following headings: name, object, when founded, management, funds from public and private sources, annual expense of management, number relieved, relief afforded, average expense of patients].

Dispensary; object: providing those who are unable to pay for it with medicine and medical advice; founded 1835; managed by a committee

of 10 subscribers of 1 pound each; funds: the average sum annually presented by the county grand jury has been 42 pounds 11s; the average sum annually subscribed has been 42 pounds 11s; annual expense of management: house rent 7 pounds per annum, surgeon's salary 46 pounds; relief afforded: medicines and medical advice; the patients are visited when unable to attend; the average expense of each patient has been 2s 8d.

Ancient Topography

Drawings

Specimen of the masonry of Doagh church, detail of 3 stones with dimensions, scale half an inch to 20 miles. [Insert note: All the stones are drawn to scale].

Annotated plan of the fort, coves and old church of Doagh, scale of 12 inches to a mile.

Draft Memoir by J.R. Ward, April 1835

Natural Features

Hills

Refer to Mr Boyle, [initialled] R.K. Dawson, 18 September 1835. Forwarded to Lieutenant Bennett, 6 February 1839 [signed] James Boyle.

The grange presents no remarkable features. It rises gradually from the Six Mile Water, where it is 164 feet, to the extreme north of it, where its elevation is 406 feet above the sea. A small hill north of Ballyclare, called the Craig hill, is 449 feet.

Lakes and Rivers

Lakes: none.

The Six Mile Water forms the south eastern boundary of the grange for 3 and a half miles (for particulars see parish of Ballylinny). The Doagh river, a considerable stream, forms the western boundary for 2 and a half miles (for particulars see Rashee).

Bogs and Woods

Bogs: there is none in the grange, but there is about 145 acres of wasteland which appears to be a cut-out bog. It is situated in Ballyclare townland.

No natural woods or remains of any. The only growing timber in the grange are the plantations above Fisherwick, once a hunting lodge of the Marquis of Donegall, situated close to the village of Doagh. It is principally fir and ash.

Climate

See accompanying register for 28 days. The crops are the same as in Ballylinny parish.

MODERN TOPOGRAPHY

Towns: Ballyclare

Ballyclare is situated in the townland of the same name, in the south eastern portion of the grange, on the banks of the Six Mile Water. That part of the town which lies on the south side of the river belongs to the parish of Ballynure. The town consists of 1 long street very irregularly built. It is in length [blank] yards and averaging in breadth 45 feet. The surrounding country is fertile and well cultivated, and the scenery is picturesque.

Present State: Buildings

There are 4 places of worship in the town.

A Presbyterian meeting house: is a plain stone building 70 feet long and 36 broad. It will accommodate about 500 persons. The date and expense of building are not known.

A Methodist meeting house: it is a plain stone building 36 feet long and 18 broad. It will accommodate 180 people. It was built in 1834 at an expense of 150 pounds, which was defrayed by subscription.

A Roman Catholic chapel: it is a plain stone building 36 feet long and 24 feet broad. It will hold about 170, though the congregation is not more than 90 persons. It was built in 1833.

A Covenanters' meeting house, which is in the parish of Ballynure. It is a plain stone building 70 feet long and 36 broad. It will accommodate 600 persons. The date and expense of building are 1833 and 200 pounds.

The town, as before said, consists of but 1 very irregularly built street. The houses are small; there is not a good-looking one in it. The general appearance is slovenly. No new houses have been built for several years, nor are there any building at present.

PRODUCTIVE ECONOMY

Occupations

A great part of the people are farm labourers. Some are employed in the mills of the neighbourhood and the remainder dealers, for which see table: publicans 19, grocers 13, doctors or apothecaries 3, saddlers 2, glaziers 2, bookbinders 1, smiths 3, carpenters 4.

Fairs and Markets

Fairs are held here on the second Tuesday after the 12th of the months of May, July and November, and on the last Tuesday in January. They are principally for the sale of cattle and horses.

Markets are held on the third Wednesday in every month, which are supplied with vegetables and cotton merchandise. No tolls are levied.

There are no insurances of any kind, no hospitals or dispensaries, nor any charitable institutions, but it is a post town.

MODERN TOPOGRAPHY

Towns: Doagh

Doagh is a small village situated near the south western extremity of the grange, about 2 miles west of Ballyclare and 90 Irish or 114 and six-eleventh British miles from Dublin. The only public building is a small Methodist meeting house built in 1795. It is capable of holding about 150 people. The congregation is about 60; they have no regular preacher. The building is plain stonework. It is 30 feet long and 20 feet broad, the expense of building not known.

The village is small, containing about 30 stone houses. There is 1 large inn and post house. It is chiefly supported [by] the gentlemen of the Antrim Hunt, who meet there during the season.

Gentlemen's Seats

Fisherwick, once a hunting lodge of the Marquis of Donegall, now the property of Squire Agnew but at present uninhabited, is situated close to the village of Doagh. It was built in 1805. It is of considerable extent and built in the cottage style. There is a large quantity of plantation about it and a lake of 7 acres in the front.

Manufactories and Mills

[Table contains the following headings: townland in which situated, nature of mill, dimensions and nature of wheel].

Doagh, iron works, diameter of wheel 14 feet, breadth 2 feet 6 inches, breast wheel.

Doagh, corn mill, diameter of wheel 14 feet 6 inches, breadth 3 feet 2 inches, overshot wheel.

Doagh, flax mill, diameter of wheel 14 feet, breadth 1 foot 10 inches, breast wheel.

Doagh, beetling mill, diameter of wheel 15 feet 6 inches, breadth 3 feet 7 inches, breast wheel.

Coggrey, corn mill, diameter of wheel 14 feet, breadth 6 feet, breast wheel.

Ballyclare, corn mill, diameter of wheel 14 feet 4 inches, breadth 2 feet 8 inches, breast wheel.

Communications

There are 3 main roads traversing the grange, one from Broughshane through Ballyclare to Belfast, though it is now seldom used for communication between the first and last mentioned towns. Its length in the grange is 1 and a half miles on the east side, and its breadth 28 feet [insert marginal query by J. Boyle: 25 feet?]. It is in good repair.

A second main road from Belfast through Doagh to Ballymena and Broughshane passes through the south west extremity for about 1 mile. Its breadth is 27 feet.

The third, which is from Antrim to Ballyclare, traversing almost parallel to the Six Mile Water for 2 miles: it is about 26 feet broad [insert marginal query: 23 feet?].

These roads were made by the county and are kept in good repair by the half-barony, Upper Antrim.

General Appearance

The general appearance of the grange is fertile and well cultivated. The scenery is rather pretty. The wooded ground of Fisherwick and Holestone relieve the eye of the traveller from that sameness of scenery which is to be met with in the parishes north and east of the grange, while the distant mountains of Divis and Agnew's hill add much to the effect.

SOCIAL ECONOMY

Early Improvements: Agricultural Society

There is an agricultural society which meets in Farrell's Hotel, Doagh, twice in the year. Prizes are given at the first meeting (which generally takes place in the beginning of March) for the best ploughing, and at the second meeting for cattle. The society is composed of persons who must contribute 5s per annum, and a president, who must also be a member of the North East Society in Belfast, of which that held in Doagh is a branch. The amount contributed for the support of the Doagh branch by its members is doubled by the parent society.

Obstructions to improvement: none.

Local Government

The magistrates are James Owens Esquire of Holestone and Thomas Adair Esquire of Loughermore. They are firm and respected by the people. A manor court is held by the Marquis of Donegall's seneschal, Mr Williamson, at Farrell's Hotel, Doagh, once each month, for the trial of petty cases.

Dispensaries: it is intended to establish one in Doagh.

Schools

[Table contains the following headings: name of townland in which situated, number of pupils divided by religion and sex, remarks as to how supported].

Doagh, Protestants 90, Catholics 3, males 49, females 44, total 93; receives 10s per annum from the National Board and the scholars pay from 1s 1d to 3s 6d per quarter.

Poor and Habits of the People

No provision for poor.

Habits of the people: the same as the parish of Ballylinny.

Fair Sheets by J. Bleakly, April 1837 to January 1839

MODERN TOPOGRAPHY AND SOCIAL ECONOMY

Presbyterian Meeting House

Forwarded to Lieutenant Bennett, Royal Engineers, 6th February 1837 [signed] James Boyle.

The Ballyclare Unitarian or New Light Presbyterian meeting house is situated in the centre of the town, slated, 1-storey high, and contains in the lower part 34 pews, viz. 6 double pews each 9 by 5 feet and 28 single pews each 9 by 3 feet. 2 galleries, 1 on each end; each gallery contains 20 pews single, each 10 by 3 feet. Total pews in the meeting house 74, viz. 68 single pews and 6 double pews. The aisle is flagged and 5 and a half feet wide, covered with a mat. A few of the pews are boarded, but very old.

There are 2 large Gothic windows in front and 4 square ones, but small, and 4 small windows on the rear of the meeting house. 2 doors, 1 on each end, viz. 1 leading to the gallery and 1 leading to the under part, each 3 and a half feet wide. The pews are in middling repair. This meeting house was built by subscription, but so old that its date and cost cannot be ascertained.

The average collection for the poor on each Sunday amounts to 5s.

Presbyterian Congregation

The Presbyterian congregation of Ballyclare consists of about 120 families, average at 5 to each family, and composed of persons from the parish of Ballynure, grange of Doagh, parish of Ballylinny and liberties of Carrickfergus. From the Reverend William Heron, minister, and Robert Greenfield, elder.

Income of Minister

The annual income of the minister, the Revd William Heron, is 75 pounds regium donum Irish currency and 50 pounds stipend. His residence is in Henryfield, parish of Ballynure, a quarter of a mile from the town, on the road leading from Ballyclare to Larne and Carrickfergus. From Robert Wilson and Robert Greenfield, elders. 14th April 1837.

Original Presbyterian Clergy

The following are the Presbyterian clergy of the Presbyterian meeting house of Ballyclare. The first is said to have been the Revd Futt; 2nd, the Revd Thomas Wilson; 3rd, the Revd James Marshall; 4th, the Revd Futt Marshall; 5th the Revd William Heron, who came about 22 years ago and still continues, and belongs to the Presbytery of Antrim and Remonstrant Synod. From James Gault.

Presbyterian Collection

Monthly collections are given to 16 poor persons on the first Sunday of each month by the Presbyterian congregation of Ballyclare. From James Gault, 26th April 1837.

Mondays are the days appointed to help the poor in the village and neighbourhood of Ballyclare. 27th April 1837.

Covenanting Meeting House

This meeting house is situated at the north east end of the town. On a stone over the door is the following inscription: "Reformed Presbyterian meeting house, built AD 1832." It is slated and 47 by 24 feet inside; contains 31 single pews each 9 by 2 and a half feet, all quite new; 2 doors, square, 1 on each end, each 3 and a half feet wide, 8 arched windows. The aisle is 6 feet wide. The floor is not flagged or boarded; nothing but earth. Built by subscription of the inhabitants and supposed to have cost 400 pounds. Slated, but not finished from want of funds.

Minister and Collection

There is no stationed minister to this congregation, but are supplied by the synod from Belfast. The collection for the poor of this congregation amounts to 3s each Sunday.

Covenanting Clergy

There is no regular appointed Covenanting minister at Ballyclare, but are supplied from Belfast. The income of the minister amounts to 20 pounds per annum. Collection at the meeting house on each Sunday amounts to 2s 6d per [week]. Worship is only held on every second Sunday. Congregation consists of 100 persons. There are no original Covenanting clergy in Ballyclare, nor any placed minister. The income of the minister who attends is 20 pounds per annum, paid by the congregation. The congregation consists of 100 members.

Social Meeting

A social meeting is held in the meeting house on every second Sunday and Thursday for the purpose of reading and expounding to each other the Scriptures. It was established in 1832 and consists at present of an unlimited number of members, both male and female, and held from 12 till 3 o'clock on Sundays. Commences with singing and prayer and concludes with the same.

There is only a service in the above meeting house on every second Sunday. On Thursday the meetings are held from 3 till 5 o'clock p.m. From William McClelland and Robert Witherhead, members. 14th April 1837.

Unitarian Meeting House

Unitarian meeting house is in the centre of the village and was built 68 years ago by subscription. It measures 68 by 27 feet in the clear, slated, in middling repair, and contains 50 single seats. Each would contain 8 persons, making the congregation 400 persons. The steps to the gallery are of stone and *outside*. Windows are nearly square, except 2 large ones, which are lancet-arch. 4 doors, 2 below and 2 above on each end of the house; stone steps outside.

Original Clergy

Original clergy remembered by the oldest inhabitant: 1st, Revd Wilson; 2nd, Revd James Marshall; 3rd, Revd Futt <Foot> Marshall 50 years ago; 4th, Revd William Heron, who is 24 years ordained.

Wesleyan Methodist Meeting House

At the south end of the town, on the opposite side of the river, stands the Wesleyan Methodist meeting house, 3-storey high, slated. The understorey is occupied as a schoolroom and the preacher's apartments. There is no school held in this at present, neither does the preacher reside here, but comes from Antrim to preach here every Sunday. Total dimensions of the house inside 50 by 36 feet, with 30 single seats each 8 by 2 feet. These occupy the centre of the house, with a few forms. The span occupied by the pews is 36 and a half by 16 and a half feet. The floor is boarded. There are 14 arched windows on the 2 upper storeys, which light the preaching room, 2 arched doors on the end, each 4 and a half feet wide, 9 oblong windows on the lower part.

The house was built by subscription in 1828 and supposed to have cost 1,200 pounds, collected by Mr Alexander Mackey, a late preacher of the Methodist Society. Upwards of 150 members attend this meeting house.

The wall round the yard is 6 feet high, the wall in front 3 feet high. The iron paling <palling> is 3 feet high. The front is ornamented with evergreens and flowers.

2 poor boxes of copper have been presented to this congregation. On each is written the following inscription: "Presented by Mr Angus Clarke, Mary Street, Belfast, to the Wesleyan Methodist congregation, Ballyclare, October 1828." From Samuel Moore Thompson and John Cannon, members, 12th April 1837.

Methodist Chapel

The Methodist chapel is situated in that part of the village called Lea Ballyclare or Wee Ballyclare, on the opposite side of the Six Mile Water, which passes through the village. It was built in 1828 and is 3-storeys high, of stone, slated, built by subscription and measures exteriorally 54 by 39 feet. The windows are circular-segment arch, except those on the lower floor which are square. There are 30 windows on the house, with 3 doors, viz. 2 on east end and 1 on west end; brick round each window and door. Yard wall, which is 6 feet high, enclosing a yard of 180 by 60 feet of ground, which is ornamented with evergreen and palisading <pallasading>.

Boys' schoolroom in the Methodist chapel measures 35 by 37 feet, but no school held in it at present. An infant school is held in a room at the lower end of the house.

There is no stationed preacher, but are supplied by the conference, who pay each preacher 16 pounds per annum and 16 pounds per annum for his wife, with a certain sum for each child from the time they begin to go to school. The congregation is upwards of 40 years established and at present consists of 150 members. Collection on each Sunday consists 2s 6d per [week].

The social meetings are for prayer, which are held in the Methodist chapel on every Thursday evening, and regular preaching on every Sunday morning and evening, and also regular preaching once a month.

Methodist Collection

The collection for the poor on each Sunday in the Methodist chapel amounts to 2s each Sunday, but service is only on every alternate Sunday. From Samuel Moore Thompson.

Roman Catholic Chapel

The Roman Catholic chapel is situated a short distance from the town, on the road leading from Ballyclare to Doagh. It was commenced in 1833 but is not yet finished. There are no seats or pews in it yet. Its total dimensions interiorally is 48 by 24 feet, slated. Built by subscription, the money chiefly collected by Dr Crolly in Belfast, who also gave 50 pounds for the ground. Its supposed cost when finished will be about 250 pounds. It contains 4 Gothic windows. The wall in front is 5 and a half feet high, but not finished. There is no appointed priest, but supplied from Belfast. From Andrew Blair, James Straighter and Robert Rice.

Roman Catholic chapel windows are Gothic arch.

Catholic Collection

The collection for the poor on each Sunday in the Roman Catholic chapel amounts to 2s 6d. From Robert Rice and James Courtney. 15th April 1837.

Paper and Corn Mills

The water wheel of the paper [mill] is 22 feet in diameter and 12 feet broad at the buckets. The other water wheel is 16 feet in diameter and 12 feet at the buckets; overshot, 22 feet fall.

The corn mill is attached. The water wheel is 16 feet in diameter and 4 feet at the buckets. Machinery is contained in a 2-storey house, slated and in good repair, and can work all seasons of the year. 14 feet of a fall, overshot. From Mr Robert Greenfield, proprietor.

Old House

There is a house at the south end of the town, the roof of which is of boards covered with paper and stiffened with tar, but not beneficial. From John Archabald. 26th April 1837.

Bridge

The bridge which [runs] across the river or stream which passes through the town of Ballyclare has 4 arches, each 14 feet in the span, and on the top of the bridge is 21 feet broad. The walls are 3 feet high and 1 and a half feet broad, and in good repair.

PRODUCTIVE AND SOCIAL ECONOMY

Fairs and Market

There are 4 fairs held in Ballyclare in the year, viz. 2 for business chiefly and 1 in August and May for pleasure and business. The above are celebrated horse fairs. There is also a market held on the third Wednesday of each month.

Temperance Society

About 3 months ago the Temperance Society was re-established in Ballyclare, through the instrumentality of Mr Benjamin Bailey, a Methodist preacher, and held in the Methodist chapel, and consists of about 60 members. From Mr George Bell, Samuel Moore Thompson and James Locke. 15th April 1837.

Mason Lodges and Book Clubs

There are 4 Mason lodges held in the town of Ballyclare.

There is also a book club held in the town of Ballyclare, which was established about 30 years ago and was originally held on the upper part of the national schoolroom, but is for the last 2 years held in the house of Mrs Murdock. About 20 members connected, each member pays 6d per month, which sum goes to purchase books; chiefly historical books and novels are read.

Book Clubs

The Ballyclare Book Club was established in 1824 and was held in the upper room of the schoolhouse, but discontinued in 1836 in consequence of the falling off of its members. For number of books see catalogue of books.

There is another book club held in the house of Mrs Murdock in the village of Ballyclare, established in 1833 and consists of 9 members only, who meet occasionally, but is also falling off;

there are 55 volumes. From Samuel Curry, librarian, from Dr Agnew and John Archibald.

Public Cars

There are 2 cars in the village of Ballyclare, viz. one which goes every Monday, Wednesday and Friday from Ballyclare to Belfast and returns each day, fare 1s, and to Ballymena every Saturday. The other goes when called on, but no regular days appointed. These are the only conveyances in the village for the public. From John Wilson, proprietor of the car. 28th April 1837.

Conveyances

There are 3 cars in Ballyclare for hire. The fare to Ballymena is 1s and 1s to Belfast, and if engaged on other days than Fridays and Saturdays (i.e. Fridays to Belfast and Saturdays to Ballymena), 7d per mile is charged.

There are 2 public cars for hire in the village of Doagh. The fare is the same as the Ballyclare cars, both to Ballymena and Belfast.

Constabulary

There are 3 constabulary in Ballyclare, viz. 1 sergeant and 2 privates, charged from Ballynure.

Book Clubs

The book club, which is held in the national schoolroom in Ballyclare, is on the decline, chiefly owing to the members being in debt. It is about 30 years established, and was broken up for a short time and was re-established in 1824, and given up in 1836 and again re-established in 1837, but, from want of funds, is declining. The members of the book club held in Mrs Murdock's pay each 1s per month.

The book club held in the Methodist chapel is 8 years established and consists of 20 members. Each pay 6d per quarter and 1s entrance money. Consists of 100 volumes of religion, history and biography. Monthly meetings are held.

Temperance Society

A temperance society was established in 1835 and is held in the Methodist chapel in Ballyclare, and consists of 60 members. It is increasing considerably. A soiree is held in January and one in July each year.

Local Government

That part of the village called Lea Ballyclare is in

the Whitehouse district of petty sessions and dispensary, and the other part of the village is in the Parkgate district of petty sessions and dispensary at Doagh.

Ballyclare: Markets and Fairs

Ballyclare ceased to be a linen market about 40 years since and ceased to be a butter market about 15 years ago. The chief articles exposed for sale at the markets in Ballyclare are pigs, cows a few, yarn, sheep, coopers' vessels of wood, baskets, all kinds of soft goods and hardware, delf and crocks, dulse, gingerbread, cheese, fruit in the season and wool hats. About 40 pigs sold at each market and about 80 at each fair, and about 50 horses sold at each fair, some at so high a price as 150 pounds.

The May and November fairs are the greatest for the sale of horses of high price; the other 2 fairs are for the sale of farm horses. Old clothes is sometimes sold in the street in market days and fair days. Turf is brought chiefly from Glenwhirry and Ballybole on every day in the week, and sold at present at 4s 6d per load containing about 2 cwt. No meal market nearer than Antrim or Belfast. Oatmeal is sold in the shops.

Post Office and Pumps

Post office established in Ballyclare about 37 years ago.

There are 3 pumps in the street of Ballyclare, which contain excellent water, at the expense of the inhabitants. From Dr Agnew and James Cortney. 27th April 1837.

Trades and Occupations

The following are the trades and occupations of the inhabitants of the village of Ballyclare: attorney 1, surgeon and apothecary 3, publicans 12, grocers 12, postmaster 1, gauger, superannuated 1, woollen drapers 3, linen weavers 14, blacksmiths 2, carpenters 2, wheelwright 1, tailors 2, tinsmiths 2, shoemakers 3, hucksters 2, cobbler 1, lodging houses 3, butchers 3, blue dyers 1, hosiers <hoziers> 1, dealer 1, paupers 2, labourers 22, bonnetmakers 1, farmers 3, ragman and dealer 1, widows 10, clerk of meeting house 2, old spinster 1, saddlers 2, reedmakers 2, besommaker 1, nailers 2, stone masons 2, slaters 1, farmer and chandler <chandelor> 1, flax dresser 2, linen draper 1, confectioner 1, leather cutter 1, pensioners 1, private 1, schoolmasters 2, excise officer 1, dressmakers 2, car drivers 1, victualling store hand 1, constabulary officer 1, general mechanic 1, stables 1, schoolhouses 2, empty houses 7, Presby-

terian meeting house 1, Seceding meeting house 1, Methodist meeting house 1, Roman Catholic chapel 1, total 153.

Houses

Total houses in the village of Ballyclare 153, viz. 139 inhabited houses and 14 not constantly inhabited. There are 28 2-storey houses slated, 1 3-storey house slated and 2 are 2-storeys high, thatched. 35 houses are 1-storey high, slated and 76 1-storey, thatched. The oldest house in Ballyclare is John Gillespie's, opposite the pump, thatched. Within the last 10 years 20 new houses have been built.

Street in Ballyclare

In 1833 about 120 paces in length was taken off the street of Ballyclare, i.e. the hill, which is the fair green, which reduced it 4 feet from its original height, that is 4 feet reduced in the highest part, at the expense of the county. A row of [blank] trees is said to have formerly stood on the west side of the street of Ballyclare. The last of them was standing about 45 years ago.

The village is not improving, chiefly owing to the failure in trade. The houses have a dark and gloomy aspect, not much appearance of neatness about them.

Ballyclare has increased considerably for the last 50 years, but has not increased much for the last 5 years, chiefly owing to the want of capital. The introduction of book clubs and Sunday schools have improved the habits and morals of the people very much, with the introduction of temperance societies.

Remarks on Ballyclare

About 15 1-storey houses slated, a Covenanting meeting house and a Methodist chapel, and 3 2-storey houses have been built within the last 10 years in Ballyclare. The village is not increasing much at present in neatness or cleanliness, as the houses in general have rather a gloomy aspect and are not white or comfortable or clean inside or outside, chiefly owing to a want of taste, the poverty of the inhabitants and the want of encouragement given by the proprietor, the Marquis of Donegall.

Origin of Ballyclare

Ballyclare, or anciently Ballybullian, means "a cover or lid", which is said to have covered that part of the Six Mile Water where the bridge now stands in Ballyclare, as at that time there was no bridge there. This lid was a trapdoor to let foot passengers walk on while his [their] horse, which was laden with goods on the back, on panniers or back suggans, walked in the water. As at that time there was no roads or carts or cars, all the goods were carried on the horse's back. This was before there was a house in Ballyclare.

Poor

On every Monday the poor of the town and neighbourhood are relieved by the inhabitants of Ballyclare. There are about 20 poor persons in the grange of Doagh, but not more than 10 are resident.

Clothing Society

Ballyclare and Ballyeaston Clothing Society was established in 1837 and consists of 3 members, viz. 1 gentleman and 2 ladies. The following are the subscribers, with their amounts of subscription: James Owens Esquire, John Owens Esquire, James Agnew Esquire, George Langtry Esquire and Mrs Smyth each give 1 pound per annum; Mrs Bell, Miss Allen and Mrs Fergusson each give 10s per annum. Clothes are given to the poor without any charge, and consist of blankets and flannel chiefly.

Labourers' Wages

The daily wages of a labouring man in a farmhouse in summer is 1s without meat and 1s per day in winter without meat. They are seldom fed by their employers. The half-yearly wages of a servant man in a farmhouse is from 3 pounds to 4 pounds 10s with their meat. Female servants in a farmhouse receive 30s per half-year with meat, and females who work by the day receive 6d per day without meat, and sometimes 8d per day, during summer and winter.

Cottiers

The rents paid by cottiers for the cot or house with a small garden, and permission to keep pigs and poultry (except geese), is from 30s to 2 pounds per annum. The agricultural labourers are sufficiently numerous, but not too much so. They are generally fed only during the harvest by their employers and live in his farm, supplied with buttermilk by them at 1d per gallon in summer and 1d ha'penny per gallon in winter, which is paid generally in work and sometimes with money. The cottiers' houses are not in good repair.

Private School

There is a private school held in a room in a private house in the village. It measures 16 by 10 feet in the clear; established in 1831. Income of the master is 8 pounds per annum, paid by the pupils. Books are *Manson's Primer and spelling book*, with *Gough's Arithmetic*, with the Authorised Version of Scripture and catechism on Saturday by the master. Total pupils 20, viz. 17 males and 3 females; boys from 10 to 15, 6 and 11 under 10; girls under 10, 3; Established Church 3, Roman Catholics 3 and 14 Presbyterians. Patrick Gault, a Presbyterian.

Schools

The Ballyclare national schoolroom no.1 is 15 feet 9 inches by 15 feet 9 inches inside.

The Doagh national schoolroom is 22 and a half by 16 feet inside.

Tradition

There is a common saying among the inhabitants of this part and all through the country "Sweet Ballyclare, where they keep no Sunday." This originated from a little boy some centuries ago who was an apprentice in Ballyclare, and used to go to Ballybolly to see his mother on Sunday. His mother insisted on his reading the Bible instead of breaking the sabbath, and kept him too close to it. When he went out of the house and looked towards Ballyclare [he] exclaimed, "Sweet Ballyclare, where they keep no Sunday."

Fairs

There are 4 fairs held annually in Ballyclare, viz. one on the second Tuesday in May, July and November, old style, and one on the last Tuesday in January, old style. No tolls paid; they were abolished 15 years ago. The people refused to pay tolls as there was no enclosed place for the fair. Tolls at that time were paid to the Marquis of Donegall. A monthly market is held on the third Wednesday of each month, for yarn chiefly.

Newspapers

About 50 newspapers pass daily through Ballyclare post office, chiefly *Belfast News Letter* and *Northern Whig*.

MODERN TOPOGRAPHY

Village of Doagh

The village of Doagh contains 46 houses, viz. 11

slated and 35 thatched. 7 are 2-storeys high and 39 are 1-storey high. The oldest house is that 2-storey house occupied by James Harper, a farmer, upwards of 100 years built. It was originally a carman's inn. Hotel was built about 40 years ago by Edward Jones Agnew Esquire. The late additional part was built in 1815 by Lord Donegall, for the club to meet and dine. It is called the Antrim Clubroom.

Hotel is 2-storeys high, slated, but now unoccupied. It is 3 years since the hunting club ceased to meet in it. Hotel was built 40 year ago. The hunting clubroom was built in 1815.

The village is rather on the decline, not improving, chiefly owing to a failure in trade.

Origin of Doagh

Doagh or Duagh means "the order of the black friars", as duagh means "black", and as a friary was at the old graveyard at Doagh.

Trades and Occupations

The following are the trades and occupations: schoolmasters 2, publicans 2, grocers 2, sawyers 2, weavers 3, smiths 3, carpenters 2, wheelwright 1, carmen 1, widows 1, labourers 6, milliners 2, old spinsters 4, farmers 5, bleachers 1, cotton printer 1, empty houses 4, 2 schoolhouses, 1 forge, 1 dispensary. Hotel is 68 by 26 feet in the clear, in good repair. The street is 38 feet wide.

Methodist Chapel

The Methodist chapel at Doagh is 1-storey high, of stone and lime, slated, and in bad repair. It was built by subscription of the Methodist congregation 35 years ago, and measures exteriorally 21 by 18 feet, with 2 oblong windows (small) and 1 door. Meetings are held in it on every Sunday morning and on every Tuesday evening, and regular preaching once a fortnight. Except the preaching, the other meetings are led by laymen. There is no regular preacher appointed. Methodist chapel is nearly attached to the national schoolhouse.

Methodist Meeting House

The Methodist meeting house at Doagh is attached to the schoolroom and is 16 by 11 feet inside, but no pews. The people sit on forms; no stationed minister.

Gentlemen's Seats: Fisherwick

Fisherwick House was built about 38 years ago by Lord Donegall for a hunting lodge. It is 1-storey high, slated, and in good repair. It was used as a hunting lodge for 33 years. James Agnew Esquire is about 5 years in it.

Bridges and Roads

The bridge between Doagh and Coggry mill has 2 arches, each 12 feet in the span by 5 high, wall 1 and a half thick by 3 high; 21 feet broad on top and 36 feet long, in good repair, 15 years built.

Bridge south of the village of Doagh was built 1764 on the Antrim road. One on Ballymena road north of village is 20 years built, on [the] new line; one on old road is 38 years built; one below dispensary was built 1764. All the arches are circular-segment arches.

All the leading roads are in very good repair, and a sufficient quantity of them, both by and public. The by-roads are not kept in such good repair as the others.

Bridges

The arches of all the bridges are circular-segment arches. The range wall of Ballyclare bridge is 171 feet in length from the extremity of one abutment to the other.

The bridge which divides Ballywalter from Ballylinny, opposite Greenfield's mills, has only 2 arch[es], which are circular segment. Each arch measures 7 feet in the span by 5 feet high and is 21 feet wide on the top. The wall is 3 and a half feet high by 18 inches thick and 165 feet long, in good repair.

Manufactory: Steam Carriage

The Speedwell forge or manufactory for machinery is a short distance from Doagh. Established in 1824, John Rowan and sons proprietors. 16 men are employed daily at this forge. The turning and fitting-up shop is 35 and a half by 16 feet inside. The grinding shop is 25 by 10 feet and the other apartments is 45 and a half by 18 feet, and the other 29 by 18 feet. The water wheel by which the machinery is worked is 16 feet in diameter and 2 and a half feet broad across the buckets; 6 horsepower.

Mr John Rowan and sons are the inventors of the first steam engine or locomotive carriage ever invented in this country. This machine is 21 horsepower and has travelled to Belfast and through all the principal streets in it. The houses are all slated and in good repair; undershot wheel. From John Rowan and sons, at the factory.

Paper Mill

The paper mill is in the grange of Doagh. It was built on the site of a flour mill about 3 years ago by the present proprietor, Mr Robert Greenfield. Consists of 3 lofts in good repair, each 34 and a half by 29 feet. The machinery of the paper mill is propelled by 1 water wheel, a breast, and 24 feet in diameter by 12 feet broad at the buckets. The fall is 22 feet, and about 30 horsepower. The smaller water wheel, also a breast, and 16 feet in diameter by 2 feet across the buckets; fall 16 feet, and 6 and a half horsepower. All the engine wheels are of metal. Established 2 and a half years, but the house built 3 years, of stone and lime, slated, all in good repair.

The flour mill which stood here was upwards of 20 years built, and about 7 years ago it ceased to work. There are 32 males and 15 females employed daily.

Corn Mill

The corn mill is nearly attached to the paper mill, only 2 or 3 feet distant. It is upwards of 150 years a corn mill, but about 20 years rebuilt, of stone and lime, slated, and measures 30 by 20 feet inside. Double geared, 2 pair of stones, and is 2-storey high, in middling repair. Propelled by 1 water wheel, which is a breast and 14 by 2 feet, and with a fall of water [of] 14 feet. Robert Greenfield, proprietor; can work all seasons of the year.

Machinery in Doagh

Beetling engine at Doagh, in the village, is slated and measures 45 by 24 feet in the clear; propelled by a water wheel 26 feet in diameter by 6 feet 2 inches broad at the buckets; a breast wheel, fall of water 18 feet, established in 1835. Previous to that time it was a corn mill. Can work all seasons of the year. The water is calculated to drive 12 horsepower, but at present only 4 horsepower is driven; worked by a stream which proceeds from Bracknahill in the parish [sic] of Ballyeaston and falls into the Six Mile Water; all in good repair. Hugh Swan is the proprietor; 1 loft.

The flax mill at Doagh: Hugh Swan is proprietor. Breast wheel, 14 feet in diameter by 1 and a half feet broad at buckets; fall of water is 13 feet; 1-storey high, thatched, and in good repair; on the same stream.

The bleach mill of Henry Bragg Esquire at Doagh is 2-storey high, slated, in good repair, on the same stream, and can work all seasons; breast wheel 13 feet in diameter by 3 feet broad at the buckets, fall of water is 6 feet, dimensions 60 by 21 feet in the clear.

Corn Mill and Bridge

The corn mill at the Coggry is the property of Mr William McFerran. It is propelled by 1 water wheel, which is a breast and 14 feet in diameter by 6 feet at the buckets; double geared, 2 pairs of stones, fall of water 14 feet; can work all seasons of the year; 3-storeys high, slated, and in good repair. 15 years built and measures 62 by 26 feet in the clear, with 2 corn kilns attached with iron heads.

Bridge at this mill has 2 arches each 12 feet in the span by 8 feet high and 21 feet broad on top; wall is 3 and a half feet high by 1 and a half feet thick by 42 feet long, in good repair.

NATURAL FEATURES

Stream and Foot Stick

The stream or river which passes through Doagh, in rear of the village, divides the ancient rectory of Doagh and Ballyhamage.

The foot stick across the stream [near?] the 2 mills at Doagh under the old graveyard is 3 years built, at the expense of John Dickey of Ballymena. It measures 43 feet in length by 1 and a half feet broad at the bottom or plank, by 3 feet wide at the top or hand-rail. The present depth of the ford or stream at the stick is about 2 feet.

PRODUCTIVE AND SOCIAL ECONOMY

General Economy

3 pounds 10s per half-year is paid for grazing a cow and 3 pounds for beef cattle per [half-year]. Merchandise is purchased in Belfast and Larne <Larn>, viz. timber, slates and other commodities. Labourers or tradesmen do not suffer from want of employment at any season; all have plenty of work. There are no more roads required, nor bridges, in the grange of Doagh. Trade is decreasing, chiefly owing to the failure in the linen trade and want of capital.

Longevity

Sarah Ardis died 6 years ago at the advanced age of 90 years. John Ewing died 10 years ago at the age of 84 years age. Mr James Gault is still living and is 82 years of age. Dr Agnew is 86 years of age.

John McClelland died 10 years ago at the age of 95 years. John Rowan died 38 years ago at the age of 85 years. Andrew Rowan is 3 years dead and was 85 years of age.

Prevailing Names

Crawford is the most prevalent name, Gault is the most ancient name. Ewing is also a very ancient and prevailing name. Robinson, Todd, Johnstone, Blair and Wilson are prevalent.

Fuel

Turf is generally used as fuel and brought from Ballyholly mountain, and some [from] Ballywalter bog, which they purchase per gauge containing 3 feet high by 3 feet wide, for 1s 3d or 15 per [use ?], or 13d in summer, and from 1s 8d to 2s in winter, brought to the house and is very scarce.

Amusement and Publicans

The only amusement now practised is dancing, and card-playing and shooting at Christmas and Easter. There is only 1 publican and 2 shebeen <sheban> houses in the country parts of the grange of Doagh (petty).

Lime and Crops

Lime is brought from Whitewells and is laid down for 14d per barrel.
    Green crops are very little cultivated.

Carriage

Cost of carriage of goods from Belfast to Ballyclare is 6d per cwt, and the same from Larne. There are 3 carmen in Ballyclare and 3 post cars, who charge each 1s from Belfast to Ballyclare for each passenger, or 7d per mile for each single person. Only 3 post horses in Ballyclare; no public conveyance in Ballyclare but those cars.

Tithe

The grange of Doagh has never paid any tithe. It belongs to the manor of Moylinny and the Parkgate district of petty sessions.

Disease

Included in the Doagh district of dispensary. Influenza and whooping cough, with lumbago, is the most prevalent disease.

Springs and Farms

Remarkably well supplied with good spring water. There is upwards of 50 springs in the grange of Doagh.

The Marquis of Donegall is the proprietor. Extent of farms from 75 acres to 4 acres; usual extent of farms is from 7 to 20 acres. There are about 20 old hawthorn trees in the grange of Doagh.

Frosts and Crops

Early frost chiefly along the water edge and marshy ground. This year the frost in August was very injurious to the potato crops. The crops usually cultivated are potatoes, wheat, flax, sometimes a little barley, very little green feeding.
    Potatoes are planted in March, April and May, and dug in August, September. Oats is sown in March and April, and reaped in August and September. Wheat is sown in November and December, and reaped in August and September. Barley is sown in April and May, and reaped in August and September. Flax is sown in April and pulled in July. Upland hay is sown in March and April in the same ground with the oats, and cut 2 years after, in June and July.

Weaving and Spinning

There are about 40 looms in the grange of Doagh, all for linen except 5 looms which are for calico.
    Chiefly owing to the introduction of the spinning mills, there is very little hand-spinning done in this parish.

Doagh Book Club

The Doagh Book Club was established in 1760 through the instrumentality of Mr William Gault, then a schoolmaster at Doagh. At that period it consisted of 45 members, but from death and forfeiture it has been reduced to its present number, 30 members, and about 1,000 volumes, purchased by subscription, which is 1s 6d per quarter from each member. Admission money is 3 pounds. Each member at its commencement paid half a guinea to purchase books, and also 1 guinea from each member to defray the expenses of erecting the clubroom, which is above the national schoolroom and is of the same dimensions, 22 and a half by 16 feet inside.
    There are 40 ancient maps round the walls of the room, all Bowle's *New pocket map of the world*, with very ancient large globes, viz. a celestial and a terrestrial by Jameson. The book purchased in Dublin and Belfast, the globes from London and cost 20 pounds. Before the book room was built the meetings were held in the schoolroom.

On Sunday morning after the Irish rebellion of '98, some of his majesty's troops came from Carrickfergus and destroyed and carried away many of the books, with many valuable jewels belonging to the Mason lodge which is held in the clubroom. Information obtained from James Love, librarian, whose income for such is 2 pounds per annum paid by the members. Night of meeting on each Sunday. For further particulars see catalogue of books. 25th April 1837.

Farming Society

The Doagh Farming Society was established in 1818 under the patronage of the Marquis of Donegall, and continued for several years, when it became annexed to the North East Society. It embraces nearly all the extensive farmers in an extent of several miles. From its commencement a considerable improvement in the production of the soil, as well as in the moral and social condition of the cultivators.

On the dissolution of the North East Farming Society in 1836, it was formed into the Doagh branch; John Owen Esquire, J.P., patron. It consists of 45 members. Ploughing match takes place in spring and the cattle show in autumn, at which all the members dine together at Mr Young's, Parkgate, but previously at Doagh Hotel before it became vacant.

Trade: Paperworks

The decrease in trade in Ballyclare was much greater than it now is. Its increase is chiefly owing to the revival of Mr Greenfield's paperworks, as that establishment was completely idle for some months past, and all the workers dismissed, chiefly owing to his failure in business.

Migration

There is very little migration from the grange of Doagh, as the people have employment at home, both by manufacturers and agriculture. By migration is meant those who go periodically from Belfast port, or any port, to Scotland and England to reap the harvest only and to seek work, and return when the harvest is ended. Their wives and families generally remain at home and work for the farmers and others who employ them, and some of the poorest of them are compelled to beg.

Wages

A labouring man at agriculture receives 1s per day in summer without meat and 10d per day in winter without meat. Some get 1s per day the year through, without meat, but those must be able-bodied men who understand all the branches of agriculture, particularly ploughing. In winter 11d per day is given to agricultural labourers in general. Females receive 6d per day in summer and winter at outdoor work. A maidservant in a farmhouse will receive 1 pound 5s per half-year, but generally receive 30s per half-year.

Commodities

Timber, slates, coals and iron are brought from Belfast, and bricks chiefly from Carrickfergus and some from Belfast, also all the other goods from Belfast occasionally.

Clothing Fund

About 60 individuals receive clothing annually from the Ballyclare Clothing Fund.

Schoolmistress and Medical Attendant

Mary Curran, a Methodist, is the mistress of the infant school in Ballyclare.

Income of the medical attendant at Doagh for last year amounted to 46 pounds 10d, amount of subscription 43 pounds 9s, amount of county grant 43 pounds 9s.

Farming Society

The Doagh Farming Society was established in 1818 under the patronage of the Marquis of Donegall and continued to be conducted with undiminished zeal for several years, when it was annexed to the North East Farming Society. During that period, and prior to its connection with that body, it acquired a prominent distinction by the regularity of its exhibitions and the respectability of its members, embracing nearly all the extensive farmers in an extent of several miles. From its very commencement a considerable improvement in the production of the soil, as well as the social and moral condition of its cultivators, was apparent throughout the several localities to which the society's influence was extended. On the dissolution of the North East Society in 1836, the members of the Doagh branch (considering the beneficial results arising from the development) lost no time in recommencing the society anew under its former appellation, the Doagh Farming Society, and its original founder and patron, the Marquis of Donegall, who was at that time in a bad state of health. John Owens Esquire, J.P., Ballyvoy, was nominated to the presidency, which he accepted.

The society has advanced considerably under his patronage and at present consists of 45 members. The ploughing match takes place in spring each year and the cattle show in autumn, at which the several prizes are awarded to the successful candidates with the strictest impartiality, and all dine together at Parkgate, where they communicate such information in the arts of husbandry and system of agriculture as they may have acquired.

A sensible change for the better is going forward in every department of agriculture through the neighbouring district. The amount of last year's subscription was 13 pounds, which is also the sum granted by the parent society. 5 pounds 15s 6d was the sum awarded at the cattle show. This society is prospering, chiefly owing to a spirit of emulation among the people in general. From John Rowan, secretary.

MODERN AND ANCIENT TOPOGRAPHY

Wall

Wall round Fisherwick House is 40 years built and is 8 feet high.

Original Boundary of Parkgate

There was another Parkgate at the eastern entrance to the park, at a place locally called the Thorn Ditch, near the small stream at the hamlet or cluster of houses on the road between Doagh and Ballyclare, nearly half-way. The gate stood exactly on the right-hand side of the road to Ballyclare. The wall commenced at the Six Mile Water, exactly below the pound at the village of Parkgate, and passed up through Durhamsland, enclosing the townlands of Ballywee and nearly all the townlands of Kilbride, Holestone and Ballyvoy, passing on by Coggry near the corn mills, and by the Thorn Ditch, where the eastern gate or entrance stood, and ending at the Six Mile Water between Greenfield's paper mill and Bessie Graw's bridge, nearly three-quarters of a mile above the bridge.

The wall (parts of which remain standing on its original foundation at the eastern entrance) measures 6 feet in thickness by 5 feet high, and was originally planted with old blackthorn, some of which remain standing at the Thorn Ditch. At that time there was no whitethorn known in this country, but was shortly after introduced and brought from Dublin, and cost 1 guinea per 1,000, and was planted on a farm in the parish of Kilbride and townland of Kilbride, now occupied by Robert Wilson, but so scarce that they were stolen several times out of the ditch. This hedge now stands,

after being once cut, one of the largest in the county. One ha'penny was paid by each person passing through the 2 Parkgates from Antrim to Carrickfergus, as there was no other way to go at that time, or no other road.

SOCIAL ECONOMY

Dispensary

The Doagh dispensary was established on the 1st April 1835. The following is an abstract of the report from the 1st April 1835 till the 11th January 1836.

Patients admitted 735, prescriptions filled 1,025, patients visited at their houses 212, deaths 8, on the books 41. Amount of subscription 41 pounds 13s 6d, amount presented by the grand jury 41 pounds 13s 6d, total 83 pounds 7s. Balance in treasurer hands 10 pounds 16s 6d, which sum was given to the medical attendant as his salary, after defraying the expenses connected with the establishment. Archibald Hawthorn M.D. was the medical attendant.

There has been no registry kept of the diseases in the Doagh dispensary during the years 1835 and 1836. The report for the year 1836 cannot be ascertained, as the documents connected with it are lost.

The Doagh dispensary at present is under the superintendence of a committee of 10 subscribers of a guinea annually each. There are 49 subscribers at present connected with it. District comprises the parishes of Donegore, Kilbride, Ballycor, Rashee, granges of Doagh and Nilteen. 14th July 1838.

Admissions from the 19th January 1837 till the 5th March 1838 1,003: discharged cured 966, died 13, incurable 8, remaining on the books 16, total 1,003. Of the above, there were 93 influenza and 90 fever patients, all of whom required attendance at their dwellings. Amount of subscriptions 43 pounds 9s, county presentment 43 pounds 9s, total 86 pounds 18s.

Expenditure: account for medicine 23 pounds 2s 2d, rent of dispensary 7 pounds, attendant on dispensary 5 pounds 4s, stationery 1 pound 5s, incidental expenses and repairs 2 pounds 6s, printing advertisements 2 pounds, total 40 pounds 17s 2d, leaving a balance as medical attendant's salary of 46 pounds 9s 10d; gratuitous visits 400.

Dispensary open on each Monday, Wednesday and Saturday from 10 in the forenoon until 1 o'clock in the afternoon. The county presentment is as much as the subscription. Income of the medical attendant for the last year, ending 19th

January 1837, 86 pounds 18s. From William Alley D.M., medical attendant.

Table of Schools

[Table contains the following headings: name, situation and description, when established, income and expenditure, physical, intellectual and moral education, number of pupils subdivided by age, sex and religion, name and religion of master and mistress].

Ballyclare national school and classical seminary, at the north end of the town, held in a good room fitted up for the purpose by subscription and is 24 and a half feet by 18 and a half feet inside, established 1826 under National Board; income: from the National Board 8 pounds, from pupils 40 pounds; physical education: none; intellectual education: books published by the National Board, with *Thompson's Arithmetic, Simpson's Euclid, Murray's English grammar, Thompson's Geography, Goldsmith's History of England*; classical authors are Homer, Livy, Sallust, Ovid, with Greek authors; moral education: visited by the Presbyterian clergy only, Authorised Version of Scripture is taught; number of pupils: males, 14 under 10 years of age, 8 from 10 to 15, 6 above 15, 28 total males; females, 2 under 10 years of age, 7 from 10 to 15, 1 above 15, 10 total females; total number of pupils 38, 36 Presbyterians, 2 Roman Catholics; master Robert Miness, Presbyterian.

Ballyclare private school, held in the room of a private house in the town, established for 8 weeks; income from the pupils 2s 7d per week; intellectual education: *Manson's Spelling book and primer*; moral education: not visited by any of the clergy, Authorised Version of Scriptures taught and catechism by the mistress; number of pupils: males, 3 under 10 years of age, 3 total males; females, 9 under 10 years of age, 2 from 10 to 15, 11 total females; total number of pupils 14, all Presbyterians; Ellen Taylor, Presbyterian. Report for April 1837.

Schools

Doagh national school is held in the village of Doagh, in a good 2-storey house, slated. The schoolroom is under the Book Club room and measures 22 and a half by 16 feet 3 inches in the clear. The house was built by subscription in [blank]; only connected with the National Board since 1832. The income of the master is 42 pounds 2s, viz. from the National Board 10 pounds per annum, from the heirs of the late Edward Jones Agnew Esquire 2 pounds 2s and 30 pounds from the pupils per annum. The books used are those published by the National Board only. Visited by the Revd William Heron, Unitarian minister, and by all the other clergy occasionally. Total children at present 45, viz. 18 males and 27 females; males from 10 to 15, 4, and 14 under 10 years of age; females above 15, 1, from 10 to 15, 10, and 16 under 10; Established Church 6, Presbyterians 39. This school is upwards of 100 years established. William Johnstone, a Presbyterian.

There is a night school held in the day schoolroom, established 7 years ago. Consists of 24 pupils, viz. 16 males and 8 females; males above 15, 11, from 10 to 15, 5; females above 15, 5, from 10 to 15, 2, and 1 under 10, all Presbyterians. Day school books are used. Income of master for night school 4 pounds 16s per annum. William Johnstone, Presbyterian.

Ballyclare Roman Catholic Sunday school is held in the Roman Catholic chapel; established 6 years. Only 2 teachers, viz. 1 male and 1 female. Hours of attendance from 10 till 1 o'clock p.m. Connected with no society. The day school books are used. No scriptural books are used in the school. Total scholars 50, viz. 36 boys and 14 girls, all Roman Catholics. About 36 are exclusively Sunday school scholars. Does not commence with either singing or prayer. Superintended by the Revd Mr Hannah, parish priest. From Patrick Kirwin, a Roman Catholic.

Ballyclare national school no.2 is held in a thatched house 16 by 16 feet in the clear; established in 1833. Income of the teacher is 18 pounds per annum, viz. 8 pounds from the National Board and 10 pounds from the pupils. National books are used. Visited by the Revd William Heron, a Unitarian. Total pupils 50, viz. 27 males and 23 females; males above 15, 10, from 10 to 15, 7, and 10 under 10 years of age; girls from 10 to 15, 8, and 15 under 10; Roman Catholics 16 and 28 Presbyterians, and 6 of other denominations. Thomas Kelly, Unitarian.

There is an infant school held in the lower part of the Methodist chapel in the village of Ballyclare. The room measures 14 by 12 feet in the clear. Established on the 8th June 1838. Income of the mistress amounts to [blank] pounds per annum. Each child pays 1d ha'penny per week. Total children 28, viz. 14 males and 14 females. All the males are under 10 years of age; girls above 10, 5, and 9 under 10 years of age; Roman Catholics 3 and 3 Methodists and 22 Presbyterians. *Manson's Primer and spelling book* are used, with the Authorised Version of Scripture. Visited by Miss Bell, a Methodist.

Ballyclare Methodist Sunday school is held in the Methodist chapel. Established in October 1838, superintended by Mr Samuel M. Thompson, a Methodist. 3 teachers, viz. 1 male and 2 female. Hours of attendance from 2 till 4 p.m. The Sunday School Society for Ireland give books. 30 scholars, viz. 15 males and 15 females, Presbyterians 20 and 10 of other denominations. Commences with singing and prayers and concludes with the same by the superintendent.

Ballyclare private school is held in a small room in a private house 12 feet square, thatched; 6 years established. Income of the mistress is 1d ha'penny per week from each scholar, or about 6 pounds per annum. Total scholars 20, viz. 12 males and 8 females; Established Church 8, Presbyterians 8 and 4 Roman Catholics; all under 10 years of age. Not visited by any; books used are *Manson's Primer and spelling book*. Martha Henderson, a Presbyterian.

A Sunday school is held in the above day schoolroom, established 1838. Superintended by the mistress, who is the only teacher. Day school books are used, not visited by any; hours of attendance from 10 till 3 p.m. Total scholars 12, viz. 2 boys and 10 girls; Roman Catholics 4 and 8 Presbyterians. All day school scholars.

Emigration in 1835

List of persons who have emigrated from the town of Ballyclare during the year 1835. [Table gives name, age, townland in which resided, religion, port to which emigrated].

Samuel Kelly, 20, Roman Catholic, to New York.

John Robinson, 22, Presbyterian, to New York.

Alexander Quinn, 19, Roman Catholic, to New York.

William Murdock, 20, Presbyterian, to New York, returned.

Thomas McBride, 32, Presbyterian, to Philadelphia.

Emigration in 1836

List of persons who have emigrated from the town of Ballyclare during the year 1836.

David Robinson, 20, Presbyterian, to New York.

Joseph Robinson, 24, Presbyterian, to New York.

Robert Baron, 20, Presbyterian, to New York.

Mary McBride, 10, Eliza McBride 8, Nancy McBride 6, Presbyterians, to Philadelphia.

John Beggs, 32, Presbyterian, to Quebec.

Migration

List of persons who migrate annually from the town of Ballyclare to Glasgow: Titus Neeson, 25, Roman Catholic, Charles Neeson, 20, Roman Catholic, William McCray, 30, Presbyterian, John Morrisson, 24, Presbyterian, James Millar, 25, Presbyterian.

ANCIENT TOPOGRAPHY

Old Road

There was an old road locally called the Irish Lonan, from Carrickfergus to Antrim. The track of it may still be seen between Doagh and Bessie Graw's bridge near George Shaw's, or below the village, not more than 7 feet wide. The Six Mile Water takes its name from this road, as it [?] rises 6 miles from Antrim to where it crossed the river, and the same distance from Carrickfergus.

Forts and Coves

There was a fort of earth called Ewingtown Fort, between Doagh and Ballyclare, on the farm of William Martin, but all demolished; also one on Robert Wilson's farm below the road, but all demolished; also 2 coves on the same farm, but closed up; also 3 coves on James Jamison's farm, but closed up, with many other coves, but are all demolished.

Forts

Fort of earth above the river near old graveyard on James Harper's farm is 50 feet in diameter on top by 84 feet at base, by 12 feet high by 5 above the level of the field at upper side, and about 27 feet above the level of the stream; parapet is 1 foot high.

PRODUCTIVE ECONOMY

Farming Society

Doagh Farming Society remained 8 years before it became connected with the parent society. The average annual amount of local subscription for the last 7 years was 14 pounds per annum, except the last year, 1838, when the amount was only 13 pounds. The parent society always gave a sum equivalent to the amount of local subscription. The number of members in 1830 was 51, in 1831 45, in 1832 46, in 1833 44, in 1834 47, in 1835 48, in 1836 50, in 1837 51, and in 1838 45. John Owen, Ballyvoy, James Owens Esquire, George Langtry Esquire and William Ferguson Esquire each pay 1 pound annual subscription. All the other members are of the farming class and pay each 5s per annum.

The society is prospering both in members and funds, and increasing in both. The prizes are awarded to farmers at the ploughing match for good implements of husbandry for farmers. The farmers' servants have for good ploughing from 5s to 1 pound 5s for good ploughing alone at the ploughing match.

Cattle Show

Cattle show in autumn: 1st prize for the best brood mare and foal 10s, second best brood mare and foal 5s; for best 2-year old colt or filly 10s; for best 1-year old colt or filly 7s 6d; for best milk cow for dairy 10s, for second best milk cow for dairy 5s, for best grass-fed cow 10s; for best bull 10s, for best 2-year old bull 7s 6d, for best 1-year old bull 5s; best 2-year old heifer 7s 6d, best calf according to age 5s; best ram 5s, best ewe and lamb 7s 6d; best sow for breeding 7s 6d, best boar 5s; best firkin of butter 7s 6d, second best firkin of butter 5s. Information obtained from Mr John Rowan, secretary at Doagh.

Fair of Ballyclare

Ballyclare fair was held yesterday, 29th January 1839. There was about 100 horses, chiefly for farming, and younger ones, prices from 18 pounds to 6 pounds, and about 120 head of black cattle from 10 pounds to 3 pounds, and about 100 pigs and a few sheep, about 20 head.

Gingerbread stalls 6, stalls for soft goods 6, 1 stall for delf, 1 stand for besoms, 3 tents for sale of whiskey. Very small fair; *severe day*. Best fair in summer. [Signed] John Bleakly, 29th January 1839.

School and Dispensary Statistics by James Boyle, 4th February 1839

Social Economy

Table of Schools

[Table contains the following headings: name, situation and description, when established, income and expenditure, physical, intellectual and moral education, number of pupils subdivided by age, sex and religion, name and religion of master and mistress].

In a suitable schoolroom built by local subscription in the house in which the library is kept in the village of Doagh; established more than 60 years, placed under the Board of National Education in 1833; income: from the National Board annually 10 pounds, from Miss Jones of Kilwaughter 2 pounds annually, [total] 12 pounds, from pupils 24 pounds; expenditure on salaries 36 pounds; intellectual education: the females learn needlework, spelling, reading, writing, arithmetic, geography, book-keeping, mensuration, books of the National Board; moral education: Authorised Version of Scriptures at stated hours, Presbyterian catechism on Saturday; number of pupils: males, 15 under 10 years of age, 12 from 10 to 15, 27 total males; females, 19 under 10 years of age, 14 from 10 to 15, 33 total females; total number of pupils 60, 7 Protestants, 52 Presbyterians, 1 Roman Catholic; master and mistress William and Mary Johnson, Presbyterians.

In a small house purchased by subscription for the purpose and situated in the town of Ballyclare, established 1833; income: the Board of National Education grants to the master an annual gratuity of 8 pounds, 14 pounds from pupils; expenditure on salaries 22 pounds; intellectual education: spelling, reading, writing, arithmetic, books of the Board of National Education; moral education: Authorised Version of Scriptures and Presbyterian catechism on Saturdays; number of pupils: males, 10 under 10 years of age, 12 from 10 to 15, 2 above 15, 24 total males; females, 16 under 10 years of age, 9 from 10 to 15, 2 above 15, 27 total females; total number of pupils 51, 3 Protestants, 38 Presbyterians, 10 Roman Catholics; master Thomas Kelly, Presbyterian.

In a suitable room rented by subscription and situated in the town of Ballyclare, established 1832; income: the Board of National Education grants the teacher an annual gratuity of 8 pounds, from pupils 30 pounds; expenditure on salaries 38 pounds; intellectual education: Homer, Horace, Virgil, Lucian and the preparatory classics, mensuration, geography, history, reading, writing, arithmetic, the books of the National Board and others; moral education: Authorised Version of Scriptures and Presbyterian catechism on Saturdays; number of pupils: males, 2 under 10 years of age, 21 from 10 to 15, 4 above 15, 27 total males; females, 11 under 10 years of age, 11 total females; total number of pupils 38, 37 Presbyterians, 1 Roman Catholic; master William Minnis, Presbyterian.

Held on Sunday in the Methodist chapel in the village of Doagh; said to have been the first Sunday school established in Ireland, about the year 1760; intellectual education: spelling and reading; moral education: Authorised Version of the Scriptures; number of pupils: males, 5 under 10 years of age, 5 from 10 to 15, 1 above 15, 11 total males; females, 5 under 10 years of age, 9 from 10 to 15, 14 total females; total number of pupils 25, all Methodists; gratuitous teachers.

[Totals]: income from public societies or benevolent institutions 28 pounds, 68 pounds from pupils; expenditure on salaries 96 pounds; number of pupils: males, 32 under 10 years of age, 50 from 10 to 15, 7 above 15, 89 total males; females, 51 under 10 years of age, 32 from 10 to 15, 2 above 15, 85 total females; total number of pupils 174, 10 Protestants, 127 Presbyterians, 12 Roman Catholics, 25 other denominations.

Dispensary

[Table contains the following headings: name, management, number relieved, funds from public bodies and private individuals, annual expense of management, annual expenses of patients, when founded].

Dispensary; management: a committee, secretary and treasurer; number relieved: 1,000 on an annual average; funds: 35 pounds per annum from the county grand jury, 35 pounds annual amount of local subscriptions; expenditure: 3 pounds annual house rent; salaries: 50 pounds per annum to the surgeon, 3 pounds 5s per annum to a porter, total 53 pounds 5s; annual expenses of patients 70 pounds; founded 1834; this dispensary embraces in its district the parishes of Ballycor, Rashee, Ballynure, Ballylinny, Killead and this grange.

Parish of Donegore, County Antrim

Statistical Report by Lieutenant R. Stotherd,
November 1832 and February 1833

NATURAL STATE

Name and Derivation

This parish is written in some ancient records
Dunnager, Donegor, Dunnigore, etc. The orthography selected is from Beaufort's and Lendrick's
maps. Query Dun-achar, or aichear, "the sharp
hill" alias "conical hill", from the singular conical
hill called the Donegore Moat <Donnagorr Mote>.

Situation

It is situated in the barony of Upper Antrim,
county of Antrim, and lies about 3 and a half miles
east north east of Antrim. Previous to the baronial
division of this county Donegore was included in
the district of North Clandeboy.

Union

It is in the diocese of Connor, province of Armagh, and was episcopally united in 1775 to the
parish of Kilbride. The cure of the grange of
Nilteen, to which it is annexed, is also served at
this parish. It is one of the parishes which constitute the corps of the archdeaconry, the rectorial
tithes being held by the archdeacon, the vicarial
tithes only by the vicar. The reputed patron is the
bishop of the diocese.

[Insert note: Since writing the above, I have
heard that the parishes Donegore and Kilbride are
no longer united: that they now constitute 2 rec-
tories. I cannot speak with confidence on this
point. 6th February 1833].

Boundaries, Extent and Divisions

It is bounded west by the parishes of Antrim and
Connor, north west by the parish of Connor, east
and north east by the parish [of] Kilbride and
south by the grange of Nilteen. It is of a triangular
form, extending from north to south about 4 and
a half British statute miles, from east to west about
3 and a half [miles] and contains 6,650 acres and
12 perches statute.

It is divided into the following 18 townlands,
namely Donegore, Ballywee, Ballygowan,
Ballynoe, Ballyclaverty, Ballywoodock,
Ballysavage, Browndod, Cromy and
Taggartsland, Drumagorgan, Dunamuggy,
Durhamsland, Halftown, Fergusonsland,
Freemanstown, Rathmore, Rathbeg and Tobergill.

A portion of Rathmore, Rathbeg and Donegore
extend into the grange of Nilteen.

Property and Tenure

This whole parish was included in the grant from
King James I to Sir Arthur Chichester, then Baron
of Belfast, of his estates in Antrim, Down and
Carrickfergus, dated 20th November 1620 in the
19th year of his reign, from whom the lands have
descended to the present proprietor, the Marquis
of Donegall. The greater portion of this parish,
however, is leased on lives renewable forever at
a very low rent and a fixed small fine at each
renewal, and the renewal is then for the remainder. A large portion of the property is again sublet,
reducing the farms to a small extent.

NATURAL FEATURES

Surface and Soil

From its northern extremity to Donegore hill its
surface is very irregular and hilly, the highest
point being in the townland of Browndod, 861
feet above the level of the sea. From Donegore hill
to its southern boundary the slope is regular and
gradual, the lowest ground in the parish towards
the Four Mile burn being 170 feet above the sea.
This gradual slope is continued to the Six Mile
Water, which bounds the grange of Nilteen to the
south.

A great part of this parish towards the north is
still in a wild and uncultivated state, consisting of
wet, coarse pasture-land, and is capable of great
improvement by draining and enclosing. The
arable land consists of a very good, light, stony
soil, mixed with loam, and is apparently produced
by the decomposition of trap rocks. Indeed, the
progress of decomposition is observable in the
numerous excavations for the repair of the roads,
and particularly in a small quarry in the adjacent
townland of Carnearny, in which the progressive
change is exhibited in a very satisfactory manner.

The lowest bed consists of a hard porphyritic
rock, above which appear nodules of the same
imbedded in a soft paste. These nodules are in
progress of decomposition, gradually become
more rare and finally disappear in a bed of white
argillaceous clay, which extends to the natural
soil of the district at the surface, similar to that
above described.

Produce

The usual crops, alternating with grass and clover, are potatoes and oats, and a small quantity of flax. In the southern townlands wheat is sometimes grown. The following is the average produce per Irish acre, namely wheat 1 ton, potatoes 350 to 400 bushels, oats 60 bushels, flax 12 stone dressed and cleaned, and in a state ready to be spun into yarn. The above may be considered a fair average, but has occasionally been greatly exceeded. The crop of wheat is particularly uncertain and as variable as the seasons, sometimes failing altogether. A respectable farmer in the neighbouring grange of Nilteen assured me that on one occasion he had sown 11 and a half acres of wheat and half an acre of oats in the same field, from want of seed to complete it, and his crop of oats exceeded in bulk that of wheat.

System of Farming and Succession of Crops

The nature of tenure by which the lands are held under the Marquis of Donegall, namely 3 lives renewable forever at a very low rent, is a great encouragement to improvement, and accordingly we find that where the farmers so holding do not sublet, the farms are in much better order and the farmers more respectable and comfortable.

The 4 crop system is that in common use, namely first potatoes, secondly oats with grass seed and clover, thirdly meadow, fourthly pasture, for 1 and occasionally for 2 years; sometimes oats follow the grass. Turnips as a green crop are scarcely known: in fact they would not know what to do with them if they had a crop. Sheep are rarely seen and stall-feeding of cattle is seldom heard of. The neighbouring market of Belfast should be an inducement to the farmers to fatten some cattle. I am induced to make the above remarks from the soil appearing particularly well adapted to turnips and other green crops.

Turbary

The whole parish is dependent on the parish of Connor for turbary, having no supply in itself, the few bogs that formerly existed being now exhausted.

NATURAL HISTORY

Rocks

In the greater portion of the parish, at various depths under the soil, trap rocks are found; and quarries are opened in every direction for the repairs of the roads and for building purposes.

Towards the south east, and particularly in the townland called Fergusonsland, there are considerable beds of gravel, composed of fragments of trap rocks, sand and clay.

No limestone has been found in the parish, which is dependent on the large quarries near Belfast and on that at Templepatrick for a supply.

MODERN TOPOGRAPHY AND NATURAL FEATURES

Roads

The roads, for a hilly country, are in very good order. There are but 2 principal roads, namely that from Antrim to Parkgate and Doagh, and that from Templepatrick and Parkgate to Connor and Kells, which latter traverses the most bare and unimproved parts of the parish, the former the most highly cultivated.

Rivers

There are no rivers of magnitude in the parish. The principal streams are the Four Mile burn, which bounds it in its whole extent on the east, and the Ballynoe stream, whose sources are in the townlands Browndod and Ballywoodock, and which, flowing south after bounding the townlands Ballynoe, Drumagorgan, Rathbeg, Rathmore and Islandreagh, falls into the Six Mile Water. Both these streams have a considerable fall and their water may without difficulty be applied to machinery.

MODERN TOPOGRAPHY

Villages

Parkgate, about 5 miles from Antrim, is the principal village. It is situated near the intersection of the road leading from Antrim to Doagh with that from Templepatrick to Kells. It consists of 1 wide street, one-half of which is in the grange of Nilteen, the boundary running down the centre of the street. It is a very neat, clean and thriving little place, under the personal superintendence of William Ferguson Esquire, whose residence, Thrushfield, is close to the village. This gentleman has a patent for a market, but none is held. There are 4 fairs annually; that in the month of February is famed for the sale of horses.

It is a police station and the petty sessions are held once a fortnight. There is also a stamp office in the village.

There are 2 other hamlets to be noticed, namely Donegore and Four Mile Burn. The former contains about 100 inhabitants. The latter, situated about three-quarters of a mile east of Parkgate, on the road to Doagh, is partly situated in the parish [of] Donegore and partly in the grange of Nilteen.

Houses

The farmers in this parish, being independent of their landlord and holding in general large farms, are a very respectable class and the houses are in consequence neat and comfortable, many of them having a first floor. They are constructed of stone, in general thatched but sometimes slated, and the windows are always glazed.

Social Economy

Inhabitants

The inhabitants are principally Dissenters, there being very few Roman Catholics and as few of the Established Church in the union. Agriculture is the principal pursuit of the men; in consequence they have a fine and healthy appearance. Some linen is woven, but this trade has much fallen off of late years.

There are no gentlemen's seats in the parish.

Donegore Moat

Modern Topography

Churches and Places of Worship

A new church has within a few years been built in the village of Donegore. There is also a Presbyterian meeting house in the village of Parkgate and a Seceding meeting house in Dunamuggy townland. There is neither glebe or glebe house in the parish.

There are 3 schoolhouses attached to the above-mentioned places of worship.

Mills

On the Four Mile burn there are 2 corn mills, 1 flax mill and the ruins of a bleach mill. On Ballynoe stream there is also a flax mill not at present worked.

Productive Economy

Planting

Towards the south and south west there is a little planting, but in general the parish is very bare of trees.

Ancient Topography

Antiquities

One of the most remarkable features in the country is Donegore Moat, constructed on a lofty isolated crag. The moat is of that kind Spencer appears to mean when he uses the word "ban-ne." The raths or mounds commonly called Danish forts are thickly scattered over the parish. The two most remarkable are Rathmore Trench and Ballywoodock Fort, both of which are very perfect. 27th November 1832.

[Insert note: In the townland Drumagorgan there is also a large flat stone about 6 feet in length which is known by the name of the Giant's Grave in the country. It is said to have been excavated some years since and bones of large dimensions and a broken sword to have been found; the latter reported to be in the Belfast museum. [Signed] R.J. Stotherd, Lieutenant Royal Engineers, 7th February 1833].

Memoir by James Boyle, May 1838 and January 1839

Memoir Writing

Composition of Memoir

Commenced 6th May 1836, completed to and on 31st May 1838; total time employed 506 hours (57 days). [Signed] James Boyle, 31st May 1838.

Natural Features

Hills

The surface of this parish presents considerable variety, its character being hilly and its northern districts approaching almost to mountainous, while its elevations vary from 250 to 860 feet above the level of the sea.

With the exception of a narrow strip along its southern borders, this parish includes the ridge known as the Donegore hills, which extends southerly through the centre of the parish from Carnearny mountain in the more northerly and contiguous parish of Connor. A broad valley watered by a trifling stream extends along the eastern and western sides of the ridge which, at its extreme point, rises to an elevation of 540 feet above the former and 460 feet above the latter.

The outline of the ridge is varied by 2 little valleys or gorges which intersect it near its northern end. One of these, the northern end of the western valley, almost disconnects it from the mountain and unites with another in the parish of Connor. The second is parallel and near to the other with which it unites, and with it forms an almost separate and isolated feature called Browndod hill.

The declivities of the hills towards the north east and west are in general smooth and but little varied. Towards the east they are generally rapid and sometimes steep. The slopes towards the south are much varied by the cropping out of the trap <trapp>, which almost invariably reaches a crest at the extremity of the features and breaks their declivity into several successive steps. The southern extremity of the Donegore hill is a strong exemplification of this, its descent from an elevation of 780 to 320 feet being broken by 3 successive steps or terraces. Browndod hill is another instance, a basaltic hummock on its summit presenting a craggy declivity on its southern side. This character is well preserved, even its minor features, throughout the parish.

The valleys and sides of the hills are cultivated, while their summit is under pasture interspersed with heath.

The principal points in the parish are: Browndod, 860 and Ballygowan, 633 feet above the sea, near its northern side, and the Standing Stone, 787 and Donegore hill, 780 feet above the level of the sea, towards the southern extremity of the parish.

Rivers

There are no rivers and but 2 little streams in the

parish. The largest of these, known as the Four Mile burn, takes its rise in the mountains in the more northerly parish of Connor, at an elevation of about 900 feet above the level of the sea. From this it pursues an irregular course for a short distance and, descending to a level of 474 feet, enters on the eastern boundary of this parish, along which it flows southerly for 5 miles, separating it from the parish of Kilbride. It then, at an elevation of 164 feet above the sea, quits this parish and enters the grange of Nilteen, through which it passes, and discharges itself into the Six Mile Water at an elevation of 148 feet above the sea.

Its total length is 7 miles, its extreme breadth 27 feet and average breadth 13 feet. Its depth varies from a few inches to 3 feet, but is very irregular, owing to the ruggedness of its bed and depending upon the proximity of numerous rapids and the effects produced on its bed by the very violent floods, to which, owing to the height of its source and the rapidity and inequality in its inclination, it is subject.

Its average fall is 1 in 40 feet in this parish and 1 in 46 feet in its entire course. Its bed is alternately rocky and gravelly. Its banks are generally high and steep enough to confine its floods and prevent their being mischievous or making any deposit. They rise very rapidly and subside equally so.

It affords a constant supply of water, however, to the little corn mills along its banks. Its situation in this respect is advantageous and might be rendered as much so, in that of draining the springy and wet districts along the eastern side of this parish.

The Ballynoe stream takes its principal source from Carnearny mountain in the adjoining and north westerly parish of Connor, at an elevation of about 800 feet above the level of the sea. This, being joined [by] several other rivulets from the north east, descends to a level of 530 feet above the sea [and] enters the north west side of the parish. From this it flows southerly for 2 and a half miles, occasionally forming its western boundary and separating it from the parish of Antrim. Having descended to a level of 232 feet, it enters the grange of Nilteen, through which it flows for 1 and three-quarter miles, and discharges itself into the Six Mile Water at an elevation of 128 feet above the level of the sea.

The extreme breadth of this stream in this parish is 14 and average breadth 9 feet. Its depth varies from 1 to 2 and a half feet but, owing to the unevenness of its bed, is very variable. Its inclination is very variable but averages 1 foot in 39 feet. Its bed is occasionally gravelly but for the most part rocky and stony. Its banks are in a few instances steep and high, but in general they are low. Its floods are very impetuous, rising very rapidly and, owing to the velocity of its fall, subsiding equally so. They therefore do not spread, and commit little or no injury to the lands along its banks, but immense quantities of stones and gravel are rolled down by it. In this parish it is in only one instance applied to machinery, but it might with some trouble be still further converted to that purpose, to a trifling extent. It might with considerable advantage and little trouble be employed in draining the marshy lands along its banks.

Springs

The parish is amply supplied with spring and river. Springs are numerous in all its districts and there is scarcely a farm which is not watered by, or in the vicinity of, a rivulet.

Bogs

There is not in this parish any bog which is cut for fuel, nor are there any tracts of bog. Occasionally a small patch of bog is to be found, either in a marshy hollow where water has lodged, or along the acclivity of a hill where a spring may have oozed forth. These patches are shallow and of very trifling extent. There is not any timber to be found in them.

Woods

There is not any natural wood in the parish except a few stunted old hawthorns and a very little hazel brushwood.

Climate

The climate of this parish varies in its different districts. Along its southern side, where it is highly cultivated and possesses a southerly aspect, it is dry and warm, and the seasons are early; while towards the northern side it is damp and, from its more mountainous character, subject to mists and rains attracted from Lough Neagh. The moisture of the ground along its western side also tends towards that of the climate.

Soil and Crops

Along the sides of the hills towards their summit the soil is light and shallow, and consequently warm; but as it approaches the valleys along their eastern and western sides, the soil becomes moist and almost marshy and abounding in springs. The growth of wheat is therefore almost confined to the southern district of the parish, where it is sown soon after the raising of the potatoes in November.

Oats is sown throughout the parish during the latter part of March and the month of April. Along the south side of the parish its reaping commences about the last week in August and terminates by the middle of September. The harvest becomes gradually later towards the north of the parish and is seldom quite finished by the middle of October.

The general planting of potatoes takes place during the month of May and their raising during the month of November.

The climate of the parish has improved perceptibly within the last 10 years, owing to the cultivation of the land along its northern and western sides, and is gradually becoming less subject to mists and rain.

MODERN TOPOGRAPHY

Village of Parkgate

There is no town in the parish.

The neat little village of Parkgate is situated at the southern side and near to the south western corner of the parish. It is built along both sides of the road from Antrim to Carrickfergus through Doagh and Ballyclare. This road forms the boundary between the parish of Donegore and the grange of Nilteen, in each of which a portion of the village is situated. Its full description will, however, be found in the Memoirs of this parish.

Parkgate: Situation

Parkgate is situated on the direct and ancient road from the town of Antrim to that of Carrickfergus, in the diocese of Connor, manor of Moylinny, barony of Upper Antrim, and townland of Durhamsland in the parish of Donegore and Moyadam in the grange of Nilteen. It is 5 miles east of Antrim, 14 miles west of Carrickfergus and 13 miles north west of Belfast.

Its extreme length from east to west is 402 yards and its breadth 19 yards. It consists of 31 houses and cottages, of which 11 are situated in this parish.

Parkgate is rather prettily situated near the base of the Donegore hills, which form the northern side of the rich and populated valley of the Six Mile Water, from the opposite side of which its whitened houses and cottages can [for] a considerable distance be seen peeping through trees.

Nothing concerning its origin or history can be locally ascertained. Its name would imply its being of modern date, and the patent for holding 12 monthly markets on the second Monday in each month, and 4 annual fairs on the 7th February, 7th May, 7th August and 4th November, is also of comparatively modern date, having been granted, 1787, to William Ferguson Esquire of Thrushfield (near the village), the present proprietor.

The road on which Parkgate is situated is said to have at one time been the only communication between the garrison of Carrickfergus and those at Antrim and Toome; that it passed through a vast deerpark, at one extremity of which this village was erected; and that it took its name from the gate at the entrance to the park being erected in it. This is in some degree borne out by the circumstance of there being another place of the same name 2 miles further on the road towards Carrickfergus, where the gate at the entrance to the park at its opposite side is said to have stood. There being no townland of the name still further strengthens this tradition.

Parkgate was formerly a little larger than at present, and has been almost entirely rebuilt within the last 32 years by its present proprietor. It had, however, never been of more importance than at present. On the contrary, it has since its rebuilding improved almost [in] every respect.

There are not any ancient buildings nor remains of antiquity in its vicinity.

Public Buildings

The only public building in Parkgate is a Presbyterian meeting house situated at its north eastern end. It is a plain, substantial old building, built of stone and roughcast. It consists of a main aisle standing east and west, and measuring externally 65 by 28 feet. To the centre of this, at its southern side, is a small addition measuring 28 by 27 feet. It is pretty comfortably fitted up internally with pews and has a spacious gallery, the entrance to which is from the outside by a flight of stone stairs. It contains accommodation for 1,000 persons.

A neat 1-storey cottage is fitted up as a barrack for constabulary and contains accommmodation for 4 men.

Houses

Parkgate contains 8 2-storey houses and 27 cottages. All the houses are slated and so are 19 of the cottages, and all are substantially and neatly constructed of stone and lime, roughcast and kept neatly whitened. The appearance of the entire village is cleanly and cheerful.

SOCIAL AND PRODUCTIVE ECONOMY

Population

The population are all of the middle and lower grades, and is almost exclusively made up of petty dealers and tradespeople, there being but 1 agricultural labourer in the village (see Table of Trades and Occupations, Appendix). They amount to 156 persons and are remarkable for their industry and good conduct. They are all comparatively comfortable in their circumstances and manner of living.

Petty Sessions

Petty sessions are held in Parkgate on every alternate Monday. The magistrates who form the bench are Thomas Benjamin Adair of Loughermore and John Owens of Ballyvoy, Esquires. A statement of the cases tried at these sessions will be found in Appendix.

Fairs and Markets

A patent was granted to the present proprietor in 1787 for holding 12 monthly markets on the second Monday in each month, and 4 annual fairs, namely on 7th February, 7th May, 7th August and 4th November. The markets are not held but the fairs are.

The February fair is the most important: from 600 to 700 horses, besides a considerable number of cows and pigs and some sheep, are usually exposed for sale at it. The horses brought to this fair are principally of the description required by the farmer and might average 12 pounds each in value. There are, however, always a few of a better description and some of them are purchased by the Scotch and English dealers, who always attend this fair. The numbers of cows and pigs exposed for sale are also considerable.

At the May fairs not quite half the number of horses are offered for sale. It is a much better fair for cows, being the season for purchasing cattle for grazing, and is well attended by dealers. The August fair is principally for beef cattle and the number brought to it is considerable, as is also that of sheep. Very few horses are brought to this fair. The November fair is very inconsiderable.

As no tolls or customs are levied at these fairs, a more accurate statement of the number of cattle brought to them cannot be obtained. They are, however, on the increase. Some stalls of pedlar's goods, old clothes, fruit and huxtery complete the fairs at Parkgate.

MODERN TOPOGRAPHY

Hamlet: Four Mile Burn

There are 2 little hamlets in the parish. One of them, Four Mile Burn, is situated on the road from Parkgate to Carrickfergus, 1 mile from the former and on the stream which forms the eastern boundary of the parish, and from which the hamlet takes its name. It merely consists of 3 2-storey houses and 11 1-storey cottages, besides a corn mill. Though pretty comfortable and neat in their appearance, [they] are built without the slightest regard to regularity or uniformity. One of them contains a grocery and another a spirit shop, and the rest are occupied by 2 farmers and by 9 agricultural labourers.

The entire population consists of 73 persons, who are quiet and industrious. The labourers are rather poor and their dwellings are neither neat nor comfortable, but the other families are rather independent in their stations and exhibit some taste in the keeping of their houses.

Four Mile Burn is very prettily situated in a little valley and quite embosomed in trees. There is nothing in it worthy of further notice.

Hamlet: Donegore

The hamlet of Donegore occupies rather an extraordinary position on the steep acclivity, and near the summit, of Donegore hill, in the townland of Donegore and 500 yards north of the road forming the southern boundary of the parish. A by-road from the latter to Kells, Connor and Ballymena passes through the hamlet.

The houses constituting the hamlet are of comparatively modern erection and their number has been doubled within memory. There are no marks of antiquity about it, nor is there any reason to suppose that it has any claim to it further than its church, which is said to be of ancient erection and to have [been] used successively [by] Roman Catholics, Protestants of the Church of England, Presbyterians and again by members of the Church of England, in whose possession it now is. It is much smaller than formerly and does not possess any architectural ornament.

Almost overhanging the church is an ancient mound known as Donegore Moat, which forms a conspicuous object in the landscape. It is not, however, in any way connected with the village.

Donegore consists of 4 2-storey houses and 7 1-storey cottages scattered irregularly in every direction within a few yards of the church. They are all constructed of stone and lime, and most of them are slated. They are substantial and roomy, but few of them are cleanly or comfortable in their appearance. They are occupied by 2 spirit dealers, 1 grocer, 1 schoolmaster and parish clerk, a sexton and 6 farmers. There are also several cabins and cottages scattered about the hamlets. They are occupied by agricultural labourers who are rather poor in their circumstances.

The parish church is the only public building. It forms, as it were, the nucleus for this cluster and is an uninteresting-looking building without tower or belfry, having merely a little arch, from which a bell is suspended, elevated on its western gable. It stands east and west, and measures externally 46 by 31 feet. The walls are 3 feet 6 inches thick. It [is] pretty well fitted up with pews, but is cold, damp and comfortless; contains accommodation for 120 persons. It is in tolerable repair.

The present church stands on part of the foundations of the former one, which was 21 feet longer than it. It bears the date 1659 inscribed on it over the doorway.

Public Buildings

The one public building in the parish, besides those already described, is the Seceders' meeting house in the townland of Dunamuggy, near the eastern side of the parish and on the left of the road from Parkgate to Kells and Connor. It is a plain and substantial old structure, measuring externally 55 by 28 feet. It is pretty well fitted up with pews and contains accommodation for 280 persons. It bears the date 1788 inscribed on it and was repaired in 1830 by the congregation, at an expense of 110 pounds.

Machinery

The machinery of the parish consists of 1 corn and 2 flax mills.

The corn mill is situated in the townland of Fergusonsland. It is propelled by a breast water wheel 15 feet 3 inches in diameter, 2 feet 4 inches broad, and having a fall of water of 16 feet.

The flax mill in the townland of Freemanstown is propelled by a breast water wheel 15 feet 8 inches in diameter, 2 feet 6 inches broad, and having a fall of water of 12 feet.

The flax mill in the townland of Fergusonsland is propelled by a breast water wheel 13 feet in diameter, 1 foot 6 inches broad, and having a fall of water of 12 feet.

Communications

This parish possesses in all its districts every facility of communication and intercourse with those adjoining it, and with the neighbouring towns and villages, by means of numerous roads traversing it.

Considering the inequality of its surface and the remoteness of some of its districts, they are not so hilly or in such indifferent repair as might be expected. The soil of the higher grounds is generally light and dry, and the material with which they are repaired is a hard description of basalt, which is very abundant. Except by the carts of the farmers, they are but little frequented and they might therefore, by a little attention in not letting get too far out of repair, and by avoiding 2 steep hills, be easily kept in excellent order.

There are not any main roads of consequence in the parish. The principal leading road is that [from] Antrim to Doagh and Ballyclare. This road extends all along the southern side of the parish, a distance of 3 and a quarter miles, and forms the boundary between it and the grange of Nilteen. Its average breadth is 24 feet. It is a good hard road and runs almost in a right line. There are 2 very steep hills on it, at its western end; they might easily have been avoided by carrying the road a little lower down the hill. This road was formerly the leading one from Antrim to Carrickfergus and, it is said, it was the only communication between the latter town and the garrisons at Antrim and Toome Bridge.

The road from Templepatrick to Kells, Connor and Ballymena through Parkgate traverses the parish near its centre from north to south for 3 and a third [miles], its breadth 24 feet. It is for the most part a good hard road and kept in tolerable repair. There are several hills on it which with little difficulty [could] be avoided. Its direction is almost rectilineal.

By-Roads

The latter road is intersected near its centre by a by-road branching from that between Antrim and Ballyclare, and traversing the summit of Donegore hill from the northern to the southern extremity of the parish. Its length in this parish is 3 and a half miles and its average breadth 20 feet. It is not kept in good repair, nor well laid out, being very hilly. In ascending the southern end of Donegore hill, its inclination for 616 yards averages 1 foot in 7 feet. There are 2 other hills on it, but they are not of so much consequence. This road is very rarely used by conveyances.

A road extends northerly from the latter for 4 miles. Its average breadth is 20 feet. It is in tolerable order but is very hilly.

A road extends along the western side of the parish from that at its southern to the road leading to Connor. There are 3 and an eighth miles of it in this parish; its average breadth is 18 feet. Speaking comparatively, it is not hilly, but it might have, with as little difficulty, been laid out in an almost level and direct line, and thereby have been more easily kept in repair. For the mighty rains which fall in hilly and mountainous districts must naturally produce a much greater effect upon roads with rapid inclinations, their floods acquiring increased velocity and committing increased mischief in their progress. This road is much torn up in rainy weather and, but for its hard bottom, could with difficulty be kept passable. It is kept in very middling repair.

A road leading towards Kells and Connor passes through the north of the parish from south east to north west. There are 2 miles of it in this parish. Its average breadth is 19 feet. It runs in a direct line, but is rather hilly and not kept in good repair.

All these roads are kept in repair at the expense of the barony of Upper Antrim, in which they are situated.

Bridges

There is no structure in the parish to which the term of bridge can be properly applied, but there are numerous pipes over the little streams which flow through it. They are sufficiently numerous and are in general in good repair.

Scenery

Except along the southern extremity of the parish, there is nothing [in] its own immediate appearance which could arrest the attention or interest the eye of the traveller. Though its northern districts are hilly, still there is nothing bold or striking in their formation, and their partially cultivated state renders them still more uninteresting, as they neither possess the wildness they should otherwise present, nor are they sufficiently cultivated to convey an idea of their fertility or the industry and comfort of their inhabitants. The almost total want of hedgerows and planting is sadly perceptible and gives them a dreary and desolate appearance.

To this, the southern extremity of Donegore hill presents a striking contrast, in its fertile and highly cultivated state. It is thickly peopled and ornamented with a large clump of thriving planting. Its moat and crags which break its steep[ness]

stand out from it in high relief and form a conspicuous and singular ornament to the landscape. It is to be seen from a distance of 18 miles, and from it, as well as from the summit, a magnificent prospect of the entire of Lough Neagh and a view bounded only by the Mourne Mountains on [the south], those of Derry and Tyrone on the west, and nearer home by the Belfast mountains on the east, may be had.

The rich and populous valley of the Six Mile Water (of the northern side of which this hill forms a portion), studded with comfortable residences of a wealthy yeomanry, may be seen from almost one extremity to another. This part of the parish is thickly inhabited, while its northern districts are but thinly sprinkled with the less tasteful habitations of a scanty population.

SOCIAL ECONOMY

Early Improvements

The parish of Donegore forms a portion of the vast estates granted to the Chichester family by James I about the year 1605. As this was the means of establishing a Scottish colony in it, it may perhaps be regarded as the primary cause of the improvements which have subsequently taken place in it.

A Protestant congregation was soon after established here, as would appear from an entry in the Ulster Visitation Book in the year 1622, and the adjoining parish of Kilbride seems to have been at that period, as it still is, united to it. The entry in the Visitation Book states that "the Reverend John Sterling M.A. is resident in Kilbride and serveth the cure, the church decayed." These parishes are still episcopally united. The church, which bears the date 1659, is situated in that of Donegore. It had at one time been much larger and was until the latter part of the 17th century used by the Presbyterians.

In the settlements which took place here, the original possessors of the soil seem to have been wholly extirpated, there being at present not the slightest trace of the aboriginal inhabitants; and within the last 10 years there was not a Roman Catholic landholder in the parish.

The southern portion of the parish only would appear to have at first been inhabited, as its northern and more remote districts are still very thinly inhabited and partially reclaimed or cultivated, while the former is populous and the land in a very high state of culture.

Progress of Improvement

A recent source of benefit to the farmers in this

parish was the embarrassed circumstances of their landlord, the Marquis of Donegall, who, to enable him to raise money, was obliged to grant leases in perpetuity at an almost nominal rent. This had for some time been foreseen, and many of the tenants in this parish by their frugality and industry were enabled to take advantage of the opportunity by paying the necessary purchase. Some indeed have embarrassed themselves by borrowing money without making any exertion to liquidate their debt and have been obliged either to mortgage or sell their property.

The opening of communications by means of roads with the more remote and hilly districts has led to their colonisation and cultivation. Within memory their appearance has been almost wholly altered, they having formerly been only fit for pasture, while now the sides of the hills are chequered with fences and present all the indications of an agricultural district.

The parish is advantageously situated with respect to markets for its produce. The great weekly market for every description of farm produce, at Ballymena, is 10 miles from its centre, and Belfast, in returning from which the farmers can bring lime from the kilns at Carnmoney, is 14 miles distant. Besides these, there is in the season a good weekly grain market at Antrim, which is within 5 and a half miles from the centre of the parish.

Though the inhabitants of this parish have been, as in the generality of Scottish districts, an enlightened and civilised people, still a much stronger taste or spirit for information has latterly been excited by the establishment of a book club in the year 1834, which holds its meetings in [the] village of Parkgate and consists of 35 members. A further proof of an increased desire for information is evinced in the more extended course of education now afforded at the schools in the parish. The people, however, are not improving so rapidly as might be expected. They certainly are rather a moral race, but their dogged and obstinate manners and ideas cause them to look on every newly introduced improvement as an innovation, their prejudices against which can be removed only by time and custom.

The names of the inhabitants of this parish would almost be a sufficient indication of their Scottish extraction. Those of Ferguson, Agnew, Boyd, Beck, Donald, Crawford, Sloan and Campbell are among the most prevalent.

Obstructions to Improvement

It cannot be said that there is any actual obstruc-

tion to improvement, either as to the morals or circumstances of the people. Still, however, the unsettled state of matters between the rector and parishioners as to tithes has created a litigious taste and hostility to the Established Church which is much to be lamented, and the more so as it might, if not altogether avoided, at least have been greatly diminished by a little prudence and conciliation.

The tithes of the union, including the parishes of Donegore and Kilbride, have within memory been raised from about 120 pounds to nearly 700 pounds per annum. The last increase took place under the present incumbent, when the parish was viewed by a commissioner sent by government, who it is alleged, raised the tithes to their present amount without any reference to the average of the 7 years preceding. This the people refused to pay, and with a very few exceptions have persisted in refusing. A lawsuit brought by the rector 2 years ago, and which is still pending, was the inevitable result. The parishioners united and raised a sum to defray the expenses of the suit, and there the matter rests.

A spirit of opposition to the system of tithes has hereby been raised in the parish, and it is by no means allayed by the circumstances of the rector being non-resident, merely coming over from the county Down to assist his curate in performing the service on Sunday.

Local Government

There are no magistrates actually in the parish, but there are 3 residing within a mile of its confines. Petty sessions for the district in which the parish is included are held in Parkgate on every alternate Monday. At these, 2 magistrates always attend, namely Thomas Benjamin Adair of Loughermore, in the adjoining grange of Nilteen, and John Owens of Ballyvoy, in the adjoining parish of Kilbride, Esquires, who are universally and deservedly respected, and possess the confidence of the people. The cases tried at these sessions are generally trivial and unimportant, relating chiefly to petty assault and disputes about wages and trespasses. A detailed account of them will be found by referring to Appendix.

4 constabulary are stationed at Parkgate.

The parish is included in the manor of Moylinny, the courts of which for this portion of the manor are held at Doagh, [blank] miles distant, once in 3 weeks. Sums under 20 pounds late Irish currency are recoverable at these courts by civil bill process.

Courts leet are held at Doagh once in 6 months. The Marquis of Donegall is lord of the manor, Mr Arthur Adair Gamble, seneschal.

No outrages of any kind have been committed within a recent date, the parish being quite free from crime and disturbance. There is neither illicit distillation nor smuggling. There are not any fire or life insurances, nor have losses been sustained by fires for several years.

Dispensary

This parish is included in the district of the Doagh dispensary, which is 2 and a half miles distant from its centre. This dispensary was established in the year 1834 and is supported in the usual manner, namely by the local contribution of a sum to which a similar one is added by a presentment of the county grand secretary. In cases of accidents the dispensary has proved of use in the ready and more skilful assistance it affords.

Still, there is no perceptible change in the health of the people: on the contrary, the village and greater portion of the townland of Donegore has never for the last 12 months been free from a virulent fever, which has in several cases proved fatal. It commenced with some poor labourers' families and, not having been checked in time, it quicky communicated itself to those of some of the neighbouring farmers. It is supposed to have been induced by want of sufficient nutritive food in the spring of 1837, and from a want of attention to cleanliness in the habits and abodes of those with whom it commenced. It is now, however, happily disappearing. The people are generally healthy and hardy, and comparatively free from disease.

A statement of the funds of this institution, and a table of diseases for the district it embraces, will be found in the Memoir of the grange of Doagh, in which the dispensary is held; but no separate list of the cases in this parish is kept.

Schools

The people of this parish have always been a comparatively enlightened race, that is, with few exceptions they have been educated to a greater or less extent. A reference to Appendix will show that the parish possessed a school more than a century ago, and the establishment of the 2 others in it has not been a matter of recent date. Their effects on the people cannot therefore be now spoken of comparatively. The system of education has been latterly much improved and its extent less limited. A spirit or taste for acquiring

knowledge and information has thereby been excited, as is evinced in the establishment of a book club in Parkgate, in the year [blank].

Another circumstance proves the desire for education in this parish, namely the much greater proportion of children between the ages of 10 and 15 to be found in its schools. There are at present 150 children attending the schools in this parish, being almost precisely one-tenth of its entire population.

Poor

In the united parishes of Donegore and Kilbride, and the grange of Nilteen, there are 17 persons resident who depend for their support upon the charity and benevolence of the people. These 17 mostly confine their wanderings to the union and are cheerfully supported by the voluntary contributions of the farmers, generally consisting of a few potatoes or a "gowpen" of meal. [Insert footnote: A gowpen signifies as much as can be contained between both hands].

The collections at the parish church, amounting annually to 9 pounds, are distributed among the poor of the union, as are also the principal portions of the collections at the 2 meeting houses in this parish, that at Parkgate amounting annually (on an average) to 15 pounds 12s and that in the townland of Dunamuggy to 9 pounds 2s. The parish is, however, subject to the visits of strolling paupers from the neighbouring districts.

Religion

About four-fifths of the population of this parish are Presbyterians, rather more than one-fifth are Protestants of the Church of England and the remainder are Roman Catholics.

There are 2 congregations of, and 2 places of worship for, Presbyterians in the parish. One of these congregations worships at the meeting house in Parkgate and is in connexion with the Synod of Ulster. The stipend paid annually by the congregation to their minister amounts to 55 pounds 7s 8d farthing and the regium donum to 92 pounds 6s 1d. The congregation is at present vacant.

The second congregation is [in] connexion with the Secession Synod. They worship at the meeting house in the townland of Dunamuggy. Their minister receives from them an annual stipend of 35 pounds, besides 50 pounds regium donum.

The members of these congregations are not confined to any particular parish or district, nor do all the Presbyterians in this parish worship at the meeting houses in it, many of them being members of those in the neighbouring ones.

In the Established Church this parish is episcopally united to the adjoining one of Kilbride and the adjoining grange of Nilteen, the united tithes of which have been valued under the Composition Act at nearly 700 pounds. This valuation having been resisted by the inhabitants as illegal, but a small portion of them is paid, in consequence of which a lawsuit was brought about 2 years ago by the rector, and is still pending. The inhabitants of the grange of Nilteen refuse on the grounds that the grange had never paid tithe.

The rector resides in the county Down but attends at the parish church here every Sunday. He keeps a curate to whom he pays 75 pounds per annum. He resides in the grange of Doagh, 2 and a half miles distant from the centre of the parish.

There is neither glebe nor glebe house in the union. The average attendance at church does not exceed 35 persons throughout the year.

In the Roman Catholic Church this parish is united to those of Antrim and Drummaul, the parish priest of which resides at Randalstown, 8 miles distant. There is no place of worship for Roman Catholics in the parish. The nearest is that at Antrim, where most of them worship. The priest is supported in the usual manner by his flock. His income, according to his own statement, amounts to but 150 pounds, while the general impression is that it exceeds 500 pounds. He has a curate to whom he pays an annual salary.

Habits of the People: Houses

In general the style of the houses and cottages throughout the parish, but more particularly in its southern districts, is substantial, dry and warm. All are built of stone and lime, and about one-third of them are slated. Some of the better description of farmers have neat 2-storey houses with roughcast and whitened fronts, slate roofs and good sash windows. They are roomy, cleanly and comfortable, and are usually enclosed in a little planting of sycamore or ash. They are well furnished and have suitable offices attached to them.

The more common description of farmhouse is 1-storey, generally slated, and consists of a kitchen and from 2 to 3 other apartments, pretty comfortable, though [not?] kept very neatly either internally or externally, nor with much regard to cleanliness. They are generally lit by lead windows and seldom have more than 1 fireplace, consisting of a large hearth at one extremity of the kitchen. They are usually surrounded by a little cluster of trees.

The cottages and cabins are in general dry, warm and sufficiently roomy, but rather deficient in cleanliness and neatness, and not nearly so comfortable as they might easily be rendered without expense or trouble. Most of them are thatched. They generally consist of 2 apartments, one used as a kitchen and the other as a sleeping room. Their furniture is scanty, consisting of a table, 1 or 2 chairs and a couple of "creepies" (stools). 2 beds on low stocks are considered sufficient for a family, no matter how large, and 1 very frequently is all that is required. These cottages generally have a couple of lead windows of tolerable size, and a single hearth with a wide chimney serves for a fireplace.

Agriculture

This parish is almost exclusively an agricultural district. It is inhabited by 307 families (1,701 individuals), of which 180 families are chiefly employed in agriculture and 73 are employed in trade, manufactures and handicraft. There [are] 107 agricultural labourers, 2 labourers not employed in agriculture and 38 female servants; 849 are males and 852 are females.

The farms usually consist of from 7 to 30 acres, and a further idea may be formed of their extent from the circumstance of there being 151 occupiers of land who do not employ labourers and only 26 who do.

Except in its southern district, agriculture is in a rather backward state as regards the actual culture of the ground, but still there are striking indications of a civilised and improving people to be found in the modern cart and other farming implements; nor is the low-backed Irish car, with its primitive harness, so common in retired and mountainous districts, ever to be seen here.

Food and Dress

The farmers are generally independent in their circumstances, industrious in their habits and frugal in their manner of living. Their food consists of stirabout or potatoes according to season, some salt or hung meat, eggs and baker's bread, to which the oaten cake has almost wholly given place. Tea is, in winter, in general use among them, but in summer it is not so much used. Though there is much comparative comfort in their mode of living, still they have not much idea of domestic economy or neatness.

They dress very neatly and respectably when attending their places of worship or of amusement or business, and in a manner little inferior to that of the inhabitants of almost any other part of the neighbourhood.

General Character

Generally speaking, they are a moral race, and perhaps more so than in the more frequented and southern districts. To a casual observer their morality and apparently strict observance of the sabbath would appear striking. They are regular in their attendance at their meeting houses, where in summer they hear 2 services, with an "intermission" of about half an hour in between them; but this half-hour, as well as another or two after service, are by the majority spent in the ale house, an establishment almost invariably to be found in the immediate vicinity of the northern places of worship. With this exception the sabbath is most properly observed.

They are rather prone to drinking spirits though they are seldom to be found in a state of actual inebriety. In other respects there is still room for further improvements.

They are considered as being remarkably honest and rather punctual in their engagements. In their manners they are anything but prepossessing. To a stranger they would appear rude and ungracious, but this is only manner. They are very uncommunicative, and even in the lowest grade in no way outwardly evince any respect for their superiors or for those on whom they may be dependent for their support.

There are not any political societies, but the Presbyterians are very bigoted in their religious and political ideas, [being] warmly attached to their own and hostile to any other form of worship, particularly that of the Established Church. In 1798 the inhabitants of Donegore took a conspicuous part by joining, almost to a man, in the rebellion of that year, and they were the first to commence the attack in the town of Antrim on the 7th June, for a day or two previous to which they were encamped on Donegore hill.

Amusements

The pressure of the times has almost totally deprived them of their taste for amusements. Dancing formerly was their favourite one. It is now almost given up and their only recreation now consists in attending the summer fair.

They are not remarkable for marrying particularly early in life.

Fuel

Turf, which, though not abundant in this parish, is to be had in the neighbouring ones, is their sole fuel. The poorer class, owing to its distance, are badly off in winter for fuel.

General Remarks

The foregoing remarks refer to all classes, except as to their living. In this respect the cottiers and labourers differ from the farmer in consuming very little animal food, their diet chiefly consisting of potatoes and milk with salt herrings, and occasionally a little pork or bacon.

The average number in a family is 5 and 166/307.

They are rather a long-lived race: persons of from 70 to 85 are to be found in almost every townland. The only remarkable instance of longevity was that of John Drummond of Tobergill, who died a short time since at the advanced age of 111 years.

Customs

Being a Presbyterian district, such things as patrons or patrons' days are unknown. There are no legendary tales or stories of any interest, as they relate merely to the sayings and doings of the fairies, in whom an implicit belief exists. This, however, is confined to the very old and the unenlightened.

Their only peculiar custom, and one which indeed exists in most of the neighbouring districts, is that of issuing invitations to all whom they wish to attend at the funerals of their deceased friends, and none other are expected to attend them. Their wakes, which formerly had been scenes of amusement, are now observed with decorum and propriety, the evening being spent in reading aloud the Scriptures. During the night refreshments, consisting of bread and cheese, whiskey, pipe and tobacco, are handed about.

Their christenings are occasions of mirth and feasting, the family usually inviting as many "sitters" (as the guests are termed) as the house can accommodate. Their weddings, though generally followed by feasting, are much quieter scenes.

Dialect

Their dialect, particularly in the more remote parts of the parish, is strongly Scottish, as are also their idioms and old saws, which are very quaint and pithy, and plainly indicate their extraction. In these respects they do not differ from the inhabitants of the adjoining parishes, from whom they can in few others be distinguished.

Emigration

There is but little emigration from this parish: only 7 individuals emigrated during the year 1837, 8 during the year 1836 and 5 during the year 1835. Those who have gone have taken little or no capital with them, having gone out merely from the inducements of friends who had been settled abroad. The United States of America are usually their ultimate destination, but they generally embark for Canada at Liverpool.

Remarkable Events

None upon record, nor has it given birth to any remarkable person.

ANCIENT TOPOGRAPHY

Donegore Church

The church of Donegore, situated in the townland of the same name and near the south centre of the parish, is the only remnant of ecclesiastical antiquity in it. Its situation, in a little valley traversing the steep acclivity of Donegore hill, is very singular, retired and picturesque. It stands immediately under the base of the conspicuous mound called Donegore Moat, which springs from the impending hill of Donegore, rising abruptly on its northern side to an elevation of 151 feet above it, while on its southern a thickly planted craggy knoll almost totally conceals it from the view.

This church has undergone several alterations, the last of which, in 1817, curtailed its length by 21 feet, its present dimensions being 46 by 31 feet. It is perfectly plain and without any architectural ornament. According to an entry in the Ulster Visitation Book in 1622, this church was then "in a decayed state"; and according to the traditions of the inhabitants of the parish it had existed long previous to that period, though the date inscribed over the doorway is 1659. It is said that from the earliest ages of Christianity a religious house had stood here, that it had been used by the Protestants from the period of the Reformation until the settlement of the Presbyterians in the neighbourhood, when it was occupied by the latter, who held it until the revolution of 1688, when it was restored to the Established Church.

There are not any tombstones of earlier date than 1617. A stone erected to the memory of the Reverend Archibald Stewart, Presbyterian minister of Donegore, still remains in the outside of a fragment of a wall, of the portion taken off the church in 1817.

The only names inscribed on the tombstones in the burial ground of this church are those of the Scottish and English settlers and their descendants. No family of note bury here, nor is [it] the place of interment of any family. The burial ground, though well enclosed, is kept in a most disorderly and neglected state.

Ancient Abbey

In the townland of Rathmore, near the south west corner of the parish and a few yards to the west of the fort known as Rathmore Trench, is a field called the Castle Field, in which an abbey and castle are said to have formerly stood. Their foundations are now with much difficulty to be imperfectly traced, but within memory fragments of walls, said to have been of exceeding strength and thickness, have stood there.

Tradition asserts that a communication through the mountains at one time existed between this abbey and the celebrated one at Connor (6 miles north of it), but of this no trace can now be discovered. Quantities of human bones and some silver coins (not now forthcoming) have been dug up about these foundations.

Military: Castle Field

The Castle Field just alluded to and the foundations of the alleged castle in it are now the only military remains in this parish.

The Castle Field occupies the summit of a little swell on the bank extending along the south side of the parish and forming a portion of the northern side of the valley of the Six Mile Water, above which it is elevated 224 feet, and of which, as well as of the southern districts of the county west of the Belfast mountains, it commands a very extensive view. The prospect northwards is less extensive and terminates in the neighbouring mountains. There is not any eminence within a mile by which this position is commanded.

Pagan Remains

Numerous remains of pagan antiquities are still to be found in the more retired and uncultivated districts of this parish, particularly in its northern and western districts. Many have been destroyed within memory and those which still remain have been so much mutilated that of either but an imperfect description can now [be] afforded.

Druidical Altars

At the north western extremity of this parish, and at the northern extremity of a broad valley formed by the hilly ridge extending northward from Donegore hill in this parish, and by that extending north and south from Carnearny mountain in the more westerly parishes of Connor and Antrim, stands an almost isolated feature known as Browndod hill, taking its name from the townland in which it is situated. The southern extremity of this hill is situated in this parish, its northern being in that of Connor. From the valley alluded to, 2 little defiles extend northward along the eastern and western sides of the hill and, uniting again at its northern side, expand into 1 wide valley extending into that watered by the Kells or Glenwhirry river.

The high road from Templepatrick and Parkgate to Kells, Connor and Ballymena runs through the western defile and immediately along the base of Browndod hill, which is 5 miles south east of Connor and 5 and a quarter miles north east of Antrim.

MODERN TOPOGRAPHY AND NATURAL FEATURES

Scenery of Browndod Hill

The country in the vicinity of Browndod hill is hilly and mountainous, and but partially cultivated and inhabited, but through the numerous glens and valleys extending from it in almost every direction, extensive and beautiful views of the more distant scenery of Lough Neagh and the counties whose shores it washes are to be had.

The northern and eastern districts of Antrim, the Derry and Tyrone chain of mountains from their northern to their southern extremity, and the still more distant mountains of Mourne form the leading features in the views from this hill, though its summit does not exceed an elevation of 860 feet above the sea, nor 200 feet above the valleys on either side of it.

This hill is of trap formation, rearing an abrupt head at its southern extremity and descending southwards by a succession of steps or terraces. Towards the north the descent is gentle and more gradual. Its eastern declivity is steep and smooth, while its western is broken by the outbreaks of the strata and rendered still more rugged by the detached stones and rocks which have rolled down from the basaltic cap on its summit. The summit of the hill is almost tabular, being but slightly varied by a few trifling swells. The western side of the hill is coated with heath, while its summit and eastern side are covered by a mossy sward.

The hill just described seems to have been particularly selected for some special purpose by a rude though religious people, if any idea can be

formed from the number of altars, circles, portions of circles and other enclosures and standing stones still to be found on it, and which, from their imperfect state, must be but the remains of works of considerable and still greater extent. By referring to the Appendix, plans of the ground and plans and views of these structures will be found.

ANCIENT TOPOGRAPHY

Altars on Browndod

The remains on this hill consist of 2 comparatively perfect altars and 1 imperfect one, 4 tumuli, 15 enclosures of various forms, the foundations of 2 buildings, a standing stone, and several ancient roads and paths. An idea of the altars may be formed from the views given in [Appendix], and their dimensions and style of structure from the plans at the end of the Memoir.

The altar at A on the summit of the hill is the most perfect and seems to have been the principal one. That at B is less perfect and seems to have been of less extent. The stones shown at C seem to have formed a third altar, but now few of them seem to occupy their former positions.

They are all formed of the rude undressed stone of the mountains. In the construction of that at A, more care seems to have been taken, the stones being more regularly set and closely fitted. The lane or row of stones is 40 feet in length and is divided into 4 almost equal compartments, each measuring inside 8 feet by 3 and a half feet. Their separation is only indicated by the stones at each side of the lane being placed nearer each other, at the extremity of each compartment. The lane seems to have at some period been covered with small stones, an immense quantity of which now lie along it. There is no appearance of the altar or semicircle having been covered, but about it are several stones which, from their longitudinal form, may probably have at one time been in an upright position.

The large flat stone in the centre of the altar measures 5 and a half feet by 3 feet. It is not raised nor set upon other stones. This altar stands south east by north west.

The altar at B differs in its bearings from the former, by standing due east and west. The enclosure at its eastern end is also less regular in its form and there is no avenue of stones but merely a confused heap lying in every position and covering, with the altar, a space measuring 100 by 41 feet. The stones in it are generally larger, but more shapeless, than in the altar at A, and from several of them lying about it, it may probably have been

Altar on Browndod

more extensive than at present. A copious spring issues from a rock about 100 yards below the altar.

The altar, or rather the collections of stones at C, are situated 110 yards to the north of the altar at B. With the exception of 3 they are all now lying, but from their longitudinal forms it is probable that they had originally been in an upright position. Several have been removed to a neighbouring fence, but from the positions of some of those still remaining, and from some marks in the ground, there seems to have been some kind of structure, if not an altar, here. Neither bones, urns, nor any other articles of antiquity have been found about these altars, though many stones have been removed, particularly from that at A, about which a careful search has been made.

Enclosures on Browndod

There are 15 enclosures on this hill. Of these, 5 are circular, 9 elliptic and 1 approaching in form to an ellipse. They are all formed of earth and stones used indiscriminately, except in 2 instances (at I and Y) where they consist of a single row of large

stones a little apart, which either have been partially sunk or, what is more probable, have been grown over by moss and other herbage. With the exception of the large enclosure at E, none of them appear more than from 4 to 8 inches above the surface of the ground, and some of them can with much difficulty be traced. [Insert footnote: I have carefully examined all these enclosures by digging them inside and outside, without making any discovery].

The enclosure E, shown in Appendix, consists of 3 compartments separated from each other by an earthen parapet similar to that enclosing the entire figure and varying in its elevation from 10 inches to 2 feet. The compartment occupying its south western portion is of a somewhat elliptic form. Across its northern side a semi-elliptic figure extends, while its south eastern portion is included in a figure more nearly approaching to a square. The extreme dimensions of the enclosure are 521 feet from north to south, 453 feet from east to west.

The western side of the enclosure occupies a little terrace or plateau running along the eastern side of the hill under a trifling bank which supports its summit, while its eastern side extends down the acclivity on that side of the hill. It is situated 518 yards north north west of the altar at A, with which there seems to have been communication by means of a beaten path or road extending between them.

The south west portion of the enclosure measures 350 feet in length from north to south by 222 feet in breadth from east to west. Its entrance is at its southern side. It is enclosed by a parapet from 5 to 14 feet in thickness which, from the fall in the ground, is from 2 to 3 feet high in the exterior along its eastern side, while in the interior its height does not exceed a few inches. It is for the most part formed of earth.

In the exterior it is founded on a row of stones varying in length from 1 foot to 3 feet 7 inches. They are rather carefully laid and are covered with earth in which a large stone occasionally appears. In the parapet along the southern side of this portion of the enclosure are 12 little hollows and attached to its exterior side are 2 more. [Insert footnote: I have searched these hollows by digging, but without making any discovery]. With the exception of one, these have been square and all have been more or less carefully faced inside with stones. The circular [one] is now the most perfect. It is 8 feet 9 inches in diameter and 22 inches deep. It is faced with a single row of stones averaging about 1 foot square. The other hollows are much less perfect in their structure and form, having been greatly mutilated by the removal of the facing stones and also by some investigation or search which seems to have taken place among them.

The enclosures outside the parapet are nearly square in their exterior and interior. The eastern one measures in the extreme 14 by 11 feet and the western one 11 feet 9 inches by 5 feet 7 inches. They are formed of earth and stones. The latter, which are rather small, seem to have been laid with some care. They do not, however, appear more than a foot above the ground. Plans of these will be found by referring to [drawings].

The northern side of this portion of the enclosure is formed by an earthen parapet from 6 to 7 feet thick and from 1 to 2 feet high. Connected with this are 3 small enclosures or mounds of earth, a few inches higher than the parapet. There are not any stones used in their construction nor can any further idea be conveyed concerning them except by referring to the plan.

A little tumulus (or what appears to have been one), consisting of a circle of 6 large stones 12 feet in diameter, is situated inside and near to the western side of this portion of the enclosure. The stones are rude, undressed and lying, and do not seem to have been laid with any degree of care.

Further Description of Enclosures

The compartment at the northern side of the enclosure measures 370 feet in [diameter] from east to west and 182 feet from north to south. It seems to have at some period been divided by an earthen parapet which extends northward for a few feet from the eastern side of the south western compartment, and in a line with this are several large stones which may have formed the base of the parapet. Within this compartment are 2 little elliptic enclosures (N) and a little tumulus (R), 21 feet in diameter and composed of 7 stones, forming an imperfect circle. The ellipses are scarcely discernible as they appear but a few inches above the ground. They consist merely of an earthen parapet about 2 feet thick and measure respectively 41 by 18 feet and 34 by 14 feet 9 inches.

The south east compartment or portion of the enclosure measures in the extreme 277 feet from north to south and 259 feet from east to west. Its form is almost square. It is enclosed on 3 sides by a stone and earthen parapet similar to that already described. On its northern side it is separated from the northern compartment by an ancient sunken road 228 feet in length and from 6 to 11 feet wide. It is sunk from 2 to 4 feet below the surface of the adjacent ground.

At the north west angle of the last compartment, and at the western end of the road just alluded to, are the foundations of a square building marked O. It measures in the extreme 41 feet 4 inches by 31 feet. It is divided into 2 chambers or compartments, that at its northern end measuring in the inside 24 by 21 feet and sunk to a depth of 6 feet below the adjacent ground.

The chamber at the southern end of the square is unenclosed at its eastern and western sides, through which there seems to have been a passage from the road leading to it. The foundations of this building appear but a few inches above the ground. They are 4 feet thick and formed of large stones laid in earth and faced in the interior. Many of them have, however, been removed and the foundations are now so much mutilated that nothing further can be conjectured or communicated concerning them.

A portion of an earthen parapet extends northerly in a curvilinear manner from the north east side of the enclosure for 270 feet. It evidently has formed a part of it and if so would have added 190 feet to its length.

108 feet to the northern side of the enclosure are the foundations of a square building (F) measuring 86 feet from east to west and 37 feet from north to south. They are situated on the verge of a little crag or cliff about 7 feet high and from the base of which a stream issues. The foundations measure 4 feet thick. They are formed of stones only, without earth or cement of any kind. The stones are large and carefully laid. It is divided into 2 compartments and there is a small fragment of a foundation which may probably have formed a third. An enlarged plan of this will be found [at end of Memoir].

The little enclosure in form resembling a horseshoe, shown at H, is probably of modern date and seems to have been formed as a place of shelter by a herdsman. It is merely an excavation in the face of the bank within feet of the north western side of the enclosure, and the earth thrown up forms a sort of parapet around it. In this a few large stones appear, but they have not been laid with any care. Its dimensions internally are 38 by 31 feet. An enlarged plan of this will be found [later].

There are 4 tumuli (as such they appear to be) on Browndod hill. They are marked in the plan G, L, R and S. That at G is the principal. It is situated on a little slope on the summit of the hill and in a trifling hollow formed by the converging of 2 roads or paths which, leading from the principal altar (at A) to the enclosure, unite immediately below the tumulus.

Its form is conical. Its circumference at the base is 66 feet and at the summit 27 feet. Its height is 4 feet. On its summit is a trifling hollow 14 inches in depth, enclosed by a row of small stones about 18 inches thick, 12 inches deep. The tumulus is with this exception constructed solely of earth. It does not contain bones, urns, ashes, nor any article of antiquity or curiosity. An enlarged plan of this will be found [later]. [Insert footnote: I have carefully examined all these structures, but without making any discovery].

The other tumuli are merely clusters of from 12 to 16 large stones thrown in a somewhat circular though otherwise irregular heap, but without earth or anything else. On searching these heaps nothing whatever could be discovered which could in any way lead towards determining their object or intention. There are several other lesser clusters of stones to be found on the hill, but as their position bears no reference to each other, it is impossible to conjecture what they may have been intended for.

Beside the enclosures before described, there are [blank] others, of which 9 are elliptic in their form. They are shown at K, N, V and at the altar at A. They consist merely of a little earthen parapet appearing but a few inches above the ground and varying in thickness from 18 inches to 3 feet. Their dimensions vary from 133 to 21 feet in length, and from 96 to 12 feet in breadth. In only one of these (an imperfect one at P) are stones used. In this one there are 5 large stones partially overgrown with moss. The enclosure at V contains a lesser one within it.

There are 5 perfect circular enclosures and 1 imperfect one, which will be found by referring to [Appendix]. Their diameters vary from 89 to 131 feet. In 3 of them a single row of stones, some distance apart and covered with earth, form the parapet. In other respects these enclosures do not differ from the ellipses.

Fragments of foundations of fences or enclosures which must have been of considerable magnitude are to be found on several parts of the hill. They will be found laid down in [the] plan.

Standing Stone

There is one remarkable standing stone on a trifling swell on the summit of the hill. Its position will be found in plan, and a sketch of it. It stands 280 yards north west of the principal altar. It has been carefully set there and beside it is another stone of much smaller dimensions.

Ancient Roads

A sunken road or path, varying in width from 5 to 9 feet, traverses the western side of the hill in a tolerably level direction for rather more than a mile. It is not paved or formed of stones, but merely by throwing up the earth on its lower side. It commences at the southern side of the hill and extends northward by the 2 lesser altars until all trace of it is gradually lost in the heath. It has not within memory been used, except casually.

A strongly marked road or path leads from the principal altar to the large enclosure at E, a distance of 538 yards. It is less strongly marked than the former path as it has not been sunken, but in crossing a little hollow near the enclosure, where it is raised from a foot to 18 inches and thereby rendered almost horizontal, at this place it is 11 feet wide, but elsewhere its breadth does not exceed 6 feet. It is not paved or formed of stones.

A road or path diverges from the former near the altar and again unites with it near the enclosure. It is less strongly marked than the latter and more resembles a beaten path. It is about 5 feet wide.

There are several other paths and portions of ancient roads on the hill, the principal of which diverges from that first described and extends northward for about half a mile, when it is finally lost in the heath.

The remains which have just been described are all that are now to be found on this hill. They have not undergone much change within memory, but it is likely that many traces have been obliterated by the growth of the heath and herbage. Those remaining still furnish ample evidence of the hill having at some period been frequented for some purpose, while now a solitary herd or peasant is the only one to disturb the peaceful seclusion of this retired and almost unfrequented spot.

The district surrounding the hill is still but partially cultivated and inhabited. Its few inhabitants, who are of Scottish extraction, must have been for but a comparatively short time occupiers of it, and it is not therefore to be wondered at that no information concerning these curious structures can be obtained from them. Neither bones, urns, nor any articles of antiquity have within memory been found here, though it is evident from their mutilated state that they have undergone some investigation, probably in the hopes of finding some of the treasures so implicitly believed to be concealed under such structures.

Druidical Circles

In the townland of Tobergill, about 150 yards east of the road from Templepatrick to Connor and Ballymena, and near the west centre of the parish, are situated upon a gentle acclivity 11 stones forming about one-half of a very fine druidical circle which within memory stood there. The diameter of the circle is 46 feet. An avenue or double row of standing stones, averaging about 3 feet high and closely fitted together, extended for 18 feet east north east from the eastern side of the circle and for 32 feet west north west from its western side, terminating at a stone measuring 3 feet 9 inches by 5 feet 11 inches by 4 feet 2 inches; but all traces of these avenues are now removed. The stones which have been removed from the circle were used in forming a fence near it. One of them was subsequently converted into a tombstone for the owner of the farm on which it stands. The stones are quite rude and undressed. They seem to have been brought from a little crag about 60 yards distant.

A very fine druidical circle, with an avenue leading from it, stood in a field in the townland of Donegore and near the summit of the hill, until about 3 years ago, when, in consequence of it having interfered with the cultivation the ground, it was totally destroyed.

The Priest's Craig, of which a description will be found hereafter, is within 200 yards of the site of this altar. Neither bones, urns, nor any articles of antiquity have been found about these structures.

Standing Stones

There are 4 remarkable standing stones in this parish which preserve an almost right line from north to south, commencing at that which stands on the mearing between this parish and the north west one of Connor, and at the point where the townland of Browndod in this parish meets those of Tardree and Carnearny in the parish of Connor. The second stone is 7 degrees south by east of the former and 572 yards distant from it, and the third is 5 degrees south by east of, and 748 yards distant from, the latter. The fourth, or rather fourth and fifth, are due south of the last-mentioned stone and occupy a conspicuous position on the summit of Donegore hill, and at an elevation of 700 feet above the sea. They are 2 miles distant from the third stone.

The first stone is of the white porphyry known in the neighbourhood as Tardree stone, the quarry being in the townland of Tardree, which is two-thirds of a mile distant. The stone is unhewn and bears no marks. Its erection must have cost considerable trouble, it being on a conspicuous position in the uncultivated mountain, at an elevation of 787 feet above the sea. It measures 7 feet 9 inches high above the ground and 3 feet 6 inches broad.

The second and third stones are also on conspicuous points of the mountain. They are of the basalt of which the mountain is formed. The former measures 2 feet 11 inches high and 1 foot 7 inches broad. The other measures 3 feet 9 inches high by 3 feet. It stands on the top of Browndod hill, 280 yards west of the principal druidical altar.

The stones on Donegore hill are of basalt and resemble in form large slabs which are quite undressed. They stand on the eastern side of a little mound 36 yards in circumference and (at present) 9 feet high. It seems to have once been conical, but it is now much mutilated. The stones, which measure respectively 4 feet 2 inches high, 3 feet 10 inches broad and 18 inches thick, and 4 feet high, 4 feet 10 inches broad and 17 inches thick, are 3 feet 7 inches apart at their base. They incline outwards and stand with their faces north and south. The only other stone is under the outside of the southern of these slabs. This may probably have been a tumulus, but nothing is known of it by the country people, nor has it any name or legend connected with it.

At 462 yards east north east of the last-mentioned stones and in the line of a very old fence now nearly razed, and within 208 yards of that which forms the mearing between the townlands of Donegore [and] Tobergill, in the latter of which it is situated, is a standing stone measuring 2 feet 10 inches high by 2 feet 4 inches by 1 foot 7 inches, seated on a rock (which just appears above the ground) and carefully secured by stones which are firmly built about its base. Its situation, which is 702 feet above the sea, is not nearly as conspicuous as that of the last-mentioned stones, but it can still be discerned from the neighbouring hills east of it in this parish.

Forts

There are in this parish 15 of the structures to which the name of forts has been indiscriminately given. In this parish there is considerable variety in their form and construction, and in some instances attention seems to have been paid to the selection of their situation, particularly in their proximity either to a stream or spring, one of which is invariably to be found in their immediate vicinity. They seem to have been the works of different races at different periods, and to have been intended for a variety of purposes. Almost every variety of fort known in the neighbourhood is to be met with in the parish, namely the cyclopean, tumulus, dun and rath, and some of these are perfect specimens of their kind. They are indebted for their preservation chiefly to the superstitious dread of the consequences attending their removal or mutilation, instances of which have been noted under the head of Social Economy; few therefore have been removed within memory.

Donegore Moat

Donegore Moat, one of the most conspicuous objects in the country, is from its situation and construction a singular structure of its kind. It occupies a position 515 feet above the sea, on the steep acclivity of Donegore hill, which rises rapidly from the right bank of the Six Mile Water to an elevation of 575 feet above it, forming a portion of the northern side of that valley. The face of the hill is broken into 3 little trap steps or hummocks which jut out from it, and on the second of these the fort or moat has been raised.

Its form (at present) is that of the lower frustum of a cone. It had formerly been almost conical and about 6 feet higher, but since its cultivation commenced (about 10 years ago) its figure has been sadly deformed. It is at present 44 feet in height from the point where the rock on which it is raised makes its appearance. At its base it is circular and rises at an angle of 40 degrees to its summit, which is oval. Its major diameter is 98 and its minor diameter 82 feet. It seems to be entirely constructed of earth taken from about its base, but no traces of its removal are now to be found about it.

A vertical pipe descends (it is said) to a depth of 33 feet from the southern extremity of its summit. A crowbar having disappeared from the hands of a farmer led to its discovery a few years ago. Several of the neighbouring inhabitants descended the pipe, which they found to be square, about 2 feet wide at the top but gradually widening to about 3 feet square at the bottom. It is built of stone and mortar made of badly burned lime, in which pieces of charred wood were found. The style of masonry was rude and the stones rather small and undressed. The bottom of the pipe was covered to some depth with mud, formed by the rain oozing into it. Nothing further is known concerning it and as it is now closed at the mouth, it cannot be explored.

The prospect from this fort is very extensive, embracing all the districts of this county south of it and west of the Belfast mountains, and extending into the more southerly counties of Down and Armagh, and the westerly ones of Tyrone and Derry. It forms a singular and conspicuous feature in the landscape, and may in clear weather easily be distinguished from points in the county Derry 25 miles west of it.

The traditions concerning Donegore Moat are vague and unsatisfactory. Some say it derived its name from Dun-a-gor, signifying "the fort of goats", from the number of these animals formerly kept about it; while others say that Dun-a-gor signifies "the bloody fort" and that this name was given it in consequence of its being the spot on which those attacked by some dreadful pestilence, which is said to have committed awful ravages in the country, were driven to die, to prevent the disease from spreading.

Cyclopean Forts

There is one fort in this parish to which, from its style of construction and unusual dimensions, the term cyclopean may perhaps be applied. It is situated in the townland of Ballywee, towards the eastern side of the parish and occupying a gentle acclivity near the base of Donegore hill. The ground about it abounds with springs, a stream from one of which now passes through the fort. Though considerably mutilated, a good idea can be formed of the extent of this fort and the scale on which it was constructed.

Its figure is an oval, the extreme diameter of which from north to south is 266 feet and breadth from east to west 185 feet. This figure is divided into 2 portions, the greater or southern one being an oval, the major diameter of which (from north to south) is 163 feet and the minor diameter 185 feet.

North of this is a circular segment, the radius of which is 81 feet. The former portion consists of an area slightly inclined to the east, enclosed on its eastern and southern sides by a rampart, now nearly razed, and on its western by 2 ramparts and 2 ditches, the interior rampart containing a portion of a gallery which once had extended along that side of the fort, ramified into its body, and communicated with the galleries which occupy the entire of the segment or northern portion of the fort, but most of which are now in such a mutilated state, either from the removal of the stones or their having fallen in, that but little of them can be explored.

The style in which the galleries are constructed is nearly similar to that used in other structures of the kind in the neighbouring districts, the stones being longitudinal and their extremities forming the face of the wall. They are rudely piled together without earth or cement of any kind, but the faces of the walls are pretty well kept and the same degree of inclination or arch carefully preserved throughout. The roofs are formed of enormous longitudinal slabs, varying in length from 6 to 7 feet and averaging about 2 feet broad and 14 inches thick. The roof does not exceed 3 feet in width, and these stones therefore not only extend considerably beyond its sides but from their length and weight render the entire structure more firm and secure. The stones in these galleries are much larger than those to be met with in any of the neighbouring districts.

The dimensions of the chambers seem to be generally similar, from 5 to 6 feet high, 4 to 7 feet wide at the bottom, 3 feet wide at the top and 13 feet long. Their sides gradually converge, each forming an elliptic segment. Their ends are circular and converge in a degree similar to their sides. The passage or communication between the chambers is by means of a square pipe, varying in width from 19 to 24 inches and in height from 20 to 22

inches, affording just sufficient room for an ordinary sized man to creep through. Some of these pipes are from 7 to 8 feet long. Some of the galleries are constructed so that the coping stones appear on a level with the summit of the rampart, while others have from 2 to 3 feet of earth over them.

Within memory a ditch of considerable width and depth encircled the entire fort, but of this only a few vestiges now remain on its western side. It is probable that the little stream which now flows through the fort is of modern origin, and that it has been turned in that direction since the fort or galleries had ceased to be occupied.

About 10 years ago an attempt to cultivate the interior of the fort and to level some of the ramparts was made by a man named [blank], who lived within a few yards of it, but this was attended by his wife's partially losing her intellects, which she has not since recovered. The fort therefore is likely to remain in its present state.

Fort in Dunamuggy

In the townland of Dunamuggy, and within a few yards of the stream forming the eastern boundary of the parish, are the remains of a cyclopean fort consisting of one-half of the rampart and ditch which encircled it, and a gallery which is constructed in the rampart and also extends nearly across the body of the fort. The remaining portion of the parapet has been removed and the fort partly cultivated. The form had been circular and its diameter from the exterior of the rampart 106 feet. The body of the fort had been slightly raised above the adjacent ground; the ditch is 9 feet wide and 4 feet deep, and the rampart varies in height above the ditch from 4 to 5 feet. It is 12 feet thick at the base and the coping stones of the gallery appear at its summit.

The gallery, which extended nearly half-way round the fort from the entrance on the north side and also diverged right across the fort, is constructed similarly to that just described in the townland of Ballywee, the stones being much smaller; those forming the roof are not exceeding 5 feet in length and averaging 4 feet. Its width at the bottom is 5 feet and at the top 3 and a quarter feet. Its height is 4 feet. It does not appear to possess any chambers, but as the stones have in many places fallen in, it cannot be thoroughly explored. The entrance to the gallery seems to have been in the inside and near to that of the fort.

Silver coins have been occasionally picked up about the fort, but none of them are now in the country. It is considered by the inhabitants who live near it as a very gentle place (that is, frequented by fairies) and some strange sights are sometimes seen about it, and delightful music is frequently heard proceeding from it. Strange to say, no misfortunes have as yet befallen those concerned in its destruction.

Fort in Browndod

On the summit of a little knoll, forming a sort of tongue and rising gradually to an elevation of 73 feet above 2 little streams which unite just below it and water the valley extending southwards from it, stands a very fine and tolerably perfect fort. It is situated in the townland of Browndod and near the northern side of the parish. The body of the fort, which is almost on a level with the ground around it, is circular, 150 feet in diameter, and is surrounded by 3 ramparts and 2 ditches. The inner rampart varies in height from 5 to 9 feet above the fort and from 9 to 14 feet above the ditch outside it. The second rampart varies in height from 3 to 9 feet above the inner ditch, the one outside being 2 feet lower than that inside it. The third or outer rampart is almost razed and nowhere exceeds 2 feet in height. Its thickness at the base is 7 feet, that of the second 16 feet and that of the inner one 22 feet. The first ditch is 16 and the outer one 9 feet wide.

The entrance to the fort is in the eastern side and is 8 feet wide. Near to its southern side, and in the inner rampart, a gallery commences which can be traced for only 71 feet, though it is probable that it extends all round, as occasionally a large stone presents a part of its surface in the face of the rampart; and had not some of the coping stones fallen in, the gallery might still, from the depth of earth above it, remain unknown. Its entrance was from the inside by a little approach which juts out from it.

The stones used in it seem similar in size to those in the last-described fort and their style of construction also seems to be similar; but as it is impossible to enter it in its present state, not[hing] further concerning it can be ascertained. Except in the gallery, earth alone seems to have been used in its construction.

Near its southern side are the faint traces of a little earthen enclosure, and from under the outside of its inner rampart a little spring issues.

In the description and plan given of this fort the depth of the ditches are given as they had originally been. They are now covered with a coat of mud and vegetable matter to a depth of from 2 to 3 feet. On clearing them out on a former occasion

the brazen pin shown in [drawings] was found at a depth of 5 feet below the bottom of the ditch at that time, and from that depth the present plan and description has been given. It is at present one of the most perfect forts in the county.

Unusual care seems to have been bestowed in selecting the situation of the fort. It seems to have been the main one in a line of forts extending along the ancient line of communication (by the defile between Carnearny and Browndod mountains) between the castle at Rathmore and the abbey at Connor, as mentioned as the tradition concerning Rathmore Castle and Abbey, though the line of forts had not been noticed before.

This fort is near the slack between the hills and at the head of the valley extending from it nearly to Rathmore Trench, which is 2 miles south of it. It commands a view of the valley and also of the 8 forts intervening along its side, and of 3 in this parish along the line to Connor, but there are no other local evidences in support of this conjecture or of the tradition alluded to.

Rathmore Trench

The fort known as Rathmore Trench is situated at the south western corner of the parish, in the townland of Rathmore, and at an elevation of 344 feet above the sea. It occupies the summit of a little swell rising from the high bank or ridge forming the northern side of the valley of the Six Mile Water, of which, as well as of the south western districts of this county and portions of those of Down, Tyrone, Armagh and Derry, with Lough Neagh, it commands a magnificent and extensive view.

The form of the fort is oval, its extreme major diameter being 161 and its minor 129 feet. At its eastern extremity it is 16 feet and at its western 12 feet elevated above the adjacent ground. A parapet of clay extends round its summit, varying in height from 3 to 6 feet. At its eastern end a mound seems, from the thickness of the parapet, to have been raised, but it is now almost wholly removed. A shallow ditch 18 feet wide encircles the fort.

In the construction or elevation of this fort advantage seems to have been taken of a little basaltic hummock upon which the clay had been afterwards heaped, and its formation considerably facilitated. Its entrance is by a steep ascent through a passage 10 feet wide in its western end.

Underneath the ascent to the fort is the entrance to an artificial cave excavated in the rock and extending in an easterly direction under the fort for 428 feet. The mouth of the cave is 5 feet wide and 5 feet 6 inches high. The cave at first descends about 4 feet, but afterwards pursues a more level line, alternately rising and descending, while the roof inclines and heightens so that in some places difficulty is found in creeping through the passages between the chambers into which it occasionally expands. Its extreme height does not exceed 9 feet and its breadth 15 feet, but both are very variable.

In the bottom of the cave, and near its mouth, is a spring which has formed a good well about 1 foot deep.

Tumulus

In the townland of Dunamuggy, in a level tract extending along the eastern side of the parish, is a tumulus or mound 18 feet high, 48 feet in diameter at the summit and 122 feet at the base, surrounded by a ditch 45 feet wide, outside which is a parapet varying in height from 2 to 6 feet. The ditch is from 2 to 5 feet lower than the ground about it.

The mound is to all appearance formed of earth, but on examining its southern side it seems that the earth merely forms a coating and that it is constructed of stones. It is almost flat on the summit. A few inequalities resembling the traces of foundations are the only vestiges of a building which is said to have once stood on it.

Neither ditch nor rampart retain their original shape or dimensions, the former varying considerably in depth and width, and the latter bearing evident marks of having at one time contained a gallery, a portion of one side of which, consisting of a row of large stones, still remaining on its eastern side. There is also the appearance of its entrance having been on the south east, as the remains of a sort of approach to the gallery can still be traced, but except the foundation stones, all the others have been removed and the rampart almost totally razed <raised>.

In the ditch, and on the south side of the mound, is a little square enclosure measuring 6 by 2 feet and denoted only by the single row of stones forming it. It bears east and west, and from its dimensions, position and proximity to a structure of the kind, it may probably be a grave.

The mound has not in itself or its enclosure suffered any injury within memory. No discoveries have been made about it, nor is any[thing] locally known concerning it. The ground about it is spouty and abounds in springs, a stream from one of which flows by its southern side. This tumulus is within 210 yards to the [?] south and west of the cyclopean fort.

Raths

There are, besides those already described, 9 earthen forts or raths in this parish. They have all been more or less mutilated and some of them are cultivated. Except one which is square, they are circular in their form and usually consist of a platform or space enclosed by a rampart and ditch, or by one of these without the other. A reference to [drawings] will more clearly illustrate their forms and relative size.

Coves

The parish of Donegore was within memory remarkable for the number of its coves and artificial caves, and also for their magnitude. Many of the former have, from time to time, either been removed or so filled up or covered, from their interfering with the cultivation of the ground, that they can be described from memory only. The cave under Rathmore Trench and the 3 coves which have been described with the forts with which they are connected are now the only accessible ones in the parish.

In the townland of Ballynoe, towards the north west of the parish, is a cove which would seem to have been discovered by the formation of a road over the summit of the little knoll in which it is constructed. The entrance appears in the fence on the roadside, but it is so blocked up with stones and brambles as to prevent ingress. It does not seem to be of great extent and can be traced externally for not more than 23 feet.

63 yards east south east of, and nearly on a level with, the base of Donegore Moat is the entrance of a cove which is now quite blocked up. The cove consists of 4 chambers, each measuring about 12 feet long, 6 feet wide at the bottom and 5 feet high. A narrow passage, just wide enough to admit a man creeping through, and about 3 feet long, forms the communication from one chamber to another. The direction of the cove is northerly and, as it preserves an inclination parallel to that of the hill, each chamber rises a step of about a foot higher than the preceding one. Its construction resembles that of the other coves in the parish.

In the townland of Ballyclaverty, and near the eastern boundary of the parish, there had been, until within a few years, an extensive cove which, in consequence of its interfering with the cultivation of the ground, was totally removed. Neither coins, weapons, ashes, bones, nor vessels of any kind have within memory been found in any of these coves.

Cairn

In the townland of Drumagorgan, and near the western boundary of the parish, is a pretty conical-shaped hill which rises to an elevation of 452 feet above the sea and about 100 feet above the adjacent country north and west of it. This hill takes its name from the townland in which it is situated. On its summit there had within memory been a cairn which, from its interfering with the cultivation of the ground, was wholly removed. It had been composed of small stones collected from the neighbouring land and piled together in a conical heap. Neither bones nor any article of antiquity were found in this cairn. From the regular form of the summit of the hill it would appear as having been artificially reduced to its present shape.

Giant's Grave

On the south side of the summit of the hill, and 130 yards from the cairn just described, is a tabular stone measuring 6 feet 6 inches by 5 feet and averaging about 1 foot in thickness, lying flat, from north to south, and partly buried in a stone fence. It seems to have been formerly almost, if not entirely, covered by a heap of small stones, many of which lie scattered about it. This conjecture is strengthened by its being, or seeming to be, the upper stone of a cromlech, from its southern end being raised about a foot from the ground and resting on a pillar. Its northern end is concealed by the ditch.

It is probable that its discovery took place on the formation of the fence. There is not any tradition connected with it, except that a giant is buried under it, and it is commonly known as the Giant's Grave or the Broad Stane.

Priest's Chair

In the face of a basaltic hummock, known in the country as the Priest's Craig, and near the summit of Donegore hill in the townland of Donegore, is an almost square recess commonly called the Priest's Chair. Though it may in all probability have been used as its name implies, its formation, as it at present appears, may have been accidentally or mechanically caused by ejecting the square mass of rock which had filled the "chair." The recess is 2 feet wide, 2 feet 5 inches deep and it is 2 feet 7 inches high at the back. It faces south and commands a magnificent and extensive view. It is said that a large slab formerly extended across the top of the chair and formed a covering for it, but

that it had been removed to be used in building a neighbouring house.

There are not any traditions concerning the "chair." It may probably have been connected with a druidical altar [which], until within the last 6 years, stood about 200 yards west of it; or its name may have been occasioned by its having been used by some Roman Catholic priest previous to the repeal of the Penal Laws.

Square Enclosures

The square enclosures shown occupy a gently inclined plane on the eastern side of and near the summit of Donegore hill, and in the townland of Tobergill. The trace of an ancient fence runs along their southern side, extending from a circular enclosure at the western [side] to a standing stone at the eastern side, and from the same circular enclosure a sod fence extends northward along their western side. The ground is smooth and covered with a sward of pasture.

These enclosures do not exceed 9 inches in elevation above the surface of the ground. They are formed exclusively of earth thrown up from an almost imperceptible hollow or trench surrounding the little parapet. Faint marks of entrances or gaps can be distinguished, but no other vestige that can in any way lead to an idea of their purposes or uses.

The circular enclosure resembles the others in its construction. It occupies the highest point in the plane and is only 4 feet lower than that on the hill, 715 feet above the level of the sea.

The only conjecture concerning them is that in former times sheep were kept in them at night and that when the ground enclosed in one part was sufficiently manured by them, they formed another enclosure and planted potatoes in the former. This certainly bears some degree of probability, but is still unlikely: palings must have been used for enclosing the sheep; the squares are too small for the purpose; and there is no trace of cultivation.

Miscellaneous: Coins

Old coins, both of silver and copper but principally the former, are frequently picked up in the fields in removing old fences about forts, and indeed in almost every part of the parish; but they soon find their way out of the country, either into the hands of watchmakers and ragmen, or are mislaid and none are now forthcoming. About Donegore Moat both silver and copper coins have frequently been found.

Brazen Hatchet

The brazen hatchet of Corinthian brass was found under a stone, which required 3 men with crowbars to move it, in a field on the side of Browndod hill in the townland of Browndod. The field seemed as if it had not been disturbed for ages.

Stone Hatchets

The flatter of the 2 stone hatchets shown in the same page was found in Browndod hill, within 50 yards east of the druidical altar on the summit of that hill. The stone is close grained, of a dark green colour and is somewhat similar to the greenstone of the country.

The other stone hatchet was found in a field in the townland of Ballynoe. It is a very perfect specimen and seems to have been but little used. The stone of which it is formed is of a deep black colour, very close in the grain and quite dissimilar to any found in the country.

Amulet and Ring

In levelling a portion of the street of Parkgate about 10 years since, the stone celt or instrument (of which 2 views are given), the circular stone shown in the same page and a highly polished ring about 2 inches in diameter, and apparently of jet, were found about 4 feet from the surface and in a bed of gravel which seemed to be then for the first time disturbed. These articles were found lying together.

The celt is of a close-grained stone, very hard, and resembling greenstone. It seems to have been but little used and is in a good state of preservation.

The circular stone is of red porphyry, very hard, weighty and quite smooth. Opposite to each other are 2 circular hollows, each half an inch deep and five-eighths of an inch in diameter.

The ring is 2 inches in diameter in the inside and half an inch in thickness, of a substance resembling jet or asphaltum, quite perfect and highly polished, in which state it was found.

Iron Spear

The iron spear was found in the townland of and near the summit of Donegore hill. It is considerably corroded, but does not seem to have been any longer than at present. It may probably have been one of the pikes used in the rebellion of 1641.

Flint Arrows

Flint arrowheads are frequently picked up through-out the parish. Those of which drawings are given were found on Donegore Moat. The arrowheads found in this parish are said to be all of similar form and of a similar description of white flint. They are termed "elfstones" by the country people, who imagine that the fairies used them in shooting at their cattle and thereby depriving them of their milk. A drink in which one of these stones, a little salt and sometimes a sixpence are thrown is the cure to the animal, which has never been known to prove inefficacious.

Brazen Pin and Celt

The brazen pin, of which a drawing is given, was found 5 feet from the bottom of the inner ditch of the cyclopean fort in the townland of Browndod. It is rather neatly finished and seems to have been a good deal used. 2 little grooves run down its 2 sides from the centre to the point and there is a little ornament work on the eye through which the ring passes. The metal of which it is made bears in its colour more resemblance to copper than to brass.

The brazen celt was found in a field a little to the east of Donegore Moat in the townland of Donegore. It is in good preservation.

Quern

The ornamented quern, of which a drawing is given, was found somewhere in the townland of Durhamsland. It is in excellent preservation. The stone of which it is formed is a sort of hard gritty sandstone.

Querns are said to have been used in the retired parts of the parish within the last 80 years.

Appendix to Memoir by James Boyle

SOCIAL ECONOMY

Petty Sessions

[Table] A statement of the description and number of cases tried at the petty sessions at Parkgate during the years 1833-7.

Number of summonses issued: 190 in 1833, 190 in 1834, 153 in 1835, 106 in 1836, 239 in 1837.

Number of cases of assault: 21 in 1833, 30 in 1834, 10 in 1835, 35 in 1836, 18 in 1837.

Number of breaches of excise law: 3 in 1833, 6 in 1834, 2 in 1835, 2 in 1837.

Number of disputes about wages: 12 in 1833, 6 in 1834, 4 in 1835, 12 in 1836, 8 in 1837.

Number of cases of trespass: 7 in 1833, 2 in 1834, 4 in 1835, 6 in 1836, 10 in 1837.

Number of cases of theft: 4 in 1833, 2 in 1834, 1 in 1835, 2 in 1836, 3 in 1837.

Number of cases of rescue: 1 in 1833, 1 in 1834, 1 in 1835, 2 in 1836, 2 in 1837.

Number of miscellaneous cases: 20 in 1833, 41 in 1834, 17 in 1835, 25 in 1836, 76 in 1837.

Number of cases sent for trial to assizes: 3 in 1833, 4 in 1834, 3 in 1836, 13 in 1837.

Number of cases sent to quarter sessions: 5 in 1833, 3 in 1834, 9 in 1835, 2 in 1836, 16 in 1837. 31st May 1838.

Table of Trades and Occupations

Parkgate: carpenters 2, constabulary 4, farmers 7, grocers 3, old clothes sellers 2, public house keepers 4, pensioners 2, labourers (agricultural) 10, blacksmiths 1, mantuamakers 2, tailors 1, shoemakers 1, watchmakers 1, wheelwrights 1, female servants 2, total 43.

Four Mile Burn: farmers 2, grocer 1, spirit dealer 1, agricultural labourers 9, total 13.

Original Clergy and Ministers

The following is the only information which can be locally obtained concerning the original clergy and ministers of this parish. It is derived merely from verbal authority, there not being any document which can be referred to on the subject.

The earliest remembered clergyman of the Established Church was the Revd [blank] Bennet. To him succeeded the Revd Bernard Lindon, the Revd Lindsay Hall, the Revd Edward Ross, the Revd [blank] Alexander and the present incumbent George Henry Johnstone.

In the Presbyterian Church in connection with the Synod of Ulster, the first clergyman remembered was the Revd John Wright, to whom succeeded the Revd [blank] Ledlie, the Revd Dr Henry Cooke (now of Belfast), Dr John Seaton Reid (now of Carrickfergus), John Doherty, who resigned in 1837, since which time the congregation has been vacant.

The first Seceding minister in this parish was the Revd Josias Wilson, ordained to it about the year 1788. He was succeeded by the present minister, the Revd William Wallace, ordained to this congregation about the year 1806.

Table of Schools

[Table contains the following headings: name, situation and description, when established, in-come and expenditure, physical, intellectual and moral education, number of pupils subdivided by age, sex and religion, name and religion of master and mistress].

This is a private school held in the session house of the Presbyterian meeting house in the village of Parkgate, established upwards of 100 years; income from pupils 40 pounds; intellectual education: the classics, mensuration, book-keeping, spelling, reading, writing, arithmetic, various authors; moral education: Sunday school, Authorised Version of Scriptures and Presbyterian catechism, visits from the Presbyterian minister; number of pupils: males, 24 under 10 years of age, 31 from 10 to 15, 5 above 15, 61 total males; females, 18 under 10 years of age, 21 from 10 to 15, 39 total females; total number of pupils 100, 7 Protestants, 90 Presbyterians, 3 Roman Catholics; master William Campbell, Presbyterian.

In a room in the dwelling house of the teacher in the townland of Donegore, established 1816; income: from the rector annually 2 pounds, 6 pounds from pupils; intellectual education: spelling, reading, writing, arithmetic, Kildare Society's books; moral education: Authorised Version of the Scriptures daily, Protestant and Presbyterian catechisms; number of pupils: males, 6 under 10 years of age, 7 from 10 to 15, 13 total males; females, 3 under 10 years of age, 4 from 10 to 15, 7 total females; total number of pupils 20, 8 Protestants, 12 Presbyterians; master Robert Reed, Protestant.

In a house built from subscriptions for the purpose in the townland of Dunamuggy; when established: unknown; income: 18 pounds annually from individuals, 18 pounds from pupils; intellectual education: spelling, reading, writing, arithmetic, Kildare Society's books; moral education: Authorised Version of the Scriptures daily, Protestant and Presbyterian catechisms, Sunday school visits from the Presbyterian minister; number of pupils: males, 11 under 10 years of age, 7 from 10 to 15, 18 total males; females: 6 under 10 years of age, 6 from 10 to 15, 12 total females; total number of pupils 30, 29 Presbyterians, 1 Roman Catholic; master John Campbell, Presbyterian.

[Totals] income: 2 [sic] pounds from private individuals, 64 pounds from pupils; number of pupils: males, 41 under 10 years of age, 45 from 10 to 15, 5 above 15, 102 total males; females, 27 under 10 years of age, 31 from 10 to 15, 58 total females; total number of pupils 150, 15 Protestants, 131 Presbyterians, 4 Roman Catholics. 28th May 1838.

ANCIENT TOPOGRAPHY

Drawings

Donegore Moat and landscape looking from the west, 5 miles distant.

Map of Browndod hill, townland of Browndod, scale 12 inches to a mile.

Plan of Browndod hill, townland of Browndod, showing location of antiquities with key and annotations, scale 12 inches to a mile.

Plans and sections of 4 druidical altars, 3 in townland of Browndod and 1 in Tobergill, with orientation, scale 1 inch to 64 feet.

Ground plan of a druidical altar, townland of Browndod, scale 1 inch to 20 feet. [Insert note by Boyle: The stones are all drawn to scale. The figures annexed to them denote their height].

Druidical altar at point A, showing figure of man standing with stick, townland of Browndod.

Ground plan of druidical altar at point B, townland of Browndod, scale 1 inch to 20 feet.

Ground plan of druidical altar, townland of Tobergill, scale 1 inch to 20 feet. [Insert note by Boyle: The figures prefixed to them denote the altitude of such stones as are standing, their dimensions otherwise being laid down to scale].

Druidical altar at point B, townland of Browndod, showing figure of a man standing.

Plan of enclosures at point E, townland of Browndod, with sections of 3 sides, scale 1 inch to 80 feet.

Enlarged plan of enclosure at point E, townland of Browndod, showing positions of tumuli, with section, scale 1 inch to 20 feet.

Enlarged plans and sections of enclosures at points O, F; enlarged plans and sections of tumuli at H and G, scale 1 inch to 20 feet.

Plans of enclosures, townland of Browndod, with dimensions, scale 1 inch to 40 feet.

Standing stone, townland of Browndod, height 3 feet 9 inches.

Standing stone, townland of Browndod, main dimensions 7 feet 3 inches by 3 feet.

Druidical altar, townland of Tobergill.

Map of Donegore Moat, townland of Donegore, showing position of monuments, scale 6 inches to 1 mile.

2 standing stones, townland of Donegore, dimensions 4 feet by 4 feet 10 and 4 feet 2 inches by 3 feet 10 inches.

Plan of Donegore Moat, townland of Donegore, with 2 sections, scale 1 inch to 40 feet.

Annotated plan of cyclopean fort, townland of Ballywee, with sections of 4 sides and orienta-tion, scale 1 inch to 20 feet. [Insert note by Boyle: Where the sides of a cove are shaded alike, it can be traced externally only; but where the side from the light is darkened, it can be explored].

Plan of cyclopean fort, townland of Ballywee, with sections of 4 sides and orientation, scale 1 inch to 40 feet.

Enlarged plan of cove in cyclopean fort, townland of Ballywee, with sections of 2 sides, scale 1 inch to 10 feet.

Style of construction of cyclopean fort, townland of Ballywee: vertical section of gallery, dimensions 5 feet 6 inches by 6 feet; extremity of a chamber and entrance of a pipe; interior of the side wall; scale 1 inch to 4 feet. [Insert note: NB The stones are all drawn to scale].

Fort and cove, townland of Dunamuggy, with section, scale 1 inch to 20 feet.

Enlarged plan of cove, townland of Dunamuggy, with detail of style of construction, main dimensions 5 feet by 11 feet 9 inches, scale 1 inch to 20 feet.

Browndod Fort, townland of Browndod, plan with 2 sections, scale 1 inch to 80 feet.

Tumulus in townland of Dunamuggy, plan with section and plan of grave at point B, main dimensions 6 feet by 2 feet, scale 1 inch to 80 feet.

Rathmore Trench, townland of Rathmore, plan with section, scale 1 inch to 80 feet.

3 forts in townland of Ballynoe and 1 in Ballysavage, plans with sections, scale 1 inch to 60 feet.

2 forts in townland of Tobergill, plans with sections, scale 1 inch to 60 feet.

2 forts in townland of Browndod and 1 in Ballygowan, with sections, scale 1 inch to 60 feet.

Artificial cave under Rathmore Trench, townland of Rathmore, ground plan with vertical section and 5 transverse sections, length 428 feet, scale 1 inch to 40 feet.

The Priest's Chair, townland of Donegore.

Plan of enclosures on Donegore hill, townland of Tobergill, showing position of ancient fence and standing stone, scale 1 inch to 160 feet.

Brazen hatchet and 2 stone hatchets, full size.

Brazen pin, townland of Browndod, iron spear and 3 flint arrows, townland of Donegore, all full size.

Brazen celt, townland of Donegore, full size.

Ornamented quern, overhead view and section, townland of Durhamsland.

2 views of stone celt, townland of Durhamsland, full size.

Stone amulet, townland of Durhamsland, full size.

Brief Memoir by James Boyle, January 1839

Ballygowan Fort

Ballygowan Fort occupies the summit of a gravelly ridge or feature which is included between 2 little streams flowing along its eastern and western sides and uniting at its southern extremity, about 450 yards from the fort which is elevated about 46 feet above them. It is situated in the townland of Ballygowan and near the eastern boundary of the parish.

The situation of the fort seems to have been selected with reference to military purposes, as it may very probably have been chosen from its commanding the pass at the northern end of the valley between the parishes of Kilbride and Donegore, and which is said to have been the ancient route between Belfast and Connor. The little feature on which it stands is situated right in the centre of this narrow valley, on each side of which the ground rises rapidly to an elevation of from 700 to 800 feet above the sea.

The fort is constructed of earth. It consists of an almost circular platform 151 by 146 feet in diameter and from 5 to 9 feet above the ditch, which is 9 feet wide. The summit of the platform is not raised higher than the natural height of the ridge. It inclines considerably towards its eastern side.

Along the outer margin of the ditch are the remains of a parapet which has been formed by the clay thrown up. It is from 7 [to] 13 feet in height above the bottom of the ditch and from 3 to 5 feet high on the outside. The entrance to the fort is at its eastern side. 13 yards north of the fort is a circular earthen mound 66 feet in diameter at the base and 31 feet at the summit, and 13 feet high. It has been much injured by mutilation.

In the southern side of the platform the entrance to a gallery, which seems to extend round a portion of it, was found. However, the stones have long since been removed and the extremities which had been laid open have been quite covered up. No remains were found about this fort.

[Plan of Ballygowan Fort and other tumulus, townland of Ballygowan, with sections, scale 1 inch to 40 feet].

Memoir Writing

Composition of Memoir

Detailed account of the time employed in completing the Memoir of the parish of Donegore, to the 31st May: Natural Features, 6 pages, 24 hours; Modern Topography, 14 pages, 38 hours; Social Economy (with appendix), 24 pages, 45 hours; Ancient Topography, 4 pages of information and 3 sheets of plans and drawings, 307 hours; total 414 hours.

Time expended at Plans and Drawings

Sheets numbered 1 to 31: sketch of Donegore Moat, 5 hours; hill sketch of Browndod hill, 50 hours; survey of Browndod hill, 16 hours; sheet of plans of altars, 5 hours; plan of altars at A, 3 hours; view of altars at A, 8 hours; plan of B and another altar, 6 hours; view of altar B, 6 hours; large enclosure (E), 12 hours; details of large enclosure (E), 7 hours; sheet of lesser enclosures, 6 hours; sheet of standing stones, 5 hours; view of altar in Tobergill, 6 hours; hill sketch of Donegore, 12 hours; standing stones of a tumulus, 6 hours; plan of Donegore Moat, 3 hours; large plan of a cyclopean fort, 12 hours; lesser plan of a cyclopean fort, 6 hours; detailed structure of a cyclopean fort, 9 hours; fort and cove in Dunamuggy, 4 hours; Browndod Fort, 6 hours; sheet of forts, 8 hours; sheet of forts, 4 hours; sheet of forts, 2 hours; cove under Rathmore Trench, 4 hours; Priest's Chair, 6 hours; square enclosures, 4 hours; hatchets, 5 hours; sheet of weapons, 7 hours; celt and quern, 4 hours; amulet and celt, 7 hours; total 244 hours.

The time thus given (414 hours) only, was actually expended on the Memoir as now sent, but to account for the remaining 92 hours I beg to state that they were expended on drawings, from which most of those now given were (by desire) substituted. For instance, the hill sketch of Donegore is now given on a scale double that of the former one. Etched views of the druidical altars and etched plans of the forts and enclosures, and another drawing of the articles have been substituted for the views and plans drawn in sepia with the brush in the former Memoir. These alterations will account for the 92 hours which make up the time changed. Added to this, the entire Memoir, with the exception of 22 pages, has been written out afresh during my private hours and it has in every respect been made complete up to the present day.

It is the second Memoir on the Ancient Topography of which I was employed, and as this section of the work was not added to my duty until after I had finished the others, much more time was expended in revisiting the parish than had I been able to have collected the information for the different sections at the same time. [Signed] James Boyle, 31st May 1838.

Fair Sheets by J. Bleakly, May to August
1838

MODERN TOPOGRAPHY

Church and Meeting Houses

Commenced 8th May 1838, completed 1st August 1838, 31 and half hours employed.

Donegore church is situated in the townland of Donegore. It was built in 1659 on the site of a Presbyterian meeting house and measures externally 46 by 31 feet; the walls are 3 and a half feet thick.

The meeting house is in the townland of Dunamuggy and measures externally 55 by 28 feet, in good repair. The Seceding meeting house at Dunamuggy was built 40 years ago.

The Presbyterian meeting house is in the village of Parkgate and is of this shape: [ground plan, "T" shape] and measuring externally from a to b 66 feet by 28 feet wide, and from c to d 28 by 18 feet.

Presbyterian Meeting House

The last repairs of Donegore Presbyterian meeting house was in 1834, cost of which was upwards of 140 pounds. Repairs was a new roof and ceiling. The congregation consist of 703 families, 3,452 individuals, from the parishes of Donegore, Kilbride, grange of Nilteen, grange of Doagh and a few from the parish of Antrim. Meeting house contains 80 single pews, each would contain 8 persons, and 5 double pews, each would contain 20 persons. Average collection for each Sunday amounts to 9 pounds per [week].

There are 13 names of poor persons on the books of the congregation, who receive each 1s per fortnight by the session. From Mr John Lawther, session clerk and elder.

Original Clergy

Original Presbyterian clergy of Donegore parish as far back as remembered by the oldest inhabitant, and from documents in the possession of Mr John Lawther, session clerk and elder. First of Donegore was the Revd Andrew Stewart; he died [?] 1634; 2nd was the Revd Thomas Crawford, died 1670, aged 45; 3rd was the Revd William Shaw, ordained 1671, continued 16 years; 4th the Revd Francis Iredall, resigned in 1699, removed to Dublin (Capel Street); 5th Revd Alexander Browne, ordained 1702 and continuing till 1754, 52 years; 6th the Revd John Wright; he was 52 years in connexion with the congregation, de-

ceased; 7th Revd James Crawford Ledlie, from April 1806 till July 1808, now a minister in Dublin, a Unitarian; 8th Revd Henry Cooke, from July 1811 till July 1818, now in Belfast; 9th Revd James Seaton Reid, from July 1819 till August 1823; 10th Revd John Doherty, from 21st December 1824 till March 1836, deceased.

NB The above is *more correct* than the former list of original clergy.

Machinery

The corn mill at the Four Mile burn, Mr Ferguson, proprietor: the water wheel is 15 feet 8 inches by 2 and a half at buckets, Fergusonsland, fall 16 feet.

The flax mill is in Fergusonsland. Its water wheel measures 13 by 1 and a half at buckets, fall 12 feet [insert marginal note: breast wheels all].

Donegore corn mill at Burnside, Charles Lawder, proprietor: water wheel is 16 feet in diameter by 2 feet 4 inches wide at buckets, fall 16 feet. The flax mill wheel is 14 by 3 feet, fall 12 feet, [all] breast wheels.

Beetling engine of Mr William Beck, Donegore: breast wheel 17 feet in diameter by 5 feet broad, fall 14 feet.

SOCIAL ECONOMY

Nonconformist Clergy

The first minister of the Seceding congregation of this parish was the Revd Josias Wilson, who ceased 36 years ago and was succeeded 32 years ago by the present, the Revd William Wallace. From the Revd William Wallace, Seceding minister.

Presbyterian clergy: the first remembered was the Revd John Wright about 32 years ago, second was the Revd Ledlie, third the Revd Dr Henry Cooke now of Belfast, 4th Revd Dr Seaton Reid of Carrickfergus, 5th Revd John Doherty. The congregation has no stationed minister since his resignation. From Thomas B. Adair Esq. and William Ferguson Esq. [Insert marginal note by Boyle: [Original Clergy is more correct].

The annual income of the Seceding minister, the Revd William Wallace, is 30 pounds per annum stipend. 8th May 1838.

Established Church Clergy

The original Established Church clergy are as follows: first of them remembered was Revd Burnett, 2nd Revd Bernard Lindon about 30 years ago, 3rd the Revd Lindsay Hall, 4th the Revd

Edward Ross, 5th Revd Alexander, 6th the present, the Revd George Henry McDowell Johnstone; he is 20 years here. [Insert footnote: For further particulars of original Established Church clergy, see Mr Skelton, Provincial Bank, Antrim].

Collections

The average collection at the Presbyterian meeting house at Parkgate amounts to 9s per Sunday; collection at the Seceding meeting house amount to 3s 6d per Sunday; collections at church 3s 6d.

Book Club

There was a book club held in the townland of Donegore and consisted of 35 members. It was established in 1834. Monthly meetings were held; now dissolved. 9th May 1838.

Parkgate Reading Society

Was established in 1832 and consists of 35 members including a chairman, secretary, treasurer and 6 committee men. Monthly meetings are held, at which each member contributes the sum of 6d. Total number of volumes in the library is 192 religious, historical and novel books. For further particulars, see Book of Rules.

Origin of Covenanters

Alexander Peden, an enthusiast, preached at a place called the Howes, a little above the meeting house in Parkgate. He is supposed to have been the founder of Covenanters in Ireland.

Marriages, Baptisms and Communicants

Marriages for the last 5 years are as follows: number married in 1833 amounted to 16 couples; in 1834, 23 couples; in 1835, 29 couples; in 1836, 18 couples; in 1837, 13 couples; total 99.

Baptisms: in 1833, 99; in 1834, 83; in 1835, 86; in 1836, 75; in 1837, 62; total 405.

Communicants: for 1833, 420; for 1834, 582; for 1835, 491; for 1836, 222 (only 1 communion this year); communicants for 1837, 514; total 2,229.

There are always 2 communions each year in the Presbyterian Church. 31st July 1838.

Bequest

A bequest of 2 pounds was left by Nathaniel Orr to purchase cheap religious books for the benefit of the congregation of Presbyterians of Donegore and to be given out by the members of the session.

Longevity

The only remarkable instance of longevity remembered is that of John Drummond of Tobergill, who died at the advanced age of 111 years.

Henry McDowell, a pauper, townland Rathmore is 90 years of age. Andrew Davison of townland Durhamsland, 94 years of age.

Patent for Fairs

A patent for the fairs of Parkgate is in the possession of William Ferguson Esq., the proprietor of Parkgate. Patent coming 7th June 1787, through the instumentality of Samuel Ferguson Esq., father of the present. It is affirmed by many that markets have been originally held here also. From William Ferguson Esquire.

Migration

James Gibbin, 25 years of age, Presbyterian, landed in Glasgow.

Anne Gibbin, 25 years of age, Presbyterian, landed in Glasgow.

Samuel McMaster, 30 years of age, Presbyterian, landed in Liverpool. All from the townland of Drumagorgan.

James Loughlin, 20 years of age, Seceder, landed in Liverpool.

Thomas Gourly, 17 years of age, Presbyterian, landed in Glasgow.

Hugh Connor, 30 years of age, Presbyterian, landed in Glasgow.

ANCIENT TOPOGRAPHY

Coves

This is the outline of an artificial cove on the farm of William Beatty at his house in the townland of Ballysavage: [plan with orientation]. It runs north and south, 13 feet in length by 3 feet wide by 5 feet high. Appears to have run a considerable distance further with rooms turning off at right angles, as stated by the inhabitants; but the entrances into these rooms are so obstructed by stones and earth that it is impossible to excavate them; entrance 12 inches by 14 inches.

The above [drawing with key] is the outline of an artificial cove which is on the stock farm of James Allison, 2 fields above the meeting house in Parkgate: (a) is the inner room; it measures 10 feet in length by 5 and a half high by 5 feet wide; (b) is the entrance into it and measures 5 feet 10 inches in length, 2 and a half high and 2 feet wide; (c) is the large room; it measures 25 feet in length by 5 and a half high by 5 wide at the bottom, 4 at centre or middle and 3 at the top; (d) is the entrance into this room and it measures 4 feet in length by 2 high by 2 broad; (e) is the outside room and it is 9 feet long by 6 wide by 6 feet high; (f) is the mouth; it is 3 feet high by 2 wide.

This cove was much longer, but long since dug away. Other rooms are supposed to run under the dwelling house but are closed up.

Memoir Writing

Notes on Townlands

I have carefully examined the townlands of Browndod, Halftown, Ballyclaverty <Ballycloferty>, Ballywoodock, Rathmore, Freemansland, Cromy <Cromy's> and Taggartsland, Ballywee and Durhamsland, and find nothing worth notice in them but what has been ascertained before. [Signed] John Bleakly, 10th May 1838.

Draft Memoir by J.R. Ward, April 1835

Natural Features

Hills

From the northern extremity to Donegore hill its surface is very irregular and hilly, the highest point being in the townland of Browndod, 861 feet above the sea. From Donegore hill to the southern boundary the slope is broken and gradual, the lowest ground in the parish, towards the Four Mile burn, being 170 feet above the sea. [Insert addition: On a close inspection it is found to be greatly broken, although from the road it appears smooth]. This gradual slope is continued to the Six Mile Water, which bounds the grange of Nilteen on the south.

Lakes and Rivers

Lakes: none.

There are no rivers of magnitude in the parish. The principal stream is the Four Mile burn, which bounds the parish on the east for [blank] miles. Flowing south its average breadth is 20 feet; it is very shallow. It rises in Rashee parish. Its source is [blank] feet above the sea. It is usefully situated for draining and water power. There are no falls or any considerable rapids on it. Its general fall is 100 feet in a mile. It is subject to floods which soon subside; they do no injury to the land. It impedes communication, flows over a gravelly

bed. The northern banks are used for grazing; the southern are well cultivated and are fertile.

Bogs and Woods

There is no bog.

Woods: none. The parish is in general very bare of trees. Towards the south and south west there is a little planting, principally fir and ash. They are planted in a prominent situation below the moat in Donegore townland and in Fergusonsland.

Climate and Crops

Climate: no register kept.

The general crops are wheat, oats and potatoes. Wheat is sown in November and reaped in August; oats are sown in April and cut in September; potatoes are put down in April and May, and dug in October and November. Very little wheat is grown in the northern part of the parish, but the ground is improving and there is hopes of its being able to bear it. In general they are a fortnight later than in the southern part, with the crops.

Modern Topography

Parkgate Village

The principal village, Parkgate, is situated 5 miles east of Antrim, near the intersection of the road (which passes through it) between Antrim and Doagh and that which leads from Templepatrick and Kells. It is in length 393 yards. The houses, being whitewashed and generally neat and clean, give the village a pleasing appearance which is improved by the trees in it and about it, and the fertility of the surrounding country.

Public Buildings

The only public building is a Presbyterian meeting house, a plain stone building. The shape and dimensions are: [ground plan, main dimensions 66 feet by 47 and a half feet, "T" shape]. It will hold upwards of 1,000 persons and the general attendance is between 700 and 800. It was built about the year 1735; the exact date and the expense of building are not known. The minister receives 100 pounds Irish or 92 pounds 6s 1d ha'penny farthing British from the government and 60 pounds Irish or 55 pounds 7s 8d farthing British from the congregation.

There is a police barrack in the village; the force residing is 1 sergeant and 3 men. A school which has been established upwards of 100 years (see table).

Houses

The village consists of but 1 street in which there are 10 houses of 2-storeys and 16 of 1-storey. About 14 of these are slated, the remainder thatched and are all built of stone and lime and have a cleanly appearance. No new houses have been built for the last 7 years; none are building. The population in 1831 was 156.

SOCIAL AND PRODUCTIVE ECONOMY

Present State of People and Occupations

Petty sessions are held here once a fortnight. The magistrates are Mr Adair of Loughermore and Mr Owens of Holestone; [insert addition: not stipendiary]. They are within convenient distances and are firm and respected by the people. The neighbourhood is very peaceable.

The trades in Parkgate are as under: grocers 3, publicans 4, carpenters 2, wheelwrights 1, watchmakers 2, tailors 1, shoemakers 1, stamp offices 1.

Fairs and Markets

William Ferguson Esq., whose property the village is, has a patent for 12 markets to be held in it, but none are held. There are 4 fairs annually, viz. 7th February, 7th May, 7th August and the 4th November. That which is held in February is famed for the sale of horses. The traffic on the other days is cattle, pigs and sheep.

The village has been much improved and is a thriving little place under the personal superintendence of William Ferguson Esq., whose residence is close to the village, in the adjacent grange of Nilteen.

MODERN TOPOGRAPHY

Donegore and Four Mile Burn

There are 2 other hamlets, viz. Donegore and Four Mile Burn. The first contains 6 cottages and a neat church. The second is a collection of 18 houses, 3 of which are 2-storeys and slated; the remainder are thatched. The road between Antrim and Doagh passes through it. The houses are tolerably clean in appearance. There is in it a grocer's shop and a public house.

Public Buildings

Beside the meeting house, of which a description is given in Parkgate, there is a church and Seceding meeting house.

The church is in Donegore village. It is a neat stone building 45 feet long and 30 feet broad; it bears the date of 1659. It holds 200; the average attendance is 45. The [insert addition: Seceding] meeting house is situated in the townland of Dunnamuggy; it is a plain stone building and bears the date of 1788. It is 56 feet long and 28 broad, was repaired in 1830 at a cost of 110 pounds, which was defrayed by the congregation. The seatholders are 220 and the average attendance 110 persons.

Table of Mills

Flax mill, Donegore, diameter of wheel 13 feet, breadth 1 foot, breast wheel.

Flax mill, Freemanstown, diameter of wheel 15 feet, breadth 3 feet, overshot wheel.

Corn mill, Fergusonsland, diameter of wheel 15 feet 3 inches, breadth 2 feet 4 inches, overshot wheel.

Communications

The principal roads are those from Antrim to Ballyclare through Parkgate, and from Templepatrick to Parkgate and Connor. Of the former, there is 4 miles in the parish and its average breadth is 25 feet. Of the latter, there is 3 and a half miles and its average breadth is 25 feet. These roads, though hilly, are very good. They were made by the county, are kept in repair by the half-barony, Upper Antrim.

General Appearance

The northern part of the parish is of a mountainous character and is chiefly used for grazing. The greater part might be drained and cultivated as there is every facility for doing so. The south is in general well cultivated and fertile. The scarcity of trees makes the scenery of the parish unpicturesque in itself, but the views of the surrounding country are very pretty.

SOCIAL ECONOMY

Local Government

Obstructions to improvement: there are none. Illicit distilling is not carried on; no insurances are effected.

Schools

[Table contains the following headings: name of townland, number of pupils subdivided by religion and sex, name of master, how supported, date established].

Parkgate, total 100 pupils; the pupils pay from 2s 6d to 7s per quarter; established upwards of 100 years.

Donegore, 62 Protestants, 26 males, 36 females, total 62; [insert addition: master Robert Ried [sic]; supported by payment from the scholars; when established: not known.

Dunnamuggy, 29 Protestants, 1 Catholic, 18 males, 12 females, total 30; supported by the scholars paying from 2s 6d to 4s per quarter; when established: not known.

Poor and Religion

No charitable institutions. The inhabitants are mostly Presbyterians. The proportions may be made by the congregations of their meeting houses and that of the church. There are very few Roman Catholics.

The clergyman of Donegore church [insert addition: Mr Johnstone] receives 700 pounds per annum tithe from this and Kilbride parish.

The minister of the meeting house in Parkgate receives of regium donum 92 pounds 6s 1d ha'penny farthing and 55 pounds 7s 8d farthing from the congregation per annum.

The minister of the meeting house in Dunnamuggy [insert addition: Mr William Wallace] receives of regium donum 50 pounds per annum and from his congregation 35 pounds.

Habits of the People

The description given in the grange of Nilteen will answer for this parish. [Insert footnote by J. Boyle: I think there is some difference between the inhabitants of these districts].

Extracts from Draft Memoir by Several Authors

NATURAL FEATURES

Rivers and Bogs

The principal streams are the Four Mile burn, which bounds the parish on the east, and the Ballynoe stream, whose sources are in the townlands of Browndod and Ballywoodock. Both these streams run southwards and fall into the Six Mile Water. They have a considerable fall and their waters may without difficulty be applied to machinery.

The Four Mile burn is usefully situated for drainage. Its average breadth is 17 feet and it is very shallow. It falls at the rate of 70 or 80 feet in a mile. It rises in wet weather, soon subsides and does not injure its banks. It runs over a gravelly bed and through banks which have not a very fertile or cultivated appearance, and are not steep.

There is no bog: what formerly existed has been cut away.

Climate and Crops

The climate of Donegore parish is very healthy. In consequence of its elevated situation it is rather colder than others surrounding it, especially Connor. There is no barley grown in the parish. Wheat is sown in October and November, and reaped in August. Oats are sown in April and cut in September. Potatoes are put down in May and taken up in October and November. The crops are in general a fortnight later than in Doagh or Nilteen.

MODERN TOPOGRAPHY

Parkgate Presbyterian Meeting House

There are 700 families attached to it, and the entire number of the congregation is about 3,400. It is built of stone, and its dimensions are: [ground plan, main dimensions 66 feet by 47 and a half feet, "T" shape]. Mr Doherty, its minister, receives from government 100 pounds (Irish) and from his congregation 60 pounds (Irish) per year.

Town: Parkgate

The population of the village in '31 was 156.

The town consists [of] 1 wide street, one-half of which is in the grange of Nilteen. It is about 118 feet in length. It consists of about 26 houses, of which 10 are 2-storeys high and 14 slated. No new houses have been built within the last 7 or 8 years.

The houses are built of stone and have a cleanly appearance. None of them are insured. It is a very neat, thriving little place, under the personal superintendence of William Ferguson Esq., whose residence is close to the village. This gentleman has a patent for a market, but none is held.

Gentlemen's seats: Thrushfield, the seat of William Ferguson Esq., is in the grange of Nilteen.

Bleach Greens, Manufactories and Mills

On the Four Mile burn are 2 corn mills, 1 flax mill and the ruins of [a] bleach mill. On the Ballynoe stream is another flax mill which belongs to J. Agnew. It is in the townland of Donegore and the wheel is 13 feet in diameter and 1 foot broad; it is a breast wheel.

The following mills are on the Four Mile burn. [Table contains the following headings: name of townland, dimensions of wheel, nature of wheel, nature of mill].

[Crossed out: Ballywee, diameter of wheel 12 feet, breadth 1 foot 10 inches, breast wheel, flax mill.

Ballywee, diameter of wheel 14 feet, breadth 1 foot 10 inches, breast wheel, corn mill. Insert marginal note: These mills are in Kilbride parish].

Freemanstown, diameter of wheel 15 feet, breadth 3 feet, overshot wheel, flax mill.

Fergusonsland, diameter of wheel 15 feet 3 inches, breadth 2 feet 4 inches, overshot wheel, corn mill.

Communications

The principal roads are those from Antrim to Parkgate and Doagh, and from Templepatrick and Parkgate to Connor and Kells. Considering the hilly nature of the country, they are in very good order.

General Appearance

From the summit of Donegore hill, about an English mile from the moat, there is a fine and extensive view of the surrounding country. On a clear day I should think that the 6 counties of Antrim, Down, Armagh, Tyrone, Londonderry and Donegal may be seen from it. A fine view of the Lough Neagh may also be had from this part. The northern part of the parish is uncultivated but forms very good pasture-land. The southern and eastern parts, which lie low, are well cultivated, and the land is very good but still much inferior to that of the grange of Nilteen.

SOCIAL ECONOMY

Habits of People

The houses in general consist of 2 or 3 rooms, are built of stone and thatched. They have glass windows, but have little appearance of comfort. Porridge made of oatmeal, milk and potatoes forms their principal diet. 4 or 5 is the usual number in a family [insert marginal query: 6].

I could not hear of any amusements. [Insert footnote: They have very few: dancing and sometimes parties for singing, and attending fairs, markets etc. are their only recreation].

Blue coats with brass, fustian trousers and old black hats form the usual dress of the men.

Early improvements: There are none. [Insert marginal note: Query this].

School Statistics

SOCIAL ECONOMY

Table of Schools

[Table contains the following headings: name of townland where held, name and religion of master or mistress, free or pay school, annual income of master or mistress, description and cost of schoolhouse, number of pupils subdivided by religion, sex and the Protestant and Roman Catholic returns, societies with which connected].

Donegore, master Robert Reed, Protestant; pay school, annual income 22 pounds; schoolhouse a good house; number of pupils by the Protestant return: 7 Established Church, 73 Presbyterians, 9 other denominations, 5 Roman Catholics, 56 males, 38 females; connected with Kildare Place Society.

Donegore, master John McClean, Presbyterian; pay school, annual income 13 pounds; schoolhouse stone and mortar, cost 100 pounds; number of pupils by the Protestant return: 67 Presbyterians, 10 other denominations, 1 Roman Catholic, 41 males, 37 females; associations none.

Parkgate, master James Heffron, Presbyterian; pay school, annual income 25 pounds; schoolhouse stone and lime, cost 40 pounds; number of pupils by the Protestant return: 59 Presbyterians, 1 Roman Catholic, 40 males, 20 females; associations none.

Rathmore, master John Bradshaw, Presbyterian; pay school, annual income 20 pounds; schoolhouse stone and lime, cost 30 pounds; number of pupils by the Protestant return: 30 Presbyterians, 18 males, 12 females: by the Roman Catholic return: 30 Presbyterians, 18 males, 12 females; associations none.

Ballyno, master Samuel Hyndman, Presbyterian; pay school, annual income 20 pounds; schoolhouse stone and lime, cost 24 pounds; number of pupils by the Protestant return: 46 Presbyterians, 34 males, 12 females; associations none.

Dunnymuggy, master Francis McCrumm, Presbyterian; pay school, annual income 10 pounds; schoolhouse stone and lime, cost 16 pounds; number of pupils by the Protestant return: 43 Presbyterians, 25 males, 18 females; associations none.

Parish of Kilbride, County Antrim

Statistical Report by Lieutenant Edward
Durnford, October 1832

NATURAL STATE

Situation

It is situated in the barony of Upper Antrim and
county of Antrim; is of a long narrow form,
extending from Collin mountain on the north to
the Six Mile Water on the south, having the small
village of Doagh near its south east extremity.

It is a rectory united to that of the adjoining
parish of Donegore <Donnegorr>, is in the diocese of Down and Connor, and province of Armagh. No composition has yet been entered into
for the tithes.

Boundaries, Extent and Divisions

It is bounded on the north west by the parish of
Connor, on the north and north east by that of
Rashee, on the east by the grange of Doagh, on the
south by the parish of Templepatrick and grange
of Nilteen, and on the west by the parish of
Donegore. It extends from north to south about 4
and three-quarter British statute miles and from
east to west about 2 miles.

The parish contains 5,641 British statute acres.
It is divided into 17 townlands, all of which are in
the manor of Moylena, the property of the Marquis of Donegall.

NATURAL FEATURES

Surface and Soil

The northern end of the parish is mountainous,
running partly up Collin mountain, but the ground
is generally dry pasture with heath and is much
used for hunting during the season by the gentlemen of the Antrim Hunt. A racecourse was commenced by the Marquis of Donegall about 20
years ago round Drumadarragh hill, but it was
never completed and consequently never used.
The southern portion of the parish is well cultivated, there being very little wasteland.

Produce and Turbary

The general crops are potatoes, oats and flax. The
former yield generally from 300 to 400 bushels
per acre, and corn yields from 14 cwt to a ton of
meal per acre. Flax is only sown in small quantities for the use of the growers. The land is chiefly
held on leases of lives, renewable for ever, about

1 pound 5s to be paid at the fall of each life, and
the rent from 3 to 7s an Irish acre. The rent is thus
low in consequence of fines having been paid to
the Marquis of Donegall, who then reduced it.
The leases given by the underlandlords are generally for 20 or 31 years, at from 30s to 2 pounds an
acre.

There is no turbary in the parish. The inhabitants are supplied from the neighbouring parishes
of Donegore, Connor and Glenwhirry, and
Ballyboley.

NATURAL HISTORY

Geology

Basalt is the prevailing rock throughout the parish. It is used both for building and for road-
making. There is, in the townland of Holestone, a
remarkable boulder of basalt, with a hole through
it, placed on its end, but for what purpose it was
erected I could not find out.

Sandybrae porphyry is found in the north west
corner of the parish and is much used in road-
making. In a sand pit in the same situation is a
substance similar to the above, called by Sir C.
Giesecke "black pearl stone."

MODERN TOPOGRAPHY

Towns and Villages

There is no town or village in the parish, nor is
there any place of worship. The rector has, however, recently commenced having service performed at a schoolhouse by the graveyard in
Kilbride townland.

Manufactories

There is a manufactory in the townland of Walkmill
for spinning flax, and a large cotton mill in the
townland of Burnside, used for the same purpose.
The flax is brought from Belfast and the yarn is
sold at Antrim, Ballymena and Ballyclare markets.

There is a large bleach mill in Drumadarragh
townland (called the Fence), also a print mill, but
they are neither of them in use at present.

A good deal of linen is made by the inhabitants
and most of the females are employed in spinning
flax.

Roads

The old road from Doagh to Ballymena traverses the parish from Doagh to the north west extremity of it and, though hilly, is a good road. There is another road to the same place which is much more level. This runs out of the parish on the western side and passes through Donegore parish.

The road from Ballyclare to Antrim, passing through Doagh, crosses the parish from east to west.

There are several crossroads which are generally very good.

NATURAL FEATURES

Rivers

The Six Mile Water forms the southern boundary of the parish for a short distance, and the Doagh river forms the eastern boundary, running into the Six Mile Water at the south east extremity of the parish. A stream called the Four Mile burn forms the western boundary of the parish.

Bogs and Woods

There is no peat bog in the parish.

There is a good deal of planting about Holestone, the residence of James Owens Esquire, and some fine trees about Springvale, the residence of Mr Watt.

SOCIAL ECONOMY

Population

By the census of 1831 the population of the parish amounted to 2,188, and was by townlands as follows.

Ballybracken, 73 males, 90 females, total 163.
Ballyhamage, 118 males, 121 females, total 239.
Ballywee, 154 males, 178 females, total 332.
Burnside, 61 males, 74 females, total 135.
Crawfordsland, 38 males, 38 females, total 76.
Drumadarragh, 76 males, 62 females, total 138.
Douglassland, 40 males, 35 females, total 75.
Duncansland, 24 males, 27 females, total 51.
Fifty Acres, 30 males, 34 females, total 64.
Holestone, 217 males, 241 females, total 458.
Kilbride, 83 males, 88 females, total 171.
Loonburn, 37 males, 40 females, total 77.
McVickarsland, males 26, females 27, total 53.
Moss-Side, 12 males, 16 females, total 28.
Owensland, males 34, females 34, total 68.

Strawpark, males 16, females 14, total 30.
Walkmill, 15 males, 15 females, total 30.

ANCIENT TOPOGRAPHY

Antiquities

In Holestone townland, near Mr Owens' house, were several caves in some of which were found urns containing bones.

There is an old graveyard in Kilbride townland, in which are the remains of a building, but when it ceased to be used is not known. [Signed] Edward W. Durnford, Lieutenant Royal Engineers, 15th October 1832.

Memoir by James Boyle, June 1836 to February 1839

MEMOIR WRITING

Composition of Memoir

The information contained in this Memoir is complete to this date. It was originally commenced 29th June 1836 and was completed on the 28th January 1839. The total time expended on it was 173 hours, equals 20 days. [Signed] James Boyle, 29th January 1839.

NATURAL FEATURES

Hills

The parish of Kilbride embraces a ridge or feature extending southwards from Collin mountain (to which it is connected by a narrow neck) in the adjoining northerly parish of Rashee and terminating in a low holme at the right bank of the Six Mile Water. A low valley extends along the eastern and western sides of the ridge, that on the former being watered by the Doagh river and that on the latter by the Four Mile burn. Towards these the ridge declines somewhat rapidly, particularly on its eastern side, while its western declivity, though less rapid, is somewhat broken and varied.

The highest point in the parish, 929 feet above the sea, is near its north centre, where the character of the district is hilly and almost mountainous. From this it descends gradually northward to a level of 780 feet. The declination of this ridge southward is very gentle. Its outline is occasionally varied by a little trap step, but with this exception it is almost imperceptible, until near the southern side of the parish where its descent becomes much more rapid and finally terminates in a low holme on the bank of the Six Mile Water.

Along the southern base of this feature the surface of the ground is much diversified by numerous little gravelly swells.

Along the northern side of the parish, and on the summit of the ridge, the country is wholly under pasture and uncultivated, but as it approaches the valleys along its southern, eastern and western sides, the face of the country gradually alters and presents an appearance of extreme fertility and superior husbandry.

The principal points are Drumadarragh near its northern side, 929, and Quarry near its centre, 870 feet above the level of the sea.

Rivers

The Six Mile Water, which gives its name to the extensive and fertile valley which it waters, flows for 1,210 yards along the southern boundary of this parish, separating it from the parish of Ballymartin. This stream issues from several sources in the south west side of Shane's hill, in the more easterly parish of Kilwaughter, the principal of which is about 1,000 feet above the level of the sea and 952 feet above Lough Neagh, into which it discharges itself. After pursuing a south westerly and rather irregular course for 7 and a half miles, it descends to a level of 162 feet above the sea and enters the south east corner of the parish. On quitting it its elevation is 149 feet. It afterwards pursues a more westerly course and finally, after passing through the town of Antrim, discharges itself into Lough Neagh, five-sixths of a mile west of that town.

Its total length is 18 and a half miles. Its breadth in this parish varies from 18 to 30 and averages 22 feet. Its ordinary depth is 4 feet. Its average inclination is 1 in 279 feet. Its bed is soft and consists of loam and fine sand. Its banks are low, and it frequently in winter overflows them, inundating the low level holme through which it flows, rendering it marshy and profitless, though its deposit rather enriches it; but it materially retards the cultivation of the land. It is applicable to machinery and irrigation, but is not in this parish applied to either purpose.

The Doagh river is a small stream which takes its rise from several sources (the principal of which is 830 above the sea and 662 feet above the point where it discharges itself into the Six Mile Water) in the adjoining north eastern parish of Rashee. After a short course it enters the eastern side of this parish and flows southerly for 4 and a quarter miles, separating it from the parish of Rashee and grange of Doagh, and discharges itself into the Six Mile Water at the south east corner of the parish, at an elevation of 162 feet above the sea. Its total length is 4 and a half miles, its average breadth 10 feet and ordinary natural depth 2 feet. Its average inclination is 1 in 46 feet, but its depth and inclination are very irregular owing to the inequality of its bed and in some instances to the proximity of carries for turning off water for machinery.

Its bed is stony and rough, from the quantity of loose stones rolled down by it in its very violent and impetuous floods, which rise and subside with great rapidity without committing any injury. Its channel is gradually deepening, being worn by it between steep banks which in some instances attain a precipitous height of 40 feet above its bed. In the neighbourhood of Doagh the scenery along them is very pleasing, their steep declivities being there diversified by planting.

It is usefully situated for the purposes of machinery and drainage, to both of which it is applied, and it is also applicable to irrigation. It does not impede communication.

The little stream known as the Four Mile burn takes its rise in the contiguous and westerly parish of Connor, at an elevation of about 900 feet above the sea and 736 feet above the point where it discharges itself into the Six Mile Water. After a short course it enters this parish at its north western corner and pursues a southerly course along its western boundary for 5 and a half miles, separating it from the parish of Donegore. It then enters the grange of Nilteen and, after flowing for 600 yards through it, discharges itself into the Six Mile Water, at an elevation of 164 feet above the level of the sea.

Its total length is 5 and three-quarter miles. Its average breadth is 13 feet. Its depth varies from a few inches to 3 feet. Its average inclination is 1 in 41 feet. Its bed is pebbly and formed of loose stones rolled down by it in its violent floods, which rise and subside, owing to its velocity, with great rapidity, without committing any injury further than eating away its banks, which in many instances are high and precipitous, and are generally of sufficient elevation to confine its waters.

It is rendered applicable to the machinery of the country and is also applicable to irrigation. It might be rendered very valuable in carrying off the water from the moist lands from which it issues and through which it flows.

The parish is abundantly supplied with water from springs and rivulets.

Bogs

The few trifling patches of bog in this parish are

either cultivated or under pasture. They are insignificant both as to extent and depth, and do not contain any timber.

Woods

The natural wood of this parish is now confined to a little stunted hazel brushwood, chiefly to be found along the edges of the streams, and in the waste grounds near the north of the parish. There is also a little holly and some ash saplings, merely sufficient to indicate their being indigenous to the soil.

Climate and Crops

The climate in the southern districts of the parish varies considerably from that in the northern. The seasons are from a fortnight to 3 weeks earlier in the former than in the latter.

The southern district of the parish possesses a fine aspect in its broad southern declivity, the soil of which is rather light but warm, and is wholly under cultivation. Towards the north of the parish the higher grounds become gradually less cultivated, until finally, at its northern extremity, cultivation is confined solely to the valley which encompasses it. In this district of the parish, which adjoins the mountains in Connor and Rashee, the country is, from its partially drained and uncultivated state, subject to mists, rains and early frosts. The seasons also are late and the air humid, while in the southern side of the parish the air is pure, dry and rather mild.

The crops cultivated are principally oats and potatoes, with a little wheat. In the southern districts oats are sown during the months of March and April, and reaped during the latter part of August and commencement of September.

The planting of potatoes is concluded generally about the 12th May and the general raising of the crop by the middle of November.

Wheat is sown immediately after the raising of the potato crop and is reaped during the latter part of August. In the northern districts wheat is not cultivated, owing to the moisture of the climate.

The other crops in it are sown much about the same time, but are from a fortnight to 3 weeks longer in coming to maturity than those in the south of the parish.

The climate of this parish could easily be improved by the drainage of the grounds along its northern, eastern and western sides, for which there is every facility in the streams which encompass it and in the numerous rivulets trickling down its sides.

Modern Topography

Towns

There is neither town nor public building in the parish.

Gentlemen's Seats

Holestone, the residence of James Owens Esquire, J.P. and D.L., is agreeably situated on the declivity of a considerable eminence in the townland of the same name, at the southern side of the parish and within 1 mile of the road from Antrim to Doagh and Ballyclare. The view from the house is spacious and interesting, including a considerable portion of the rich valley of the Six Mile Water.

The house is a spacious and modern-looking 2-storey edifice, presenting 3 stone-finished fronts. The offices, though not extensive, are suitable. There is a tolerable garden and a small extent of tastefully laid out pleasure grounds. The demesne, including a spacious and handsome lawn, includes about 300 acres. It is almost entirely under cultivation, but is much diversified by numerous and extensive belts and clumps of thriving young planting, which form a very striking ornament to the scenery of the valley.

Holestone takes its name from the remarkable remnant of pagan antiquity which also gives its name to the townland. The stone stands about half a mile north of the house. Holestone was rebuilt and considerably enlarged in 1827 by its present proprietor.

Ballyvoy, the residence of John Owens Esquire, J.P., occupies a retired situation in the townland of Owensland, near the centre of the parish. The house is not spacious, nor are the grounds of any extent. There is, however, some thriving young planting about it. Ballyvoy had been a thatched cottage until 1828, when it was enlarged by Mr Owens.

Brookfield, the residence of Thomas Lyle Esquire, is situated in the townland of Burnside, on the bank of the stream forming the eastern boundary of the parish. The situation is low and retired, and the view very confined. The house is 2-storeys high and neither modern nor spacious. There is neither demesne nor pleasure grounds attached to it.

Drumadarragh, in the townland of the same name and in the mountainous and very retired district towards the north east of the parish, is the residence of George Langtry Esquire. Its situation, besides being low and disagreeable, is on the very edge of the public road. The house, though large, is by no means modern or neat in its appearance, nor is there a lawn or demesne attached to it. It is said that the original house was erected in 1641, rebuilt in 1742 and, on coming into the possession of Mr Langtry, again rebuilt in 1827.

There is a small, and by no means a neat-looking, 2-storey house, the occasional residence of the Reverend Samuel Johnstone, the rector of the parish, situated in the townland of Ballyhamage at the southern side of the parish, and near the road from Antrim to Doagh. There is a trifling lawn attached to it.

Machinery

The manufactories and machinery of the parish consist of 2 mills for spinning linen yarn, 1 beetling mill, 1 flax mill and 1 corn mill. The spinning mills are the property of Messrs Watts and Lyle, and are situated on the Doagh river.

Brookfield mill is situated in the townland of Burnside. The machinery is contained in 1 house, 3-storeys high and measuring 75 by 24 feet. It is propelled by a breast water wheel 34 feet 3 inches in diameter and 4 feet 4 inches broad, having a fall of water of 25 feet. This mill was burned about 7 and rebuilt 6 years ago. 20 men and 30 women are kept in employment at it.

Springvale mill in the townland of Drumadarragh is contained in a 3-storey house measuring 146 by 27 feet. The machinery is propelled by a breast water wheel 24 feet in diameter by 7 feet broad, having a fall of water of 20 feet. This mill gives employment to 6 men and 64 women. It was originally used as a beetling mill and was converted to its present purpose in 1827.

The beetling mill (the property of Mr Henry Bragg) is situated in the townland of Ballyhamage and on the Doagh river. The house consists of 2 floors and measures 60 by 21 feet. The machinery is propelled by a breast water wheel 13 feet in diameter by 3 feet 4 inches broad, having a fall of water of 6 feet. This mill has been nearly a century established.

The corn mill is situated on the Four Mile burn and in the townland of Ballywee. The machinery is propelled by a breast water wheel 16 feet in diameter and 2 feet broad, having a fall of water of 12 feet.

The flax mill is situated on the same stream and in the same townland. The machinery is propelled by a breast water wheel 14 feet in diameter and 2 feet broad, having a fall of water of 7 feet. The last 2 mills are idle during summer from want of a sufficient supply of water.

Communications

This parish is amply supplied with the means of communication. It contains 5 miles 7 furlongs of main roads and 12 miles 1 furlong of by and crossroads, all of which are kept in repair at the expense of the barony of Upper Antrim.

The main roads are: the direct and main road from Antrim to Doagh, and which formerly was the main road to Ballyclare and Carrickfergus. It is said to be one of the oldest roads in the county and to have formed the means of communication between the garrisons of Carrickfergus and Toome. It passes for 1 mile and 5 furlongs along the southern side of the parish. Its average breadth is 23 feet. It is tolerably level, but is not kept in very good repair.

A road from Kells and Connor through Doagh to Belfast traverses the parish diagonally, from north west to south east, for 4 miles and 2 furlongs. The average breadth is 22 feet. Its direction is bad and it is also hilly and kept in but middling repair.

The by-roads are not generally well laid out, being in many instances unnecessarily crooked, while in others they traverse steep declivities in almost right lines. They are, however, suited to the wants of the country. Their average breadth is 19 feet. All the roads in the parish are repaired with broken stone, chiefly a hard whin, which is everywhere abundant, either in field stones or quarries.

Bridges

There are 3 small bridges and several pipes which afford every facility of intercourse between the districts along the different streams in the parish. The bridge on the road from Antrim to Doagh, across the Doagh river, consists of 3 circular-segment arches, each of 10 feet span. Its extreme length is 120 feet and its width 18 feet.

The bridge on the road from Kells and Connor to Belfast, and across the same stream, consists of 2 circular-segment arches of 12 feet span. It is 36 feet long and 20 feet wide.

The bridge on a crossroad over the same stream, and between the former bridges, consists of 3 circular-segment arches of 12 feet span. It is 50 feet long and 21 feet wide.

These bridges are plain, substantial structures and are in good repair.

General Appearance and Scenery

The southern side of this parish forms a portion of the northern [side] of the rich and beautiful valley of the Six Mile Water, which traverses the county from its western almost to its eastern side. Here, and along the eastern side of the parish, the country presents an appearance of extreme fertility and good husbandry, its fields being large and enclosed by thick hedgerows, and its broad slopes being diversified with numerous plantings and clusters of trees about the gentlemen's seats and the substantial residences of the farmers, which not merely ornament this immediate district but add considerably to the scenery of the surrounding country.

Along the western and towards the northern side of the parish the scenery becomes gradually less interesting, and finally bare and cheerless, the ground being moist, partially cultivated, thinly inhabited and almost wholly destitute of planting. Its features, though large, are tame and want diversity, and are almost entirely under pasture.

SOCIAL ECONOMY

Early Improvements

The parish of Kilbride constitutes a portion of the manor of Moylinny, which was granted to the Chichesters (the ancestors of the Marquis of Donegall, the present proprietor) in the reign of James I and was, in common with all the surrounding districts, colonised by the Scottish settlers of the 16th and 17th centuries, but particularly by those who came over in the years 1610 and 1641. Among the present inhabitants there is not a single descendant of the former, nor is there the slightest trace of them, either in their religion, manners, dialect or customs. The present occupiers of the soil are almost exclusively Presbyterians. There is not a Roman Catholic landholder in the parish, and there are only 2 members of the Established Church who hold farms.

There are still to be found in the parish indications of its having, at a very early period, been inhabited by a rude and uncivilised people. There are few districts in which coves are so numerous, there being scarcely a townland in the parish in which there is not at least one of these structures. There are also 4 earthen raths still remaining in it. It is said that a famous church, dedicated to St Bridget, and from which the parish took its name, formerly stood in the old burial ground near its centre. Its foundations could within memory have been traced.

To the settlement of the Scots, who brought over their ministers with them, may be attributed the present improved state of the parish.

The early settlers have evidently been of a respectable class, and different from those in most of the adjoining districts, inasmuch as that they seem to have brought some capital with them. The strongest indication of this is the names of the townlands, which appear to have been derived from those of the families to whom they were allotted, each townland having evidently been the tract given to the individual whose name it bears, for instance Crawfordsland, Duncansland, Owensland, Douglassland, Kerrsland. This is still further confirmed by the prevalence of many of these names. Those most prevalent are the names of Ferguson, Beck, Douglass, Donnel, Colman, Warwick, Boyle and Barefoot, which is a corruption of Beresford.

The establishment of Presbyterian congregations and schools were immediately consequent on the colonisation of the parish.

Progress of Improvement

The construction of roads in it is said to be of comparatively modern date. Within a century it is alleged that the only road in the parish was that passing through its southern side, and which formed the means of communication between the garrisons of Carrickfergus and Toome; and that so deficient was the parish in the means of communication, that it was cultivated only to such an extent as was actually necessary for the support of its inhabitants. It now possesses every facility of communication with the neighbouring towns and districts, and for the transmission of farm produce to market, and is now becoming a flourishing agricultural district.

Belfast, which is 11 and a half miles from the centre of the parish, is now their market, and to it they send their grain, potatoes, pork, milk and butter. The situation of the extensive lime-works at Carnmoney enables them to bring back lime when returning. Lime is much used by the farmers. The kilns are 7 and a half miles distant from the parish and at them lime costs 14d per barrel.

The establishment, in 1818, of a farming society at the neighbouring village of Doagh has produced a very perceptible effect in their system and method of farming. Green crops such as turnips, clover and vetches are now generally cultivated and found to succeed. Their mode of farming is also more systematic than formerly.

An important event, to which many may attribute their present independent circumstances, occurred about the year 1824, when, in consequence of the very embarrassed circumstances of their landlord (the Marquis of Donegall), who, to relieve his difficulties, granted leases in perpetuity at a mere nominal rent to such of his tenants as could purchase. This had for some time been foreseen by the tenantry, almost all of whom availed themselves of the opportunity. Many, by living frugally, were enabled of themselves to pay the necessary fine. Some were obliged to borrow money for the purpose, and have subsequently by their industry and frugality liquidated their debt, but some have also been embarrassed, and in order to discharge their encumbrance have been obliged to sell their lease and leave the country; but to the great majority of the numerous tenantry it has been an important benefit, and to it most of them are indebted for their present independent circumstances.

Obstructions to Improvement

Though it cannot be said that there is any actual obstruction to improvement, still there is one circumstance connected with the parish which has been productive of rather unfortunate results. This parish, with several others, formed the corps of the archdeaconry, and had paid rectorial and vicarial tithes, which at a period within memory did not amount to 100 pounds per annum.

An alteration in the ecclesiastical connection of the parish took place some years since, and this parish was united to that of Donegore and the grange of Nilteen, the tithes of which were gradually increased, until (a few years ago) they were jointly raised to between 700 and 800 pounds. The land is said to have been valued by a commissioner, sent by the government, who was quite unqualified for the duty. A lawsuit, still pending, immediately ensued between the incumbent and his parishioners, and for so far little or no tithe has been paid. The very worst feelings, which since 1798 (when to a man the people of this parish were actively engaged as rebels) had slumbered and were beginning to be forgotten by the passing, and had as yet been unknown to the rising generation, were aroused. Meetings denouncing tithes were held, subscriptions, to which the neighbouring districts contributed, were raised to defend the prosecuted, and a political feeling of the very worst description was excited throughout the neighbourhood.

To make matters worse, the incumbent is non-resident. He comes here merely on Saturday, attends church on Sunday and departs to his residence in the county Down on Monday. He keeps one curate who resides in the adjoining grange of Doagh.

There is not a clergyman or place or worship in the parish. There is a want of religious instruction among all denominations, but particularly among the members of the Established Church, who, though they be few and of the humbler grade, are daily becoming even less numerous from neglect.

Local Government

There are 2 magistrates residing in the parish, namely James Owens of Holestone Esquire, J.P. and D.L., and John Owens of Ballyvoy, Esquire, whose residences are conveniently situated and who possess the confidence and respect of the people. Petty sessions for the district in which this parish is included are held at Parkgate, in the adjoining grange of Nilteen, on every alternate Monday.

This parish is quite free from crime or outrage, and rarely furnishes more serious legal business than a case of trespass or a dispute concerning wages. There is neither smuggling nor illicit distillation.

Kilbride is included in the manor of Moylinny, the manor courts for which are held at the village of Doagh (2 miles distant) on every third Tuesday, and at Antrim (7 miles distant) on every third Thursday. Sums not exceeding 20 pounds are recoverable at these courts by civil bill process.

The Marquis of Donegall is lord of the manor. Mr Arthur Adair Gamble is the present seneschal.

Insurances

The insurance of property from fire is unusual and extends only to the yarn-spinning mills. There are not any life insurances.

Dispensary

Kilbride is included in the district of the dispensary established in the village of Doagh in the year 1835. The effects of this institution, though not perceptible, still have been attended with beneficial results in this parish, particularly during the year 1837 and the summer of 1838, when fever was very prevalent here. In cases of accident it has also, from the distance of other medical advice, proved useful.

With the exception of 1837 and 1838, the parish has been comparatively free from disease. There is but little indigence. The labouring class are in pretty regular employment. They are rather cleanly in their dwellings and are comparatively well fed.

A statement of the funds of this institution and a table of the cases treated at it will be found under the proper head in the Memoir of the grange of Doagh.

Schools and Book Club

There are 2 day schools in the parish, at which 80 children are receiving instruction. This would give a proportion as to the population of 1 to 33 and a half. Many of the children from this parish are being educated at the schools in Doagh, and there is not perhaps any district in which all classes are more generally educated. There are few, if any, who cannot read, and most of the males can also write.

The establishment of schools, either in the parish or in its immediate vicinity, does not seem to have been of recent date, but on the contrary almost coeval with the colonisation of the country by the Scots.

The usual course of education consists in spelling, reading, writing and arithmetic. English grammar is now generally taught, and the system of teaching has of late years been much improved; but on the other hand, the children are taken from school at an earlier age than formerly, in fact as soon as they are capable of being of the slightest use at home. This is particularly the case among the lower class.

There is much taste for acquiring knowledge. Several individuals are members of the excellent book club which was established in Doagh in the year 1754 and consists of 750 volumes, and many of the farmers subscribe to some of the Belfast newspapers; see Table of Schools, Appendix.

Poor

There are only 6 actual paupers or beggars residing in the grange, and these receive their portion of the collections at the different places of worship in the parish of Donegore. The parish is much frequented by strolling beggars from the western districts of this county and also from the counties of Derry, Tyrone and Donegal. The farmers are generally humane and charitable. The farmer's wife usually dispenses the alms. She feels a degree of pride in doing so and in receiving the beggar's benison, though she little values the beggar's curse.

Religion

With a few exceptions the entire population are Presbyterians. There is a Roman Catholic and only 2 Protestant landholders, the few members of these persuasions being confined to the cottiers or labourers.

In the Church of England this parish is united to that of Donegore and the grange of Nilteen, and constitutes a rectory in the gift of the bishop. The united tithes amount to 787 pounds. There is neither glebe nor glebe house. The parish church is situated in Donegore and is 3 miles from the centre of this parish. The present incumbent, the Reverend Samuel McDowell Johnston <Johnson>, is non-resident. He has a residence in the parish, to which he comes from his seat in the county Down on Saturdays and returns on Mondays. He keeps a curate, who resides in the adjoining grange of Doagh and to whom he pays an annual salary of 75 pounds.

The Presbyterians are members chiefly of the congregation in the adjoining parish of Donegore, the places of worship in which are conveniently situated. One of these congregations is in connection with the Synod of Ulster, the other is in connection with the Secession Synod. The Presbyterians of this parish contribute in the usual manner to the support of their ministers.

The few Roman Catholics in the parish worship at the chapel near Ballyclare in the grange of Doagh, which is 3 and a half miles distant.

There is not a place of worship, nor is there a clergyman resident in this parish.

Habits of the People: Population

According to the enumeration returns of 1831 the population of this parish amounted to 491 families, consisting of 2,680 individuals, giving an average of 5 and a half to a family; and with reference to the extent of the parish (5,641 acres 15 perches), of 1 individual to [blank] acres. Of the families, 318 are chiefly employed in agriculture and 93 in trade, manufacture or handicraft. 69 occupiers of land employ and 182 do not employ labourers. 213 labourers are employed in agriculture and 2 in labour not agricultural. 144 individuals are employed in retail trade or handicraft, as masters or workmen. 3 individuals are employed in manufacture or in making manufacturing machinery. There are 12 capitalists, 4 male and 123 female servants.

PRODUCTIVE AND SOCIAL ECONOMY

Spinning

From the foregoing analysis of the population it will be seen that this is an almost exclusively agricultural district, the only exceptions being confined to the individuals employed at the spinning manufactories, with about a dozen linen weavers. The weaving of linen was formerly more general and, previous to the introduction of mill-spun yarn, almost all the females were engaged in spinning. There was not a house in the parish in which there was not at least 1 wheel. In the farmers' houses the female servants spun while otherwise unoccupied, and the women of the family were similarly occupied; but now their spinning is for domestic use and the yarn is generally manufactured into linen for their own wear.

Farms

The farms vary in size from 20 to 60 acres of arable land, but to many of them, particularly in the northern districts of the parish, a considerable extent of mountain grazing is attached.

The system of farming is Scottish and of a tolerably improved description. Cultivation is, however, confined to the southern districts of the parish and to the valleys along its eastern and western side, its northern end being chiefly under mountain pasture. Towards the summit of the ridge cultivation is in a less forward state. The ground is but partially broken in, the houses are smaller and less numerous, the fields are less spacious, and dry stone walls and sod fences are almost the only descriptions of enclosure. Towards the base of the ridge, particularly at its southern and eastern side, the aspect of the country gradually improves and finally becomes very cheerful, its broad slopes being laid out into spacious fields, well squared and enclosed by high hawthorn hedgerows.

There are several very neat-looking houses, occupied by an opulent class of farmers or "small gentry", which are almost secluded in planting; and though the eastern district of the parish is very retired, its inhabitants are among the most affluent and enlightened in the parish.

Houses

All the houses and cottages are built of stone and lime. The majority of the former are 2-storeys high and are slated and roughcast. The latter are roofed with thatch. The houses of the more affluent farmers are of a very excellent description, being roomy, commodious and substantial, and evincing much attention to comfort and taste in their exterior keeping and interior arrangement. They consist of 2 spacious floors and are furnished in modern style. They have each a good garden with a greater or less extent of pleasure ground or lawn, and some little shrubbery or

planting. Their offices are in keeping with the dwelling house as to substance of construction and extent, but are not neatly kept.

The houses of the humbler class of farmers are 1-storey high, generally thatched, and though sufficiently roomy, dry and warm, are by no means neat-looking nor kept in good order, nor is there much regularity in the arrangement of their offices or homesteads. Their gardens are small and contain merely a few early potatoes and some cabbage and leeks. There is very little regularity in their internal arrangement, but they are generally more cleanly than they appear. They usually consist of 3 apartments with earthen floors, and receive light from 3 or 4 lead windows.

The cottages and cabins, though substantial and dry, are neither neat nor cleanly in their appearance. They consist mostly of 2 small apartments and are lit by a couple of lead windows. Their furniture, though of an indifferent description, is not scanty. Each cottage possesses a small garden, in which a few early potatoes, some cabbage, leeks and onions are raised. Towards the north of the parish the cottages and cabins are in every respect much inferior to those in the southern district.

Food

The better class of farmers live right well and with much comfort. At their tables most of [the] comforts of life, so far as eating is concerned, are to be found, though at the same time not without a proper attention to economy.

Among the humbler class of farmers there is a good deal of animal food, either salt or dried bacon and hung beef, consumed, which, with eggs, butter, milk, oatmeal and potatoes, constitute their food. Tea is not generally used by this class, nor is the same quantity of baker's bread consumed by them as by those in the neighbouring districts. They are more homely, but not less substantial in their manner of living than the people of the more frequented southern parishes.

The cottiers live principally upon potatoes, salt herrings and milk, with oatmeal occasionally and a very little animal food. Though very few of them keep a cow, still milk, from the extent of pasture, is rather plentiful. In harvest, and at some other seasons, labourers are generally fed by their employer. On these occasions their food is nutritive and wholesome.

Fuel

Turf is almost exclusively burnt. It is procured from the bogs in the adjoining parish of Connor, which are 4 miles distant from the centre of this parish. It is both dear and scarce, and among the cottiers much privation is endured from want of a sufficiency of firing. Turf when laid down costs 13d per gauge (a cubic yard).

Dress

The dress of the farmers of the better class, and that of their families, is particularly neat and respectable, being of the best materials and of modern make. The women dress very well. Silk gowns, handsome leghorn or straw bonnets, neat boots, gloves and shawls constitute their usual attire. They sometimes sport parasols and boas. Among the other classes dress, particularly with the females, is a matter of paramount importance, and on Sundays, at fairs, or on other public occasions their appearance is but little inferior to that of the inhabitants of any of the neighbouring districts. During the week their attire is coarse and homely, and among the lower classes slovenly. Their children are almost in a state of nudity and by no means cleanly in their persons.

Longevity

Speaking generally, the inhabitants of Kilbride are a long-lived race. There is not perhaps any district in the county of similar population in which there are more instances of individuals who have attained the age of 80. In the year 1837 James Drummond died at the age of 100. In 1835 Mrs Watt died at the age of 100. In 1837 Mary Bryson died at the age of 96. In 1838 Alexander Bell died at the age of 89. Mr James Watt of Springvale is now in his 91st year.

Early Marriage

Though they do not generally marry at a very early age, still there have been 2 remarkable instances of early marriage in this parish: Mary Bryson (still living) was married in 1829 at the age of 13 and Margaret Boyd was married in 1821 at the age of 13.

Amusements

The taste for amusements has within the last 12 or 15 years considerably declined. Their recreations are now of a higher order than formerly. Card-playing has been almost given up and the barbarous sport of cock-fighting, which was formerly, particularly at Easter, kept up, has also been abandoned. On the other hand an excellent book club has been established here (in 1838). It con-

sists of 17 members (16 males and 1 female), who pay 1s per quarter each. It at present contains 44 volumes of well-selected works on historical and religious subjects only. Besides, several of the better class of farmers are members of the book club in the village of Doagh.

They are fond of dancing and dances are not infrequent among all classes. Those in the farmers' houses are in generally well got up.

Attending singing schools for the purpose of learning sacred music is another recreation. A singing school, which is held once a week in the farmhouses, has recently been established here. There are 13 male and 14 female pupils, who pay 2s 6d per quarter each.

Going to one or two of the summer fairs at some of the neighbouring towns is, particularly with the lower classes, a favourite amusement.

Christenings

Their christenings, particularly among the more wealthy farmers, are scenes of festivity and mirth, and are much more so than their weddings. On these occasions as many guests as can be crammed into the house are invited to dinner, and the evening is spent in feasting and dancing, but generally without excess or intemperance.

They have neither patrons nor patrons' days.

Character and Party Feeling

There is no such thing as party spirit, but there is a very violent and general prejudice to episcopacy, but more especially to the Established Church. In no part of Ireland is this feeling stronger or more deeply rooted than in this and the adjacent districts.

In the year 1798 the people of this neighbourhood signalized themselves by the active part which they took in the proceedings of that period. Their political feeling, which had for a long time lain dormant, was lately aroused by the increased applotment of their tithe, and at the present moment the great bulk of the population are in a state of rancorous excitation. They never appeal to violence, but their opposition is not on this account the less powerful or determined.

With the exception of a few of the better description [of] farmers, the general character of the people is that of a bigoted race of republicans, whose education and independence as to circumstance has, in their own estimation, placed them on a par with those whom fortune or birth have elevated to a higher sphere. They inherit much of their notions of independence from their Scottish forefathers. Their leases in perpetuity and their low rents contribute still further to them. The extent of information which they have acquired by reading has not been matured by intercourse with strangers. Their notions are therefore illiberal and their ideas contracted.

On the subject of religion they are very bigoted and they pique themselves on a regard for morality to which they are in nowise entitled. It is true that they make a point of regularly attending meeting, but they rarely return from it without having indulged at the ale house, either "between sermons" in summer or "after sermon" in winter. In other respects they strictly observe the sabbath.

They are by no means a temperate or abstemious race. The farmers who can afford it use spirits almost daily and the other classes whenever they can obtain it. They are, however, otherwise moral, and are very punctual in fulfilling their engagements.

Their manners are by no means pleasing. Their accent is strictly Scottish, as are also their idioms, manners and customs, but there is a degree of doggedness and silence, mixed up with no small share of inquisitiveness and suspicion, which is disagreeable. Courtesy they consider as servility.

Without possessing talent they are very shrewd and cautious, and are tolerably conversant on subjects which are seldom thought of by such classes. Their taste for studying works on religious subjects, particularly those which are Calvinistic, is remarkable.

They are social and rather hospitable, and are also charitable. They are very industrious, but among the lower class there is little or no idea of domestic economy.

Funerals and Wakes

A singular custom, which, however, exists in the contiguous districts, and one which they must have derived from their Scottish ancestors, is prevalent here with respect to their funerals, which are not attended by any except by those specially invited by letter.

Their wakes are conducted with much decorum. They are attended by the neighbours and friends of the deceased, who sit up all night and listen to the Scriptures being read aloud. During the night whiskey, punch and biscuits are handed round.

Situation of Farmers

There is a great deal of comfort and substance, without much actual wealth, among the farmers. Many of them have neat gigs or jaunting cars.

Every house has a clock and a gun, and almost all the men have watches.

Cottiers

The cottiers, or agricultural labourers, are hardworking and honest, but they are by no means an interesting class. Their habits and manners, speaking comparatively, resemble those of the farmers, except that they have little or no idea of comfort or economy.

They are by no means provident. They are rather intemperate in their habits whenever an opportunity offers, and they are apathetic and dull in their intellects.

Each cottier has at least 1 pig; many of them have 2, besides some poultry; but a few of them have cows or hold any land.

Their children they send to school at a very early age and take them from it before they can have acquired any permanent information. They are not regular in their attendance at meeting. Among them there is much ignorance on religious subjects.

Superstition

Superstition is almost wholly confined to the lower class. With them it is as general as in any of the neighbouring districts, and their belief in fairies, brownies, enchantments, the black art and witchcraft is quite common.

Appearance

In stature the farmers exceed the middle size and are rather robust and well made. From the early age at which they are set to work, the labouring class, particularly the rising generation, are rather below the ordinary stature. They are not very well made, but they are very strong and wiry, and capable of enduring much fatigue. They would make very good soldiers, but scarcely anything could induce them to enlist. There is nothing peculiar in their physiognomy. Their foreheads are rather low, their hair is generally dark and their cheek-bones are commonly high.

Some of the females are really handsome and speaking generally they are good-looking. Their eyes and hair are dark, and their complexion is good. Their features are strongly marked, but their expression is pleasing.

Emigration and Migration

Within the last 7 years not more than 20 individuals have emigrated from this parish. No capital has been taken out of it, nor have any emigrants returned. None have emigrated during the last 2 years.

Migration does not prevail here.

Remarkable Events

There is no record or tradition of this parish having been the scene of any remarkable event, nor of its having given birth to any remarkable individual.

ANCIENT TOPOGRAPHY

Ecclesiastical: Burial Ground

The parish of Kilbride is said to have formerly possessed an extensive church or monastery, which was dedicated to St Bridget, and from which the parish derived its name. Of this, not the slightest vestige, except its burial ground, now remains.

The burial ground occupies a conspicuous and elevated position, commanding a very extensive prospect. It is situated in the townland of Kilbride and near the centre of the parish. The foundations of the church were wholly removed about 6 years since. The church, which stood near its centre, measured 68 by 30 feet and stood east and west.

The burial ground includes a quadrangular area measuring 114 by 123 feet. It is but indifferently enclosed by a dry stone wall and is not neatly or regularly kept. The graves are very numerous, in fact as much so as possible, and from them it seems to have from an early period been a favourite place of interment.

No families of any note are buried here, but the members of several who had formerly resided in the neighbourhood are brought to it. Among others are the respectable family of Stephenson, of which 13 individuals are interred here, and over whom a handsome mausoleum was last year erected at a cost of 300 pounds.

The oldest tombstone bears the date of 1674. There are several others bearing dates from 1676 to 1699. The name of Smith is that on the oldest stones.

Near the graveyard, and at the intersection of 2 old roads, extensive foundations have been dug up. They are said to have been those of a village (the intermediate one between Belfast and Connor) which stood there and had been destroyed during the wars of 1641.

Military Remains

There are not any military remains in the grange, nor have there been any in it within memory.

In the townland of Drumadarragh, at the north east corner of the parish, is a spot locally known as the Trench: why, it is neither (locally) known nor conjectured, nor are there any works or remains from which any idea can be formed. There is, however, in a neighbouring parish a tradition that during the troubles of 1641 a stand was made here by the Protestant or English, who threw up some works and constructed a large house on the site of that now the property of George Langtry Esquire, and that from these works the place derived its name.

At the point alluded to the valley is narrow and formed by 2 high and tolerably steep ridges. It is watered by a small stream, which seems to have formerly rendered the valley marshy. The situation is one capable of being defended against a superior force, and as the valley is said to have in old times been the pass or route between Connor and Belfast and Carrickfergus, it may on some occasions have been contested, and the Trench in consequence have been erected.

Pagan: Giant's Grave

Near the summit of the uncultivated mountainous ridge at the northern end of the parish, and in the townland of Drumadarragh, are the imperfect remains of [a] giant's grave. The adjacent ground is thickly overgrown with heath and has probably never been cultivated. The mountain is of basaltic formation and is studded with numerous little basaltic hummocks, from which the materials for the grave have with facility been procured. Until about 6 years ago the structure was quite perfect and had been undisturbed. It then was somewhat injured, and was in 1838 totally destroyed by the removal or displacement of the stones to form the enclosure for a stockyard which is partly built on its site.

The grave (see plan, Appendix) consisted of a double row of standing stones bearing south west and north east. The row or avenue is 47 feet in length; its sides are 3 feet 6 inches apart. There were formerly 11 standing stones, 6 of which were in one row and 5 in the other. They were almost equidistant and varied in height from 2 to 6 feet, but few of them now retain either their original position or situation.

Near the south west end of the row a stone measuring 7 feet 5 inches long, 3 feet 8 inches broad and about 15 inches thick is laid transversely across the row. At one extremity it rests on a stone 1 foot high and at the other on one 2 feet 4 inches high. No other coping or tabular stones have been remembered here. The stones are quite rude and undressed, and do not bear any marks or inscriptions. They resemble those commonly known as "pillar stones."

About 6 feet south east of the south western end of the row is a large unshapely stone, measuring 5 feet by 5 feet 6 inches and 2 feet high. It stands at right angles to the row and seems to have been connected with it, the intermediate ground being covered with small stones which seem, from constant pressure, to have been firmly bonded together. Along the sides of the avenue there are similar indications of its having been partly buried in a heap of small stones. [Insert footnote: I have in several instances found giant's graves almost buried in a heap of small stones, for instance the giant's grave in Drummaul, that in Donegore, the "Avenue" in the same parish and the circle in the grange of Nilteen].

About 41 yards north west of the grave is a large stone of a pyramidical form, which seems formerly to have been in an upright position. It measures 4 feet 3 inches long by 2 feet by 2 feet 4 inches thick. It appears to have been set on 3 stones which lie at its base. There are 4 others, each about a foot from it, around it.

Standing Stones: Holestone

Occupying a very conspicuous position on a knoll on the summit of the ridge, and towards the southern side of the parish, is a remarkable stone familiarly known as the Holestone, which name it gives to the townland in which it is situated.

This stone is nothing more than an undressed slab of basalt 5 feet 4 inches high, 2 feet 9 inches broad at the base and 2 feet broad about half-way from the top. It varies from 10 to 14 inches in thickness. At a distance of 1 foot 10 inches from the top, and precisely in its centre, is a circular hole which gradually diminishes in diameter from 8 inches at each side to 2 inches at the centre. It is carefully and smoothly cut, and seems to have been worn by something passing frequently through it; but except this, there is not the slightest mark of any kind on the stone.

It is finely set in a little square heap, which is securely confined by large stones laid along its edges. The base of the stone is also secured by stones which are firmly and closely set round it.

No discovery of any kind has been made about this stone, nor is there legend or tradition connected with it. A drawing of it will be found in the Appendix.

230 yards south of the giant's grave, and in the townland of Drumadarragh, is a standing stone 2 feet 8 inches high by 2 feet 3 inches by 2 feet thick.

Its position is by no means conspicuous. Its form is somewhat oval. Its sides are smoothly worn by the weather and has evidently been intentionally set in its present position.

Coves

Coves are very numerous in this parish. The light gravelly soil of its southern districts is such as seems to have usually been selected in the construction of such structures, which are seldom to be found in heavy or clayey ground.

Upwards of 20 coves have been remembered by the present inhabitants. With 6 exceptions they have either been wholly or partly removed, or their mouths have been blocked up and the ground levelled over them, so as to render their situation a matter of uncertainty. Several of them have been entered and explored, and were found to be precisely similar in construction and form to those in the adjacent districts of Donegore, Nilteen, Doagh and Ballyclare; and it may be remarked that these and the other parishes and granges included in the valley of Six Mile Water are remarkable for [the] extraordinary number of coves which have from time to time been discovered in them, and which bear every indication of their having been the works of the same race and probably of the same age.

The only remains which have been found in them were the bones of sheep, small cows and a deer, some of them partially calcined but most of them in a sound state. Ashes of wood and of the husks of corn have been found in a few of them. In one in this parish there are evident marks of a fire having [been] kept up, as several stones in the floor of the cove (though they are not paved) are quite black and seem to have formed a hearth. Though their sides and roofs are dingy and almost black, their colour appears to have been caused more by damp than by smoke. Clay pipes about an inch long in the stalk, but in others respects similar to those in common use, have been found in many of them.

In a cove in the townland of Ballyvoy which has a rocky bottom there is a spring well which quite obstructs its narrow entrance. In this townland there are not less than 5 coves, 3 of which, now closed up, are said to contain several chambers. Of the 2 coves which are accessible, plans will be found in Appendix which will sufficiently illustrate their style of construction.

Forts

There are 6 forts in this parish. They are all circular

and vary in diameter from 45 to 80 feet. They are constructed of earth and are by no means remarkable either as to their situation, dimensions or construction. Plans of them will be found in Appendix which will sufficiently illustrate them.

Enclosure

The enclosure shown in Appendix is situated on the wild and uncultivated summit of Drumadarragh hill, at the northern extremity of the parish. It is quite overgrown with heath and moss, and seems to have suffered some mutilation. It measures 93 feet square in the clear. The parapet is 5 feet high in the exterior and 3 feet in the interior. It averages about 9 feet thick and is chiefly composed of earth. There are, however, some large stones which appear in its exterior and interior face. They vary from 1 and a half to 2 feet in length and are about 1 foot deep. They are laid longitudinally but are not always contiguous. There is but 1 row or course of them.

The parapet contains 18 hollows, which have been intentionally formed and have been faced with stones, but they have been mutilated and their original form thereby destroyed. They appear to have been square, about 2 feet deep, and to have been from 3 and a half to 10 feet long and from 3 to 4 feet wide. Most of the stones which face them have been removed. The entrance, which is in its eastern side, is 5 feet wide. There are faint vestiges of a ditch outside the parapet.

It is difficult to conjecture what this structure may have been or for what purpose it had been intended. In the adjacent parish of Donegore there is an elliptical enclosure which contains little hollows similarly formed, but its use is equally unknown.

There is a tradition that during the wars of 1641 an encampment took place on Drumadarragh hill, where this enclosure is situated, and that on the opposite side of the valley, in the parish of Rashee, an encampment of the Irish or rebel party took place at Dunamoy Moat. It is said that several cannon-balls have been found about both places.

The summit of Drumadarragh hill is intersected by the foundations of numerous old fences which, from the dense coat of heath, are now but indistinctly to be traced.

Ancient Park and Boundary

The townlands of Fifty Acres, Ballywee, Holestone, Kilbride, Douglassland and Ballyhamage were included in the bounds of an ancient park, the remaining portions of which are in the adjoining parish of Donegore and grange of

Doagh. The boundary of this park is still at intervals to be traced in these parishes.

It commenced at the Six Mile Water, immediately south of the village of Parkgate in the adjoining western parish of Donegore, and, proceeding northwards through the village, soon after crossed the stream which [separates?] the latter parish from that of Kilbride. It ran along the northern side of the townlands of Ballywee, Holestone and Douglassland, and from thence extended eastward into the adjoining grange of Doagh, and soon after struck suddenly towards the south and terminated at the Six Mile Water, at a point 3 miles and 3 furlongs from that from which it started.

The park included an area of about 3 miles from east to west by 2 miles from north to south. One gate stood on the site of the present village of Parkgate. The other, at its eastern side, was on the same road (that from Antrim to Carrickfergus through Doagh and Ballyclare), about half-way between Doagh and Ballyclare.

This site is also known as the Parkgate, and also as the Thorn Dyke, from the massive fence which formed the boundary and which was planted with large sloe thorns, some of which still remain. Small portions of the ditch are still to be traced on the summit of the hill in the townland of Holestone. It is formed of stones and earth, rather rudely constructed. It is from 5 to 6 feet thick at the base, but nowhere now exceeds 3 feet in height.

This park is said to have been formed and the wall built by Sir Arthur Chichester, Lord Deputy of Ireland, in the reign of James I. Each person passing through the gates paid a toll of a ha'penny, but it is not known whether this was his perquisite or that of the Crown.

The summit of Drumadarragh hill, in the townland of Drumadarragh, though it does not bear the slightest evidence of ever having been cultivated and though it is densely covered with heath, is traversed by the foundations of numerous fences, some of which have been partly constructed of stones, but most of them solely of earth. From the length of the heath they are now scarcely discernible, but with little trouble they may be found to be both numerous and running in almost right lines.

Miscellaneous Discoveries

Flint arrowheads and stone hatchets of different styles of workmanship as to their finish, brazen celts and brazen pins with a ring at one end have frequently within memory been found in the fields in this parish. Clay pipes similar to those now in common use, only a little shorter, have been found in the coves.

Coins

Coins of silver and copper of various reigns, but principally of that of Elizabeth, are picked up almost daily in the cultivation of the ground. The silver coins include those of the reigns of Edward I, II and III, Henry II, III, VII and VIII, Alexander III, David Bruce, Baliol and Elizabeth. The copper coins are chiefly Scottish. A few of James I and II have been found.

Appendix to Memoir by James Boyle

Drawings

Giant's grave in Drumadarragh, gound plan with annotations and dimensions, scale 1 inch to 10 feet. [Insert note: All the stones are drawn to scale. The figures prefixed to denote their height. Those to which none are prefixed formerly were upright].

The Holestone, townland of Holestone.

Forts: 2 in McVickersland, 1 in Ballybracken, Loonburn, 2 in Drumadarragh, scale 1 inch to 10 feet.

Square enclosure in Drumadarragh, showing hollows in parapet, with section, scale 1 inch to 20 feet.

Coves in Douglassland, with transverse and longitudinal sections with dimensions, scale 1 inch to 5 feet.

SOCIAL ECONOMY

Table of Schools

[Table contains the following headings: name, situation and description, when established, income and expenditure, physical, intellectual and moral education, number of pupils subdivided by age, sex and religion, name and religion of master and mistress].

Held in a house in bad repair, measuring 31 feet by 14 feet, originally built for the purpose by subscription, situated in the townland of Kilbride, established 1818; income from pupils 30 pounds; expenditure: the teacher receives this sum, 30 pounds; intellectual instruction: spelling, reading, writing, *Manson's Primer and spelling book*, *Thompson's and Gough's Arithmetic, Jackson's Book-keeping, Murray's English grammar*; moral instruction: not visited by the clergy, the Authorised Version of Scriptures read daily, Presbyterian catechisms on Saturdays only; number of

pupils: males, 12 under 10 years of age, 22 from 10 to 15, 6 above 15, 40 total males; females, 5 under 10 years of age, 5 from 10 to 15, 10 total females; total number of pupils 50, 31 Presbyterians, 10 Roman Catholics, 9 other denominations; master Joseph Orr, an Independent; visited 10th December 1838.

In a small thatched house (the schoolroom being 15 feet by 13 feet) in bad repair, the property of the teacher, situated in the townland of Ballybracken, established 1828; income from pupils 14 pounds; expenditure: 14 pounds in salaries; intellectual instruction: *Manson's Primer and spelling book*, *Thompson's and Gough's Arithmetic* and *Murray's English grammar*, with writing; moral instruction: not visited by the clergy, Authorised Version of Scriptures daily, Presbyterian catechisms on Saturdays; number of pupils: males, 8 under 10 years of age, 7 from 10 to 15, 15 total males; females, 3 under 10 years of age, 12 from 10 to 15, 15 total females; total number of pupils 30, all Presbyterians; master John Craig, Presbyterian; visited 10th December 1838.

[Totals]: expenditure 44 pounds in salaries; number of pupils: males, 20 under 10 years of age, 29 from 10 to 15, 6 above 15, 55 total males; females, 8 under 10 years of age, 17 from 10 to 15, 25 total females; total number of pupils 80, 61 Presbyterians, 10 Roman Catholics, 9 other denominations.

[Insert addition: In a suitable house built for the purpose by subscription and situated in the townland of Kilbride; when established: unknown; income from pupils 24 pounds; intellectual education: spelling, reading, writing, arithmetic, mensuration, book-keeping, books of the London Hibernian Society; moral education: Authorised Version of Scriptures daily, Presbyterian catechism on Saturday, visits from the Presbyterian clergyman; number of pupils: males, 13 under 10 years of age, 17 from 10 to 15, 2 above 15, 32 total males; females, 7 under 10 years of age, 8 from 10 to 15, 17 total females; total number of pupils 49, 3 Protestants, 42 Presbyterians, 4 Roman Catholics; master James Gawin, Presbyterian].

Fair Sheets by J. Bleakly, July to December 1838

NATURAL STATE

Boundaries

Commenced 12th July 1838, completed 10th December 1838, 105 hours employed.

This parish is bounded on the north by the parish of Rashee, on the south by the grange of Nilteen, on the east by the grange of Doagh and on the west by the parish of Donegore. 19th July 1838.

Parkgate Boundary

The old Parkgate boundary commenced at the Six Mile Water below Parkgate and ended at the Six Mile Water, and ran in a straight line to Donegore hill, and turning northerly to the parish of Kilbride and forming a boundary between the townlands of Kilbride and the townland of Ballyvoy, and then turning south east and running in a straight line forming the boundary between Kilbride and Cogry, and from thence to the Six Mile Water, dividing Doagh and Ballyclare.

This boundary consisted of only stones and clay rudely put together, with a quantity of sloe thorn growing on it; now demolished.

This was the Park wall, which is now all demolished except a few perches, which is nothing more than a ditch. It commenced at the Six Mile Water and ended at the Six Mile Water, enclosing a regular park.

NATURAL FEATURES

Springs

The parish of Kilbride is well supplied with excellent spring water: not less than 40 good springs in it.

Hawthorns

There are 4 old hawthorn trees in the parish.

Crops

The crops usually cultivated are potatoes, oats, flax a little and wheat a little. Not so much wheat as in Donegore parish or in the grange of Nilteen, as the soil is lighter. The seasons are the same as in Ballymartin, Ballyrobert, Ballywalter and Donegore, except near the mountain district, which is always much later. The early frosts are chiefly on the mountain district, Six Mile Water and on the banks of the Kilbride river.

MODERN TOPOGRAPHY

Gentlemen's Seats

Holestone is the residence of James Owens Esquire. The house was rebuilt in 1827. The house is of a modern style, has 3 fronts, 2-storeys high and slated previous to 1827, on a hill near the stone from which the townland takes its name. In 1817 it was also also a 2-storey house, but not so large.

Ballyvoy is the residence of John Owens Esquire. The house is also 2-storeys high and slated, situated near the mountain. It was rebuilt in 1828. Previous to 1828 it was a 1-storey house, slated.

Springvale is the residence of James Watt Esquire; house 2-storeys high and slated.

Mr Langtry's house is 2-storeys high, slated; built in 1641. It was then only 1-storey high, slated. It was rebuilt in 1742 and rebuilt again by George Langtry, the present proprietor, in 1827 (by Patrick Allen, architect).

The house occupied by Thomas Lyle Esquire is locally called Brookfield House. It is 2-storeys high, slated, and upwards of 40 years built and in good repair.

Mr Watt's house, near Mr Lyle's, is 3-storey high, slated, and upwards of 50 years built and in good repair.

Machinery

The beetling engine is the property of Henry Bragg Esquire, in the townland of Ballyhamage. It measures 60 by 21 feet in the clear; 2 lofts. The water wheel is a breast wheel 13 feet in diameter by 2 feet 4 inches across the buckets; the fall is 6 feet. Can work all seasons and is slated, in good repair, on a stream which proceeds from Brackna hill in the parish [sic] of Ballyeaston and falls into the Six Mile Water; about 100 years built. From James Johnstone, workman.

Bleach Houses

There are 3 old bleach mills, all 2-storeys high, slated, in the townland of Drumadarragh, on Mr Langtry's property, but all dilapidated and in disuse these [blank] years.

Mills

There is a corn mill in the townland of Ballywee, the property of Jackson Beard. Water wheel is 16 feet in diameter by 2 feet broad at the buckets; breast wheel, single geared, fall of water 12 feet; slated, in good repair.

The flax mill is the property of the same person; also a breast wheel 14 feet in diameter by 2 feet at the buckets, fall of water 7 feet; thatched and in middling repair.

Both mills are idle in summer from want of water.

In Springvale, in the townland of Drumadarragh, there is a flax spinning mill the property of Watts and Lyle. The machinery consists of 1 water wheel 24 feet in diameter by 7 feet across the buckets, fall of water 20 feet; breast wheel, single geared, can work all seasons of the year. The houses are 2-storeys high, slated and in good repair; about 11 years established as a spinning manufactory, was originally a bleach mill; the houses are insured. About 70 persons are employed at present, viz. 6 males and 64 females.

In Brookfield, in the townland of Ballyvoy, there is another spinning mill which is also the property of Messrs Watts and Lyle, and was established at the same time. The water wheel is a breast wheel 34 feet 3 inches in diameter by 4 feet 4 inches at the buckets. The fall is 25 feet, single geared. The houses are 3-storeys high, slated, all in good repair, and can work all seasons of the year, also insured. This mill was burned about 7 years ago and was rebuilt about 6 years ago by the present proprietors. There are 50 persons employed here, viz. 20 males and 30 females. 270,000 spangles of yarn, of 4 hanks to the spangle, are the annual quantity spun; grist from 2 and a half to 8 and a half hanks to the lb of flax; all for home consumption. Both foreign and home materials are manufactured. Information obtained from the manager, Mr Hugh McKeown, 12th July 1838.

There is a flax mill, the property of Thomas Bayne, in townland Ballywee. Breast wheel 15 and a half feet in diameter by 3 broad, with 12 feet of a fall, but all in a state of dilapidation.

Bridges

The bridge which divides the grange of Doagh from the parish of Kilbride, on the road from Doagh to the old graveyard at Kilbride, has 3 arches, each 12 feet in the span by 8 feet high and 21 feet broad on the top. The range wall is 2 and a half feet high by 1 and a half feet thick, in good repair.

Also the bridge leading from Doagh to the Ballymena road by Holestone has 3 arches, each 12 feet in the span by 6 and a half high; range wall is 3 feet high by 1 foot thick, by 45 feet long, in good repair; about 20 years built.

Also the bridge which divides Ballyhamage from village of Doagh, at Doagh, has 3 arches, each 12 feet in the span by 12 feet high; 16 feet on top by 2 and a half high, i.e. range wall, by 1 foot thick by 120 feet long, in good repair.

Schoolhouse and Bridges

The new schoolhouse is situated at the boundary

mearing near the parish of Kilbride and is 24 by 18 feet in the clear, but not roofed.

The bridge at the schoolhouse has 2 arches, each 10 feet in the span by 5 feet high; range wall 3 feet high by 1 and a half thick and 27 feet broad on top; in good repair.

Also the bridge at Mr Langtry's house has 1 arch 15 feet in the span by 8 feet high; wall 2 feet by 1 and a half thick and 21 on top, in good repair. It divides Drumadarragh townland from parish [sic] of Ballyeaston.

Social Economy

Union and Tithe

The above parish is united to the parish of Donegore. It pays both rectorial and vicarial tithes to the Reverend Henry [sic] McDowell Johnstone. Its amount is calculated at 700 pounds per annum, including Donegore, but the inhabitants have heretofore refused to pay the rector his demand.

Manor and Petty Sessions

Kilbride is included in the manor of Moylinny. Manor courts held at Doagh (see report of manor courts). Kilbride parish is included in the Parkgate district of petty sessions. The petty sessions are held on every second Monday in a room fitted up for the purpose in Parkgate village.

Dispensary

The parish of Kilbride is in the Doagh district of dispensary. Fever is, and has been, a prevailing disease during the last year, 1837, and the summer of this year, 1838. There are still cases of that disease through the parish.

Paupers

There are about 6 paupers in the parish of Kilbride, resident. There are many others who lodge in the parish, but natives of the county Derry and Donegal and Tyrone.

Amusements

The amusements are almost all extinct, except singing schools and dancing schools and a little card-playing, but none are carried to any great extent. Horse-racing and cock-fighting used to be carried to a great extent about 20 years ago, but now not practised.

Cottiers

Cottiers in general pay from 30s to 2 pounds per

annum for a house, and sometimes a garden, small, and keep a pig and poultry (except geese).

Labourers

Agricultural labourers are sufficiently numerous, but not too much so. They are generally fed during the harvest by their employers and sometimes during the winter, but in general they are fed by their employer and live on his farm, and are cottiers; supplied with milk by their employers, buttermilk at 1d per gallon in summer and 1d ha'penny per gallon in winter; paid with work generally and sometimes with money.

Longevity

James Drumond died in 1837 at the advanced age of 100. Mary Byers died in 1837 at the advanced age of 96 years. Alexander Bell, 89, 1 year dead; Mrs Watt, 100 years, 3 years dead; James Watt Esquire, 91, living.

Margaret Downs of Ballyhamage is still alive at the age of 80 years. Margaret Byers deceased <diseased> at 90 years of age.

Early Marriage

Mary Bryson (still living) was married at the age of 13. Margaret Boyde was married 17 years ago at the early age of 13, still living.

Prevailing Names

Wilson, Brison and McClelland are the most prevalent names. The 2 former are the most ancient.

Population

Kilbride contains 2,680 inhabitants, viz. 1,302 males and 1,378 females, and 488 inhabited houses and 18 uninhabited houses.

Reading Club

There is a reading club held in Alexander Byers' house. Established 1838, contains 44 volumes, history and religious only. The religious works are all Calvinistic. It contains 17 members, viz. 16 males and 1 female. 1s per quarter is paid by each member. Meetings once each month, on the Monday before full moon.

Schools

Kilbride school is situated at the old graveyard and held in a thatched house in bad repair, 31 by 14 feet in the clear, built by subscription about 20 years ago. Income of the teacher about 30 pounds per annum, paid by the pupils. Books used are *Manson's Primer and spelling book, Thompson's and Gough's Arithmetic, Jackson's Book-keeping, Murray's English grammar*, with the Authorised Version of Scripture and catechism on Saturday by the master; no regular visitor. Total pupils 50, viz. 40 males and 10 females; 6 males above 15 years of age and 22 from 10 to 15, and 12 under 10 years of age; girls from 10 to 15, 5 and 5 under 10 years of age; Roman Catholics 10, Presbyterians 31 and 9 of other denominations. Joseph Orr, an Independent, is the teacher.

There is not a Sunday school in existence at present in the parish. There was 2, viz. 1 in Kilbride schoolhouse and 1 in Ballybracken schoolhouse, but both are discontinued these 4 years from want of teachers and from want of clothing for the children.

A singing school is held for sacred music through the houses, one night in each week; consists of 27 pupils, viz. 13 males and 14 females, all above 15 years of age; established 2 weeks ago; Hugh Smith, teacher; 2s 6d per quarter is paid by each.

Ballybracken private school is held in a small thatched house 14 feet 9 inches by 13 feet in the clear, established 7 years ago; income of the teacher is 14 pounds per annum, paid by the pupils; *Manson's Primer and spelling book, Thompson's and Gough's Arithmetic* and *Murray's English grammar*, with the Authorised Version of Scripture and catechism on Saturday by the master; not visited by any. Total pupils 30, viz. 15 males and 15 females; 30 are Presbyterians; males from 10 to 15, 7 and 8 under 10; females from 10 to 15, 12 and 3 under 10 years of age; John Craig, a Presbyterian, is the teacher.

Migration

James Armstrong, age 20, Kilbride townland, Methodist, to Glasgow.

Joseph Steen, age 26, Kilbride townland, Presbyterian, to Glasgow.

Alexander Thompson, age 25, Kilbride townland, Presbyterian, to Glasgow.

PRODUCTIVE ECONOMY

Proprietor, Farms and Leases

The Marquis of Donegall is the proprietor of the parish of Kilbride. The farms are all various in size, from 20 to 60 acres, not including the mountain district, which is chiefly the property of [blank] Langtry Esquire, under the Marquis of

Donegall. The leases are [in] perpetuity or lives renewable for ever.

Trades

There are 3 bonnetmaking establishments in the parish. There are 2 publicans and 2 grocers in the parish.

There is no place of worship in the parish.

Linen Manufacture

There are about 12 hand-looms for linen weaving only. There is very little spinning carried on, chiefly owing to the introduction of Lyle and Watt's spinning machinery, where 50 hands are at present employed, in Brookfield, including 24 hacklers or flax dressers, which are all males.

In the Brookfield spinning mill for flax there are 1,200 spinning spindles in use.

In the Springvale mill there are 2,496 spindles in use and 70 hands employed, viz. 6 males and 64 females; grist of yarn from 2 till 9 hanks per lb, which is all chiefly sold in Ballymena market.

Brookfield House, which contains the machinery, has 3 floors and measures 75 by 24 feet in the clear.

The Springvale machinery is contained in a 3-storey house with 3 floors. It measures 146 by 27 feet in the clear, including the boiler house, wheel house and office, which are all under 1 roof.

Leases

The old leases were for 41 years and 3 lives, i.e. about 50 years ago. At that time the leases were [for the lives of] the 3 sons of George III, viz. George IV, the Duke of York and William IV. At his death they expired. In 1805 almost a general renewal took place for 61 years, and in 1824 the marquis offered leases renewable for ever, of which the majority of tenants accepted. A debt was on the estate at that time, when the marquis and Lord Belfast agreed to renew the lease forever, until the renewal, and fines would make up the amount of 70,000 pounds, which was the amount of the debt due on the estate.

Fuel

Fuel is principally from Ballybolley mountain bog and Ballywalter or Ballycor bog, which the cottiers purchase, but many of them are not able to do. Therefore they have to burn sticks, which they gather through the ditches and hedges. The cost of a gauge or a load of turf, containing 3 feet high or deep by 3 feet wide, will cost from 13d to 15d in summer and from 20d to 2s in winter. Cottiers purchase a few, but burn sticks occasionally. Turf brought to the house will cost from 13d to 15d per gauge and from 20d to 2s in winter.

Lime

Lime is generally brought from the Whitewells and laid down at the houses at 14d per barrel, and some for 1s per barrel.

Wages

Female servants in a farmhouse receive 30s per half-year. The daily wages in summer for labourers, agricultural, males, is 1s per [day] without meat and 6d per day in winter with meat, and 1s per day in winter without meat. Females during the summer and harvest receive 6d per day without meat and sometimes 8d per day, and very few give 10d per day without meat. Half-yearly wages for a labourer hired in a farmhouse amounts to from 3 pounds to 4 pounds 10s per half-year. Female servants in a farmhouse receive 30s per half-year.

ANCIENT TOPOGRAPHY

Ancient Graveyard

There is an ancient graveyard in this parish, in the townland of Kilbride, in the centre of which stood a church which is said to have been dedicated to St Bridget. Not a vestige of this edifice remains, which formerly stood east and west 68 by 30 feet. About 6 years ago part of the foundation stones was dug up.

Near the centre of the graveyard there stands a very fine monument, erected in 1837 to the memory of the Stephenson family, in which 13 of that family are interred. It was built at the expense of the late Dr Stephenson (author of an *Historical essay on the parish and congregation of Templepatrick*) and cost 300 pounds. It is built of Tardree cut stone and displays much architectural beauty.

There is another vault at the north corner of the graveyard, which was built by subscription of the inhabitants as a protection vault, to prevent exhumation. The dead bodies are deposited in this vault for 6 weeks before interment; subscriptions from 1 guinea to 1s, non-subscribers pay 10s, which sums are kept. It is supposed to defray the expense of building a new wall round the graveyard, which is now in contemplation.

The most prevailing names on the gravestones are Stephenson, the old[est] of which died at the age of 96 years; Ferguson 11, Bryson 9.

Oldest stone 1676, to the memory of Robert Smith; the next, 1699, James Smith.

Giant's Grave and Cromlech

[Ground plan of L-shaped grave and cromlech. [Insert note: These 3 stones, e, f, and g, are west of the above]. The above is the outline of a giant's grave and cromlech which is situated on the mountain part of the townland of Drumadarragh, on the property of George Langtry Esquire and about 50 perches nearly north west of the mountain road leading from Belfast to Connor. The following is a description of it.

A. is that part of the giant's grave which is undisturbed. It measures 22 feet in length by 5 feet broad and 1 and a half feet high. The stones are regularly laid and runs easterly.

B. is the north west part of the grave, which is said to have run 20 feet, but is all demolished and the stones taken to make a wall round the haggard, in which wall the stones of the cromlech stand.

C. is the largest stone of the cromlech, which is said to have formerly stood perpendicular, but is now in a reclined posture, supported near the top by a pillar 2 feet high by 1 and a half and 1 foot thick. The stone itself is 7 and a half feet long by 4 feet broad and 2 feet thick at the base, and becomes smaller to the top.

D. is that part of the wall which contains 3 of the largest stones of the cromlech. The largest of them measures 4 by 8 long by 4 and a half broad and 1 foot thick. It stands about 9 feet from the base of the large stone. The next is 5 and a half feet long by 2 feet high and 1 foot thick, 4 by 9 distant from the former. The third is much smaller.

The proprietor, taking advantage of the situation of these stones, made them to form a part of the wall.

NB The above cromlech is well worth drawing.

Standing Stones

The most remarkable standing stone in the parish is one locally called the Holestone. It is situated 26 yards south of the old line of road leading from Parkgate to Ballyclare. It is placed on a rock and measures 5 feet high by 3 feet broad at the base, 2 and a half feet at the middle by 1 and a half at the top, and 1 foot thick. The hole, which is 3 inches in diameter in the centre, is 2 feet from the top and exactly in the centre of the stone. It is on the property of James Owens Esquire of Holestone.

There is a standing stone conspicuously situated on a mount on the farm of Mr William Fulton, townland of Moyadam or Holestone Lower, about 30 perches south of the road leading from Parkgate to Doagh. This stone stands 5 and a half feet high by 2 and a half feet broad and 2 feet thick; well worth drawing. [Insert marginal note by J. Boyle: This stone is in the grange of Nilteen].

Tumuli

There are 12 of these small tumuli (similar to those on Browndod hill) in the townland of Drumadarragh, on the mountain a short distance north east of the herd's house, on the property of George Langtry Esquire. The largest of them is 10 feet in diameter, with a parapet of stones chiefly about 3 feet broad.

Coins

Ancient silver coin of 2s 6d magnitude of James I, in a perfect state of preservation, with a smaller one of 6d magnitude of Edward, but almost defaced, with a silver coin of 6d mag[nitude] of Anne, in a good state of preservation, found in the above parish in 1837.

Ancient Town

A village is said to have stood at the crossroads near the old graveyard in the townland of Kilbride. The foundations of houses have been dug up. Tradition states it was the second town (between Belfast and Ballymena) to Connor. It was destroyed during the 1641 war.

Camp

During the '41 war a camp is said to have stood on Drumadarragh hill, on Samuel Robinson's farm, supposed to have been the loyal party; and on the Castle hill which is opposite, in the parish [sic] of Ballyeaston, on the moat, stood another camp. Many cannon-balls have been found at both places.

Coves

There are 4 artificial coves on the farm of James Bryson in Ballyvoy townland, but all closed up except one, which is 18 feet long by 3 and a half wide by 3 and a half high; mouth is only 1 and a half feet wide; only 1 apartment. There is one at his house, but closed up except the mouth, which is an excellent spring well. The other coves have rooms turning off at right angles, some 5 feet high by 4 wide. All situated on a rock, but closed up. From James Bryson.

There is a cove, artificial, on the farm of Robert Wilson, townland of Kilbride, but closed up.

This is an outline of a cove on the farm of John Lawson, townland of Kilbride, a short distance east of the graveyard: [ground plan, cruciform, head to the north]. It measures from north to south 40 feet by 4 feet high by 4 wide, from east to west measures 10 feet by 3 wide and 2 high; nearly closed up by earth.

Part of the wall (connected with the origin of Parkgate) runs along and forms the boundary between Kilbride and Ballyvoy townlands, and is built of stones without mortar. From the schoolmaster at Doagh.

Forts

There is a fort of earth in the townland of McVickersland, on the farm of Robert Bryson, near his house. It is circular, 50 feet in diameter on the top by 62 at the base, and 4 feet high from the bottom of [the] trench to top of parapet, and 1 and a half feet high inside by 4 feet thick. All undisturbed except the parapet, which was taken away; no trench.

There is also a fort of stones and earth in the townland of Ballybracken, on the farm of Thomas Watt, at the edge of the stream, in marshy ground and very low. The stream divides the parish of Donegore from the parish of Kilbride. This fort is circular and 96 feet in diameter; trench is 4 feet wide; parapet is 5 feet high in the highest part and not 1 foot in the lowest part. The parapet is a regular circle, chiefly of stones; made in the low ground and quite undisturbed.

There is something in the form of a fort on the heath in the mountain of Drumadarragh, on George Langtry's farm (Esquire), near the giant's grave. It is 90 feet in diameter, but no trench or parapet and quite irregular, with 6 small tumuli inside, each 6 feet in diameter. In fact it is not like a fort.

Parkgate

The old Parkgate wall, which commenced at the Six Mile Water and ended at the Six Mile Water (as before described), was made by Lord Chichester, then Lord Lieutenant of Ireland.

I have carefully examined the townlands of Loonburn, Ballybracken, Crawfordsland and Strawpark, and find nothing in them worth notice. 18th July 1838.

Draft Memoir by J.R. Ward, 1835, with insertions from Office Copy

NATURAL FEATURES

Hills

Received 23rd April 1835 [signed] J. McGann; refer to Mr Boyle [signed] R.K. Dawson, 18th September 1835.

There is a long ridge springing from Collin and running down the centre of the parish. The northern part of it is of a mountainous character. Drumadarragh, the principal point, is 929 feet above the sea and 720 above the village of Doagh.

Lakes

None. There is a large mill-dam [insert addition: through which the north boundary passes. It contains 11 acres 21 perches, of which there are 5 acres 3 roods 16 perches in the parish] (see parish of Rashee).

Rivers

The Six Mile Water forms the southern boundary of the parish for half a mile [insert addition: running south east. It is usefully situated both for drainage and water power. There are no falls or rapids of any consequence on it]; for particulars, see parish of Ballymartin.

The Doagh river forms the northern and eastern boundaries for about 6 miles [insert addition: running into the Six Mile Water at the south eastern extremity of the parish]; see parish of Rashee.

The Four Mile burn forms the western boundary of the parish for 5 and a half miles. [Insert addition: It flows in a southern direction. Its average breadth is from 15 to 20 feet. It is very shallow. It rises in the parish of Rashee and is usefully situated for drainage and water power. Its fall is about 200 feet in a mile. It is subject to floods which soon subside and leave no injurious deposits on the land. It impedes communication and flows over a gravelly bed. The northern lands are used for grazing, the southern are well cultivated and fertile]; see parish of Donegore.

Bogs and Woods

There is no peat bog in the parish.

There are no natural woods, or remains of any. There is a good deal of planting about Holestone, the residence of James Owens Esquire, and some fine trees in Springvale, the residence of Mr Watt (linen thread spinner), and some in Drumadarragh. There is also some young plantations in Owenland, principally fir.

Climate

See register for Doagh. The crops are the same as in Donegore parish.

Modern Topography

Towns and Public Buildings

Towns: none.
     Public buildings: none. There is a graveyard in Kilbride townland.

Gentlemen's Seats

Holestone, the residence of James Owens Esquire, is situated in the townland of the same name, near the southern extremity of the parish. It was built in 1830. It is in the modern style of country seats and has an elegant appearance. There is some ornamental ground about it.

Bleach Greens, Manufactories and Mills

[Insert addition: The bleach mill in Drumadarragh townland: there is no such thing in the townland, but there are ruins of several mills in it.
     The print mill: ruins].
     A flax spinning mill in Walkmill townland, breast wheel 30 feet diameter by 6 feet broad.
     A flax spinning mill in Burnside townland, breast wheel 34 feet diameter by 4 feet broad.
     A flax mill in Ballywee townland, breast wheel 12 feet diameter and 1 foot 10 inches broad.
     A beetling mill, Ballyhamage townland, breast wheel 13 feet 6 inches diameter, 2 feet 9 inches broad [insert alternative: 13 feet 7 inches diameter, 2 feet 7 inches broad].
     A corn mill, Ballywee townland, breast wheel 14 feet diameter and 1 foot 10 inches broad.

Communications

The old road between Doagh to Ballymena traverses the parish from the former to the north west extremity of it. There is 4 miles of this road in the parish. Its average breadth is 26 feet. Though very hilly, it is a good road and kept in very good repair, though it is now seldom used by travellers.
     There is another road between the towns above mentioned which is much more level. It traverses the parish north west and runs [out] of it on the west side [insert addition: and passes through Donegore parish]. Its length in the parish is 3 miles and its average breadth is 26 feet. It is in very good repair.
     The road from Ballyclare to Antrim passes through Doagh, crossing the parish, forming part of the southern boundary for three-quarters of a mile. Its whole length is 1 and three-quarter miles in the parish, its average breadth 27 feet, and it is in tolerable good repair.

There are besides several crossroads in good repair which, with the main roads, were all made by the county and are kept in repair by the half-barony, Upper Antrim.

General Appearance

The north of the parish, from its mountain character, has a bleak appearance. The southern is well cultivated and appears fertile. In the vicinity of Doagh, there being a little planting, the [scenery] is pretty and the surrounding scenery is picturesque, being varied with mountain and undulated ground.

Social Economy

Local Government

Obstructions to improvement: none.
     James Owens Esquire is one of the magistrates and resides in the parish. [He] is firm and respected by the people. There is no police [?force] in this parish.
     No dispensaries.

Schools and Poor

There is 1 school in Kilbride townland, which is generally well attended [table]: Protestants 45, Catholics 4, males 32, females 17, total 49; the scholars pay from 2s to 4s per quarter; books are got from the Hibernian Society; when established: not known.
     No provision for the poor.

Religion

The greater part of the inhabitants are Presbyterians. Tithe is paid to the clergyman of Donegore.

Habits of the People

Similar to the parish of Rashee. Emigration does not prevail.
     Remarkable events: none.

Ancient Topography

Pagan: Holestone

About a mile north of Mr Owens' residence there is a curious upright whinstone slab called the Holestone. It gives the name to the townland in which it is situated. It stands, almost perpendicularly, in the centre of a base evidently made for it, about 3 feet 6 inches in length and 3 feet in breadth. The slab is 5 feet high and measures little more than 6 feet 6 inches in circumference at the